UNITING AMERICA

ALSO BY PETER SHINKLE

Ike's Mystery Man

UNITING AMERICA

How FDR and Henry Stimson
Brought Democrats and Republicans
Together to Win World War II

PETER SHINKLE

ST. MARTIN'S
PRESS

NEW YORK

First published in the United States by St. Martin's Press, an imprint of St. Martin's Publishing Group

UNITING AMERICA. Copyright © 2022 by Peter Shinkle. All rights reserved. Printed in the United States of America. For information, address St. Martin's Publishing Group, 120 Broadway, New York, NY 10271.

www.stmartins.com

Library of Congress Cataloging-in-Publication Data

Names: Shinkle, Peter, author.
Title: Uniting America : how FDR and Henry Stimson brought Democrats and
    Republicans together to win World War II / Peter Shinkle.
Description: First edition. | New York : St. Martin's Press, 2022. | Includes bibliographical
    references and index.
Identifiers: LCCN 2022021352 | ISBN 9781250762528 (hardcover) | ISBN 9781250762535
    (ebook)
Subjects: LCSH: Roosevelt, Franklin D. (Franklin Delano), 1882–1945. | Stimson, Henry L.
    (Henry Lewis), 1867–1950. | World War, 1939–1945—United States. | Political leadership—
    United States—History—20th century. | Polarization (Social sciences)—United States. |
    United States—Politics and government—1933–1945.
Classification: LCC E806 .S513 2022 | DDC 973.917—dc23/eng/20220525
LC record available at https://lccn.loc.gov/2022021352

Our books may be purchased in bulk for promotional, educational, or business use. Please contact your local bookseller or the Macmillan Corporate and Premium Sales Department at 1-800-221-7945, extension 5442, or by email at MacmillanSpecialMarkets@macmillan.com.

First Edition: 2022

10 9 8 7 6 5 4 3 2 1

To all patriotic Americans—of any political party—who
have the integrity to search for the truth, the honesty to
say that an opponent is right and the courage to cross
partisan lines for the good of the country and democracy

CONTENTS

UNITING
AMERICA

DEMOCRATS

FRANKLIN D. ROOSEVELT
President

HENRY WALLACE
Vice President 1941–1945

HARRY TRUMAN
Elected Vice President 1944
President 1945–1953

HENRY MORGENTHAU JR.
Secretary of the Treasury

HARRY HOPKINS
Special Assistant to FDR

FRANCIS BIDDLE
Attorney General

ELEANOR ROOSEVELT
First Lady
Unofficial Adviser to the
President
Associate Director,
Office of Civilian Defense

CORDELL HULL
Secretary of State 1933–1944

JAMES BYRNES
Secretary of State 1945–1947
Director,
Office of War Mobilization
1943–1945

REPUBLICANS

FRANK KNOX *Secretary of the Navy*	**HENRY L. STIMSON** *Secretary of War*
WENDELL WILLKIE *GOP Presidential Nominee 1940*	*War Department Appointees*
WILLIAM DONOVAN *Director,* *Office of Strategic Services (OSS)*	**ROBERT PATTERSON** *Undersecretary of War*
	ROBERT LOVETT *Assistant Secretary of War for Air*
ALLEN DULLES *OSS Switzerland Director*	**JOHN McCLOY** *Assistant Secretary of War*
FIORELLO LA GUARDIA *Director,* *Office of Civilian Defense* *Mayor of New York*	**HARVEY BUNDY** *Assistant to the Secretary of War*
	COLONEL ROBERT CUTLER *Coordinator of Soldier Voting*
NELSON ROCKEFELLER *Assistant Secretary of State*	**CHARLES TAFT** *US Community War Service*
JOHN WINANT *Ambassador to the United Kingdom*	**WILLIAM KNUDSEN** *Director,* *Office of Production Management*
PATRICK HURLEY *Ambassador to China*	
HAROLD ICKES *Interior Secretary*	**JOHN O'BRIAN** *General Counsel,* *Office of Production Management*

With the exception of Willkie and Cutler, all these Republicans sought positions with the Roosevelt Administration prior to the Pearl Harbor attack on December 7, 1941.

Introduction

After tearing through Belgium, the Netherlands and France, Adolf Hitler's armies had surrounded British and allied troops at Dunkirk in early June 1940. Fearing Germany would attack Great Britain next, Prime Minister Winston Churchill appealed to President Franklin D. Roosevelt for arms so the British could defend themselves from Nazi fascism. In America, however, isolationists bitterly condemned FDR, accusing him of dragging the United States into another costly European war. On June 3, Representative Hamilton Fish, a New York Republican and ardent isolationist, took the floor of the House of Representatives and hurled a rhetorical bomb, suggesting that Democrats were encouraging FDR to "set up a dictatorial government in the United States."[1]

Amid a drumbeat of attacks on FDR's war policies, the Republican Party prepared to select a presidential nominee at its national convention in Philadelphia in late June 1940. If a staunch isolationist won the election that fall, America might refuse to send aid to any allies; the prospect of a Nazi empire spanning *all* of Europe loomed.

On June 20, 1940, FDR launched a bold strategy to undercut the isolationists. In a surprise announcement, he appointed two prominent Republicans—both strong supporters of aiding America's European allies—to critical posts in his cabinet. Henry L. Stimson, who had been secretary of state under FDR's Republican predecessor, President Herbert Hoover, would be secretary of war, and Frank Knox, the Republican vice-presidential nominee in 1936, would be secretary of the navy. The White House said the appointments, setting partisan politics aside in the name of defending the country, were intended to create "national solidarity."[2]

By their example, Stimson and Knox encouraged other Republicans to support the Democratic president. The appointments immediately set off an uproar among Republicans. On the day of FDR's announcement, Republicans lambasted Stimson and Knox at their national convention. They were, some said, "read out" of the party and no longer spoke for it. Yet days later, in a stunning volte-face, the convention rejected the leading isolationist candidate and instead chose Wendell Willkie, whose war policy was closest to FDR's, as the party's 1940 presidential nominee.

The Stimson and Knox appointments were a daring and risky move that placed a bipartisan political relationship at the very center of America's defense against fascism. The gamble paid off. Stimson and Knox cultivated an appearance of nonpartisan leadership, and their support ultimately helped FDR win the 1940 presidential election. The nation's capital gained a new spirit of solidarity, and many bills passed Congress over the next five years with strong backing from both parties. The bipartisan coalition worked effectively to unite the nation, rapidly expand and strengthen the American military and secure victory in World War II.

Stimson, despite his relatively advanced age—he accepted FDR's appointment at seventy-two—spearheaded the bipartisan alliance and carried it through the end of the war. Other prominent Republicans soon joined forces with FDR, including his recent opponent Willkie, New York City mayor Fiorello La Guardia and William Donovan, who was appointed to lead the Office of Strategic Services, the wartime spy agency. Each of these men chose to stand with FDR to defend democracy at a time when doing so meant losing favor with large numbers of Republicans.

The alliance was in full swing long before the December 1941 attack on Pearl Harbor spurred the nation to widely support the war effort and abandon isolationism. It arose at a time when isolationists held sway in Congress and blocked preparations for war—a time when it was not easy for Republicans to side with the Democratic president. Yet even after Pearl Harbor, FDR found significant benefits in bipartisanship and sought to work with more Republicans as the war went on. He even imagined a future in which liberals in the Republican Party would convert to the Democratic Party, which would in turn send its conservatives over to the Republicans.

This embrace of bipartisanship—as Hitler's war machine savaged Western Europe—stands as an act of audacity and brilliance that was instrumental in leading America and her allies to victory in World War II. Yet it has been all but forgotten. One reason for this national amnesia is that FDR and Stimson were so skilled at creating unity that their party differences faded into the background. Another is that political partisans typically attract adherents and campaign contributions by demonizing their opponents as irrational and intransigent—not by celebrating shared goals achieved through collaboration with opposing parties. There is an old saying that success has many fathers, but failure is an orphan. To this one might add: compromise, even for the national good, is a neglected child.

I first learned about the FDR-Stimson alliance years ago while writing a biography of Robert Cutler, a Boston Republican and closeted gay man who served under President Dwight D. Eisenhower as the nation's first national security adviser. A decade before that service, Cutler had gone to Washington to work in the War Department.[3] I was amazed to discover that there was something of a Republican brigade in command of the War Department under FDR's Democratic administration and set out to unearth the story of this partnership. The logical starting place was Stimson's diary, an authoritative contemporaneous account often cited by historians yet never fully mined for a picture of his wartime collaboration with FDR. Among the remarkable things I found was a letter revealing that Stimson considered becoming secretary of war akin to taking the War Department as a "hostage" of the Republican Party.

The FDR-Stimson alliance was informal—it had no founding charter, no written agreement. It also expanded beyond FDR to include First Lady Eleanor Roosevelt and cabinet members like Secretary of State Cordell Hull and Treasury Secretary Henry Morgenthau Jr. The two major parties still dominated politics in Washington, and partisan disputes—even very acrimonious ones—still arose, yet they did so against a backdrop of leadership in the White House that constantly worked for bipartisan agreement.

Today, it may seem a matter of course that—at a time when the nation's existence was threatened—Republicans and Democrats would set aside partisan disputes and work together. But it was never a matter of course. A lifelong Republican, Stimson had publicly criticized Roosevelt, and many Republicans denounced his acceptance of the post of secretary of war. On the other side, FDR had fought innumerable battles with Republicans over his long career. He could have secured wavering Democratic voters in 1940 by appointing a prominent Democrat.

Stimson and FDR, both students of history and admirers of President Abraham Lincoln, surely knew of the pitfalls of bipartisanship revealed by events seventy-five years earlier. Lincoln, the heroic Republican, sought to build a spirit of national unity in the midst of the Civil War by choosing a pro-Union Democrat, Andrew Johnson of Tennessee, to be his vice-presidential running mate. They won the 1864 election. After the war ended the next year, Lincoln was assassinated and Johnson became president. The new Democratic president eventually fired his Republican secretary of war, Edwin Stanton—causing a storm of protests among Republicans. Republicans in the House of Representatives impeached Johnson over Stanton's firing; although the Senate acquitted Johnson, the party divide that Lincoln had hoped to close grew wider again. This was a searing cautionary tale of the risks of bipartisan control of the executive branch. Nonetheless, three-quarters of a century later, a Democratic president and a Republican secretary of war chose the path of bipartisanship in an effort to unite America. This was neither an obvious choice nor a preordained one; it was a courageous decision by both men that ran contrary to partisan pressures, political convenience and the lessons of history.

Over nearly five years of war, Roosevelt and Stimson labored together over hotly contested matters such as initiating a military draft, invading North Africa and a long dispute with Churchill over whether to invade Nazi-occupied France. Sometimes their work was amicable, sometimes marked by anger and discord, but their relationship—underlain by a bond of trust—only grew stronger through the years. Ultimately, as FDR wrote his friend in November 1944, "we both have faith and that is half the battle."[4] FDR and Stimson also struggled with issues for which they are widely and correctly faulted—their refusal to desegregate the armed forces even as Black soldiers fought and gave their lives to preserve America's freedom, their internment of Japanese Americans and their sometimes halting response to the Nazi genocide of European Jews.

After FDR's death in April 1945, Stimson sought to continue his collaboration with the Democrats by working closely with FDR's successor, President Harry Truman. The relationship faltered when Truman diminished Stimson's role in the decision to drop the atomic bomb, but Truman ultimately embraced bipartisanship in creating the North Atlantic Treaty Organization (NATO) to defend democracy.

Just as it was in 1940, the United States is once again riven by extreme partisanship. And once again, in America and elsewhere around the world, democracy faces enormous threats. The following chapters tell the compelling story of the wartime bipartisan alliance—marked by both brilliant achievements and haunting failures—a legacy that may guide and inspire those who have hopes of uniting America today.

PART I

FORGING THE
BIPARTISAN ALLIANCE

1

The Hunter and the Strategist

On the morning of January 9, 1933, Republican secretary of state Henry L. Stimson took a train north from New York City along the Hudson River through falling snow. He got off at Hyde Park, then rode in a car sent by Franklin D. Roosevelt to Springwood, Roosevelt's estate overlooking the Hudson. FDR, the Democratic governor of New York, was preparing to take office as president, and the elegant mansion was cluttered with packages from his recent election campaign and the Christmas holiday. Despite the relaxed setting, both men were in suits and the occasion had the air of a diplomatic visit. Before FDR won the presidential election the prior November, Stimson, at the urging of Republican president Herbert Hoover, had attacked Roosevelt publicly. Yet after defeating Hoover in the election, FDR asked Stimson—not Hoover—to meet with him in Hyde Park.

FDR received him "with great cordiality," Stimson noted later that day in his diary. "We both spoke with the utmost freedom and informality." Stimson marveled at FDR's handling of his paralysis from polio. "I was much impressed with his disability and the brave way in which he paid no attention to it whatever." They agreed to reveal no details of their conversation to the press—an accord they held to when reporters were at last ushered in and photos were taken as the two men had lunch. A photo the next day in the paper showed Stimson as bolt upright while FDR appeared relaxed and garrulous. Resisting questions with a smile, FDR said, "It was delightful to have the secretary of state here for lunch. . . . Everything in relation to foreign affairs was discussed."[1]

The two men continued their friendly conversation as FDR accompanied Stimson in a car through deep snow back to New York City. Their discussion that day ranged over many topics, including particularly a mounting financial crisis—European nations had defaulted on their war debts—an issue over which FDR and Hoover had clashed. Stimson steered the dialogue to Japan's invasion of the northern Chinese realm of Manchuria, and on this point by the end of the day he had what he sought—FDR's agreement to preserve Stimson's policy of declaring Japan's invasion of Manchuria a violation of international law and refusing to grant recognition to the puppet state Japan had established there.[2] Dismissing the concerns of his own advisers, who wanted the United States to remain strictly neutral on the Japanese invasion, FDR announced a week later that he would uphold Stimson's policy on Manchuria.[3]

The spirited meeting of FDR and Stimson that day in Hyde Park marked the start of a relationship that seven years later—as war spread across the globe—would become what is surely the most important bipartisan political alliance in American history.

The two statesmen hit it off so well at Springwood that it was as if they had long known each other. In fact, FDR and Stimson had circled each other in New York public life for decades. Yet living in the disjointed orbits of Republicans and Democrats, they had never had a conversation until that day. Both men were prominent in national politics, had gone to Harvard, were wealthy and had deep ties to Wall Street. Both men also were fierce admirers of President Theodore Roosevelt, the Republican cousin of FDR who occupied the White House from 1901 to 1909. Yet their life paths diverged, and their characters were in some ways sharply opposed.

STIMSON WAS BORN in New York City two years after the Civil War ended. His father, Lewis A. Stimson, was a Yale College graduate who had served in the Union Army during the war, and afterwards married

Candace Wheeler, who gave birth to Henry Lewis Stimson on September 21, 1867. After Candace became ill, and doctors were unable to diagnose her condition, Lewis took her to Europe in 1871 in search of a cure, leaving Henry and his younger sister with Lewis's parents. Lewis's campaign to find a cure for his wife led him to study with Louis Pasteur in Paris.[4] After the couple returned to New York, Lewis obtained a medical degree but he was unable to save Candace, who died in 1875.

Amid his grief, Lewis Stimson sold the family home and rented a small apartment to devote himself to the practice of medicine as a surgeon. He sent Henry to Phillips Academy, a historic boys school in Andover, Massachusetts. Henry reveled in outdoor life at the school, known simply as Andover. "There was football, baseball, skating, bobsledding, and walking over the hills and woodlands of northern Massachusetts," he recalled, adding that the school's academics were rigorous. "Andover fitted a boy for college and it fitted him well."[5]

After his freshman year at Yale, Harry Stimson spent the summer in Colorado hunting and fishing. He became enamored of the wilderness. "For over twenty years thereafter, I spent a portion of nearly every year in mountains or forests of the western Rockies or Canada, exploring, hunting, and traveling by horse, foot or canoe," he recalled. "I became a fair rifleman and canoeman; could pack my own horses, kill my own game, and cook my own meals."[6] In the summer of 1885, Stimson went to New Brunswick, Canada, and spent two months canoeing in the wilderness with a guide from the Mi'kmaq tribe. Stimson shot a bear and the two men survived on bear meat, fish and game as their supplies dwindled. Stimson shot a second bear and "gathering the remains of a salt barrel in an old logging camp, we salted it down and ate it to its toes."[7]

At Yale, Stimson was a member of the Phi Beta Kappa honor society and graduated third in his class in 1888, but it was after he enrolled in Harvard Law School that he found his greatest academic challenge. "The whole atmosphere was electric with the sparks of competitive argument," he recalled.[8] He completed his legal studies in 1890 and returned to New York City to work at Root & Clarke, the law firm of Elihu Root, a prominent lawyer who had served as US attorney in New York under Republican president Chester Arthur. The firm's clients included railroad magnate Frederick Vanderbilt, Standard Oil Company and an energetic Republican New York police commissioner, Theodore Roosevelt.[9]

On January 1, 1893, Stimson became a partner in the firm, ensuring him the financial wherewithal he felt he needed in order to marry Mabel Wellington White. He'd first met Mabel, the daughter of a prominent New Haven family, while he was at Yale. He was instantly smitten and the young couple soon became engaged, which they kept secret for half a decade. Stimson later recalled that his salary increase in 1893 at last permitted him, after five years of waiting, "to marry and support his wife." The couple was wed on July 6, 1893, and moved into a rented home in the city.[10]

Mabel soon joined Henry on his ventures into the outdoors. On their first trip together, they canoed through a hundred miles of New Brunswick wilderness with meager rations until Henry shot a moose. Henry later recalled Mabel "had a love of nature which developed at once into a love of nature's greatest expression—the untouched wilderness."[11] The couple would have no children, but they had an enduring love of each other and of the outdoors.

After Root was named secretary of war in 1899 by Republican president William McKinley, Stimson and another partner, Bronson Winthrop, took over the law firm, which they renamed Winthrop & Stimson. After McKinley was assassinated in September 1901, his vice president, Theodore Roosevelt, became president. Two years later, when Stimson was in Washington to attend a meeting, he went horseback riding with a friend along Rock Creek, which was swollen with heavy rains. At one point, Stimson heard Root summon him to cross the creek on his horse "on the order" of the president, who was riding with Root on the opposite side of the rushing creek. Stimson tried to cross, but both horse and rider were immediately submerged in the turbulent waters. Stimson managed to extricate himself and rode up to the president and his secretary of war. Stimson recalled: "I said, 'Mr. President, when a soldier hears an order like that, it isn't his business to see that it is impossible.' T.R. . . . laughed and said 'well it was very nice of you to do it. Now hurry home and drink all the whiskey you can.'" That night, at a dinner of the Boone & Crockett Club, a conservation group founded by TR, the president drew uproarious laughter recounting the story and hailing Stimson as "young Lochinvar," Sir Walter Scott's heroic knight who rides a mighty steed.[12]

Stimson's law practice, meanwhile, grew rapidly, providing Henry and Mabel sufficient income in 1903 to purchase a farm on more than one hundred acres in the village of Huntington on Long Island. They named the property "Highhold" because it sat atop a ridge from which one could see both north to Long Island Sound and south to the Atlantic Ocean.[13] Highhold was about six miles from TR's home, Sagamore Hill, near Oyster Bay, and the two men occasionally visited each other.

In 1906, TR appointed Stimson US attorney for the Southern District of New York, a position in which Stimson brought important prosecutions in TR's campaign against trusts, the sprawling businesses that the president accused of undermining competition and driving up prices. In May 1906, Stimson filed antitrust indictments against American Sugar, the New York Central Railroad, and four executives of the two businesses. Stimson's cases resulted in convictions.[14] In a second round of indictments, Stimson accused American Sugar of engaging in a conspiracy to falsify records on the amount of sugar it imported in order to avoid paying import tariffs. The company and five managers were convicted after trial.[15]

Not long after Stimson took office as US attorney, Wall Street was rocked by a financial collapse that would ultimately be known as the Panic of 1907. Fear spread through the markets, investors pulled money out of banks and stocks and the value of the Dow Jones Industrial Average plummeted to almost 50 percent of its peak the previous year. Within months, in early 1908, Stimson brought charges against a man seen as a chief malefactor in the panic, Charles W. Morse, who backed a failed effort to take control of the United Copper Company.[16] An indictment filed by Stimson accused Morse of fraudulently taking large sums of money from a bank he controlled. After a trial that drew wide attention, Morse was convicted and sentenced to fifteen years in prison.[17]

Among the young lawyers Stimson hired in the US attorney's office was Felix Frankfurter, a graduate of Harvard Law School. At a time when anti-Semitism was prevalent, Stimson opened the door to professional relationships with Frankfurter and others of Jewish descent.

Frankfurter, who became a lifelong friend of Stimson's, later recalled him as a "wholly scrupulous" prosecutor, noting that Stimson accompanied investigators on raids to ensure they complied with court orders and protected the rights of suspects.[18]

In 1908, TR—who had vowed not to serve more than two terms as president—backed his secretary of war, William Howard Taft, to be the presidential nominee of the Republican Party. Taft won the election and, after he was inaugurated in March 1909, Stimson resigned as US attorney and resumed his law practice at Winthrop & Stimson.

In 1910, TR urged Stimson to run for governor of New York. Stimson agreed. With the former president's backing, Stimson won the nomination and threw himself into campaigning, with TR joining the effort. Stimson attacked his Democratic opponent, John A. Dix, as subservient to Tammany Hall, the Democratic political organization in New York City that held power with the support of laborers and immigrants. Dix and his Tammany supporters, meanwhile, charged that Stimson was merely a puppet of TR, and that electing Stimson as governor would be a first step in returning TR to the White House.[19] *The New York Times* profiled Stimson in a story that likened him to TR and recounted his prosecutions of the Sugar Trust and Morse under the headline "Stimson Fighter of Big Graft Cases."[20]

ANOTHER ENTRANT IN the elections of 1910 was Franklin D. Roosevelt, who at age twenty-eight was a Democratic candidate for a state senate seat. FDR and TR both descended from a Dutchman who immigrated to New Amsterdam, as New York was then called, in the 1650s. The family eventually split into branches—one along the Hudson north of New York, where FDR lived, and the other on Long Island, where TR lived. One of FDR's forebears, Isaac Roosevelt, helped draft New York's first constitution and, with Alexander Hamilton, founded the Bank of New York.

FDR's father, James Roosevelt, was a lawyer and investor in industries such as coal and railroads.[21] After his first wife died, James Roosevelt in 1880 married Sara Ann Delano, whose family lineage included seven passengers on the *Mayflower*.[22] Franklin was born on January

30, 1882—more than fourteen years after Stimson—and he grew up at Springwood, the estate in Hyde Park, where he was tutored in French, Latin, German and other subjects. The family traveled often and spent summers at their home on the Canadian island of Campobello off the coast of Maine, where Franklin learned to sail and began a lifelong love of the sea, ships and fishing.[23]

In 1896, Franklin entered Groton School, in northern Massachusetts about thirty miles from Andover. The private school provided the children of wealthy Americans with an education infused with Christian principles and fortified with vigorous physical exercise. After completing Groton, Franklin in the fall of 1900 entered Harvard, where he would become editor of *The Crimson*, the student newspaper.[24] That December, during Franklin's freshman year at Harvard, his father, James, died at Springwood.[25] In the wake of his death, Franklin, already a great admirer of his cousin Theodore, measured himself against the public service career of TR, who had become president in September 1901.[26]

In November 1902, Franklin attended a horse show in New York City's Madison Square Garden, an event that brought together a large group of Roosevelts from both the Hudson River and Long Island branches of the family. Among them was eighteen-year-old Eleanor Roosevelt, the daughter of TR's younger brother Elliott and wife Anna. Both Elliott and Anna had died about a decade earlier, and Eleanor, who had grown up in the care of various family members, was a favorite of her uncle, TR, who was her godfather.[27] Franklin and Eleanor soon began courting.

In October 1903, while Franklin was in his senior year at Harvard, he proposed marriage to Eleanor and she accepted, although at the behest of Franklin's mother, Sara, they agreed to keep the engagement secret for a year.[28] In October 1904, while Franklin was at Columbia University Law School, the couple revealed the news of their engagement. TR wrote Franklin a congratulatory letter: "You and Eleanor are true and brave, and I believe you love each other unselfishly; and golden years open before you."[29] Franklin and Eleanor were wed in New York on March 17, 1905, the president giving Eleanor's hand away.[30]

· · ·

AFTER STARTING A career in the law, Franklin decided to run for the New York state senate seat in the district that encompassed Hyde Park in the election of 1910, the same year Henry Stimson ran for governor. FDR and Stimson must have appraised each other across the New York political landscape. Stimson was TR's protégé, promoted by the former president at campaign events across the state. Franklin was TR's cousin who ran as a Democrat but criticized Tammany Hall, the Democratic political machine in New York City.[31] Their fortunes differed: FDR won his election in 1910, setting him on a course to prominence. Stimson, competing in a year when national sentiment favored Democrats, lost narrowly.[32] He returned to his law practice, never again to run for elective office.

In spring 1911, Taft appointed Stimson as secretary of war. Taft had become increasingly conservative, creating tension between Taft and TR, and Stimson accepted the position only after getting blessing from his mentor in a meeting at Sagamore Hill.[33] In 1912, TR stunned the Republican Party by deciding to run for president again and, when he did not win the Republican presidential nomination, forming his own Progressive Party. Stimson supported Taft, believing his duty was to him and the Republican Party. With progressive Republicans supporting TR and conservatives backing Taft, the party was divided, and the 1912 presidential election was won by the Democratic candidate, Woodrow Wilson.

FDR had supported Wilson in the race, and after his inauguration Wilson appointed him to be assistant secretary of the navy, a position in which he became increasingly prominent as the Democratic Roosevelt.

When World War I broke out in Europe in 1914, TR pushed for the creation of a training camp in Plattsburgh, New York, for volunteers to enter the army and prepare for a US role in the war, at a time when Wilson argued America must stay out of the war. TR's four sons and other well-known Republicans went to Plattsburgh, and the camp was headed by General Leonard Wood, a friend of Stimson's from his days as secretary of war. Stimson, who supported preparedness for the war, visited the Plattsburgh camp, and in 1916 he enrolled for training. He was forty-eight years old.[34]

Wilson called upon Congress to declare war in April 1917. Stimson, who believed that Germany was bent on destroying democracy, publicly supported the Democratic president, displaying the political independence and straightforwardness that would be the hallmark of his public career.[35] Delivering a speech in St. Louis, Stimson said, "President Wilson is a Democrat and I am a Republican, but let me tell you, gentlemen, it is the Republican opponents who are wrong and the President of the United States who is right."[36]

FDR, despite being encouraged by TR to take up arms in the war, remained assistant secretary of the navy in Washington. Stimson, on the other hand, joined the army in December 1917 at the age of fifty and was sent to France with the rank of colonel. There he commanded the 305th Field Artillery unit, which launched the US Army's first artillery fire against the Germans in the war. As secretary of war, he had known many soldiers, but now he had his own war experience with members of his unit. "As they worked, they began to feel that heartening self-confidence that comes to a good unit sometime in its first campaign when the men in it suddenly understand that now they are veterans—now they *know*. For the only thing worse than the fear that fills all battlefields is the fear of fear that fills the hearts of men who have not fought," he later wrote.[37]

After an armistice halted the war in 1918, President Wilson ultimately negotiated a peace treaty in Paris that included creation of an international organization, the League of Nations, to prevent future wars. Yet the League of Nations failed to get enough Republican votes to pass the Senate, so the League came into being without the United States as a member.

In this period, FDR and Eleanor suffered a series of personal and professional trials. One of the couple's six children died in infancy. In 1918, Eleanor discovered that FDR was having an affair with Lucy Mercer, a young woman who had been her personal secretary. The couple was on the verge of separating when FDR's mother, Sara, stepped in and threatened him with losing his vast inheritance if he proceeded with a divorce.[38] FDR and Eleanor agreed to remain together, but from that time forward their marriage often appeared to have the character of a partnership in which she was remarkably independent from her husband.[39] FDR was the Democratic vice-presidential candidate in 1920, but Republican nominee Warren G. Harding won the election. In 1921,

FDR contracted poliomyelitis, which paralyzed his legs. Although his polio was reported widely in newspapers, he downplayed the disease's impact on him and slowly resumed his political career.[40] In 1924, he received treatment in the mineral-laden thermal waters at Warm Springs, Georgia, where he later bought a hotel to provide care to other polio sufferers.[41]

Stimson returned to his private law practice after the war, representing major industrial clients such as a coal industry association battling with the United Mine Workers of America union. Stimson accused the union of violent crimes culminating in a massacre of strikebreakers at a mine in Herrin, Illinois, in 1922.[42]

In 1927, Republican president Calvin Coolidge asked Stimson to help resolve a civil war that was devastating Nicaragua in the wake of a coup by a member of the country's right-wing Conservative Party.[43] Stimson negotiated a deal in which the Conservative Party leader agreed with the opposing Liberal Party to disarm and to honor the results of elections to be held the next year if the United States sent troops to supervise the elections.[44] Marines were dispatched to Nicaragua, and the elections of 1928 returned the Liberal Party to power.[45]

Coolidge then appointed Stimson governor-general over the Philippines, the territory the United States seized in the Spanish-American War. The Stimsons moved to Manila to occupy the Malacañang Palace, where Stimson took control of the Pacific nation. When a new Republican president, Herbert Hoover, was elected in 1928, he asked Stimson to be his secretary of state.

Stimson had become wealthy owing partly to his younger cousin, Alfred L. Loomis, who in the 1920s became a tycoon through investments in his electric utility holding businesses.[46] Loomis was both a brilliant investor and a scientist, and he ran a research laboratory at his home in Tuxedo Park, New York, where he sometimes worked with prominent physicists.[47] Loomis and his partner, Landon Thorne, had expanded their businesses rapidly in an era when electric holding companies boomed as demand in American homes soared. Loomis and Thorne hired Stimson to represent them, and Stimson also received investment advice from them.[48] In 1929, suspecting the market had become inflated, Loomis, Thorne and Stimson began selling significant amounts of shares.[49] Stimson said later that his sales of highly appreciated stocks prior to the stock market crash of October 1929 made it possible for him and Mabel to buy their Washington estate, Woodley.[50]

Perched atop a hill, Woodley had a commanding view down to the center of Washington and the Potomac River in the distance. The estate, located near the National Cathedral, had eighteen acres of gently rolling land. Built by slaves in 1801, the mansion had a series of notable owners, including President Grover Cleveland, who used Woodley as his primary residence during his second term in office.[51] The Stimsons kept horses in the estate's stable and took rides along nearby Rock Creek. Henry often invited diplomats and senior US officials to Woodley for discussions of issues such as the war debts that burdened European countries.

FDR, meanwhile, had resumed his role as a prominent figure in New York politics. After condemning Tammany Hall in his early years, FDR had changed course and built an alliance with Tammany, revealing himself as a political strategist. He supported Tammany candidates and gained their support in return. Speaking up for the working class and immigrants that Tammany appealed to, FDR won election as governor of New York in 1928. After the stock market crash of 1929, the Great Depression left many people unemployed. FDR began endorsing state programs to provide relief to the public.

President Hoover and Secretary Stimson held that any government response should be limited, but it soon became obvious that Roosevelt's approach was gathering support nationwide and he might run for president in 1932. Stimson decided to help the Republican candidate seeking to defeat FDR in the gubernatorial race in 1930. In a radio broadcast carried statewide on October 28, 1930, Stimson charged that FDR had "shown his unfitness" by blocking an investigation of state judges. "Governor Roosevelt's present position is a mere partisan excuse," Stimson said.[52] Roosevelt responded three days later by impugning the credibility of Stimson and Hoover's secretary of the treasury, Ogden Mills, and secretary of war, Patrick Hurley, who had attacked FDR. Both Stimson and Mills had run unsuccessfully for New York governor, FDR noted. "The people did not believe in them or their issues then, and they will not believe in them or their issues now," he said.[53] On Election Day,

November 4, FDR won by the largest plurality for any gubernatorial candidate in New York history.

STIMSON, AS SECRETARY of state, became deeply concerned about the rise of Japanese militaristic nationalism the following year. On the night of September 18, 1931, an explosion damaged rail lines that the Japanese Imperial Army patrolled under treaty in Manchuria, a large region of northern China. A Japanese military unit, which later claimed it was fired upon, attacked a Chinese army barracks, killing more than three hundred Chinese soldiers.[54] By the next morning, the Japanese had seized Mukden, Manchuria's largest city, and several nearby cities. China argued the Japanese attack was completely unjustified and requested help from the League of Nations.[55]

Seeking Japanese withdrawal from Manchuria, Stimson entered delicate talks with a moderate Japanese diplomat, Baron Kijuro Shidehara, who was opposed by nationalists in control of the army. "My problem is to let the Japanese know we are watching them and at the same time do it in a way which will help Shidehara who is on the right side, and not play into the hands of any nationalist agitators," Stimson noted in his diary.[56] After a murder plot targeting Shidehara and the prime minister was revealed, Stimson wrote in his diary that Japan was "in the hands of virtually mad dogs."[57] Shidehara resigned, and by January 1932 Japan controlled all of Manchuria. Stimson cabled the US embassy in Tokyo that "one of the most critical internal conditions in Japanese history has been brought about."[58] He issued a formal message to the Japanese government denouncing the invasion as an unprovoked attack in violation of international law.[59] The United States would not recognize the seizure of Manchuria, he said, proclaiming a policy that became known as the Stimson Doctrine.

Stimson's concerns about the threat of Japanese nationalism were soon proved right. In Tokyo, the former finance minister was assassinated in February 1932.[60] In March, the Japanese installed Henry Pu Yi—who decades earlier had been forced to abdicate as emperor of China—as president of a Japanese-controlled puppet regime in Manchuria.[61] In May, radical nationalist naval officers assassinated Japan's prime minister. Emperor Hirohito, who had long encouraged expansion of the Japanese Empire, selected a new prime minister who moved to bolster the new Manchurian regime.[62]

Stimson felt frustration as the global economic depression fueled the rise of extremists in other countries, including Germany, where the fascist movement gathered steam under its anti-Semitic leader, Adolf Hitler. Stimson made repeated trips to Europe in an effort to resolve the war debts, which continued to burden European economies. Discussing the war debts in April 1932, Stimson told the leader of Germany's government, Chancellor Heinrich Brüning of the Centre Party, "that the situation in the world seemed to me like the unfolding of a great Greek tragedy, where we could see the march of events and know what ought to be done, but [seemed] to be powerless to prevent its marching to its grim conclusion."[63]

The depression left millions of Americans desperate, in need of housing, work and food. In April 1932, the unemployment rate in the United States was a staggering 21 percent, almost ten times what it was in early 1930.[64] On April 7, 1932, FDR delivered a national radio address calling for recovery efforts focused on helping the "forgotten man," the least fortunate in society. Roosevelt attacked the Hoover administration for trying to address the depression through programs that would only provide "relief from the top down." In July, the Democrats chose FDR as the party's presidential nominee, and in his acceptance speech he unveiled his call for a "New Deal" to achieve a "more equitable opportunity to share in the distribution of national wealth."

As the presidential race unfolded, President Hoover asked Stimson to attack FDR publicly. Stimson resisted at first but ultimately agreed, and in October 1932, he delivered a speech at the National Republican Club charging that FDR had made a "complete misstatement of facts" about the Reconstruction Finance Corporation, an agency Hoover had established to make loans to struggling businesses.[65] In his speech, carried nationally on radio and covered on the front page of *The New York Times* the next day, Stimson accused Roosevelt of inflaming class prejudices.

FDR never responded to Stimson's attacks during the campaign. He won the election by a landslide, carrying every state except a handful of

Republican strongholds in the Northeast. The Democrats also delivered crushing defeats to the Republicans in elections for the House of Representatives and the Senate, taking large majorities in both houses and setting the stage for FDR to launch his New Deal programs.

In December 1932, Germany defaulted on World War I debts owed to the United States, France and Belgium, and the latter two countries also defaulted on war debts owed to the United States. President Hoover proposed a bipartisan committee to address the debts, asking FDR to name members, but FDR rejected the idea. Felix Frankfurter, who had become a close ally of FDR, called Stimson on December 22 and told him that the president-elect wanted him to come to see him at his home in Hyde Park. Frankfurter said Roosevelt felt no acrimony toward Stimson and believed he "didn't play politics."[66]

Thus the two men—a sixty-five-year-old Republican and a fifty-year-old Democrat—met on January 9, 1933, at Springwood. As noted above, they discussed the war debts and an array of other matters but devoted a good part of their conversation to Manchuria, and Stimson left believing that FDR would side with him on opposing the Japanese invasion. On January 16, Stimson reasserted that the Japanese invasion violated the 1928 Pact of Paris, a treaty that banned aggressive war.[67] The next day, FDR announced that he would maintain the Hoover administration's policy on Manchuria and added, "American foreign policies must uphold the sanctity of international treaties."[68]

When they met again in Washington two days later, Stimson recalled in his diary, FDR referred to their work together on the Far East and said, "'We are getting so that we do pretty good teamwork, don't we?' I laughed and said 'Yes.'"[69] After the president-elect narrowly escaped an attempted assassination in Miami on February 15, Stimson sent him a telegram later that night saying simply, "I am profoundly thankful for your escape."[70]

FDR had not yet taken office, but world events demanded his attention. On the night of February 27, a fire gutted the Reichstag, Germany's parliament. A top Nazi and Hitler ally, Hermann Göring, proclaimed at the scene that "this is a communist crime against the government."[71] Communists were arrested and, along with other critics of Hitler, sent to concentration camps, and communist newspapers were shut down.

In fact, before the fire occurred, Göring knew about Nazi plans to start the fire and prepared a list of communists to arrest for the crime, according to testimony years later at the Nuremberg war crimes trials. Nazi Storm Troopers carried fuel for the blaze from Göring's offices through an underground tunnel to the Reichstag, where they spread gasoline and self-igniting chemicals, the trials revealed. The next day, Hitler convinced Germany's eighty-four-year-old president, Paul von Hindenburg, to issue a decree suspending constitutional freedoms, including the rights of free press and assembly.[72] In this climate of fear, Hitler convinced the Reichstag to vote to surrender all of its rights to Hitler's cabinet for four years.

At the same time, a bank panic was spreading across the United States as many banks were forced to shut their doors to prevent customers from withdrawing funds. To stem the crisis, Hoover Administration officials worked with the man whom FDR planned to name treasurer, William Woodin, a Republican industrialist who had supported FDR's campaign. As the financial panic reached a crescendo, FDR was sworn in on Saturday, March 4, 1933. In his inaugural address, he made no mention of the bank panic, though he expressed confidence in the nation's ability to prosper, saying "the only thing we have to fear is fear itself."[73]

The next day, FDR issued an order closing banks for four days, and he then unveiled a plan to issue Federal Reserve notes to restore the currency supply and to permit banks to reopen after a review by the US Treasury. Congress approved FDR's plan when it passed the Emergency Banking Act—by overwhelming bipartisan majorities in both the Senate and the House of Representatives—and FDR signed it into law the same day, March 9.[74] Hailing the remarkable feat, the president gave credit to both parties in the first of his radio addresses to be known as the Fireside Chats: "I want to tell our citizens in every part of the nation that the national Congress—Republicans and Democrats alike—showed by this action a devotion to public welfare and realization of the emergency and the necessity for speed that it is difficult to match in our history."[75]

FDR successfully resolved the banking crisis, and basking in the flow of bipartisan support the following week he signed a bill repealing Prohibition. But bipartisan support for his policies dissipated after he moved on to a massive legislative effort to create New Deal programs, many of which drew severe Republican criticism as going too far in restricting industry. The new laws included the Home Owners' Loan Act, which provided loans to help homeowners who could not pay their mortgages; the National Industrial Recovery Act, which guaranteed certain trade union rights and permitted the federal government to issue regulations on a broad array of businesses; the Agricultural Adjustment Act, which provided subsidies and loans to farmers; the Civilian Conservation Corps, which put millions of young men to work protecting natural resources; the Federal Emergency Relief Act, which provided funds for states to issue as support payments to the unemployed; and the Tennessee Valley Authority Act, which provided federal funding for electric power in the impoverished Appalachian region. In all, fifteen major pieces of legislation were signed into law by FDR in the first one hundred days of his presidency, transforming many parts of the American economy and helping the nation rise from the depths of the Great Depression.[76]

FDR turned to liberal members of the Republican Party in a bid to build support for his New Deal programs, which called for a broad use of government authority to cure the nation's problems. In addition to his secretary of treasury Woodin, FDR named Harold Ickes, a liberal-minded attorney who once headed Chicago's branch of the National Association for the Advancement of Colored People (NAACP), as secretary of the interior. Ickes became a voice of support for Black Americans in the Roosevelt Administration and headed one of the largest New Deal programs, the Works Project Administration.

In Berlin, Hitler moved to destroy opposing political parties and what remained of German democracy. In June 1934, Hitler's security forces, the Schutzstaffel, or SS, led by Heinrich Himmler, carried out a bloody purge, killing hundreds of perceived opponents in the so-called Night of the Long Knives.[77] The next month, Hitler declared the Nazi party the only political party allowed in Germany, making it a crime to form other parties. Hitler told all Germans that he demanded their unquestioning obedience: "Everyone must know for all future time that if he raises his hand to strike the state, then certain death is his lot."[78]

. . .

STIMSON CONTINUED PRACTICING law and having wide-ranging conversations with FDR about national and global events. He also built a
friendly relationship with Cordell Hull, FDR's secretary of state. In the
summer of 1933, Stimson traveled to London, where he helped Hull
resolve disputes at a global monetary conference and met with British
prime minister Ramsay MacDonald and King George VI.

As Stimson and FDR spent more time together, they exchanged views
on ominous events in Germany and Japan. In a meeting at the White
House on May 17, 1934, FDR recounted to Stimson how as a student at
Harvard he met a Japanese student, a member of the samurai caste, who
told him of a long-term Japanese plan to occupy and control all Asian
nations and Australia and Hawaii. Stimson told FDR he thought Americans would rise up en masse if they believed their legal rights were
threatened. "I felt that if the American people thought there was any
danger of those being trammeled on, it would produce a tremendous
revulsion of feeling." Writing in his diary, Stimson noted that FDR "said
he agreed perfectly."[79]

The importance and challenges of defending freedom arose repeatedly in the two men's discussions. In December 1934, Stimson sent FDR
an essay by Ramsay Muir, a historian and member of Great Britain's
centrist Liberal Party. Entitled "Civilization and Liberty," Muir's twelve-
page treatise painted a broad picture of the evolution of democracy, beginning with the ancient Greeks who pursued truth and reason to craft
laws that reshaped society and improved life. During the Renaissance
period this Greek philosophy met with the Christian idea of the "equal
value of all human personalities," giving rise to a liberal movement that
prized equal rights under the law, freedom of speech, free trade, and
other liberties. Britain engaged in the evil of slavery for three centuries,
but the abolition of the slave trade in 1807 and the subsequent freeing
of all enslaved people in the British Empire in 1834 were among "the
first victories of organized Liberalism." At a time when Hitler, Communists in the Soviet Union and the Japanese Imperial Army were firmly
in power, Muir warned: "The cause of Liberty is not dead, though it

is momentarily obscured. . . . And if those who love liberty, and appreciate the magnitude and profundity of the choice which lies before humanity, are at this moment, in all countries, few, disheartened, and disorganized, that is no justification for relaxing their efforts."[80]

After returning from a trip to Georgia, FDR sent Stimson a note of gratitude: "I read that article by Ramsay Muir one night at Warm Springs after I had gone to bed. I read it through again the next night. Thank you for sending it to me. It is a splendid expression of faith."[81] Although the start of the Second World War still lay five years in the future, fascist and communist forces were rising around the world. In 1934, FDR and Stimson had already found they shared a belief in the crucial importance of taking action to defend democracy.

The Fight over Isolationism

In the summer of 1935, fascist Italian dictator Benito Mussolini was bent on revenge. Abyssinia, the East African country now known as Ethiopia, had won its independence almost forty years earlier by dealing a humiliating defeat to the Italian army. In early 1935, Mussolini garrisoned troops in Italian colonies adjacent to Abyssinia and prepared to invade.[1] Abyssinia was the only African member of the League of Nations, and its emperor, Haile Selassie, appealed to the League for protection. Great Britain urged Italy to stand down and sent warships to guard the nearby Suez Canal.

In Washington, isolationists feared an Abyssinian war could drag American forces back into combat across the Atlantic less than two decades after the Great War, the worldwide conflict of 1914–1918. Senator Gerald Nye, a North Dakota Republican who was a leading isolationist, proposed a bill that would require the president in case of war to keep the United States neutral by imposing an arms embargo on all belligerents— whether an ally of the United States or not.[2] President Roosevelt praised the bill and signed it into law as the Neutrality Act on August 31. He said it was the "desire of the government and the people of the United States to avoid any action which might involve us in war. The purpose is wholly excellent, and this joint resolution will, to a considerable degree, serve that end."[3]

Italy, which had one of the world's largest armies with a million troops under arms, invaded Abyssinia on October 2, 1935. Days later, as Italian forces assaulted Abyssinian towns, FDR issued an order banning arms exports to both nations as belligerents.[4]

Henry L. Stimson was distraught over the Neutrality Act and Italy's war in Abyssinia. His private concord with FDR on foreign policy—begun at their first meeting in January 1933—came to an end after Stimson wrote a lengthy letter to *The New York Times* condemning the president's embargo as "ineffective." Stimson's letter, published October 11, 1935, said the arms embargo actually made it possible for American exporters to profit at the expense of peace efforts. The embargo permitted US exporters to send the belligerents food and other supplies, while other nations were poised to prohibit such trade. Two weeks later, Stimson sharpened his criticism in a national radio broadcast, saying Roosevelt's proclamation "is likely to do more harm than good."[5]

Stimson took up his objections to FDR's policy with his old friend Felix Frankfurter, who he knew was in regular contact with the president. On November 1, Frankfurter spent the evening on Long Island at Highhold, where Stimson told him he had hoped FDR would work with the League to condemn the Italian invasion, just as FDR and Stimson had coordinated US policy with the League regarding Japan's invasion of Manchuria. Stimson, knowing that isolationists opposed the League, told Frankfurter he was confident the president would not "lose his leadership if he took a brave position on the League." Stimson told Frankfurter, "The president was the only person who could make the people understand the necessity of working with the League. Therefore I regretted that he didn't speak out more plainly."[6] Instead, in Stimson's view, by signing the Neutrality Act the president had appeased the isolationists and surrendered some of his latitude to join forces with the League, to build alliances with other countries and to stand up to the fascist powers.

Stimson's dispute with FDR over the Neutrality Act and resulting arms embargo against Italy and Abyssinia marked the start of an estrangement between the two men that would last for more than five years. During this period, Stimson continued sounding an alarm about fascism's rise and the need to build alliances, while FDR strategically navigated the political reality of America's strong isolationism to ensure he retained power. Stimson sometimes praised FDR for condemning

the fascist powers, but he also publicly criticized the president for actions that appeased the isolationists and undermined alliances that
might protect democracies. The men did not have an overt break. There
were no arguments, no harsh words. During this period, Stimson met
periodically with Hull, and FDR occasionally offered positions to Stimson. Yet FDR did not invite Stimson to the White House, and Stimson
did not request a meeting with the president.

THERE WAS ANOTHER matter that likely contributed to the rift between
the two men: a legal challenge fomented by Stimson against one of FDR's
New Deal programs, the Tennessee Valley Authority (TVA). Stimson
had resumed representing the electric utility companies partly owned
by his cousin Alfred Loomis and Landon Thorne, Loomis's brother-in-
law. Loomis and Thorne held significant stakes in the Commonwealth
& Southern Corp., a holding company that owned several large utility
companies.[7] The utility industry had undergone turmoil after a major
utility holding company in Chicago had collapsed amid charges of a
vast fraud scheme.[8] Congress had launched a multi-year investigation
of electric holding companies. And FDR, a proponent of public ownership of utilities, severely criticized the holding companies as driving
up costs paid by the public. FDR believed that the best solution for providing electricity to the impoverished people in the Appalachia region
was for the TVA to build and operate electric power plants. In late 1934,
however, Stimson developed an argument that the TVA, by building
plants in competition with Commonwealth & Southern, was unconstitutional. Stimson discussed these ideas with Loomis and Thorne, setting in motion a legal challenge to the TVA.[9]

In January 1935, Stimson invited David Lilienthal, the head of the
TVA, and Grenville Clark, a lawyer and mutual friend of Stimson and
FDR, to Woodley to discuss the constitutionality issue. Stimson and
Clark concluded after their talk, though, that the two sides might be
able to reach a settlement.[10] Between Clark and Lilienthal, FDR would
certainly have learned that Stimson was advocating a constitutional
challenge to the TVA. The battle over the TVA soon became a high-
profile public spectacle.

Commonwealth & Southern, with Loomis's approval, had hired as its new president a gregarious lawyer from Indiana named Wendell Willkie.[11] A pro-business Democrat, Willkie made sharp attacks on the TVA and the cost of big government under the New Deal, which soon made him a favorite of business interests. "Power is just as destructive on Pennsylvania Avenue as it is on Wall Street," Willkie said in a May 1935 speech to the US Chamber of Commerce.[12]

Lilienthal went on the offensive, charging publicly that holding companies were a "financial tapeworm," draining cash from utilities and driving up costs for ratepayers. FDR, who had called for abolishing "the evil of holding companies," signed a law in August 1935 to eliminate many holding companies and subject others to regulation.[13]

The litigation threat from Stimson, Willkie and Commonwealth & Southern hung like a cloud over the TVA. After the US Supreme Court struck down as unconstitutional the National Industrial Recovery Act, a key piece of New Deal legislation, in May 1935, Commonwealth & Southern and its subsidiaries filed lawsuits claiming that both the TVA and the new federal law restricting holding companies were unconstitutional. The dialogue between FDR and Stimson, once so warm, went dormant.

FEARS OF WAR in Europe continued rising. In March 1935, Adolf Hitler issued a decree raising an army of five hundred thousand men, renouncing the Treaty of Versailles provision that had prevented Germany from having an army. Secretly, Germany also was rebuilding its armaments.[14] Hitler also intensified his campaign against Jewish Germans. In 1933, Jews had been excluded from public office, radio and other professions, and in September 1935 Hitler signed the so-called Nuremberg Laws depriving Jews of German citizenship and barring marriage between Jews and ethnic Germans.[15]

With a presidential election approaching, FDR made a robust appeal to the isolationists. In his State of the Union address to Congress on January 3, 1936, FDR condemned autocratic leaders—obliquely referring to the Japanese, Italian and German regimes—as having "reverted to the old belief in the law of the sword."[16] To keep America safe, he proclaimed his commitment to neutrality, the legalistic expression of

isolationism. "The United States is following a two-fold neutrality toward any and all nations which engage in wars that are not of immediate concern to the Americas," he said.

With FDR's support, Senator Key Pittman, who was the Democratic
chairman of the Senate Foreign Relations Committee, proposed a bill
to extend the Neutrality Act and expand it to require embargoes on not
just arms and ammunition but also financial transactions with belligerents. Nye, not to be outdone, proposed strengthening the Neutrality Act
by banning US vessels from sailing in waters near belligerents.

US allies became concerned over the proposals, which would require
a broad embargo against a US ally even if attacked by an aggressor. If
Germany were to attack England, for instance, the act would impose
an embargo on both countries equally. "No distinction is attempted between belligerents. The aggressor and his victim stand on precisely the
same footing," said an editorial in *The Daily Telegraph* of London. "That
may be logical and it may be statecraft, yet we suspect that many American consciences will be sorely troubled."[17]

Isolationists, though, were riding high in Congress. Nye summoned
J.P. Morgan and other prominent bankers to testify before a special committee about the conduct of banks and munitions manufacturers in the
world war two decades earlier, forcing an admission that the banks had
lobbied President Wilson to change his stance and permit the banks to
make large loans to Great Britain and other allied governments for their
war efforts. J.P. Morgan & Co. made $30 million in commissions han-
dling purchases of some $3 billion in munitions from the United States
during the war, Nye's committee revealed. (Dollar figures in this book
are actual, not adjusted for inflation.) J.P. Morgan himself, appearing
before the committee, insisted that German submarine attacks—not
bank loans—brought America into the war.[18] Suspicion of foreign wars
also was fueled by former Marine Corps general Smedley D. Butler,
who accused the munitions industry of pushing war for purposes of
profit. Butler's 1935 book *War Is a Racket* warned that Americans had
become "internationally minded," with grave consequences. "It would
have been far cheaper (not to say safer) for the average American who
pays the bills to stay out of foreign entanglements." Butler toured the
country speaking publicly and delivering radio broadcasts proclaiming

his isolationist and anti-war views.[19] Polls showed strong support for anti-war policies and neutrality laws.[20]

Bolstered by concerns about war and allegations of war profiteering, Nye's neutrality bill passed. President Roosevelt, who hoped to win the votes of isolationists in the presidential election approaching in the fall, signed the bill into law on February 29, 1936.[21] FDR praised the law "for enabling this country to maintain its neutrality and avoid being drawn into wars involving other nations."

That same month in Tokyo, rebel military officers supporting Emperor Hirohito's imperialist policies carried out a coup attempt, murdering seven senior officials, including two former prime ministers.[22] More than 1,300 soldiers seized government buildings in Tokyo, though they withdrew after three days and seventeen participants were later sentenced to death.[23] Hirohito selected a new prime minister, who secured military support by granting the army control over key cabinet posts.

In Germany, Hitler again violated the Treaty of Versailles in March 1936 by moving military forces into the Rhineland, a region that had been demilitarized since the end of the First World War. In Spain, civil war broke out in early 1936, as General Francisco Franco led right-wing forces seeking to topple the democratic Republic of Spain. Hitler sent German bomber planes, fighters, tanks, antiaircraft guns, munitions and military advisers to help defeat the Spanish Republicans.[24] Benito Mussolini supplied Franco's forces with fighters, tanks, weapons and soldiers. In October 1936, Soviet dictator Joseph Stalin began sending arms to Spanish Republican forces, seeking to help the communists fighting Franco.

WITH THREATS OF war spreading around the globe, the Republican Party prepared to select its next nominee for president. Early in 1936, the progressive Republican Kansas governor Alf Landon announced his candidacy, as did Senator William Borah, a strong isolationist. Another Republican, Frank Knox, the publisher of the *Chicago Daily News* and a sharp critic of the New Deal, also threw his hat in the ring. At the June 1936 Republican national convention in Cleveland, Ohio, Landon won the nomination, and Knox was chosen as his vice-presidential running mate. In accepting his nomination, Knox charged that "hysterical" New Deal experiments had delayed recovery from the depression and that the Republican ticket would work for "preservation of free enterprise."[25] The party's isolationist platform called for maintaining peace "by all honorable means not leading to foreign alliances."

At the Democratic national convention in Philadelphia two weeks later, FDR and Vice President John Garner sought nomination for a second term in office. FDR called for a continuation of the New Deal and keeping the nation far from the wars flaring up around the world. FDR approved a draft of the party platform that called for "true neutrality" and avoiding commitments that would "tend to draw this nation into war."[26] Having signed the original Neutrality Act in 1935, and its extension in February 1936, FDR had in effect positioned himself as both a peacemaker and an isolationist.

Roosevelt and Garner won their nominations, and their campaign continued to sound isolationist notes. On August 14, giving a campaign speech in Chautauqua, New York, FDR said, "We shun political commitment which might entangle us in foreign wars; we avoid connection with the political activities of the League of Nations." He raised the familiar isolationist complaint about war profiteering: "If war should break out again in another continent, let us not blink the fact that we would find in this country thousands of Americans who, seeking immediate riches—fools' gold—would attempt to break down or evade our neutrality." Yet he also sought to straddle the issue, when he uttered a paradoxical statement: "We are not isolationists except insofar as we seek to isolate ourselves completely from war."[27]

FDR's popularity, founded on the broad appeal of the New Deal and his commitment to neutrality, overwhelmed Landon and Knox. On Election Day, November 3, FDR and Garner won forty-six of the forty-eight states, grabbing 523 electoral votes to the eight won by Landon and Knox—a humbling rout for the Republicans that was the greatest margin of defeat in a presidential race since the largely uncontested 1820 election.

The isolationists flexed their political muscle in January 1937, when

Congress, as its first act in its new session, passed a bill authored by Nye to embargo arms exports to Spain because of the civil war there. FDR signed the bill into law the same day.[28]

In early 1937, FDR, angered by the US Supreme Court rulings that had struck down some New Deal programs as unconstitutional, pushed a bill in Congress that would add six justices to the nine already on the high court. The Constitution was silent on how many justices should serve on the court, and that number had been fixed by law at nine since 1869, the president said in an address announcing the plan on February 5. The bill would also add judges across the entire federal court system, which FDR argued was overburdened. Republican critics swiftly denounced the bill as a scheme to win favorable rulings from the Supreme Court. Former president Hoover charged FDR was simply "packing" the court with allies so he could shield New Deal programs from scrutiny.[29] Joining in the objections was Stimson, who circumspectly told The Baltimore Sun, "Even if the president's proposal were made at a normal time and under normal conditions, I should not favor it."[30] Meeting privately with Hull at the State Department in early April, Stimson put it to him bluntly: "I never expected to live to see a President of the United States try to pack the Supreme Court. . . . I do not think that the president has any intention of making himself a dictator but I can only say that anyone who had such an intention would follow exactly this course."[31] Amid broad condemnation of the bill, Democrats in Congress broke with the president, and on July 22 the Senate defeated the measure by a vote of 70–20.[32] The debacle left FDR politically weakened and chastened by the proof that Democratic legislators, particularly the bloc of southern Democrats who had supported him previously, could abandon him.

Amid the political furor over FDR's judiciary bill, FDR and the isolationists moved to renew the Neutrality Act, which—after FDR extended it in 1936—was set to expire May 1, 1937. FDR maintained his pro-isolationist posture by backing a measure by Senator Pittman that would make the act permanent and also expand its reach by restricting even sales of nonmilitary items to belligerents.[33] FDR signed the bill into law on May 1.[34]

Japan invaded central China in July 1937.[35] Three months later, resistance from Chiang Kai-shek's nationalist armies bogged down the Japanese forces near Shanghai. Chiang had been engaged in a long-running civil war against the Communist Party of China, but Chiang and Communist leader Mao Zedong had entered an alliance known as the Second United Front to face their common enemy of Japan. The alliance enabled both sides to focus on attacking the Japanese.[36]

As China burned, FDR spoke out forcefully against the global toll of war. On October 5, 1937, while in Chicago to dedicate a bridge built with New Deal funds, he issued an appeal for peace. America, he said, was menaced by "the present reign of terror and international lawlessness" that has "reached a stage where the very foundations of civilization are threatened."[37] He said that "without warning or justification of any kind, civilians, including women and children, are being ruthlessly murdered with bombs from the air." The president, who adhered to his Christian faith, urged the teachings of Jesus Christ. "If civilization is to survive, the principles of the Prince of Peace must be restored." He added that wars of aggression violated the League of Nations covenant and the Pact of Paris, and he urged all nations to recognize "the sanctity of treaties." He called for "concerted action" to "quarantine" aggressor nations. However, the president made no mention of specific aggressor nations, and he identified no specific steps to be taken against them.

The next day, October 6, the League of Nations formally condemned Japan for its invasion of China. FDR had derided the League in campaigning for reelection, but the State Department now endorsed the League's finding in a statement. Thus, FDR was effectively condemning Japan and moving away from the sentiment of strict neutrality. In a sign he was edging away from his isolationist stance, he quietly refused to declare under the Neutrality Act that a state of war existed between Japan and China, which in effect permitted the United States to sell arms to China.

Stimson published in *The New York Times* that same day a lengthy letter attacking FDR's Neutrality Act and the growing isolationism of the United States while praising FDR's stance against war. Stimson, however, pushed for a more aggressive policy than FDR: he called for ending trade with Japan. As a former Republican secretary of state, his support for the Democratic president drew attention. *The Times* ran a front-page story on the letter under the headline "Stimson Favors Action on Japan."[38] Stimson praised FDR's Chicago speech, saying, "I am filled with hope that this act of leadership on his part will result in a new birth of American courage in facing and carrying through our responsibilities in this crisis." But he called for more than simply moral condemnation—he called for taking action, writing: "In this grave crisis in the Far East we not only must not fear to face issues of right and wrong but we must not fear to cooperate with other nations who are similarly attempting to face those issues." He urged US cooperation with the League of Nations to call upon Japan to end the war. He also argued that Japan's exports of raw silk and its purchase of oil, iron and rubber from the United States and other countries amounted to foreign assistance to the Japanese war machine. He suggested countries wishing to assist China "should cease helping her enemy." This bold statement, which in effect called for a trade embargo against Japan, confirmed Stimson's place as the most prominent American calling for action against Japanese aggression.

Stimson also made a broad attack on isolationism, condemning the Neutrality Act as a "policy of amoral drift." Not only was isolationism morally wrong, it was destined to fail in preventing war. In America, "there has been no excuse except faulty reasoning for the wave of ostrich-like isolationism which has swept over us and by its erroneous form of neutrality legislation has threatened to bring upon us in the future the very dangers of war which we are now seeking to avoid."

Isolationists responded swiftly. Nye charged that the United States was once again being summoned to fight a foreign war. "I very much fear that we are once again being caused to feel that the call is upon America to police a world that chooses to follow insane leaders," he said. He demanded that the president invoke the Neutrality Act in regard to China.[39] The act gave the president discretion to determine whether a state of war existed, and FDR exercised that discretion by declining.

As the war in China worsened, Stimson broke his long personal silence with FDR the next month by writing him a letter saying, "My mind is full of foreboding as to what seems to me in the Far East one of the very gravest crises that have confronted us during my lifetime. . . . China is really fighting our battle for freedom and peace in the Orient today." He implored the president to consider aiding the Chinese, and warned that imposing an embargo against China as a belligerent, as required under the Neutrality Act, would be a "serious present military blow."[40] Stimson pointed to Ramsay Muir's "Civilization and Liberty," the essay he had sent to FDR three years earlier: "That world crisis of freedom which Muir so eloquently described in his article is trembling in the balance on the fields of China today."

FDR replied a week later in a letter to Stimson saying it was not possible to pursue "measures of pressure" against Japan, suggesting the political power of the isolationists was simply too great. "I am sure neither the people of this country nor Congress would have supported it," the president wrote.[41] Stimson had called for FDR to take bold action against the Japanese invasion of China, but the president, calculating the political chances of success for such a strategy, bluntly rejected Stimson's plea.

Even as the two men corresponded, staggering war news arrived from China. The Japanese army won control of Shanghai in November 1937 and then surged west toward Nanjing. On December 5, 1937, secret orders went out under the name of the top commander of the Japanese forces attacking Nanjing: "Kill all captives."[42] The Japanese troops then unleashed a campaign of executions, torture and rapes against Chinese soldiers and civilians over the next six weeks.[43] Two Japanese soldiers garnered laudatory coverage in the Japanese press for a contest in which they vied to be the first to use a sword to kill one hundred Chinese people, and when both exceeded that number they revised their goal to one hundred and fifty.[44] Japanese soldiers raped many women, often executing them afterwards and mutilating their bodies, according to witness accounts and Japanese confessions.[45] War crimes trials later revealed that the number of people killed in the massacre was at least two hundred and sixty thousand, although some researchers have suggested the actual number may be closer to four hundred thousand.[46] US newspapers extensively covered the carnage.[47]

In Europe, in early March 1938, Hitler threatened Austrian officials, and Nazi forces quickly occupied the nation.[48] Tens of thousands of people were arrested, and the SS established a large concentration camp, Mauthausen, to hold Austrian Jews and other opponents of the regime. The Nazis established the Office for Jewish Emigration, headed by the Austrian Nazi Adolf Eichmann, to limit Jewish emigration from Austria.[49]

Hitler next turned his empire-building attentions to Czechoslovakia. In the summer of 1938, he threatened to seize the Sudetenland, a region of Czechoslovakia with significant industrial plants. In Munich on September 30, British prime minister Neville Chamberlain and other leaders signed an agreement granting the Sudetenland to Germany on the condition that it would seize no other European lands. In London, Chamberlain won cheers in Parliament when he hailed the Munich Agreement as providing "peace in our time." Critics charged that Chamberlain was engaging in a futile act of appeasement of Hitler, and his fellow Conservative Winston Churchill caused an uproar when he denounced the pact saying, "We have suffered a total and unmitigated defeat."[50]

A month later, a Jewish opponent of Nazism shot and mortally wounded a minor official of the German embassy in Paris on November 7, 1938. In response, Nazi Storm Troopers carried out violent attacks and arsons across Germany and Austria against Jewish homes, businesses and synagogues on the nights of November 9 and 10. It became known in German as *Kristallnacht,* the night of glass. On the first night in Vienna, fires and bombs wrecked eighteen of the city's twenty-one synagogues, and fifteen thousand Jews were arrested by the police.[51] Across Germany twenty thousand Jews were arrested, thirty-six were killed, and one hundred and nineteen synagogues were set on fire.[52] On November 12, the Nazi government fined all Jews in Germany one billion marks, and barred Jews from operating businesses and going to concert halls and other public places. The virulent anti-Semitism in Hitler's speeches had turned into savage dictatorial action.

In these fraught times, Stimson's relationship with Secretary of State Hull evolved into a closer bond and, in effect, a confidential collaboration. In March 1938, Stimson went to the State Department, where Hull told his Republican predecessor of his concerns about isolationism. "He was worried and troubled by the efforts of our isolationists which he said could not have been better designed to aid the governments of Japan, Italy and Germany than if they had been employed by those powers," Stimson noted in his diary.[53] As the men became closer, Stimson invited Hull to use Woodley for personal recreation after work—even when the Stimsons were not in Washington. Hull, who had caught typhoid as a young man and secretly suffered from tuberculosis and other health conditions, spent countless hours in the following years playing croquet on the lawn at Woodley.[54]

In June 1938, Hull announced a "moral embargo" against Japan by asking all American aircraft manufacturers to voluntarily stop selling airplanes to Japan.[55] American industry responded promptly and within a year aircraft exports to Japan had almost completely stopped.

Stimson continued pushing Hull and FDR to abandon neutrality. At the State Department on October 24, 1938, Stimson urged Hull to have confidence in the president's ability to win the support of the American public for international alliances. It was, in essence, a plea for the president to lead and to disregard critics and polls. "I said that the American people take their attitude towards foreign policy primarily from the president. They will follow his lead almost always and, when he gave them a good strong lead, the talk of pacifists and trouble makers usually would die away into nothing."

FDR soon began warning the American people that they might soon have to help foreign allies. In his State of the Union address to Congress on January 4, 1939, he said, "There comes a time in the affairs of men when they must prepare to defend not their homes but the tenets of faith and humanity on which their churches, their governments and their very civilization are founded. The defense of religion, of democracy and of good faith among nations is all the same fight. To save one we must now make up our minds to save all."[56] Yet the president made no attempt to overturn the Neutrality Act, nor did he call for specific alliances with other democracies.

Stimson resumed his attacks on isolationism. He launched a committee to urge an embargo of Japan, the American Committee for Non-Participation in Japanese Aggression, whose members included William Allen White, a prominent progressive Republican newspaper publisher from Kansas. Stimson also called for an end to the embargo on Spain. After Hitler's air force firebombed the town of Guernica in 1937, killing an estimated three hundred people, support for the Republican loyalists soared in western countries.[57] As the bloodshed in Spain continued, Ickes urged FDR in 1938 to push Congress to lift the embargo blocking aid to the loyalists. FDR refused, saying he feared that in the midterm elections of that year Catholic voters who supported Franco would turn against any member of Congress who voted against the embargo.[58] By early 1939 Franco's air force was bombing the loyalists in their last stronghold, the city of Barcelona and the surrounding region of Catalonia.

In January 1939, Stimson wrote Hull a letter—also published in *The New York Times*—urging him to lift the embargo on Spain and permit shipment of arms to loyalist Republican forces.[59] "If this Loyalist Government is overthrown, it is evident now that its defeat will be solely due to the fact that it has been deprived of the right to buy from us and other friendly nations the munitions necessary for its defense," Stimson wrote. Isolationists in Congress condemned Stimson's plea and argued the embargo on Spain was required by law. Representative Hamilton Fish, the hardline isolationist Republican from New York, said on the House floor that he opposed Stimson's views—and didn't know a single member of Congress who supported them.[60] FDR made no effort to overturn the embargo.[61]

Despite their discord over the Spanish embargo, Stimson saw FDR as turning against neutrality and isolationism, and he soon called for "all parties and citizens" to support FDR's foreign policy. In yet another long letter to *The New York Times*, Stimson issued a clarion call for Republicans to form a loyal opposition: he expressed complete support of FDR's foreign policy while firmly objecting to his domestic policy. By this time, there was a pattern of Stimson writing letters to *The Times*, and the newspaper publishing both the full text of the letter and an article about it. Stimson was a prominent New Yorker who had been covered by the paper for decades—ever since he was TR's top antitrust prosecutor in the city. He also was a former Republican secretary of war, secretary of state under the previous Republican president, and a man who had for years been warning the world about imperial Japan's military ambitions. His experience and authority in foreign affairs were unrivaled. Beyond his stature and experience, Stimson represented a brand of progressive Republican whose internationalist views often agreed with *Times* editorials. Stimson also had a key connection:

he was friends with Julius O. Adler, an army reserve colonel who was general manager of the paper. While Stimson was extremely adept at using the media to achieve his ends, it was clear *The Times* accorded him particular attention. His letter published in the paper on March 6, 1939, stretched across five columns and totaled nearly 3,300 words, far more than the average letter to the editor. Like many of his earlier letters, this one was treated as a news event in itself and ran on page sixteen—amid the news pages, not with other letters to the editor. More important, the story about the letter ran on the front page under the headline, "Stimson Supports US Foreign Policy."

Stimson's letter praised FDR's "affirmative action" on foreign policy. But once again Stimson went beyond FDR's policies: he called for the United States to join with Great Britain and other democracies and combine their navies in joint forces.

Perhaps most significantly, Stimson also sharply criticized the president, arguing his domestic policies undermined national unity. "In his January address to the Congress the president truly stated that the success of a national foreign policy depends upon having behind it a strong and united people," he wrote. "But national strength is not prompted by an extravagance which comes dangerously near the impairment of our national credit. It is not promoted by novel and haphazard experiments with the nation's finance. National unity is not promoted by appeals to class spirit. Nor is it promoted by methods which tend to disrupt the patriotism of either party or the effective cooperation of the two, upon which the coordinate working of the American Government depends."

Stimson's letter demonstrated how Republicans could continue their sharp criticism of FDR's domestic policies while supporting his foreign policy. But if FDR wanted Republican support in such a bargain—in essence an alliance with Republicans—Stimson made it clear he would have to avoid "the temptations common to the politics of normal times." The president "should have the support of all parties and all citizens. But he must lead toward that accomplishment. No others can." His words were addressed to his fellow Republicans on one hand and FDR on the other.[62]

Franco and his fascist allies were in control of Spain and the loyalists were defeated by the end of March 1939. The next month, Stimson testified to the Senate Foreign Relations Committee that the Neutrality Act undermined US national defense because it obligated the president to treat aggressors and victims equally, and this requirement was known to both the fascists and the loyalists in Spain. In essence, Stimson said, it was "like playing poker with your hand open on the table while the other hands are concealed."[63] His arguments fell on deaf ears. The Neutrality Act remained in place.

In May 1939, Japanese forces began an intense campaign of devastating aerial bombardments of the city of Chungking in southwest China.[64] FDR and Hull decided to protest Japan's conduct in China by abrogating a vital commercial treaty between the United States and Japan, which had been in effect since 1911 and provided most-favored-nation trading status to Japan.[65]

Yet Hull and FDR sought to avoid any sign that they would take sides in foreign conflicts. In July 1939, the ocean liner *St. Louis* approached the United States carrying more than nine hundred Jewish refugees fleeing Germany. After Cuban authorities refused to let the Jews disembark, Hull and FDR disregarded calls to permit them entry into the United States and they were returned to Europe. Many later perished in the Holocaust.[66]

THE LONG LEGAL battle over the TVA was finally resolved in August 1939. Commonwealth & Southern had lost its challenges to TVA's constitutionality in rulings by the US Supreme Court. Stimson's quiet role in the sprawling litigation was revealed in 1938, when Willkie told a congressional committee investigating the TVA that he had "consulted with Mr. Stimson for a long time."[67] At last, on August 15, 1939, the struggle ended with a ceremony attended by 250 people on the top floor of a Wall Street bank, where the TVA delivered a check to Willkie in a deal to buy Commonwealth & Southern's power company in Tennessee for $78 million. Stimson was not there—he was immersed in litigation for an oil company at the time—but this was likely the compromise settlement he had envisioned five years earlier. It was a huge payout, but Willkie nonetheless attacked the TVA, saying, "We sell these properties with regret. We have been forced to do so because we could not stay in business against this subsidized government competition."[68]

On August 24, 1939, the foreign ministers of Germany and the Soviet Union signed a nonaggression treaty as the two nations secretly planned to divide Poland. A week later, on September 1, 1939, Hitler's armies invaded Poland. The Germans bombed both military targets and cities, quickly seizing swaths of Polish territory. On September 3, Poland's allies Great Britain and France announced they were at war with Germany. A new world war had begun. The same day, a German submarine torpedoed and sank the *Athenia*, a British ocean liner. Among the 1,400 passengers aboard the ship were 292 Americans, twenty-eight of whom died in the attack.[69]

That evening, FDR delivered a Fireside Chat via radio from the White House, promising to keep America safe by proclaiming America neutral in accord with the Neutrality Act. "I trust that in the days to come our neutrality can be made a true neutrality," he said. But he also hinted at uneasiness with neutrality when he said, "Even a neutral cannot be asked to close his mind or his conscience."[70]

Two days later, the president imposed an embargo on Great Britain, France, Poland and Germany equally—on the Nazi aggressor state and its victims alike, as the Neutrality Act required. The embargo immediately halted all sales of weapons to the American allies, just as critics of the Neutrality Act had long warned. The president's embargo also targeted Australia, India and New Zealand, deemed belligerents because they sided with Britain. The Nazis tightened their grip on Warsaw, the British Navy attacked the German Navy in the Baltic Sea, and the French clashed with German troops along their shared border. In the United States, concern rose over the war and the embargo's impact on America's allies.

After four years of supporting the Neutrality Act, FDR abruptly announced on September 8 that he would call for a special session for the purpose of repealing the act's key element—its embargo provision. He disclosed this plan in a news conference called to announce an emergency order he signed increasing the size of the US military, which he carefully termed as necessary for "enforcing the neutrality of the United

States." The increase would add another 107,000 soldiers to the 120,000 currently in the army.[71] Weakened by isolationism, the US Army was small—it ranked nineteenth out of all the world's armies, just ahead of Bulgaria and behind Portugal. It was far behind such powerhouses as Germany, which had an estimated two million men under arms at that time.[72]

The isolationists quickly launched a defense of the Neutrality Act. On September 11, Senator William Borah, the isolationist from Idaho, gave a national radio address proclaiming that he would vigorously oppose any revision of the Neutrality Act. Its repeal, he warned, would "inevitably bring us into the war."[73]

Stimson attacked Borah's arguments in a letter to *The New York Times*. "Senator Borah evidently thinks that the repeal of the automatic arms embargo provisions of the so-called Nye legislation would inevitably drag us into armed participation in the present war," Stimson wrote. "I think that the repeal of those provisions constitutes perhaps the last remaining hope of our avoiding being so dragged in."[74] Because the Neutrality Act barred the sale of weapons to US allies, the nation had "played into the hands" of the aggressors, Stimson argued. He contended that by sending arms to nations attacked by aggressors, America could end the war before it reached American shores.

A popular American hero then entered the debate, taking an isolationist position sharply opposed to Stimson's. Aviator Charles A. Lindbergh, who had won international acclaim for his pioneering solo flight from New York to Paris in 1927, gave a speech broadcast nationally September 15 calling for America to maintain its isolation from the wars in the rest of the world. "If we enter by fighting for democracy abroad, we may end by losing it at home," he said. *The New York Times* ran its story on Lindbergh's speech the next day on the front page, side by side with the article about Stimson's letter condemning the Neutrality Act. Lindbergh warned that delivering arms to one side would not be sufficient to win, and America would soon be caught up in a horrific war. He then issued a harsh prediction: "We are likely to lose a million men, possibly several million—the best of American youth. We will be staggering under the burden of recovery during the rest of our lives."[75]

Lindbergh polarized the national debate. He openly lauded Nazi

Germany's military and industrial might. In 1938 he had visited Berlin, where Hermann Göring, the Nazi leader who was commander in chief of the German Luftwaffe, presented him with a medal awarded by Hitler. Now, delivering his speech over the radio September 15, the aviator said it would be madness to send American troops to fight in Europe. He insisted that "as long as we maintain an army, a navy and an air force worthy of the name, as long as America does not decay within, we need fear no invasion of this country."[76]

The European war spread as German submarines sank British ships and were sighted off the east coast of the United States. The Soviet Union and Japan concluded a peace agreement, enabling those two nations to divert armed forces to fronts other than their shared border in Manchuria. Stalin's armies invaded Poland September 17, seizing the eastern half of the country as had been secretly agreed with Hitler. More isolationists rushed to defend the Neutrality Act. Democratic senator Bennett Clark of Missouri and Republican senator Arthur Vandenberg of Michigan announced a bipartisan effort to preserve the Act. Clark sought to hold FDR to his previous support for the Neutrality Act by recounting verbatim the president's statement in 1936—"We are not isolationists except insofar as we seek to isolate ourselves completely from war."[77]

FDR responded with his own display of bipartisan support, inviting the 1936 Republican presidential candidate Landon and his running mate, Frank Knox, to meet with other Republicans and Democrats in a "unity conference" at the White House to discuss revising the Neutrality Act on September 20, the day before the special session was to begin. In the pages of his *Chicago Daily News,* Knox also had called for repealing the arms embargo and urged all Americans and all political parties to rally around the president. In a September 12 editorial, Knox called for FDR to create a "government of national unity" by bringing Republicans into the cabinet. "If we are to achieve national unity, adjourn politics, and keep this country from errors that might involve us in war, we must achieve a government of national unity—a government that in its personnel represents us all."[78]

Issuing a remarkable apology for his own role on the Neutrality Act, FDR called for its repeal on the first day the special session. "I regret that the Congress passed the Act. I regret equally that I signed that Act," he said in a speech to both chambers. "This government must lose no time or effort to keep the nation from being drawn into the war."[79] FDR aide Samuel Rosenman, who wrote the speech for FDR, later said this moment marked the start of a bipartisan wartime policy from which FDR would never waver.[80] Seeking both Republican and Democrat votes to secure the repeal, FDR urged Congress to consider the matter "without trace of partisanship."

The administration's bill, backed by Senator Pittman, would end the mandatory embargo on all belligerents, leaving the administration free to decide when to impose arms embargos on aggressors. Isolationists opposed the bill. A group of twenty-four isolationist senators—both Republicans and Democrats—met in the office of Senator Hiram Johnson, a long-standing isolationist, and emerged vowing to block the repeal by fighting it, as one said, "from hell to breakfast."

On October 2, Borah said in debate on the floor of the Senate that the Neutrality Act was a moral crusade by a hundred and thirty million Americans who believed that its adoption meant "the cause of peace had received a most substantial and permanent advance."[81] The same day, Germany warned the United States that its ships were subject to search and that if they failed to comply could be targeted for attack.

Three days later, Stimson gave a national radio address arguing the Neutrality Act threatened the security of the United States by preventing the country from aiding its allies. At this time, England and France were fighting a battle against the Nazis. But if England and France lost, it "would become our own battle," Stimson said, and so Congress must repeal the "foolish and dangerous embargo."[82]

Stimson had long called for repeal of the Neutrality Act, and now the president had joined him. More political leaders began to want to hear what Stimson had to say. Landon met with Stimson to discuss the embargo, as did Thomas Dewey, the Republican district attorney for New York City who was contemplating a run for the presidency in 1940.[83] Stimson's old friend Frankfurter, whom FDR had appointed a Supreme Court justice early in 1939, sent Stimson a letter praising his October 5 radio address as being "in your most luminous style and inescapable in the realism of its logic."[84] Knowing Stimson's heavy workload in his law practice, Frankfurter wrote, "I wish that you soon will be free of your immediate professional obligations and that you will keep yourself free. To paraphrase Milton—United States hath need of thee."[85]

Congress continued debating. No bill passed. The Nazis bombed a naval base in Scotland and launched minor attacks against French forces along the Maginot Line fortifications in eastern France.

Lindbergh took to the airwaves again on October 13, denying that democracy was in jeopardy and suggesting England and France were equally at fault with Germany for the war. He said the conflict was "over the balance of power in Europe—a war brought about by the desire for strength on the part of Germany and the fear of strength on the part of England and France."[86] In the Senate, Vandenberg and other isolationists praised Lindbergh while Pittman condemned him for defending Germany's "brutal" conquests.

The Senate finally voted on October 27 to pass Pittman's bill to repeal the embargo provisions of the Neutrality Act. The 63–30 vote cut across party lines: eight Republicans joined with fifty-four Democrats and one Independent in support of the repeal, while twelve Democrats joined with fifteen Republicans and two Farmer-Laborites and one Progressive in opposition. Six days later, the House passed the repeal by a vote of 243–181.[87] The repeal supporters included twenty-one Republicans and two hundred and twenty Democrats, while opponents included one hundred and forty-three Republicans and thirty-six Democrats. FDR signed the repeal on November 4. The British government swiftly moved to purchase American military aircraft, while Nazi leaders warned America would soon be drawn into the war.

A week later, in a speech via telephone to the Virginia Military Institute, the president suggested his objective remained peace.[88] "The only object of arms is to bring about a condition in which quiet peace under liberty can endure," he said.

Backed by Stimson and other Republicans, FDR had secured the votes of both Republicans and Democrats in Congress, and the Neutrality Act embargo had been abolished. FDR and Stimson had proved that an alliance of the Democratic president and Republicans could provide the visionary leadership—and the votes in Congress—necessary to curb the power of isolationism and lead a global defense of democracy. Isolationism, however, remained a powerful force across the country and in Congress. FDR began considering how his nascent bipartisan alliance could face the challenges ahead.

Crossing the Divide

When Frank Knox met with President Roosevelt at the White House on December 10, 1939, the two men kept the visit quiet. Reporters caught up to the former Republican vice-presidential candidate at the train station on his way out of Washington, but Knox held his words. "I consistently declined to give out any statement whatever save to acknowledge that I had been a visitor to the White House which they already knew," he wrote FDR in a letter a few days later. Rumors that the president might appoint Knox to his cabinet swirled, but FDR publicly ridiculed the idea.[1]

In fact, in their meeting that day FDR and Knox had secretly plotted a strategy for bringing Knox and another prominent Republican into Roosevelt's cabinet to lead the war effort, a bold political move that would construct a bipartisan alliance to prepare the nation for the wars spreading across the globe. Knox saw himself serving the nation best as secretary of the navy. "Like yourself, I feel intensely that our chief bulwark against aggression and for the promotion of future security must lie in sea power," he told FDR in his letter December 15.[2] "I am also keenly conscious of the great compliment you paid me in asking me to become a member of your official family, despite the fact that I have been one of the most active, and I fear sometimes cantankerous, critics of your domestic program. May I also add that it is even more a tribute to your broad gauged patriotism that you should seriously consider such action."

Knox was an intensely patriotic, dyed-in-the-wool Republican. Born William Franklin Knox in Boston in 1874, he left college in his senior year to fight in Cuba with TR's Rough Riders in the Spanish-American War. He later worked as a newspaper reporter, then editor and then founded the *Manchester Leader* newspaper in New Hampshire. He backed TR in his Bull Moose campaign against Republican president William Taft in 1912. Knox rejoined the US Army and served as an artillery officer in the First World War, rising to the rank of colonel. After the war he returned to journalism, serving for four years as general manager of William Randolph Hearst's newspaper empire. In 1931 he parted ways with Hearst and acquired a controlling stake in the *Chicago Daily News,* which he used to publish his blistering anti–New Deal and anti-Roosevelt editorials before and after the 1936 presidential race. Yet after the outbreak of the European war and the national debate over the Neutrality Act in 1939, Knox's editorials began urging the public to support FDR for the good of the country.

Knox realized that his joining FDR's cabinet could spark severe political criticism. One problem, he told FDR in his December 15 letter, was "the absence at the moment on the part of the public of any deep sense of crisis which would justify completely forgetting and obliterating party lines." Another problem was that only one Republican joining the cabinet "would not make it, in the public view, a coalition cabinet into which a member of the opposition could go without encountering overwhelming criticism which would be destructive of any reputation one may have built through a whole lifetime of pretty consistent party loyalty."

Yet Knox also noted that both of these barriers to the creation of a "coalition cabinet" might be resolved. First, it was possible the world would reach a heightened crisis, such as would occur if Nazi Germany and the Soviet Union joined to form an alliance, he said. And the second problem might be resolved by adding another Republican to the cabinet along with Knox. He urged FDR to consider Knox's friend William Donovan for this second Republican post. Donovan was a First World War hero and prominent Republican who had run unsuccessfully for

New York governor in 1932. He suggested that FDR could appoint the two Republicans as a "non-political measure" to improve military preparedness. This plan would defuse partisan criticism, he said. "In brief, if this rather radical idea which you have in mind and which you outlined to me so clearly in our talk, could be put upon an obvious and undeniable basis of all-American national defense, it would have a very different effect upon the country as a whole and would tend to subordinate, if it did not eliminate, partisan and political criticism."

Having launched the bipartisan discussion with Knox, FDR hit the brakes. Two weeks passed before he wrote Knox a sober reply: "Your suggestion that the country as a whole does not yet have any deep sense of world crisis must I fear be admitted by me—and, therefore, I must also admit that your coming into the Cabinet might be construed as a political move rather than as a patriotic move, which, as you know, was the only thing that actuated me."[3]

The president, nonetheless, noted interest in Donovan. "Bill Donovan is also an old friend of mine—we were in the law school [at Columbia University] together—and, frankly, I should like to have him in the Cabinet," FDR wrote. But there were political concerns, the president noted: "Here again the question of motive must be considered, and I fear that to put two Republicans in charge of the armed forces might be misunderstood in both parties!"

FDR put the plan on hold. "So let us let the whole matter stand as it is for a while," he wrote. But he said that if a "real crisis" should take place, then "it would be necessary to put aside in large part strictly old fashioned party government, and the people would understand such a situation. If this develops I want you to know that I would still want you as a part of such an Administration." He also noted that he would promote an assistant secretary of the navy—Charles Edison, son of inventor Thomas Edison—to fill the vacant navy secretary post. But he advised Knox to remain on alert: "I may make changes of many kinds if things get worse."

FDR and Knox had devised a secret plan for a "coalition cabinet"—a plan that FDR would activate if world events justified it. The two men appeared to agree they needed to identify a second Republican to join the cabinet, but there is no evidence either man mentioned Henry L.

Stimson, even though he was likely the most well-known Republican supporter of FDR's foreign policy. They may have considered Stimson, then seventy-two years old, ineligible because of his age. Stimson was also the best-known American statesman openly calling for the United States to aid democratic nations militarily and to prepare for war against the fascist powers. To bring Stimson into the cabinet would thus be a defiant stand against the isolationists. FDR felt the time was not right for such a step.

FDR WAS A practiced hand at building political alliances across dividing lines. In his early years, he campaigned as a critic of Tammany Hall, but he eventually embraced Tammany and its support played a key role in his elections as New York's governor. Born into America's wealthy elite, he sought to help poor and working-class Americans struggling in the Great Depression by sharply changing the federal government and imposing requirements on businesses. Now, FDR was mulling over the launch of a new alliance with Republicans if the war took a turn for the worse.

The war news indeed worsened on a daily basis. The Soviet Union had invaded its neighbor, Finland, on November 30, 1939. After Soviet planes bombed the capital city of Helsinki on December 1, FDR called for a "moral embargo" on trade with the Soviet Union like the one imposed on Japan in 1938. He also approved a $10 million loan to the Finnish government for non-military supplies.

In China, the Japanese army continued its drive to seize territory and destroy Chinese nationalist forces. Stimson remained focused on opposing Japanese aggression in China, and in early January he and Mabel hosted Weiching Williams Yen, a Chinese diplomat representing Chiang Kai-shek, at their apartment in New York City.[4] Stimson had first met Yen in 1906 during a visit to China. Yen shared with Stimson "confidentially" the substance of a letter that he was carrying from Chiang to FDR, saying the Chinese had no intention of yielding to the Japanese and apparently were seeking additional aid from the president. "Yen told me that they have munitions for at least a year and are still receiving a good deal from Russia and quite a good deal from the United States," Stimson noted in his diary.

Stimson returned to the pages of *The New York Times* to call for an embargo against Japan. In a letter to *The Times* published on January 11, 1940, Stimson said that because the United States continued trading with Japan, the "evil which we have assisted in China has been much more widespread and brutal than anything which has yet happened in Europe."[5] The paper ran a front-page story on the letter, under the headline, "Stimson Asks Curb on Arms to Japan," and printed its full text in the news pages.[6] Stimson called for passage of a bill in Congress to impose a trade ban that would be broader than FDR's "moral embargo" because it would include scrap iron, oil, aviation fuel and other items used to power Japan's war machine. Stimson said it was important for the United States to show it was "not afraid to discriminate between right and wrong." The American Committee for Non-Participation in Japanese Aggression quickly sent copies of the letter to every member of Congress. Ultimately, without support from FDR and Hull, the embargo bill urged by Stimson died.

Seeking to avert war with Nazi Germany, FDR sent Undersecretary of State Sumner Welles to meet with Hitler in Berlin on March 2. Hitler told Welles that the French and British were intent on destroying Germany, and so Germany had no choice but to continue the war.[7] As the threat of an escalating war in Europe grew, FDR and General George Marshall, the army chief of staff, urged Congress to increase US military spending by $271 million. Isolationists, however, continued opposing FDR's war strategy. On April 3, the House Appropriations Committee cut the new spending proposal by 10 percent.[8]

As the 1940 presidential election approached, the field of Republican candidates was dominated by three men—crime-fighting New York City district attorney Thomas Dewey, Ohio senator Robert Taft and Michigan senator Arthur Vandenberg. Taft and Vandenberg were committed isolationists, while Dewey's position was more moderate. The race also included a lesser-known candidate who opposed isolationism—Wendell Willkie, the Commonwealth & Southern president. Willkie had switched his party affiliation from Democratic to Republican the previous fall and, capitalizing on his fame as a critic of FDR's New Deal, declared his candidacy for the presidential nomination.

Stimson's longtime law partner and friend, George Roberts, asked him in late March 1940 to advise Willkie on foreign trade. Roberts, who had represented Willkie when he was at Commonwealth & Southern, supported Willkie's candidacy. On April 5, Stimson sent Willkie a letter praising Secretary of State Cordell Hull's efforts to reduce tariffs and increase foreign trade. Stimson also offered to meet with Willkie.[9]

Willkie was a dark horse candidate for the Republican presidential nomination—far behind the leader, Dewey, the New York prosecutor renowned for pursuing organized crime. Yet Willkie's blend of views—he was pro-business, anti–New Deal, pro-civil rights and in support of international alliances—captured the imagination of progressive Republicans like *Fortune* magazine editor Russell Davenport, who hosted parties to build interest in Willkie as a candidate. In April 1940, Davenport published Willkie's essay "We, the People: A Foundation for Political Recovery" in the April 1940 issue of *Fortune*. The essay condemned FDR's domestic policies as crushing the rights of individuals and businesses, and called for the United States to take international action to defend democracy.[10] Willkie won support from Republican media figures such as *New York Herald Tribune* publishers Ogden and Helen Reid, and Henry Luce, publisher of *Time, Life* and *Fortune* magazines. Gardner Cowles Jr., publisher of *Look* magazine, and his brother John Cowles, publisher of the *Minneapolis Star* and the *Des Moines Register and Tribune,* also became vigorous backers of Willkie. A torrent of positive press coverage in spring 1940 spurred a groundswell of support for Willkie.

On April 6, Adolf Hitler launched an invasion of Denmark and Norway. Denmark's king quickly signed a peace accord accepting the Nazi occupation of his country. Norway, however, resisted; a Norwegian ship torpedoed a Nazi cruiser as it approached the port of Oslo, sending 1,600 Germans to their deaths.[11] Great Britain and France rushed troops to help the resistance, but the Nazis swiftly seized Oslo and Norway's key ports within the invasion's first forty-eight hours.[12]

Distraught over the world situation, Supreme Court justice Felix Frankfurter took steps to return his old friend Stimson to a public leadership role in America. Frankfurter, who considered Stimson a wise and capable defender of democracy, arranged for Stimson to meet with FDR at the White House. On May 2, Stimson took a train from New York to Washington and spent the evening with Frankfurter and his wife, Marion, at their home in Georgetown.[13] The next day, the two men went to the White House for a private lunch with FDR. Frankfurter downplayed the significance of the event, telling reporters, "We are just two old friends visiting the president."[14]

It was the first time FDR and Stimson had met since 1934. FDR was relaxed and open in his conversation, Stimson later noted in his diary. "He looked older and more poised than I remembered him. He made a very pleasant impression and talked very frankly about the war situation, telling me a number of things in confidence."[15] They discussed Nazi Germany's invasion of Norway, FDR's recent warning that Mussolini should stay out of the war and aircraft purchases by the Allies. They evidently did not discuss the subjects that divided them in the past—the Neutrality Act or the Tennessee Valley Authority. Nor is there any sign that they explored the idea of Stimson or other Republicans joining FDR's cabinet. Later that day, Frankfurter sent a thank-you note to FDR about the meeting with Stimson. "He is a fine old Roman—he is, you know, close to 73 and wants to feel he is still of use to the Republic. . . . You made Stimson feel he *is* of use—and gave him fresh impulse to go on."[16]

On May 10, Hitler's armies stormed into three Western European democracies: the Netherlands, Belgium and Luxembourg. The frontline defenses of the three countries were swiftly crushed and the 237,000 troops of the British Expeditionary Force stationed in Belgium suffered losses.[17] The invading German forces then surged into northern France, bypassing the massive Maginot Line defense structure that the French had built along their eastern border with Germany after the First World War. The rapid Nazi invasion, dubbed the "Blitzkrieg," rolled over Allied armies and killed large numbers of civilians, stunning people around the world.

. . .

ON THE VERY first day of the Nazi invasion, Great Britain turned to Winston Churchill for leadership. Despite Churchill's reputation as a Conservative member of Parliament who was no friend of the working classes, he had in recent years made common cause with labor union leaders to urge Britons to recognize the threat of fascism and support military preparedness.[18] He also had condemned the appeasement of the Munich Pact and joined with members of the two chief opposing parties—the Labor Party and the Liberal Party—in sounding the alarm over fascism's rise. Harold Laski, a Labour Party leader and well-known socialist writer, had voiced support for Churchill. Though they were in opposing political camps, Laski urged Labour to create a united front with other parties and praised Churchill as a leader in the fight "against the Gestapo and the concentration camp."[19] Laski—who had taught at Harvard and was a friend of both Frankfurter and FDR—appealed to FDR in April 1939 for help in bringing British Conservatives and Labour together to oppose Nazi Germany.[20] For all their political differences, Churchill and Laski shared a passion for uniting their country against fascism.

When the crisis came on May 10, this bridge-building effort by both the right and the left yielded a great gain: Britons were primed for unity. Labour Party leader Clement Attlee announced that Labour would support a national coalition government led by the Conservative Party—but not one led by Chamberlain.[21] Chamberlain resigned, and Churchill went that same evening to Buckingham Palace, where King George VI asked him to form a new government and be his prime minister.[22]

Amid the chaos of the war, with Britons dying on foreign battlefields, Churchill swiftly announced the first members of what he called his "National Coalition Government." He proposed a cabinet that would include members of his own Conservative Party and the Labour and Liberal parties. He gave a leading role to Attlee, who had risen to the rank of major in the British Army before being wounded in France in the First World War, and as a Labour member of Parliament was recognized as a vigorous yet pragmatic advocate for his party. Churchill named Attlee his deputy prime minister and lord privy seal, a key post in the cabinet.[23]

On May 13, for the first time in its history, the Labour Party voted at a party conference to support a coalition government led by a member of the Conservative Party.[24] That same day, with Labour and Liberal leaders solidly backing Churchill, the House of Commons voted 381–0 for Churchill as prime minister. The House of Lords also gave unanimous approval.

Churchill said in a speech that day that he would form an administration "conceived on the broadest possible basis and that it should include all parties."[25] He prepared the country to face the bleak prospect of war. "I have nothing to offer but blood, toil, tears and sweat," he said. "You ask, what is our aim? I can answer in one word. It is victory. Victory at all costs—victory in spite of all terrors—victory, however long and hard the road may be, for without victory there is no survival." He ended his speech with an appeal for unity: "I feel entitled at this juncture, at this time, to claim the aid of all and to say, 'Come then, let us go forward together with our united strength.'"

Churchill distributed seats in his War Cabinet among the parties. His Conservative ally Anthony Eden was made secretary of state for war; a Labour figure, Albert Alexander, the son of a blacksmith, became first lord of the admiralty; Archibald Sinclair, leader of the Liberal Party, was made secretary of state for air. Churchill also named Ernest Bevin, a Labour leader who was a prominent union organizer, to be minister of labor a position from which Churchill hoped he would inspire the British working class to support the war effort. Churchill's formation of his National Coalition Government captured headlines around the world. Churchill's National Coalition—a stellar example of how to unite a nation by building an alliance across party lines—was a model Roosevelt could not miss.

THE HARD FACTS of war demanded FDR's immediate attention. In a cabinet meeting on May 10, General Marshall sounded a note of alarm as he urged the president to strengthen the army. Marshall said war materiel was in extremely short supply, and the US Army could support only fifteen thousand troops in combat at a time while the Germans had two million men equipped, trained and ready to enter combat. "If you don't do something, and do it right away, I don't know what is going to happen to this country," the general said.[26]

The following day, on May 14, Nazi bombers laid waste to the Dutch city of Rotterdam, killing more than eight hundred people and leaving seventy-eight thousand homeless. The Netherlands surrendered the next day to Germany.[27]

England turned to America with a plea for aid. On May 15, Churchill cabled FDR a secret letter urgently requesting that the United States lend forty or fifty older destroyers and provide hundreds of aircraft to reinforce Britain's defenses. "The small countries are simply smashed up, one by one, like matchwood. . . . We expect to be attacked here ourselves, both from the air and by parachute and air-borne troops, in the near future, and are getting ready for them," Churchill wrote.[28] "But I trust you realize, Mr. President, that the voice and force of the United States may count for nothing if they are withheld too long. You may have a completely subjugated, Nazified Europe established with astonishing swiftness, and the weight may be more than we can bear."

As newspapers and radio broadcasts carried stories about German forces advancing deeper into France, FDR went to Capitol Hill the next day and delivered a speech raising concerns about a possible attack on the United States. He called for America to boost its production of war planes from six thousand in 1939 to fifty thousand per year. He asked Congress to approve $1.2 billion in military spending, though he carefully avoided making any mention of a draft or sending ships or other aid to the British.[29]

Members of both parties greeted FDR's speech with thunderous applause. "The president in his splendid address to the Congress yesterday spoke as the leader of all the people. He is acting in the spirit of unity for which American citizens have been waiting and in a spirit which will bring him a united support in preparing our defenses," former Republican presidential candidate Alf Landon said in a radio broadcast.[30]

Despite the robust bipartisan support, FDR feared isolationists would condemn the idea of sending destroyers to Britain. He cabled Churchill: "I am not certain that it would be wise for that suggestion to be made to Congress at this moment."[31]

The leading Republican presidential candidates—Dewey, Taft and

Vandenberg—remained silent at first about FDR's speech. Willkie, however, quickly voiced qualified support of FDR's plan. At a campaign event in Iowa on May 17, Willkie admitted to the crowd that FDR's plan was "theoretically correct," but he quickly faulted his "blundering" New Deal for having "hamstrung" American industry so that it no longer had the capacity to rebuild the nation's defenses.[32]

Stimson wrote a letter to FDR the next day praising the president's speech before Congress, adding language that subtly hinted at his own interest in joining with FDR to form a national unity government. "I wanted to express my hearty sympathy and approval of what you said to Congress the day before yesterday."[33] Stimson added: "I am much gratified to see what appear to be the evidences of a truly united national feeling springing up over the country, and I feel confident that you will meet and cooperate with such a feeling. Faithfully yours, Henry L. Stimson."

Stimson wrote Churchill that day, too, expressing sympathy and encouragement. "I am confident that somehow or other the right will prevail in the end and that the forces of evil will be stopped," he wrote. "I hear rumors of political cooperation which would truly be revolutionary in a presidential year."[34] Stimson told the prime minister, "There seems to be arising a real spirit of national unity in the face of a great emergency which is now at last realized, and many men who never realized it before have suddenly and sharply awakened to the extent to which our future safety is entwined with yours."

Isolationists dug their heels in against what they continued to perceive as FDR's efforts to push America into war. On May 19, Charles Lindbergh gave a national radio address insisting there was little chance of an attack on America. He shifted blame for the threat of war from Germany to America. The famous aviator also condemned the news media and launched into a diatribe against an unidentified minority group that he said had unusual power, financial motives and foreign connections. Lindbergh's screed echoed the anti-Semitic rhetoric emanating from Nazi Germany, and it vaguely suggested violent action against American Jews. "The only reason that we are in danger of becoming involved in this war is because there are powerful elements in America who desire us to take part. They represent a small minority of the American people, but they control much of the machinery of influence and propaganda. They seize every opportunity to push us closer to the edge. It is time for the underlying character of this country to rise and assert itself, to strike down these elements of personal profit and foreign interest."[35]

Within days, a German Panzer tank corps had fought all the way to the coast of the English Channel, trapping French and English armies in northern France, including the coastal cities of Calais and Dunkirk.[36] The encircled Allied forces began a desperate battle for survival, and the Nazi assault on Dunkirk played out daily on America's front pages and on radios.

With the Nazi defeat of the French now likely, FDR apparently concluded that the moment of crisis he discussed with Knox six months earlier was approaching. But with the Republican National Convention set to begin in Philadelphia in late June, the president faced questions about how and when to appoint his new Republican cabinet members as their party prepared to nominate a presidential candidate to oppose him.

Knox planned to attend the Republican convention and work for the nomination of Willkie, and he urged the president to wait until after the convention to nominate him. FDR, however, countered that he must appoint Knox before the convention, because if the Republicans nominated an isolationist candidate, Knox's joining FDR's administration would be attacked as "an act of disgruntlement and bad sportsmanship," according to FDR speechwriter Robert Sherwood. [37] FDR wanted Knox's appointment announced before the convention to ensure that the public would see it as "an act of pure patriotism, animated by the belief that the conduct of the whole defense effort and of foreign policy in general should be placed above all partisan considerations."

On Monday, May 20, *The New York Times* carried a story on its front page saying that FDR was contemplating the idea of appointing Republicans to his cabinet, revealing that Knox had met with FDR and expressed interest in serving as the secretary of the navy, and Landon was under consideration to be secretary of war.[38]

Landon, however, immediately rejected the idea of joining a coalition cabinet, saying it would amount to an attack upon the American democratic system. "In this critical period, when free government is under attack in the world, it becomes doubly urgent that we in America safeguard and maintain the essential functions of democracy," he said.[39] "The very basis of these functions are free elections and party responsibility."

Stimson had a very different reaction. On that same day, he wrote Knox that he wholeheartedly supported the idea of Republican leaders forming a coalition with FDR. "I write you at once to express my deep gratification that you have been willing to take a step of such vital importance and historic magnitude," Stimson wrote.[40] He said it was vital for America to build national "solidarity" around the president. "I cannot conceive of any more effective step which he could take towards the creation of such real national solidity [sic] than to offer to place in the hands of responsible leaders of the opposition party the two departments which have direct supervision of the navy and the army."

Stimson's concept of a coalition cabinet differed from Knox's. Knox spoke of Republicans joining the cabinet in a nonpartisan way, in essence setting their party affiliation aside as they entered the administration. Stimson, in contrast, envisioned Republicans—fully retaining their party affiliations—taking control of the War and Navy departments as part of an alliance they would form with the Democratic president. "Such a step is not a gesture. It is the giving of a most effective hostage towards the placing of our national defense upon a truly national basis," Stimson wrote in his May 20 letter to Knox. Long concerned about the dominance of the Democrats, Stimson hoped to create bastions of Republicanism in the War and Navy departments that would give his party a role in national defense.[41]

FDR soon replied to Stimson's earlier letter that pointed to a "united national feeling springing up over the country." FDR wrote, "Ever so many thanks. That kind of note keeps a fellow going. I, too, sense an enormous growth in national unity in the last week. . . . When I read Lindbergh's speech I felt that it could not have been better put by Goebbels himself. . . . What a pity that this youngster has completely abandoned his belief in our form of government and has accepted Nazi methods because apparently they are efficient. I hope to see you soon."[42]

The war continued in France, where counterattacks by French

general Charles de Gaulle failed to stop the powerful Nazi advance.[43] British and French forces withdrew to the French town of Dunkirk on the English Channel, but their evacuation by the British Navy was halted after German dive bombers destroyed port facilities and sank numerous vessels. It was then that English citizens, braving the German attacks, began piloting their private fishing and pleasure boats across the English Channel in a volunteer effort to rescue the stranded troops.[44] Bleak news came on May 28, when King Leopold III of Belgium ordered his army to surrender.[45]

In America, Knox urged FDR to create camps to train up to 10,000 volunteer pilots along the lines of the Plattsburgh camps active during World War I. Separately, a group of Plattsburgh veterans also concluded the country must once again raise an army quickly through a draft, just as it had in the First World War. Stimson was one of these men, and another was his friend Grenville Clark, a former law partner of FDR's and founder of a Wall Street law firm.[46] After Clark urged FDR to support conscription, FDR replied pointing to the difficulty of getting Congress to pass such a bill. The president approved Knox's volunteer pilot training camps but was not ready to back a draft.[47]

Clark and another Plattsburgher, Julius Adler, the army reserve colonel and friend of Stimson's who was general manager of *The New York Times,* traveled to Washington on May 31 to meet with General Marshall and seek his support for conscription. Marshall told the men it was not his place to advocate a legislative policy that the president had not authorized. Clark and Adler left the meeting disappointed and looking for another approach.

Clark concluded that the best way to win support for a draft would be for FDR to appoint a vigorous new secretary of war.[48] The current occupant of the post, Harry Woodring, was an isolationist former Democratic governor of Kansas. Immediately after meeting with Marshall, Clark met with his friend Frankfurter. The two men compared their lists of possible candidates to replace Woodring. They quickly agreed Stimson was the best person for the job.

Frankfurter discussed the idea of appointing Stimson with FDR at the White House on June 3. The president expressed interest but raised concerns about Stimson's age.[49] The next day, Frankfurter wrote the president a lengthy letter proposing the idea of teaming Stimson with a younger man, Judge Robert Patterson, a Republican and a Plattsburgher, who would act as an assistant. Frankfurter described Patterson, then forty-nine, as "made to order" for the role. "He is young, he is vigorous, he is able." Frankfurter, who knew well of Stimson's disagreements with FDR over the Neutrality Act and other matters, assured FDR that Stimson "could be counted on to carry the responsibility of the War Department in strict conformity with your general policy." As for Stimson's age, he said, "his mind is alert and vigorous and, freed from details, you would have an extraordinarily equipped man for this vital post."[50] Stimson's experience was remarkable: Not only had he served as secretary of state to President Herbert Hoover, but he also had been secretary of war once before, under President Taft three decades earlier.

In London, Churchill directed the war effort from a bunker deep below street level. On June 1 he took time to respond to the encouraging letter from Stimson. "Thank you so much for your letter," he said in a telegram.[51] Churchill closed his message to Stimson with a simple French expression of confidence adopted by the Allies during World War I: "*On les aura*"—"We'll get them."

Churchill had reason for hope. The British Navy and the volunteer rescue effort by some eight hundred private vessels had evacuated two hundred thousand British and a hundred and forty thousand French and Belgian soldiers from Dunkirk to safety in England.[52] However, the German Army took control of Dunkirk and the rest of northern France on June 4. British casualties reached a withering toll—sixty-eight thousand soldiers dead or wounded, a quarter of the British Expeditionary Force in France. As the Germans closed their grip on Dunkirk, German planes bombed Paris and Hitler's armies stormed toward the stricken French capital.

Churchill went to Parliament on June 4 and gave a nationally broadcast speech hailing Dunkirk as a "miracle of deliverance," though he warned the English people that "wars are not won by evacuations"—and the Nazis might next invade their island nation. He exhorted his fellow citizens to keep up their courage for the war ahead. "We shall fight on the beaches. We shall fight on the landing grounds. We shall fight in the fields and in the streets. We shall fight in the hills. We shall never surrender." His speech, broadcast to the United States, ended with a subtle plea to the Americans: England would fight the war alone "until, in God's good time, the New World, with all its power and might, steps forth to the rescue and the liberation of the old."[53]

At this time, Willkie supporters sought to enlist Stimson in their campaign for Willkie's nomination. On June 10, William Loeb Jr., the son of a top aide to President Theodore Roosevelt, wrote to Stimson asking him to speak at a Willkie campaign rally set for June 19 in Oyster Bay, on Long Island, to be carried on a national radio broadcast. The idea, Loeb wrote, would be to rally votes for Willkie under the banner of TR's "vigorous stand for national defense."[54] Stimson, however, declined. Accepting such an invitation would surely have scuttled his chances of joining FDR's cabinet. Still, no offer came from FDR.

On June 14, Stimson spoke at Andover. Though the occasion was only a small school graduation ceremony, the press covered his speech, which proclaimed the importance of the rule of law and decried the unjustified invasion of peaceful nations.[55] Among those in the audience was a sixteen-year-old sophomore, George H.W. Bush, who two years later would begin training as a Navy pilot and decades later would become president of the United States as a Republican.

The White House announced the next day that the president had signed a bill to spend $1.8 billion to purchase 2,566 military planes and other munitions, and to increase the army to 280,000 men—but only through volunteer recruitment. That same day, the Nazi army occupied Paris, dealing a blow to Allied morale. French premier Paul Reynaud resigned and the eighty-four-year-old Marshal Philippe Pétain, a hero to the French for his stand at the Battle of Verdun in the First World War, took over as prime minister. Pétain's government announced on June 17 that it would surrender if the Germans granted France an "honorable peace."[56]

As France fell before Hitler's armies, Stimson gave a rousing address that was carried nationally over the radio on the evening of June 18. "The United States today faces probably the greatest crisis in its history. Not only our own safety but the continuance of the existence of the kind of world which we have been trying to create and the methods of freedom and self-government which have been ours since the foundation of our nation are at stake."[57] He invoked the individual's freedom from the state and—likely borrowing from Ramsay Muir—"the Christian principle of the equal value of human personalities." To defend these principles from the threat of global fascism, Stimson said, America must adopt compulsory mandatory military training, send arms to Britain and France in convoys protected by the US Navy, and open US naval ports to the British and French navies. He concluded that "with the old American spirit of courage and leadership behind them, I believe we should find our people ready to take their proper part in this threatened world and to carry through to victory, freedom and reconstruction."

Like FDR, Stimson articulated a vision of America as a guiding light for democracies around the world. Stimson, however, went much further than FDR, calling for activation of the draft, direct military aid to France and England and preparation for war with Nazi Germany. The next morning, June 19, Frankfurter sent the president's secretary, Missy LeHand, a brief telegram: "Hope president can find time to read full text of Stimson's speech page 17 of today's *Times*." The story had been pushed off the front page by stories on the Nazi seizure of France and a speech by Willkie demanding that the United States stay out of the war.

At some point that day, June 19, FDR decided to set in motion his plan for a bipartisan cabinet by inviting Stimson and Knox to join as the secretaries of war and navy. Bringing the two men into the cabinet offered FDR the hope of uniting America behind his plans to fight Hitler. It had the added benefit of averting any risk that the two Republicans might join forces with Willkie.

FDR called Stimson at his office in New York that afternoon and offered him the post of secretary of war. Stimson later recalled, "The president said he was very anxious to have me accept because everybody was running around at loose ends in Washington and he thought I would be a stabilizing factor in whom both the army and the public would have confidence."[58] Roosevelt said Stimson would be free to name his own assistant secretary of defense. Stimson asked the president for some time to think the matter over.

There is no evidence that Stimson and FDR discussed the fact that the Republican National Convention was beginning in four days. Yet both men surely grasped that the appointments would have political impact because they suggested that Republicans who believed that America must fight for democracy should support FDR.

The appointments posed major risks. As FDR had worried, the American public might see them not as patriotism but as political maneuvering, which would damage FDR's chances of winning reelection. Also, bringing Stimson and Knox into the cabinet could prompt the Republican Party to embrace isolationism more fervently as a means of offering voters a clear alternative to FDR's interventionism.

Later the same evening, Stimson called the president. He began by asking FDR whether his speech the night before would embarrass the president. "He replied that he had already read it and was in full accord with it," Stimson noted in his diary. He asked FDR specifically if he knew Stimson supported compulsory military service; FDR replied that he did and that "he was in sympathy with me." Roosevelt had thus expressed openness to Stimson's views that diverged from his own, a tolerance that would imbue their working relationship in the many trials to come. Stimson accepted the post. He also noted that Patterson was recommended to be his assistant secretary. FDR said he approved of Patterson, calling him a "fine man," clearing the way for Stimson's first Republican hire on his staff.

FDR announced his appointments of Stimson and Knox the next morning, issuing a White House statement that portrayed the move as solely aimed at uniting America: "The appointments to the Cabinet are in line with the overwhelming sentiment of the nation for national solidarity in a time of world crisis and in behalf of national defense and nothing else."[59]

WHEN WORD OF the appointments reached the Senate floor, one of the best-known Democratic isolationists, Senator Burton Wheeler of Montana, uttered a bitter pronouncement: "These appointments ought to be particularly appealing to the warmongers."

Republicans made furious attacks condemning Stimson and Knox and proclaiming that the party itself rejected any sort of coalition or bipartisan government. In Philadelphia, where Republicans were already

gathering for their national convention, John Hamilton, the party's national chairman, issued a verdict on the two rebels, saying, "These men
are no longer qualified to speak as Republicans or for the Republican
organization."[60] Hamilton emphasized that the party was not involved
and the decisions by Stimson and Knox to join FDR's cabinet were
"purely personal on their part." Some observers said Hamilton had in
effect ejected Stimson and Knox from the party.

Prominent Republicans issued dire warnings. Colonel Theodore Roosevelt Jr., son of the former president and a friend of both Stimson and
Knox, denounced FDR's actions as a threat to democracy. "I sincerely
hope Colonel Knox and Colonel Stimson refuse the appointments. Our
representative democracy depends for its existence on the maintenance
of a two-party system. President Roosevelt seeks to destroy this system
and substitute a single party. The history of Germany, Italy and Russia
shows what happens when a single-party system is adopted by a great
nation. First comes collectivism, then totalitarianism and then dictatorship."

Other Republicans attacked the FDR-Stimson-Knox coalition as
pushing the country into another European war, and suggested that as a
result the Republican Party should lean even more toward isolationism.
Landon said FDR's alliance with Stimson and Knox meant the Republicans should position themselves as the "peace party" and the Democrats as the "war party."

Though this was not the first time FDR had put Republicans in his
cabinet, some in the press depicted the appointments of Stimson and
Knox as a shocking strategic move by FDR to take the wind out of Republican sails and win over Republican voters. A headline in *The Atlanta Constitution* newspaper announced: "Master Stroke by Roosevelt
Stuns G.O.P." The story went on to say that FDR's appointments were a
"demolition bomb tossed into the Republican camp."[61]

News of the appointments was carried around the world. In London,
the press hailed them as a strengthening of American support for the
war effort. *The Daily Telegraph* blared the news under headlines "Roosevelt Forming Coalition Cabinet" and "Advocates of Full Aid to the
Allies in Defense Posts." *The Daily Mail* carried the headline "America's

Warning," and said, "Big things have happened in America. President Roosevelt is forming a coalition Cabinet. . . . Never in the United States has there ever been such a combination. All precedent has been swept away by the world crisis." It added that both Stimson and Knox had supported large-scale aid to the Allies, and said, "The President's action is a warning that the United States really does mean business."[62]

Frankfurter rejoiced in a telegram to FDR: "Simply grand . . . Let me express my gratitude of this new manifestation of leadership for a free people."[63] To Stimson, Frankfurter sent a telegram saying simply, "You are where the country needs you."[64]

Julius Adler of *The New York Times* wired Stimson: "Thank god the portfolio of secretary of war has been offered you and that you have accepted. Your selection is superb and my fervent prayers are answered. The right man for this key post has been found to meet the present grave emergency which confronts the nation."[65]

A wave of letters arrived at Stimson's office in response to his nationwide radio address and his nomination. Some were harsh. "We are sick and tired of you war mongers. We will not fight Europe's wars," one person wrote anonymously. "Go over and fight if they shoot you you'll never be missed." Attacking Stimson's nomination, one anonymous writer said: "After having been honored 2 times by the Rep. Party you try to stab them in the back. Traitor! . . . You deserve the hatred of everyone, Rep. & Dem." Supporters wrote, too. Edward S. Beebe of Morris Plains, New Jersey, noting he had two sons in the navy, wrote, "I heartily approve of everything you said. . . . If there is any way in which I can be of assistance in furthering your proposals please let me know."[66]

On the same day that FDR announced the Stimson and Knox nominations, Senator Edward Burke, a Nebraska Democrat, filed a bill that would launch a draft system for compulsory military service, seeking to build an army of up to four million men. Prepared with the help of Clark, the bill would require up to forty million men of ages eighteen to sixty-five to register with a selective service system.[67] The following day, a Republican friend of Stimson's, Representative James Wadsworth of New York, filed a similar bill in the House. The moves to start a military draft—an action that Stimson had called for, but which FDR had not publicly supported—grabbed headlines nationwide. The two bills, merged to form the Burke-Wadsworth Bill, showcased the bipartisan support for rapidly expanding the armed forces.

The war's rapid escalation in Europe, and America's response to it, had a profound effect on the Republican Party's presidential candidates. In late May, a poll had found that Willkie had surged to a ranking of fourth place with 13 percent of Republican voters, up from just 3 percent about two weeks earlier.[68] That poll still placed Dewey, the New York crime fighter, far ahead, with 62 percent of Republican voters supporting him, and Senator Taft in second place with 14 percent. But by the time the Republican Party kicked off its convention a month later, FDR's appointments of Stimson and Knox had forced the party to reconsider where it stood in relation to the global war. Willkie supporters saw that their candidate was "the man to beat."[69]

On Tuesday, June 25, newspapers carried banner stories about Nazi bombers striking targets across Great Britain. The drumbeat of war, combined with the defection of Stimson and Knox, appeared to undermine confidence in isolationism. On Thursday, when the convention took its first vote to select a presidential nominee, Dewey had 360 votes, far more than Taft with 189 or Willkie with only 105. The competition between the two leaders set the stage for a seismic shift of support. As additional votes were taken, backing for isolationism collapsed and Willkie gained votes. After more discussion and debate, on the fourth ballot of the evening, Willkie moved into first place with 306 votes, with Taft in second place and Dewey in third.[70] Finally, in the early hours of Friday, June 28, on the sixth ballot, Willkie won the nomination unanimously.

The Republican convention chose Senator Charles McNary of Oregon, who had support from isolationists, to be the vice-presidential nominee.[71] Willkie then took the stage and gave a speech seeking to distinguish himself from FDR but echoing the nonpartisan patriotism that FDR had been calling for: "I stand before you without a single pledge, promise, or understanding of any kind, except the advancement of your cause, the preservation of American democracy."

At Stimson's confirmation hearing before the Senate Military Affairs

Committee a week later, Senate isolationists jumped at the chance to question Stimson. Senator Edwin Johnson, a Colorado Democrat, asked Stimson whether he continued to oppose FDR's domestic policies.[72] "I retain my own mental and moral integrity as to my own convictions, but I have the right to subordinate their expression to the paramount duty which I accept from him," he replied.

Stimson warned that Germany's modern air force, artillery and tanks, combined with the force of a secret police such as Hitler's Gestapo, meant that the United States faced "an unprecedented peril" and needed to rearm quickly. He also called for swift passage of a compulsory military service bill.

The next day Knox rejected the idea that his appointment meant FDR was creating a coalition government. "We are not representing the Republican Party at all," he testified before the Senate Naval Affairs Committee,[73] "We are just two private individuals trying to do a job." He added, "I am here because I believe we should be united." The committees approved the nominations and sent them to the full Senate for final votes.

Stimson and Knox were not forming a coalition in which the Republican Party itself endorsed FDR or his administration. While their philosophies about their alliance with FDR differed, they both were Republicans who backed FDR's foreign policy—and in effect opened the door for other Republicans to do the same. Stimson had already arranged for another Republican, Patterson, to join the administration. The American people supported Stimson and Knox. A poll released July 4 found that 71 percent of voters supported the two appointments. Broken down by party, 57 percent of Republicans and 85 percent of Democrats supported the nominations.[74] George Gallup, whose American Institute of Public Opinion released the poll, said, "Despite a recent statement by John Hamilton virtually reading Stimson and Knox out of the Republican party because of their appointment to the New Deal Cabinet, the rank and file of G.O.P voters with definite opinions on the subject approve the two appointments by a comfortable majority."

Stimson invited General Marshall and Grenville Clark to Woodley on the morning of July 9 to discuss the proposed compulsory service bill and "the two sides agreed to get together again and work out a new bill," he recorded in his diary.[75] Though not yet secretary of war, Stimson's persistent prodding had already gotten US Army officials and the Plattsburghers, who a month earlier had been sharply at odds, to resolve their differences and develop a plan for conscription.

Stimson and Knox were with FDR at the White House on July 9 when word came through that the Senate voted 56–28 to confirm Stimson as secretary of war, with both parties split. Among Republicans, ten voted for confirmation and twelve against. Stimson was already drawing Republican votes to support the president.[76] Democrats split over FDR's appointment of the Republican as fourteen voted against and forty-five for it. The divided vote in the Senate was a far cry from the unanimity in Parliament that two months earlier heralded Churchill's "National Coalition," yet the new bipartisan alliance had nonetheless taken its first steps toward uniting America.

Stimson and Knox helped FDR prepare a written message to Congress supporting the draft and requesting an additional $4.8 billion to expand the army and navy. However, the president also used the speech, which he delivered July 10, to fend off concerns that—with the appointments of Stimson and Knox—he was rushing America into foreign wars. "We will not use our arms in a war of aggression; we will not send our men to take part in European wars," the president said.[77] That afternoon, Stimson went to the White House, where in FDR's presence he was sworn in.

Stimson moved into the secretary of war's office in the Munitions Building near the Lincoln Memorial. Built during World War I, the building was originally intended to be a temporary structure for the War Department, but amid disputes over military spending it had remained in use—and had grown crowded. At the end of his first day as secretary of war, Stimson returned home for a game of deck tennis on Woodley's court, he noted in his diary.[78] "The tennis made me feel much better, for I was beginning to feel the lack of exercise."

Woodley provided ample opportunities for recreation and fresh air after work. High-ranking officials began appearing regularly at the estate for discussions of national defense or for deck tennis or lawn bowling.

Secretary of State Hull continued his croquet. In the evenings, General Marshall, Patterson and many others dropped by for dinner, sometimes bringing their wives, as they would over the next five years. Woodley rapidly became an outpost of the War Department.

Uniting America

As Democrats gathered in mid-July 1940 at their convention in Chicago to select a presidential candidate, President Roosevelt continued to refuse to say whether he wanted to serve for a third term. Democrats seeking the presidential nomination—including his own vice president, John N. Garner—criticized the idea. No president had ever served more than two terms before, and Thomas Jefferson had famously opposed the idea. Beyond the controversy, the president had told friends he was genuinely exhausted and wished to retire. At the same time, many Americans had taken a liking to the Republican nominee, Wendell Willkie; one poll showed that 47 percent of voters preferred Willkie, placing him only slightly behind Roosevelt.[1] As the convention opened its doors on July 15, FDR's future was cloaked in mystery.

In Washington the next day, Secretary of War Stimson learned that Democratic isolationists at the convention wanted the party platform to oppose the military draft. He went to the White House to meet with FDR and warned him about the threat to the draft. FDR was already aware of the problem and told Stimson he was "very much alarmed," and was trying to reach the chairman of the platform committee, his friend Senator Robert Wagner of New York.[2] Anticipating new isolationist attacks, FDR wrote a platform plank saying the party would not participate in foreign wars "except in case of attack."[3]

The next morning, Stimson took the matter of defending the military draft into his own hands. Appearing in a news conference with Army chief of staff General George Marshall, Stimson urged Congress to pass the Burke-Wadsworth compulsory service bill, saying the United States needed an army of two million men. The draft is "the very foundation stone of preparedness," Stimson said. Later, he said, "To me it is so ludicrous that anyone in the United States cannot see the importance of this measure. Congress has appropriated billions of dollars for materiel to save the country, but we have not yet taken the step necessary to get the men to run the materiel."[4]

With isolationists in both parties attacking the president, FDR made no public statements that day in support of the draft. Instead, it was his new Republican secretary of war who carried the burden of making the administration's case publicly. Stimson, once again calling the nation to take action, carried authority. Their tandem attack worked: the Democratic Party platform did not oppose the draft.

FDR also made a move that made him appear indifferent to a third term—but which virtually assured his nomination. On the convention's second night, his ally Alben Barkley, the senator from Kentucky who was the Senate majority leader, read the delegates in Chicago a message from FDR. "The president has never had and has not today any desire to, or purpose to, continue in the office of president, to be a candidate for that office, or to be nominated by the convention for that office," Barkley announced from the dais. "He wishes in all conviction to make it clear that all of the delegates at this convention are free to vote for any candidate."[5] Delegates supporting FDR, quickly concluding Barkley's words meant the president would accept the nomination, marched gleefully with banners through the aisles.

The next evening, delegates brushed aside Garner and other third-term opponents and nominated FDR again for the presidency. When the voting was tallied early in the morning hours of July 18, FDR won in a landslide on the first vote. FDR chose his secretary of agriculture, Henry Wallace, a onetime liberal Republican who had become a Democrat, to replace Garner as vice president.

FDR delivered an acceptance speech via radio from the White House early on the morning of July 19 explaining his long hesitation over his candidacy. "Lying awake as I have done on many nights, I have asked myself whether I have the right as Commander in Chief of the Army and Navy to call on men and women to serve their country . . . and at the same time decline to serve my country in my personal capacity if I am called upon to do so by the people of my country."

Stimson wrote the president a note the next day voicing sympathy: "I have lived too near the burdens of the Presidency, at different times in my life, not to fully appreciate the sincerity of your desire to be relieved from such burdens, particularly at such time as the present. . . . So long as I may occupy my present post I shall do my best to alleviate the weight of those burdens for you, in a full understanding of the spirit in which you have decided to carry them on." Stimson himself had privately doubted the wisdom of the third term, but he set those concerns aside and recommitted himself to his alliance with FDR.[6]

Stimson quickly built a strong and cooperative relationship with General Marshall, the lauded military man thirteen years his junior who was the US Army chief of staff. A respected commander and military planner, Marshall had the nonpartisan patriotism expected of American soldiers that meshed well with Stimson's capacity to set political differences aside. Marshall later commented wittily on his disinterest in party politics: "I have never voted, my father was democrat, my mother was a republican, and I am an Episcopalian."[7]

Stimson plunged into myriad issues facing the War Department—contracts to purchase military aircraft, labor disputes in munitions plants, the security of radio communications with Great Britain, sharing secret weapons technology with the British, disconcerting reports the Japanese were buying large quantities of aviation oil in California and much more. There were two major issues on which Stimson and FDR particularly wanted Republican cooperation with the White House. The first was a proposed sale of fifty destroyers to Great Britain to answer Prime Minister Churchill's plea to bolster the Royal Navy's fight with Germany for naval control of the North Atlantic Ocean. The second was passage of the compulsory service law necessary to begin the draft and rapidly expand the US Army. FDR, Stimson and Knox considered these two items critical for the war effort, but they feared that Willkie would use them to attack FDR and win isolationist votes by accusing FDR of pushing the nation into war. They believed both issues would require passage of legislation in Congress, and isolationists might block them if they became campaign issues. FDR and Stimson turned to William Allen White, the Kansas Republican newspaper editor, asking him to convince Willkie not to attack FDR on these two critical points. White ardently wanted the United States to do more to help the democratic nations under attack by Adolf Hitler, and he spread that message nationally through a group he launched in May 1940, the Committee to Defend America by Aiding the Allies. He also had a key advantage in taking up the matter with Willkie—he had supported Willkie vigorously in editorials in his newspaper, *The Emporia Gazette*.[8]

Late at night on August 3, Stimson received a long-distance call from White, who said he had spoken with Willkie and urged him to support the plan to send destroyers to Great Britain.[9] The next day, Stimson called FDR at Hyde Park to update him, and learned FDR had discussed the destroyers with Churchill and the British ambassador in Washington, Lord Lothian. Stimson then sent documents on the destroyer plan to White for delivery to Willkie.

Stimson called White on August 8 at his vacation home in Estes Park, Colorado. White said the papers Stimson had sent him were "highly satisfactory," and he had delivered them to Willkie, who was in Colorado Springs.[10] White also revealed to Stimson that he had seen the major speech Willkie was preparing to accept the Republican nomination and launch his presidential campaign. While Willkie's speech "did not mention the question of the British Destroyers, the attitude which it took would justify it, which is a sensation," Stimson wrote with delight.

Stimson called again the next day, but there was still no news from Willkie.[11] His eagerness reflected the tremendous importance that he and FDR placed on winning Willkie's support of—or at least neutrality toward—both the destroyers deal and the draft. Isolationists including Senator Arthur Vandenberg, the Michigan Republican, renewed their attacks on the conscription bill on August 12. With Republicans seeking support from isolationist voters, Stimson worried Willkie, too, would attack the bill.

FDR discussed the destroyers deal again on August 13 with Stimson, Knox and two of his closest advisers, Treasury Secretary Henry Morgenthau Jr. and Undersecretary of State Sumner Welles. Later that day,

Stimson called White again, and this time there was good news. White had spoken with Willkie and "was confident that [Willkie] would not say anything in criticism of the destroyer transaction, and might say something favorable to it," Stimson reported in his diary.[12]

Had Stimson's and FDR's secret communications via White with the Republican presidential candidate on the subject of arming Great Britain been revealed at that time, it would likely have caused a scandal. Republicans could have credibly accused FDR of using Stimson to limit the speech of the Republican presidential candidate, depriving the public of a free and full debate on the draft and destroyers questions before casting a vote in the election. It is a sign of how much FDR trusted Stimson that he asked him to communicate via White with Willkie on these extraordinarily sensitive issues. FDR's trust ultimately proved right. There was no scandal, and Stimson's behind-the-scenes dealings with the Republican presidential nominee were evidently never revealed—until the publication of this book.[13]

POLITICAL COMMENTATORS ARGUED that the fate of the conscription bill in Congress depended on whether Willkie would condemn it when he delivered his speech to formally accept the nomination.[14] The issue loomed as FDR and Stimson departed on the presidential train on August 16 for an overnight ride to observe US Army troop maneuvers in upstate New York and to meet with Canadian prime minister Mackenzie King.[15] That evening, FDR hosted what Stimson described as a "very pleasant dinner—a sort of family party" with members of FDR's staff in the president's railcar.

FDR and Stimson left the train the next morning to ride in the back of an open car, observing some ninety-four thousand troops performing maneuvers near Ogdensburg, New York. FDR wore a seersucker suit and a Panama hat, while Stimson sat beside him in a dark suit and fedora.[16] The inadequacies of the America's armed forces were on display: some of the soldiers carried broomsticks instead of guns, while others drove trucks instead of tanks. Many of the soldiers were volunteers who had never fired a gun, FDR was told.[17] Democratic New York governor Herbert Lehman joined the outing, but FDR kept Stimson at his side in the car, an act of political showmanship, putting the bipartisan alliance on display for the news reporters—and stealing some of Willkie's thunder on his big day.

That afternoon in his hometown, Elwood, Indiana, Willkie delivered his acceptance speech to a crowd of two hundred thousand people. He appealed for the votes of both Republicans and Democrats, making a frank observation on America's political turmoil: "Party lines are down. Nothing could make that clearer than the nomination by the Republicans of a liberal Democrat who changed his party affiliation because he found democracy in the Republican Party and not in the New Deal Party."[18] Turning to the war, he argued that the nation needed "some form of selective service," saying it was "the only democratic way to secure the trained and competent manpower we need for national defense." And, as White had predicted, he made no mention of the destroyers deal with Great Britain.

Willkie did attack FDR on a range of other issues, including his handling of the economy and foreign affairs. "He has courted a war for which the country is hopelessly unprepared—and which it emphatically does not want. He has secretly meddled in the affairs of Europe, and he has even unscrupulously encouraged other countries to hope for more help than we can give."

Yet Willkie's support of conscription won praise from Stimson, who wrote in his diary that Willkie "has done a great act for his country, and has gone far to hamstring the efforts of the little group of isolationists to play politics with that matter."[19]

That evening, FDR and Stimson returned to the president's train, and Prime Minister King arrived. King greeted Stimson cordially and told him "how glad Canada and Great Britain had been at [his] appointment." Though independent, Canada remained closely tied to Great Britain as a member of the Commonwealth. The three men ate dinner alone in FDR's dining car, then moved to a sitting room to discuss the destroyers deal and the creation of a joint US-Canadian board to defend North America from attack.[20]

The Justice Department soon announced that the president had the authority to exchange the destroyers for a lease of naval bases that the United Kingdom controlled in the Western Hemisphere, including those in Nova Scotia and Bermuda. Three days later, in London, where waves of Nazi bombers had recently wreaked devastation on civilians, Churchill jubilantly announced the destroyers deal in the House of Commons. The prime minister said, "We should today not only feel stronger but actually be stronger than we ever have been before."[21] Though isolationists in Congress objected to the deal, opinion polls showed the public supported it. Once the deal between the two governments was signed, the ships were dispatched to the British, who quickly deployed them to protect transatlantic shipping from German submarines.[22]

MOVING AHEAD WITH his plan to expand the army, Stimson began building his team of Republican men to help him run the War Department. He moved Robert Patterson to the newly created post of undersecretary of war. Stimson hired John J. McCloy, a New York attorney and personal friend who had investigated German sabotage in the United States during World War I, to handle counterintelligence as an assistant secretary of war, though his role would soon broaden. He also brought on Robert A. Lovett, a banker with Brown Brothers Harriman in New York. Stimson asked Lovett, who had won distinction as a naval pilot during World War I, to be his assistant secretary for air power and aircraft production. He also hired Harvey Bundy, a Boston Republican and attorney who had served with him as assistant secretary of state in the Hoover Administration. Bundy, whom he called "my closest personal assistant," would handle matters including work with scientists on the development of new weapons. As Stimson sought to turn the War Department into a juggernaut that would defeat the fascist armies threatening America, these were the chief civilians to whom he turned. "All but one of them were Republicans, but none of them ever aroused partisan opposition," Stimson said in his memoirs.[23] The one exception was apparently Lovett, a registered Republican who acknowledged voting for Democrats.[24] With his team of moderate Republicans, Stimson quietly executed his plan, outlined in his letter to Knox in May, to make his department a "hostage" of the Republican Party.

Stimson later described them as men of integrity who were not small-minded about seeking credit for their labors. They also tolerated

the mercurial nature of their boss, known for sometimes venting his irritation. "These were men who knew how to laugh . . . at trying events;
nor were they put off or dismayed" by Stimson's occasional "thunderous
anger," he wrote in his memoirs. This close-knit group would remain
together as the nucleus of the War Department over the next five years.

Another Republican embraced by both Stimson and Knox was their
mutual friend William J. Donovan. After graduating from Columbia's
law school, where Franklin Roosevelt was a fellow student, Donovan
joined the US Army in 1917 to serve in World War I.[25] As a major in an
infantry unit, he was wounded while rescuing another wounded soldier,
and was awarded the Distinguished Service Cross and other medals.[26]
After the war, he served as US attorney in western New York and ran
unsuccessfully as the Republican candidate to succeed FDR as New York
governor in 1932. Donovan, a close friend and political ally of Knox,
had hosted dinners in New York in 1936 to win support for Knox's bid
for the Republican presidential nomination.[27] Donovan's fame as a war
hero soared in early 1940 when a World War I movie, *The Fighting 69th*,
depicted him and other members of his regiment.

Donovan was summoned by FDR to an urgent meeting at the White
House on July 1, 1940, with Knox, Stimson and Secretary of State Cordell Hull.[28] The immediate dilemma was the lack of reliable information
on the likelihood of a Nazi victory over Great Britain. FDR's ambassador to Great Britain, the prominent Boston Democrat and businessman
Joseph P. Kennedy, had become close to pro-Hitler circles in England
and suggested England's military collapse was certain. With FDR's approval, Knox arranged for Donovan to go to London to obtain the best
intelligence possible about Britain's defenses. Kennedy, deemed untrustworthy, was not informed of the true objective of the trip, but shortly after Donovan arrived on July 17 British newspapers described the visit as
a mission for FDR. Donovan met King George VI, visited Churchill in
his underground war rooms beneath Whitehall and examined air force
bases and coastal defenses. Kennedy, enraged at being misled, fumed
in an August 7 cable to Hull: "I either want to run this job or get out."[29]

Upon his return to Washington, Donovan discussed the findings of
his trip with Knox, Stimson and other officials.[30] On the evening of August 6, he dined at Woodley with Henry and Mabel Stimson and Robert

Patterson and his wife. He recounted British requests for armaments, including the destroyers, and "described the morale as very high now and his final summary was that if an attack was made now, the British would probably win," Stimson noted in his diary.[31] In the following days, Knox and Donovan joined FDR and his close adviser Harry Hopkins aboard the presidential yacht *Potomac* off the coast of Maine.[32] Upon leaving the yacht, Knox explained to newspaper reporters the purpose of Donovan's trip to England: "He went over as my eyes and ears to see what he could find."

By early August, with three months remaining before the presidential election, FDR had dramatically changed the face of national defense leadership by placing a triumvirate of high-profile Republicans in positions of authority.

On August 3, Knox, who was insistent on his nonpartisanship, sounded an alarm over the need to prepare for war, a message that undoubtedly bolstered FDR's campaign against isolationism. "A titanic revolutionary struggle for the domination of the entire world is being waged in Europe, Asia and Africa," he warned in a national radio address.[33] "This attack is directed at democracy, competitive trade, and individual freedom everywhere. . . . Our one hope of keeping this vast struggle out of the Western Hemisphere rests on the success of our efforts to build our defenses, on such a scale, and with enough speed, so that no combination of international brigands would dare to test our power."

FDR further expanded his alliance with Republicans in August 1940 when he appointed Nelson Rockefeller, grandson of oil magnate John D. Rockefeller, to a diplomatic post. Rockefeller, who had worked in the oil industry in South America, would work to prevent the Nazis from extending their power over Latin American countries.[34]

Republican support for FDR got a boost the next month when New York City mayor Fiorello La Guardia endorsed FDR for president. He was a progressive Republican, and Stimson had repeatedly endorsed him in political races as early as 1929.[35] A maverick who downplayed party politics, La Guardia had years earlier built a close friendship with FDR and embraced the New Deal. In endorsing FDR on September 12, 1940, the mayor said, "I belong to no party. I do not like politicians. I want nothing from either party." La Guardia had often spoken out forcefully against the rise of fascism in Germany and Italy, and in praising FDR he said, "Roosevelt has regenerated our country. Roosevelt has made America the hope of the world."[36]

THE PUSH FOR conscription, meanwhile, prompted civil rights leaders to seek equal opportunities for African Americans in the expansion of the military, which had long implemented rigid racial segregation, keeping Black and white soldiers in separate units and sharply limiting the promotion of Black officers. Over the years of FDR's presidency, the New Deal had earned him support from the Black community. Eleanor Roosevelt helped build bridges between the president and Black leaders, including Mary McLeod Bethune, a vice president of the prominent civil rights group, the NAACP. Early in July 1940, Bethune brought to Eleanor's attention "grave apprehension among Negroes" about discrimination in the armed forces.[37]

Thurgood Marshall, the NAACP's special counsel, wrote a letter later that month to Stimson calling for an end to racial segregation by the US Army in advance of the draft. "The success of the new defense program depends entirely upon the establishment of 'unity' among the American citizens of this country," Marshall wrote. "The refusal to fully integrate Negroes who constitute the largest minority group in this country tends to destroy that 'unity' which is necessary to the success of the new defense program."[38] On August 2, Stimson replied and dismissed the request, turning Marshall's argument about unity on its head. "Unity can be destroyed by attempting to establish a program which is contrary to the War Department's plans, by those who are not familiar either with the principles involved or the requirements of such plans," he wrote. Faced with a blunt refusal to desegregate the army, Walter White, the executive secretary of the NAACP, went to Hyde Park to discuss the matter with Eleanor Roosevelt, who again appealed to FDR.[39]

Thurgood Marshall sent another letter to Stimson, this time basing his argument on the reasoning that Stimson had often appealed to: the importance of defending democracy. "The present defense program is being pushed forward for the avowed purpose of protecting democracy in the United States. It is impossible to maintain such a program if the program itself is based upon un-democratic policies such as racial discrimination," Marshall wrote in his August 7 letter. "Negroes are willing to take their part in this defense program along with other American citizens, but at the same time insist that they be given the right to serve in every branch of the armed services for which they may be qualified without distinction because of race or color."[40]

Eleanor again raised the issue with FDR, who agreed to discuss it with Stimson and Knox in the cabinet meeting set for August 16. Four days after the meeting, Stimson wrote the president a letter saying induction of Black soldiers would be proportionately equal to that of white soldiers. "If selective service is approved, colored personnel will be inducted and trained in the Army of the United States in the ratio that available negro manpower bears the available white manpower," Stimson wrote.[41] He promised inclusion of Black Americans in the armed services but sidestepped the issue of segregation by failing to address whether Black soldiers would be assigned to units side by side with white soldiers. The navy had announced in August that it would not rely upon the draft, avoiding the issue of enlisting any Black sailors. Once again, the First Lady urged the president to have Stimson and Knox meet with White and other civil rights leaders.[42] The contentious debate simmered behind closed doors.

After long argumentation, Congress on September 14 passed the Burke-Wadsworth compulsory service bill with bipartisan support. The House approved the bill with forty-six Republicans joining one hundred eighty-six Democrats to vote yes, and eighty-eight Republicans joining thirty-two Democrats and four independents to vote no. The Senate reflected a similar bipartisan split, with seven Republicans joining forty Democrats to vote yes.[43] President Roosevelt signed it into law in the White House two days later as Stimson, General Marshall and the chairmen of the House and Senate military affairs committees stood behind him.[44] An estimated 16,500,000 men between twenty-one and thirty-five were expected to register by October 16. From those registrants, the first 400,000 were expected to be called to training on January 1. With African Americans constituting 9 percent of the population,

Black men would account for 36,000 of the new conscripts, a White House statement said. FDR issued a proclamation underscoring the draft's vital importance for national defense and hailing the fact that members of both parties supported the law. "The Congress debated without partisanship and has now enacted a law establishing a selective method of augmenting our armed forces. The method is fair. It is sure, it is democratic—it is the will of the people."

The NAACP, however, continued to challenge the idea of whether the new army would be fair or democratic. Walter White decided to press his case with the help of A. Philip Randolph, the president of America's largest predominantly Black union, the Brotherhood of Sleeping Car Porters, and another civil rights activist, T. Arnold Hill of the National Urban League. The three men went to the White House on September 27 to meet with FDR, Knox and Patterson to urge once again the desegregation of the armed forces.[45] The discussion resulted in no changes of positions. In his diary, Stimson revealed the racist attitudes that underlay his firm opposition to ending segregation: "Leadership is not imbedded in the negro race yet and to try to make commissioned officers to lead the men into battle—colored men—is only to work disaster to both." He also worried that desegregation would lead to racial turmoil in the army. "I hope for Heaven's sake they won't mix the white and the colored troops together in the same units for then we shall certainly have trouble."[46]

The White House issued a statement after the meeting announcing that Black soldiers would be allocated to all branches of the army but that—with the exception of the three previously established Black regiments—the officers of all new Black units would be white.[47] This release caused an explosion of criticism directed at FDR in the Black press. *The New York Age,* a Black newspaper, proclaimed in a headline across its front page: "President Roosevelt Okays Jim Crow Army; Negro Leaders Indignant Over His Treatment."[48]

Willkie, seeking to reestablish the Republican Party as the defender of Black civil rights, campaigned by calling for the end of discrimination in the armed forces. He quickly won endorsements from a prominent Black newspaper, *The Pittsburgh Courier,* and some NAACP officials. Heavyweight boxing champion Joe Louis toured making campaign appearances for Willkie.[49] FDR's allies, concerned the president was rapidly losing Black voters, began to panic.[50]

FDR and Stimson, who proclaimed a lofty vision of America defending liberty against the ravages of global fascism, faced an immense challenge on the home front: would they embrace the fight for equality that Black people were waging in the very armed forces intended to keep America free? They ultimately did not budge on desegregation, but as the election approached, they made concessions to the civil rights activists: Stimson approved a request by Walter White that a Black officer, Colonel Benjamin O. Davis Jr., be promoted to brigadier general.[51] In addition, Stimson agreed to the appointment of a Black attorney, William Hastie, as his assistant to handle matters related to Black soldiers. FDR had appointed Hastie as the nation's first Black federal judge in 1937, a post he had left to become dean of Howard University Law School in Washington, DC.[52]

FDR's ISOLATIONIST OPPONENTS, meanwhile, continued to depict the president as driving the nation into war, a charge that echoed Willkie's attacks. Among those opposing FDR was a group formed in Chicago, the America First Committee, whose members included auto industry tycoon Henry Ford, retired general Robert E. Wood, and a former Sears, Roebuck & Co. chairman, Lessing Rosenwald. America First acquired its most famous spokesman when Charles Lindbergh joined its ranks and continued his isolationist diatribes. In a national radio broadcast on October 13, Lindbergh avoided using Roosevelt's name but condemned the country's "present leaders."[53] He said, "If we desire the unity among our people that is essential to national life and strength, we must select leaders who believe sincerely in national defense, but who are wholeheartedly opposed to our involvement in foreign wars."

The war made constant headlines: Germany bombed London and other English cities, and on September 27 Japan joined Germany and Italy to form the Axis alliance. As a result, the candidates' approaches to the war dominated the race. Willkie had supported conscription, but on October 15, during a speech in Buffalo, New York, he argued that FDR failed to provide barracks for the incoming draftees, appealing for the votes of the young men who might be drafted: "Surely they will not vote to return a government that performs like that."[54]

It was Stimson—not FDR—who delivered the counterpunch to Willkie. Stimson, who had recently begun holding a weekly Thursday news conference, told the press that all the housing needs for the eight hundred thousand soldiers to be conscripted by June 1941 would be met on time. Stimson was careful to balance his attack so as to preserve the quiet concord with Willkie. "Mr. Willkie, who is usually a fair critic and who has been courageous in his support of conscription and rearmament, has recently been misled into making statements about delays in the progress of housing the men who are being called out for military training which are neither fair nor accurate."[55] This jousting on the national stage, just weeks before the election, highlighted the rift in the Republican Party.

Some of FDR's advisers urged the president to start the military draft after the election so as to avoid providing grist for the mill of isolationists attacking the president and Stimson as warmongers. FDR, however, decided to launch the draft a week before the election.[56] On October 29, FDR, Stimson and Knox strode onto a stage at a War Department auditorium for a ceremony laden with symbolism designed to signal patriotism, fairness and bipartisan support of the draft. With newsreel cameras recording and radio networks broadcasting, FDR said the draft—the first in the nation's history undertaken during peacetime—was necessary to preserve America's freedom.[57] He marked the solemnity of the occasion by reading parts of letters from three religious leaders, a Presbyterian, a Catholic and a Jew, all in support of the draft. Then the Republican secretary of war, wearing a blindfold made of fabric cut from a chair used at the signing of the Declaration of Independence in 1776, reached into an enormous glass bowl filled with 8,944 blue capsules, each holding a different registration number designating the order in which soldiers would be summoned to training and service. Stimson pulled out the first capsule and handed it to FDR. The president opened the capsule, extracted a piece of paper, and said into the microphones, the first number "drawn by the secretary of war is serial number 158." A brief cry went up from the crowd in the hall, and the number picking continued. The expansion of America's army was under way. At the end of the day, Stimson praised FDR's decision to proceed with the draft, saying in his diary that it was "good statesmanship": FDR's speech helped "change the event of the Draft into a great asset in his favor."

On Tuesday, November 5, America pronounced its judgment on FDR's strategy of uniting with Republicans to face the global conflict. Voters went to the polls and decisively reelected FDR, giving him 469 electoral votes over Willkie's 82. FDR and Wallace got 27.3 million votes while Willkie and McNary got 23.3 million.

Pleased with the outcome, Stimson wrote in his diary the following day that "the election will be very salutary to the cause of stopping Hitler." After taking a day of rest in Hyde Park, Franklin and Eleanor Roosevelt returned to Washington by train and were greeted by Stimson and other cabinet members at Union Station.[58]

Stimson immediately saw an opportunity to bring Willkie, the nominal head of the Republican Party, into the fold of Republicans working with FDR. On November 10, he wrote Willkie a letter praising the way he handled the issues of the destroyers and conscription during the campaign. "I think I have been in a position to peculiarly appreciate the courage and vision which it took for you to come out as clearly as you did in favor of helping the British and adopting the Selective Service Act, and I think you rendered a great service to your country in doing so," he wrote.[59] "I believe we are facing a very grave time, when we shall need every leader gifted with initiative, foresight and courage in order to keep our nation from missing its opportunity for the imperatively needed leadership," Stimson wrote. He closed the letter, "Very sincerely your friend."

The next evening, Willkie gave a nationally broadcast speech urging the millions of people who cast their votes for him to act as a "loyal opposition," supporting the president and the national defense yet also maintaining their own political principles and independence.[60] He said the Republican Party remained powerful and had an important role to play. "Let us not, therefore, fall into the partisan error of opposing things just for the sake of opposition," he said. "It must be an opposition for a strong America."

Stimson saw in Willkie's appeal for a "loyal opposition" an opening for the Republican leader to play a positive role in supporting FDR's administration—and he swiftly began working to make it a reality. The next day, Stimson discussed Willkie with Knox and Hull. The three men agreed that "there was great danger of an appeasement movement in this country now that the election was over from people who said that Great Britain was surely going to be beaten and that the best thing we could do would be to make peace with Hitler and accept the fact of his domination over the world," Stimson wrote in his diary.[61] "Under these circumstances Willkie would have great influence in the Republican Party to keep them from doing it—if he would take that position." The three men agreed Stimson should contact Willkie in an effort to get him to lead Republicans away from accepting Hitler's domination of Europe. Willkie would become increasingly close to the bipartisan alliance in the coming months.

FDR AND HIS Republican allies continued pushing the nation toward greater industrial production to prepare for war. On November 26, Stimson announced that in order to make more military planes, manufacturers would be prevented from expanding production of civilian aircraft. "With the Army and Navy far below their requirements in combat planes, and with the British need for American-built planes growing more serious every month, the Army and Navy believe that it is incompatible with adequate national defense to have part of the nation's productive capacity taken up with an attempted expansion of civilian business."[62] Hours later, FDR made public remarks backing up Stimson.

The Nazis continued daily bombing of London and other English cities as the Battle of Britain air war raged. Hitler also tightened his control over France and other occupied European nations. The Nazis also dominated the high seas. Between May and December 1940, fascist forces had sunk three million tons of shipping vessels.[63] Concerns arose that Britain's defenses were weakening and, unable to import food from traditional markets in Europe, the British people would begin to go hungry. The British also were running out of financial reserves. On

September 17, Lord Lothian had met with Stimson at Woodley and repeatedly mentioned the "British are reaching the bottom of their financial resources," as Stimson put it.[64] On December 10, Stimson, Marshall
and Patterson went to the Treasury Department to meet with Morgenthau and navy officials. The men reviewed a list of British requests to-
taling about $5 billion worth of munitions and concluded the British
had available resources to pay that were "considerably smaller than this
amount," Stimson noted.[65] Britain would soon be desperate and vulnerable if she could not continue purchasing American arms.

Churchill sounded the alarm over Britain's finances in a lengthy telegram December 8 to the president while he was vacationing with Hopkins on a navy cruiser, the USS *Tuscaloosa,* off the Caribbean island of
Antigua. "The moment approaches when we shall no longer be able to
pay cash for shipping and other supplies," Churchill wrote. He warned
that Great Britain would be "stripped to the bone" to pay for its war
effort, which was buying time for the United States to arm itself.[66] FDR
pondered Churchill's cable over the next two days, rereading it alone on
his deck chair aboard the *Tuscaloosa.* Finally, the president developed
an idea to provide Great Britain whatever help it needed for the war effort on the understanding that it would make repayment when it could.
This would be a massive loan to the British—one the president would
need to convince the American people to support.

On December 17, FDR explained this concept in a press conference
by offering a morality tale: "Suppose my neighbor's home catches fire,
and I have a length of garden hose four or five hundred feet away. If he
can take my garden hose and connect it with his hydrant, I may help to
put out his fire. Now what do I do? I don't say to him, 'Neighbor, my
garden hose cost me fifteen dollars; you have to pay me fifteen dollars
for it.' No! I don't want fifteen dollars. I want my garden hose back after
the fire is over."[67]

After Christmas, on the evening of December 29, FDR conveyed
his vision via radio in a Fireside Chat, warning first of the fascist plan
for world domination and denouncing "appeasers" in America calling
for a negotiated peace with Hitler. Then he laid out for the American
people the idea of manufacturing the military equipment needed for

the war and letting the nation's military leaders decide how to best to use it. "As planes and ships and guns and shells are produced, your government, with its defense experts, can then determine how best to use them to defend this hemisphere. The decision as to how much shall be sent abroad and how much shall remain at home must be made on the basis of our over-all military necessities."[68] The president called for Congress to pass a bill to carry out his plan and make America into "the great arsenal of democracy."

Despite this grand vision, Stimson and Knox found that their departments were struggling to negotiate and approve all the contracts necessary to produce the massive amounts of arms and equipment needed to fight a war. The two Republican secretaries found the seven-member National Defense Advisory Commission, which had purview over the contracting efforts, cumbersome and inefficient. Also, various War and Navy department offices had taken up different parts of the contracting workload, causing disarray and confusion, Stimson concluded. The Republican secretaries urged FDR to centralize the contracting work in an office to be led by a single person, William Knudsen, a Republican auto industry executive who already was advising FDR.

On December 18, Stimson and Knox, backed up by Patterson and Undersecretary of the Navy James Forrestal, went to the White House to make their case. "Conferences with the president are difficult matters," Stimson grumbled in his diary. "His mind does not follow easily a consecutive chain of thought but he is full of stories and incidents and hops about in his discussions from suggestion to suggestion and it is very much like chasing a vagrant beam of sunshine around a vacant room."[69] Despite this complaint, Stimson's arguments prompted the president to take action. Impressed by the need to solve the contracting problems and unleash the nation's industrial power for the cause of freedom, FDR swiftly embraced the value of a "concentration of responsibility" in the contracting process.

FDR announced two days later that he would create the Office of Production Management (OPM), which was to lead the contracting effort for the army and navy.[70] FDR named Knudsen as director of the OPM, while Stimson and Knox were made board members. Knudsen, a lifelong Republican who had been a senior executive at General Motors, had been recruited by FDR in May 1940 to serve on the Advisory Commission.[71] Labor disputes had led to strikes paralyzing auto manufacturing plans in late 1940, and FDR sought to ease labor concerns that Knudsen would have too much power by placing Sidney Hillman, a leader of the Congress of Industrial Organizations union, as associate director under Knudsen. Knudsen, Hillman, Stimson and Knox would become known as the "Big Four" in the effort to mobilize industry for the war. Stimson also would soon arrange for attorney John Lord O'Brian, a moderate Republican friend of his who had been an assistant attorney general under President Hoover, to become OPM's legal counsel.[72] Thus staffed, the OPM moved swiftly to engage American industry in creating the world's mightiest armed forces.

As Christmas approached, Stimson sent FDR a gift of a walking stick he had acquired more than a decade earlier in the Philippines.[73] The president, with his legs paralyzed, occasionally used a cane and leg braces to walk short distances. Stimson attached to his gift a handwritten note:

My Dear Mr. President,

I am very grateful this Christmastide. I have been given an opportunity to try to serve my country at a time of life when I had no right to expect such a chance. Instead of eating my heart out on the sidelines, I am busy with what I hope will be useful activity in this great crisis of the world, and my heart turns to you with thankfulness for giving me such a chance. I pray that I may not be an occasion of failure or disaster.

As a small token of Christmas, I am sending you a Philippine cane to which there is a little history. When I was there as Governor General it was given to me by a Moro princess—a niece of the Sultan of Sulu—as a token of loyalty and allegiance to the American government.

May it carry the same pledge from me to you in the great task on which we are engaged this coming year. With my very best

wishes for a Happy Christmas and New Year to both you and Mrs.
Roosevelt, I am

Very faithfully yours,
Henry L. Stimson

Stimson's gift of the cane symbolized his loyal support of FDR in
their efforts to unite America, defeat fascism and save democracy. "Dear
Harry," the president wrote in a note after the holidays. "That cane from
the Philippines is perfectly beautiful—thank you ever so much for giving it to me. This carries to you my very best wishes for the New Year."[74]
Stimson's unwavering support of FDR would be critical in the coming
years amid the ordeals of war.

A Bipartisan Call to Arms

After the New Year's holiday, Secretary of War Stimson went to the White House on Thursday, January 2, 1941, for a 10:30 A.M. meeting with President Roosevelt. The president, often exhausted due to the long-term effects of his paralysis, remained in bed, where he sometimes met close advisers. The two men talked for an hour about intelligence on German aircraft production, concerns about labor troubles on a contract with auto magnate Henry Ford for manufacturing tanks and the rising costs of constructing training camps for the army's new draftees. Stimson warned that Germany's superiority in aircraft meant that the Nazis could deliver a severe blow to Great Britain.[1] "I felt that there was great danger that Great Britain would be reduced to a crisis during the coming winter and spring and I said that it seemed to me that he should be thinking of some dramatic way of restoring their morale; otherwise they would not get through."

Stimson was at the heart of FDR's war effort, and the president would soon call upon him to drum up support for his vision of turning American industry into the "arsenal of democracy" to aid Great Britain and other allies. On January 6, the president went before both chambers of Congress to offer his State of the Union message, urging full material aid to the embattled democracies facing the fascist armies. "Let us say to the democracies: 'We Americans are vitally concerned in your defense of freedom. We are putting forth our energies, our resources and our organizing powers to give you the strength to regain and maintain a free world. We shall send you, in ever increasing numbers, ships, planes, tanks, guns. This is our purpose and our pledge.'"[2] Describing what would soon be called the Lend-Lease program, FDR said the Allied nations would repay the borrowed equipment to the United States in kind when they could.

Without making specific reference to Stimson and Secretary of the Navy Knox, the president proclaimed America's "national policy" as nonpartisan support of national defense and democracy. "First, by an impressive expression of the public will and without regard to partisanship, we are committed to all-inclusive national defense. Second, by an impressive expression of the public will and without regard to partisanship, we are committed to full support of all those resolute people everywhere who are resisting aggression and are thereby keeping war away from our hemisphere. By this support we express our determination that the democratic cause shall prevail, and we strengthen the defense and security of our own nation." He also laid out his vision of the "four essential human freedoms" that were the goals of the American war effort: freedom of speech, freedom of religious worship, freedom from economic want and freedom from fear.

Four days later, the Democratic leaders in each chamber, Alben Barkley of Kentucky in the Senate and John McCormack of Massachusetts in the House, filed bills in Congress to give the president broad authority to carry out the Lend-Lease program. The bills provided authority for Stimson and Knox—as the secretaries of war and navy—to procure arms and equipment for war and export them as needed to America's allies as needed for national defense.[3]

Isolationist critics attacked swiftly. "I am neither an appeaser nor a Hitlerite," said Senator Hiram Johnson, the California Republican isolationist. "I want to see Hitler whipped and Britain triumphant. But I regard the bill presented today as monstrous. I decline to change the whole form of my government on the specious plea of assisting one belligerent." Senator Robert Taft, the Ohio Republican, said, "The proposed bill combines all the faults of the worst New Deal legislation, including unlimited delegation of authority and blank-check appropriations.... No Congress but a rubber-stamp Congress would enact such a bill. I am unalterably opposed to it and shall do all I can to defeat it." Representative Hamilton Fish III, a staunch Republican isolationist whose New York district included FDR's hometown of Hyde Park, inveighed: "It looks as if we are bringing Nazism, fascism and dictatorship to America and setting up a Fuehrer here."

WITH LEND-LEASE FACING fiery Republican opposition, Stimson moved swiftly behind the scenes to advance his plan for Wendell Willkie, the recently defeated Republican presidential candidate, to support the war effort. Stimson learned from his friend Landon Thorne that Willkie was planning to travel to England and had invited Thorne to accompany him. Thorne was the electric utility investor and partner of Stimson's cousin Alfred Loomis, and both men knew Willkie from his involvement with Commonwealth & Southern.[4] After Loomis visited Stimson at Woodley in Washington on January 10, he arranged for Willkie to meet with Stimson and Thorne the following day at Highhold on Long Island.

Stimson flew up from Washington to Long Island that evening and got up early the next morning, a Saturday, to take a horseback ride from Highhold. In the afternoon, Willkie arrived at the estate in a limousine that Thorne had sent for him. The three men ate lunch together and discussed Willkie's planned trip to England. Stimson showed Willkie the latest intelligence reports on the European war from G-2, the War Department's military intelligence division. "He expressed himself very much concerned with the seriousness of the situation," Stimson recalled in his diary.[5] "I gave my views to Willkie on the situation and I think on the whole the meeting was a good success."

Stimson wanted Thorne to keep the Republican leader on the right track. "Willkie is all right but he is rather a prima donna and not a student and with a careful, thorough man like Thorne along, who can be made acquainted with the facts, there is a great chance to steady Willkie and keep him well informed where he wouldn't do it himself." Stimson was seeking to build a connection with Willkie that was personal and political in hopes of guiding the former Republican presidential nominee. Passage of the Lend-Lease bill was under threat, and Stimson wanted Willkie's firm support for the war effort.

The very next day, January 12, Willkie publicly announced both his trip to England and his support of the Lend-Lease bill. He said that while the bill would turn over tremendous power to the president, it was the right move for national defense.[6] "This is a critical moment in history. The United States is not a belligerent, and we hope we shall not be. Our problem, however, is not alone to keep America out of the war but to keep war out of America." His support for the Democratic president's Lend-Lease program made headlines across the country. He did call for amending the bill to limit the period for which the president would have unchecked authority to send aid to allies, with Congress having the power to extend or revoke that authority, yet he advocated vigorously for its passage. "Democracy is endangered. And the American people are so aware of the danger that they have endorsed the policy of giving full and active aid to those democracies which are resisting aggression."

Imploring the nation to rise above the partisanship gripping American politics, Willkie left no doubt that he was diametrically opposed to the isolationists: "Appeasers, isolationists or lip-service friends of Britain will seek to sabotage the program for aid to Britain and her allies behind the screen of opposition to the bill. It makes a vital difference to the United States which side prevails in the present conflict. I refute the statement that our national security is not involved in a British defeat."[7]

Willkie's remarks were a brickbat to Alf Landon, who recently had asserted that a British defeat would have no impact on US national security. Landon, who had endorsed Willkie in the 1940 race, responded critically. "There is no essential difference between Mr. Willkie's position and Mr. Roosevelt's position, which is to go to war if necessary to help England win. If Mr. Willkie had revealed it before the Republican national convention, he would not have been nominated," Landon said. More Republican leaders, including former president Hoover, soon came out in opposition to Lend-Lease. The fissure in the Republican Party over isolationism was widening.

Isolationism divided the Democrats, too. The furor over Lend-Lease escalated that same night when Senator Burton Wheeler, the isolationist Democrat from Montana, condemned the bill in a debate on a national radio broadcast. Lend-Lease, Wheeler sneered, represented another "New

Deal triple A foreign policy—plow under every fourth American boy." It was a horrifying prediction—one calculated to terrify families across the country. The next morning, FDR condemned Wheeler's remark as "the most untruthful . . . the most dastardly, unpatriotic thing that has ever been said."[8]

Willkie's statement supporting Lend-Lease, meanwhile, delighted Stimson, who said in his diary that even the demand for a time limit on the president's powers was "reasonable." With evident satisfaction, he noted that Willkie "used one expression in his statement which I had given him Saturday at Highhold—namely, that the problem was not so much to keep America out of war as to keep war out of America."[9] He moved ahead with his plan for Thorne to manage Willkie's trip to England. Stimson arranged for Thorne to come to Washington and—in the privacy of Woodley—receive a briefing from his assistant John McCloy and Army chief of staff General George Marshall.

A whirlwind of events in support of Lend-Lease began on January 16, when Stimson went to the Capitol to testify in support of Lend-Lease before the House Foreign Affairs Committee. He told the committee that Germany's seizure of weapons factories in allied countries posed a serious threat to American defense, and he warned that a defeat of the British navy could lead to an invasion of the United States.[10] The committee's senior Republican, Fish, challenged him: "Do you actually believe we are in any danger of immediate attempted invasion?" Stimson stood up from his chair, pointed at Fish and jabbed with his finger to underscore each point in his reply: "I think we are in very great danger of invasion by air in the contingency the British navy is destroyed or surrendered."

After his confrontation with Fish on Capitol Hill, Stimson went to the White House for a cabinet meeting, where he again advanced his plan to bring Willkie into the alliance with FDR—in essence playing matchmaker between the two former rivals. He told the president he "thought it would be highly advisable for the two—Willkie and Roosevelt—to get together, so at least they will have met once on a subject on which they are congenial instead of only on meetings where they were arrayed on opposite sides, such as the utility meetings." The president "gladly consented."[11] The next morning, Thorne came to breakfast at Woodley, and Stimson told him the president agreed to meet with Willkie. Thorne promised to convey the idea to Willkie.

Stimson went back to testify before the House Foreign Affairs Committee later that day, this time with Knox. Both men urged passage of Lend-Lease, warning that England faced a crisis within the next sixty to ninety days, pointing particularly to the superiority of the naval forces of the Axis powers. Fish charged the bill would permit the president to give away the United States Navy. Partisan anger over the two Republicans' alliance with FDR flared when Stimson reminded committee member George Tinkham that Stimson, too, belonged to the Republican Party. "You did," Tinkham retorted. "I think I still do," the secretary of war fired back. "I don't believe you will read me out of it."[12] As Stimson left at the end of the hearing, applause broke out among the crowd in the large room. Later, the secretary of war reviewed the events in his diary. "The general impression on me as I look back on it after the day is over was one of dismay and sorrow that one could be so blinded by partisanship and by ignorance as the Republican members of that Committee have shown themselves to be during this hearing. It augured sadly for what may happen to our country if they represent any very large percentage of our population. Their questions were puerile, silly, and blinded by an intense hostility to the president."[13]

Knox also was furious over the hearing, and he wrote a fierce editorial in his *Chicago Daily News* charging that congressional Republicans "are attempting to destroy national unity in a time of great peril. Others have tried that. And they have ignominiously failed. It doesn't pay to sell your country short."[14]

Willkie arrived at the White House on January 19 to meet with FDR and Secretary of State Cordell Hull. The three men conversed in the Oval Office on the second floor for more than an hour. It was precisely the sort of alliance-building talk Stimson had hoped for. Upon emerging from their meeting, they revealed no details of their discussion but said that Willkie would meet with Winston Churchill on his trip and that Roosevelt had given Willkie a note for the British prime minister, which was kept secret.[15]

In the note, revealed years later, FDR wrote, "Dear Churchill, Wendell

Willkie will give you this. He is truly helping to keep politics out over here," a vow of confidence in Willkie's efforts to cross partisan lines and support the Democratic president's war policies.[16] FDR's note went on to quote from Henry Wadsworth Longfellow's poem, "The Building of the Ship":

> Sail on, O ship of state!
> Sail on, O Union, strong and great!
> Humanity with all its fears,
> With all the hopes of future years,
> Is hanging breathless in thy fate!

The American poet had written the patriotic verse a century earlier, at a time when fears ran high that civil war would tear the nation apart, yet Roosevelt told Churchill it "applies to your people as it does to us." The president could count on the poem to strike a chord with Churchill, who had created his National Coalition to reduce partisan political divisions and unite Great Britain behind his defense plans. The two leaders, of course, had their political differences: Churchill was a conservative while FDR was a liberal. But both men were contending with the challenges of building a coalition with an opposing political party.[17] Roosevelt's personal note to Churchill identified Willkie as a confirmed ally in their shared struggle.

Before leaving the White House that day, Willkie once again proclaimed his strong support for the Lend-Lease bill. He told reporters, "We can't afford to make the president impotent in dealing with the emergency. We have to realize that new powers are necessary."

THE NEXT DAY was cold and sunny in Washington—and frenzied with FDR's third inauguration. In the morning, Stimson and other members of the cabinet went to church with FDR and then on to the Capitol, where the president was sworn in and delivered his inaugural address.[18] FDR's speech left aside politics, parties, war and armaments. Instead, he traced America's defense of democracy through its history. He pointed to George Washington's first inaugural address, in which the nation's first president called for the "preservation of the sacred fire of liberty." Now, FDR said, "In the face of great perils never before encountered, our strong purpose is to protect and to perpetuate the integrity of democracy. . . . We do not retreat. We are not content to stand still. As Americans, we go forward, in the service of our country, by the will of God."[19]

After eating lunch at the White House and watching a military parade on Pennsylvania Avenue, Stimson remarked in his diary that FDR's speech was "very impressive and on a very high and rather exalted spiritual plane."

Lofty speeches about protecting democracy, however, did not impress isolationists, who continued to attack Lend-Lease as a dictatorial measure that would drive America into the European war. On January 23, Charles Lindbergh denounced the Lend-Lease bill in testimony before Congress, calling instead for the nation to remain strictly neutral and to pursue a negotiated peace with Hitler.

Lindbergh portrayed the war as a struggle over the balance of power in Europe, and testified that the English and French were at fault for failing to stop Hitler years earlier from taking such steps as establishing the German air force. He laid blame for the war equally on Hitler and his opponents.[20] Asked whether he had ever criticized Hitler, Lindbergh replied, "Yes, but not publicly." He added, "There is much I do not like that is happening in the world, on both sides. Over a period of years, however, there is not as much difference in philosophy as we have been led to believe." After his testimony, the aviator received a standing ovation from members of the committee.

Willkie arrived in London on January 26, a time when civilian casualty numbers mounted steadily as Nazi bombers rained destruction on English cities. "I am very glad to be here in England, for whose cause I have the utmost sympathy. I want to do all I can to get the United States to give England the utmost aid possible in her struggle for free men all over the world," he said. He also promptly made it clear that he was not an emissary of President Roosevelt. "I am here as Wendell Willkie. I am representing no one."[21]

The next day, he met with Churchill at the prime minister's official residence at 10 Downing Street, sharing with him the note from FDR, and toured the old city district of London, which was recently damaged severely by Nazi firebombs. He also had a friendly public meeting with Ernest Bevin, the unionist and Labour Party member of Parliament whom Churchill brought into his cabinet as minister of labor. Thorne and the publisher John Cowles, who also accompanied Willkie on the trip, remained behind the scenes. Willkie met a policeman and an injured soldier, and he hailed the bravery of the English amid the war. "During the few hours I have been here," he told reporters, "I have found their spirit magnificent. I like their nerve. I have not met anybody so far who is downhearted, but I did not expect anything else."[22] Willkie's supportive words won him praise from many English people. When he toured Birmingham, where nearly 1,400 people had died in a single night of bombing in November, and visited a shattered cathedral in Coventry, crowds cheered him.[23]

In Washington, however, Willkie's support of Lend-Lease left congressional Republicans unmoved. When the House voted on the bill February 8, it passed by a vote of 260–165, largely along party lines. Voting yes were two hundred thirty-six Democrats and twenty-four Republicans, while the no votes came from one hundred thirty-five Republicans along with twenty-five Democrats and five members of small parties.[24] Among the opponents was Republican minority leader Joseph Martin of Massachusetts, who warned that the bill "will be the longest single step that this nation has yet taken toward direct involvement in the war."

The battle over Lend-Lease then moved to the Senate, where Willkie— two days after returning from his trip to England—appeared before the Senate Foreign Relations Committee in support of the bill. It offered the American people their "only chance to defend liberty without themselves going to war," he warned on February 11. "If Britain were to collapse, we would be in war a month afterward. That's my guess." Republicans questioned why he had charged FDR was leading the country into war during the presidential race but was now supporting military spending that some Republicans claimed would hasten America's entry into the conflict.[25] The isolationist senator Gerald Nye, a North Dakota Republican, asked whether it was still Willkie's view that—as he had charged during his presidential campaign—FDR would have the nation at war by April 1941. "It might be," Willkie replied. But with a smile, he conceded, "It was a bit of campaign oratory."[26]

The "campaign oratory" comment provoked a storm of controversy, as Willkie's critics portrayed it as a confession that he had misled Republicans about his true beliefs. The *Chicago Tribune* said it discredited everything he stood for. Seattle's Roman Catholic bishop called for him to apologize to his party and the nation. Republican interventionists, however, saw the remark as a dose of truth. William Allen White, the Kansas editor who had served as a go-between for FDR, Stimson and Willkie, called it "one of the most courageous things any man ever said in public life."[27]

Willkie's plea in support of Lend-Lease reaped condemnation from Republican leaders, some of whom sought to demote Willkie from his leadership in the party. Taft concluded there was "no justification in precedent or principle for the view that a defeated candidate for president is the titular head of the party." Nye called his support for Lend-Lease a "betrayal."[28] As isolationist opposition to the bill intensified, a crowd of women protesting Lend-Lease hung a two-faced effigy—one side FDR and the other Willkie—near the British embassy in Washington.[29] Republicans in Washington even discussed the idea of reading Willkie out of the party, though House minority leader Martin resisted the efforts.

FDR and his Republican allies may not have won over many congressional Republicans to support Lend-Lease, but Willkie appeared to be convincing the American public. A poll prepared by the American Institute of Public Opinion, led by George Gallup, found in a survey conducted February 14—three days after Willkie's testimony—that 58 percent of respondents wanted Congress to pass the Lend-Lease bill, up from 54 percent two days before he testified.[30] The day after he testified, the Senate Foreign Relations Committee passed the bill by a vote of 15–8, with all but one of the committee's eight Republicans voting against.

FDR, MEANWHILE, CONTINUED building his Republican alliance. Joseph Kennedy, FDR's ambassador to Great Britain who gloomily predicted a Nazi victory in England, had announced his resignation in December

1940, and to replace him FDR chose a Republican, John Winant. Born to a prosperous family in New York in 1889, Winant joined the US Army to fight in the First World War, serving as an aircraft pilot in France. After returning home, he entered politics and served two terms as New Hampshire's governor, building a reputation as a progressive Republican who backed programs such as expansion of public works and a minimum wage law.[31] Winant moved to the national stage in 1935 when FDR named him chairman of the board that launched and then ran the new Social Security program providing aid to the elderly and disabled. Later named by FDR to a diplomatic post in Europe, Winant's clear-eyed optimism stood in marked contrast to the pessimism of Kennedy. Having seen the devastating Nazi bombing of London in the fall of 1940, Winant told FDR of the English, "They will take all the bombing that comes."[32]

As ambassador, Winant landed on March 1 at an airport in the English city of Bristol, where he told a BBC reporter, "There is no place I'd rather be at this time than in England." His support of Great Britain in its darkest hour endeared him to the British. King George VI broke protocol by leaving his palace to greet the new ambassador. The king went to the Windsor train station and waited for Winant's arrival. When the American envoy finally stepped from a train car, the king extended his hand and said, "I am glad to welcome you here."[33]

Shortly after taking his new post in London, Winant sent a supportive note to his old friend Frank Knox, whom he knew from past Republican campaigns. "I would like very much to go back to the days when we were both progressives and friends working for the election of Theodore Roosevelt. We are playing on the same 'team' again," Winant wrote. "I think you are doing a great job."[34]

Stimson added another Republican to a War Department position aimed at improving soldier morale. This was Charles P. Taft, son of President William H. Taft and brother of isolationist Republican senator Robert Taft. Charles Taft had left Yale to fight in the First World War, then returned to graduate. He eventually practiced law and became a member of the Cincinnati City Council. For the War Department, his duties were to provide recreation for the large number of recruits housed at army bases around the country.[35] Stimson hailed the appointment in his diary: "Taft is a man whose chief thought is to his ability to smooth out difficulties, and . . . he will have full opportunity for exercise of that quality."

As the chief defenders of Lend-Lease, Stimson and Knox bore the brunt of the attack from the bill's isolationist opponents in the Senate. On March 8, Wheeler charged the bill would give the president the power to carry out an undeclared war. He then tried to skewer Stimson by introducing a memorandum on "Historic Parallels in the Present Drive to War," which recited Stimson's efforts in early 1917—prior to formal entry of the US into the First World War—to warn of a possible invasion of the United States, urge the nation to prepare for war, draft troops and send aid to the allies.[36]

After heated debate that day, the Senate passed the bill by a tally of 60–31. In a sign of growing bipartisanship, ten Republicans, including Willkie's former running mate, Minority Leader Charles McNary of Oregon, joined Barkley and forty-eight other Democrats in voting yes. Yet isolationism remained strong in both major parties: seventeen Republicans, thirteen Democrats and one Progressive voted no. After the House gave final approval to the Senate version three days later, FDR quickly signed the act into law and approved a transfer of war supplies to Great Britain, and also Greece, which had recently been invaded by Italy.

In the following weeks, the German Navy sank vessels in Atlantic waters close to the US coast, as Nazi bombs fell on England. On March 16, Hitler boasted in a speech that Germany would defeat England, suggesting America's Lend-Lease aid would be impotent. "No power and no support coming from any part of the world will change the outcome of this battle in any respect," the Nazi dictator said. "England will fall."[37]

Hitler's bravado undermined isolationist arguments in Congress. Like a fever breaking, the isolationist grip on congressional Republicans eased. Three days later Republicans joined Democrats in passing a bill providing $7 billion for Lend-Lease spending. The bill passed the House on a strong bipartisan vote of 337–55. House Republican minority leader Martin, who had earlier voted against Lend-Lease, joined one hundred and three other Republicans and two hundred and thirty-one Democrats in voting yes.[38] Five days later, the measure passed the

Senate by a dramatic bipartisan margin, 67–9, with seventeen Republicans and one Independent joining forty-nine Democrats to vote yes. Even isolationist stalwarts Taft and Vandenberg voted begrudgingly for the measure, noting their objections to the expansion of presidential power under Lend-Lease. "I vote for the bill with great regret," Taft said in the debate. "I vote for it simply because I am in favor of aid to England."

FDR signed the bill and publicly praised Willkie's efforts to curb partisan politics. "The leader of the Republican Party himself—Mr. Wendell Willkie—in word and in action, is showing what patriotic Americans mean by rising above partisanship and rallying to the common cause," the president said. "And now that the plain people of America have spoken their determination, Republicans and Democrats in the Congress and out of the Congress are patriotically cooperating to make that determination take positive form."[39]

Isolationism lost its intense grip on American politics largely because prominent Republicans—Stimson, Knox and Willkie—took a stand supporting FDR's war policy. Approval of the vast funding for Lend-Lease signaled that America would unleash her massive industrial might to aid her allies. Other spending measures followed, causing the total to soar. By May 1941, Congress had appropriated a total of $37.3 billion for defense, approximately four times the entire federal budget in 1939.[40] American factories were soon turning out thousands of airplanes and tanks.

Isolationists, meanwhile, continued attacking the administration's war policies, turning their fire particularly on the Republicans who supported FDR. An America First rally on May 23 filled Madison Square Garden in New York City, where Senator Wheeler condemned Stimson and Knox as "war makers," and Charles Lindbergh ridiculed the presidential election of 1940 as failing to present voters with a choice on war policy. "We in America were given just about as much chance to express our beliefs at the election last fall as the Germans would have been given if Hitler had run against Göring," the aviator said. Outside the hall, an overflow crowd listened to the proceedings over speakers, and anti-fascist protesters distributed leaflets at nearby street corners.[41] America was not at war, but her peace was uneasy.

PART II

WAR COMES

The Separate Peace

Nazi submarine and air attacks took an increasing toll on shipping in early 1941. In the first three months of the year, 302 British and Allied vessels, or more than 1.2 million tons of shipping, went to the bottom.[1] On a single day in February, German bombers attacked a group of vessels three hundred miles west of Ireland, sinking nine ships and seriously damaging seven more.[2] The Nazi attacks on shipping depleted British supplies of food, fuel and industrial materials, undermining the country's defenses. In late March, the Nazis announced a significant expansion of their naval combat zone around Britain, extending it several hundred miles westward into the Atlantic, further threatening American shipping.[3] The Nazi predations on the high seas left America in an uneasy separate peace and also sparked discord between President Roosevelt and Secretary of War Stimson.

By spring 1941, the idea of having the US Navy convoys to protect shipping vessels from attack had been under discussion for months by Stimson, General George Marshall, Secretary of the Navy Knox and Admiral Harold Stark, the navy's chief of naval operations. FDR, however, steadfastly rejected the idea, out of concern he would be accused of putting US Navy ships in harm's way to instigate a war.

Stimson grew impatient over what he perceived as FDR's lack of leadership in responding to the Nazi attacks.[4] In a meeting with FDR in the White House on April 22, Stimson urged him to lead the American people. "I cautioned him on the necessity of his taking the lead and that without a lead on his part it was useless to expect the people would voluntarily take the initiative in letting him know whether or not they would follow him." Stimson said people wanted "serious and constantly responsible attitude towards the war." He warned FDR about his press conferences drifting into "wise cracks and repartees." Stimson suggested the president should go on the offensive by defeating a Republican iso-lationist senator's bill to block the navy from using convoys to protect shipping. "'You can do so, can't you?' I said. He said, 'We certainly can.' Altogether we had a very good talk and I felt that perhaps I helped him."

Stimson's unique authority as an adviser to FDR has been noted by historians.[5] Cabinet members Henry Morgenthau Jr. and Harold Ickes spoke very frankly with FDR, as did his adviser Harry Hopkins. Yet Stimson's decades of experience as a political figure, secretary of war and secretary of state gave him unique status. In addition, his character—he valued decisive action, disliked gamesmanship and was sometimes quick to anger—inclined him to speak bluntly with the president. Being a Republican—not a Democrat speaking to his party's leader—likely also emboldened him to speak freely.

FDR, who respected and trusted Stimson, was inclined to listen to his secretary of war. The president encouraged lively debates with his cabinet members and was not irritated by disagreements. Eleanor Roo-sevelt later observed that her husband "made an effort to give each per-son who came in contact with him the feeling that he understood what his particular interest was."[6] She added that often FDR said things to show he understood, but his interlocutors mistook these as indicating he agreed. Stimson's diary is littered with reports that FDR appeared to agree with him—but some share of these may have been wishful think-ing on Stimson's part.

FDR, as a strategist, often saw benefits in confusion or even deception. Morgenthau later would recall the president saying, "You know I am a juggler, and I never let my right hand know what my left hand does. . . . I may be entirely inconsistent, and furthermore I am perfectly willing to mislead and tell untruths if it will help win the war."[7] For Stimson, the old hunter, who prided himself on straightforwardness on matters of policy, FDR's willful unclarity at times was infuriating.

On April 24, Stimson met with FDR and Knox, and argued that there was no need to keep the US naval fleet in Hawaii because army air defenses at the Pearl Harbor base were more than sufficient to defend the region. Knox told the president that Hawaii was "impregnable" and the navy supported the army's idea of moving the fleet to the Atlantic.[8] FDR believed it was important to keep the fleet in Hawaii as a "striking force" protecting the South Pacific. He also continued opposing convoys though he was open to the idea of a "patrol to watch for any aggressor."

Stimson's irritation flared. He was convinced the proper course was to send convoys to protect shipping to Great Britain. "I wanted him to be honest with himself. To me it seems a clearly hostile act to the Germans and I am prepared to take the responsibility of it." The meeting ended with no apparent resolution, and in his diary he fumed over Roosevelt's "disingenuous attitude."

During a cabinet meeting the next day, FDR and Stimson discussed using a new technology that might thwart Nazi attacks on shipping. FDR said James Conant, the president of Harvard University, had told him of progress on a fledgling system that used radio beams to locate enemy ships and aircraft, and was "called radio but was not radio."[9] This was the advent of radar, which the British military had already deployed. FDR wanted the army and navy to begin training three hundred men in its use. Stimson spoke with Conant days later and authorized Marshall to start the training, and he quickly became an advocate for its deployment.

Facing the Nazi threat to shipping, FDR announced April 29 that navy vessels would patrol waters far from the US mainland, but he stopped short of ordering convoys. The issue surged into debate in Congress, where Republicans in the House of Representatives demanded that the president clarify his plans for the patrols.[10] "We have now reached the great question," said Representative Hamilton Fish. "Shall we go into this war or stay put? The question of convoys is uppermost, for every member of Congress knows that convoys mean shooting and shooting means war." The battle over isolationism erupted again, now focused on the question of a naval tactic—convoys.

As the convoy furor arose, Stimson decided to make his argument to the American public via radio. He submitted his speech to the president, who approved it. Once again, as the two men had played their dual roles so many times over the previous years, FDR remained close to the center of the national debate while Stimson urged America to confront aggressors.

Speaking May 6 to radio listeners from his War Department office, Stimson avoided the debate over the specific tactical questions of using convoys. Instead, he renewed his attack on isolationism and called broadly for using American naval power to protect shipping. He said the US Navy "can help to hold in check the onward rush of the tide of Nazism until the other defense forces of all the democracies are completed." He asked rhetorically, "After we have taken our place definitely behind the warring democracies and against the aggressor nations in defense of our freedom; after providing for billions worth of munitions to carry on that defense and while we hold in our hands the instrument ready to make these steps effective, shall we now flinch and permit these munitions to be sunk in the Atlantic Ocean?"[11] To do that would be an "act of irresponsibility and indecision." Then he raised a hard truth, one that FDR had shied away from—that preserving American freedom would likely require American deaths. "I am not one of those who think that the priceless freedom of our country can be saved without sacrifice. It cannot. Unless we on our side are ready to sacrifice and, if need be, die for the conviction that the freedom of America must be saved, it will not be saved." For a nation steeped in isolationism and leery of war, he delivered a hard and sobering message about the reality of the conflicts facing the nation.

Stimson's argument in support of convoys to protect arms shipments was bolstered the next day when Wendell Willkie spoke to a large crowd in New York City's Madison Square Garden, urging protection of shipments to Great Britain. Speakers at the event, dubbed a "Freedom Rally," included New York City mayor Fiorello La Guardia, and its guests included diplomats from Belgium, Denmark and other countries conquered by the Nazis.[12] Willkie drew thunderous applause when he called for aid shipments to arrive safely in Britain, pausing for emphasis: "We—want—those—cargoes—protected! And we want it at once with less talk and more action." He sounded a bipartisan note in appealing for Americans from both major political parties to come together on the issue. "As Americans, Democrats and Republicans, people who voted for me and people who voted against me, I call upon you as a united people to keep that life line [the sea lanes to Great Britain] open."

Stimson pressed his case with Hopkins, urging that the fleet be moved to the Atlantic immediately. "People are asking for leadership and not more talk," he wrote in his diary.[13] Hopkins, however, told Morgenthau that "the president is loath to get into the war and would rather follow public opinion than lead it." FDR himself expressed his reluctance by telling Morgenthau, "I am waiting to be pushed in."[14]

PRODDED BY STIMSON, FDR began preparing a speech on his views. Seeking to buck up the president in advance of the speech, Stimson wrote him a letter May 24 saying the American people "are looking to you to lead and guide them . . . and it would be disastrous for you to disappoint them." He added that "expedients and halfway measures" were no longer enough, that Americans should not be asked to go to war because of "an accident or mistake" in the Atlantic.[15] "They must be brought to that momentous resolution by your leadership." The next day, he sent FDR two pages of proposed language for the speech, including an announcement of moving "sufficient strength from our main fleet in the Pacific" into the Atlantic.[16] Stimson was a bulldog who would not let go. FDR received his Republican secretary of war's advice without voicing any objection—and prepared his speech.

War was now raging in the Atlantic. On May 24, in waters near Greenland, the German battleship *Bismarck* sank the British vessel HMS *Hood,* killing nearly all of its 1,400 crew members. Three days later, British warships avenged the attack by sinking the *Bismarck,* whose two thousand crew members perished.[17]

That same evening, FDR delivered his speech, declaring an "unlimited national emergency" and that the US Navy would increase its patrols of the Atlantic. He vowed to ensure the safe delivery of supplies to England and resist Hitler's efforts to take control of the seas. "I say that the delivery of needed supplies to Britain is imperative. It must be done. It will be done," he said. He also proclaimed the importance of keeping Nazism out of the Western Hemisphere. "Adolf Hitler never considered the domination of Europe an end in itself. European conquest was but a step toward ultimate goals in all the other continents. It is unmistakably apparent to all of us that unless the advance of Hitlerism is forcibly checked now, the Western Hemisphere will be within range of the Nazi weapons of destruction."[18]

After weeks of internal debate, FDR still refused to order convoys but had come forward with a statement demanding freedom of the seas and ensuring Great Britain received munitions sent from America. In his diary, Stimson pronounced the president's points "right and praiseworthy."[19]

FDR, however, had deleted from the speech the idea of moving the fleet to the Atlantic. Frankfurter, who also had been wanting FDR to make a strong statement, told Stimson by telephone that this change came at the behest of Secretary of State Cordell Hull, who was carrying out protracted discussions with the Japanese ambassador to Washington, Kichisaburo Nomura, in an attempt to reduce tensions in the Pacific region.[20] Finally, the navy quietly moved three battleships, one aircraft carrier, four cruisers and nine destroyers to the Atlantic.[21] Yet most of the fleet remained based in Pearl Harbor, and Nazi attacks on shipping in the Atlantic continued taking a severe toll.

Seeking a strategic approach to the perils of war, FDR drew on the knowledge of William Donovan, who in early 1941 had been on a tour collecting intelligence, traveling some twenty-five thousand miles. He had visited British troops fighting the Italians in Libya, and had been to Yugoslavia, Greece and other countries. Nazi agents had trailed him, and Nazi radio broadcasts condemned him. He returned to Washington in mid-March and debriefed FDR, Stimson and Knox.[22] He also gave a national broadcast on March 26 sounding an alarm that Hitler was bent on world domination. "Our only choice is to choose whether or not we will resist and to choose in time while resistance is still possible, while others are still alive to stand by us."[23]

The next day, Prince Paul of Yugoslavia, who had been under pressure from Hitler for months, joined Yugoslavia to the Tripartite Pact of Germany, Japan and Italy. Two days later, a military coup removed him from power and placed the country's seventeen-year-old monarch, King Peter, in control of the government. The coup was led by a general whom Donovan had encouraged to organize armed resistance against Germany.[24] Enraged by the coup, Hitler ordered his forces to invade Yugoslavia and Greece on April 6. The Nazis bombed Belgrade for three days, killing seventeen thousand civilians.[25] By mid-April the Nazis had taken control of the country, and King Peter fled to form a government in exile in London.

Donovan had developed a close working relationship with William Stephenson, the head of British intelligence operations in the United States. In early June, Donovan and Stephenson traveled to London, where Britain's top intelligence official told them that Hitler planned to attack the Soviet Union on approximately June 22.[26] Donovan returned immediately to Washington and informed Roosevelt of the planned attack.

Four days after the London meeting, Donovan submitted to FDR a written proposal for the creation of a US government agency that would obtain, analyze and evaluate intelligence to help devise strategy in the face of the crisis caused by the rise of fascism. "Strategy without information upon which it can rely is helpless," he said. "Likewise, information is useless unless it is intelligently directed to the strategic purpose."[27] In a meeting with Knox and Donovan on June 18, FDR gave his approval for the new operation, to be called the Coordinator of Information (COI). A few days later, Donovan went to Highhold on a Sunday and laid out the plan, prompting Stimson to note in his diary, "I am particularly glad that the president has landed on a man for whom I have such respect and confidence as Donovan and with whom I think we can work so satisfactorily in respect to our own intelligence branches in the Army and Navy."[28]

Donovan, the new agency's director, soon began hiring a broad array of experts—cartographers, linguists and other scholars. One of the men he reached out to was his old friend Allen Dulles, a prominent New York Republican who had served in American espionage during World War I.[29] Donovan asked Dulles to run the COI office in New York's Rockefeller Center; it was adjacent to an office with a bland name, British Security Coordination, where Stephenson ran his intelligence operation. FDR a year later merged the COI into the new Office of Strategic Services, an intelligence agency for which Dulles would work in Switzerland.

Another high-profile Republican who joined the ranks of the FDR-Republican alliance was New York City mayor Fiorello La Guardia. In May 1941, FDR issued an executive order creating an Office of Civilian Defense and named La Guardia its first director. The office had a small staff, and the post permitted La Guardia to remain mayor of New York, though he traveled to Washington regularly to help coordinate efforts to prepare American cities in case of attack. In August 1941, La Guardia came to the War Department to discuss "affirmative propaganda" in support of national defense with Stimson and his assistants McCloy and Bundy. "It was La Guardia at his best," Stimson wrote in his diary.[30] A short while later, Stimson and Roosevelt endorsed La Guardia for reelection to a third term as mayor, a race he easily won with support from both Democrats and Republicans.

FDR and Stimson had sharply differing perspectives on organized labor. Stimson had a long history of pro-business stances, while FDR had signed some of the most significant laws in support of organized labor. However, the two men found common ground when they confronted labor strife that threatened to disrupt production at munitions plants. In early June, Stimson learned that unionized workers were preparing to strike over wages at the North American Aviation Company plant in Los Angeles, where planes were being made for the Army at the rate of ten per day.[31]

The union, the Congress of International Organizations, sought to prevent the strike so the wage dispute could be mediated. When employees called a strike for Monday, June 9, the union charged that "communists" led the workers to abandon mediation. That morning, FDR signed an order permitting Stimson to take control of the plant, and on Stimson's orders 2,500 soldiers carrying rifles with bayonets confronted the workers, tear gas was launched, and strikers were arrested and taken to a US Army base.[32] He also ordered that the strikers be stripped of the deferment from the military draft they had as munitions plant workers.[33] Under army control, the North American plant resumed operations later that same day.

FDR kept a low profile on the labor dispute, leaving Stimson to handle it until a month later when the president signed an order turning the plant back over to North American's control. The president issued a stiff warning against another eruption of trouble at the plant: "Should efforts be made again to interfere with this essential production, I will not hesitate to take whatever steps may hereafter be necessary to assure its continuance."[34]

ON JUNE 22, as British intelligence had foretold, Nazi forces invaded the Soviet Union across a vast front extending from the Baltic Sea in the north to the Black Sea in the south.[35] The German invasion force included three million soldiers and six hundred thousand vehicles. Stalin and his foreign minister, Molotov, had disregarded repeated warnings that the Germans were preparing to attack, and Soviet armies were caught unprepared.

In Washington, where fears had run high that Hitler and Stalin might fully join forces to assault the democracies, officials breathed a sigh of relief. Hitler's invasion of the Soviet Union would divert his forces from attacking Great Britain and other Western nations, giving them time to fortify their defenses and prepare counteroffensives. "I cannot help feeling that it offers us and Great Britain a great chance, provided we use it properly," Stimson wrote in his diary. He sent FDR a memo saying "this previous and unforeseen period of respite should be used to push with the utmost vigor our movements in the Atlantic theater of operations."[36]

FDR, however, immediately embraced a different response: sending aid to the Soviets. On the evening of the attack's first day, Prime Minister Churchill told the British people in a radio address that "no one has been a more consistent opponent of Communism than I have for the last 25 years. . . . I will unsay no word that I have spoken about it." He then proclaimed a stunning new stance on communist Russia: "Any man or state who fights against Nazidom will have our aid. It follows, therefore, that we shall give whatever help we can to Russia and the Russian people."[37]

Members of Congress voiced immediate opposition to the idea that America might provide the Soviets with military aid under Lend-Lease. The isolationist senator Robert Taft of Ohio revealed the depth of his hatred for communism when he said, "The victory of Communism would be far more dangerous to the United States than a victory of Fascism."[38]

Missouri Democratic senator Harry Truman offered morbidly, "If we see Germany is winning we ought to help Russia and if we see Russia is winning we ought to help Germany and that way let them kill as many as possible."[39]

FDR did not wait to gauge public opinion or develop a strategy to appease the isolationists; he followed Churchill's lead and called for supporting the Soviets. The president said at a news conference on June 24 that the United States would "give all the aid that we possibly can to Russia." On the same day the Treasury released $40 million in frozen Soviet credits.[40]

FDR faced another key decision at this time: whether to occupy Iceland, the island nation in the Atlantic which had broken free of the Kingdom of Denmark after the Nazis seized Denmark in 1940. Iceland's port of Reykjavík had become a critical base for US vessels carrying munitions to Great Britain. The island sat in the middle of the war zone declared by Germany, and Iceland's new prime minister had asked the Americans for protection. Stimson and Knox urged FDR to approve the plan so that America could prevent the Nazis from seizing Iceland.[41] Stimson told FDR in late June 1941 that the Nazi invasion of the Soviet Union made it highly unlikely that the Germans would try to block the Americans from occupying Iceland.[42] The American forces would replace British troops already in Iceland, permitting Britain to deploy those troops elsewhere. FDR agreed.

On July 7, the US Navy landed forces on Iceland, and FDR delivered a message to Congress justifying the occupation as a defensive action. "The United States cannot permit the occupation by Germany of strategic outposts in the Atlantic to be used as air or naval bases for eventual attack against the Western Hemisphere," the president said.[43] Isolationists howled, charging that the occupation was in fact part of a scheme to push America into the war and bypass the constitutional provision permitting only Congress to declare war. Senator Burton K. Wheeler, the Montana Democrat, said, "One reason why the American people are apprehensive is that they know secretaries Knox and Stimson are openly advocating war. These two know they cannot get a declaration of war by Congress, so they are going in by the back door, step by step. They are trying to trick the American people into the war."

FDR moved quickly to build an alliance with Stalin and provide the Soviets with weapons. In late July, FDR sent Hopkins to meet with Stalin in Moscow. Hopkins carried a letter to Stalin from FDR that said the president wanted to explore "the assistance which the United States can render to your country in its magnificent resistance to the treacherous aggression by Hitlerite Germany."[44] In a meeting with Hopkins on July 31, Stalin said "the problem of supply by next spring would be a serious one and that he needed our help." Stalin also gave him a list of items the Soviet army needed, including light antiaircraft guns, aluminum for planes and .50-caliber machine guns.

In a cabinet meeting on August 1, FDR took Stimson to task for what he saw as the War Department's failure to provide munitions rapidly to the Soviets. He said "the Russians had been promised arms for six weeks and they had been given a run-around here in Washington and nothing had been done for them."[45] He wanted a hundred or more fighters delivered to the Russians immediately, even if they had to be taken from the US Army: "Get the planes right off . . . with a bang next week."[46] Stimson responded gruffly, faulting the president himself. "I thought it was due largely to the uncorrelated organization which the president set up that this should happen. I told him frankly that the list of Russian wants which he spoke of in his outburst had never been seen by me nor presented to me nor to anyone of the War Department so far as I knew." Afterwards, he began working to send fighters to Russia and meet FDR's other demands.

FDR, MEANWHILE, LEFT Washington for a trip that was announced as a ten-day fishing vacation off the New England coast. On August 3 in New London, Connecticut, he boarded the presidential yacht *Potomac* and the next day hosted the Danish and Norwegian royal families on board. Late that night, the president secretly boarded a navy cruiser, the USS *Augusta*, which took him to Placentia Bay, Newfoundland, for a meeting with Churchill.[47] Joining FDR aboard the *Augusta*—under a shroud of secrecy—were General Marshall, General Hap Arnold and Admiral Stark. Undersecretary of State Sumner Welles and diplomat Averell Harriman also participated. Hopkins, having flown from

Moscow to London, joined Churchill on his voyage aboard the battleship HMS *Prince of Wales,* which arrived in Placentia early on the
morning of August 9.

For his secret summit with Churchill, FDR had left out the Republican men upon whom he had relied so heavily—Stimson, Knox and
Donovan, all of whom were recognized widely for their leadership in
the war effort, their pro-British views and their public calls to challenge
the Nazis on the open seas. This was to be the first meeting between
FDR and Churchill—with the exception of a brief meeting in 1918 that
Churchill did not recall. FDR, in laying a foundation for his future relationship with Churchill, evidently wanted no debates with his Republican allies, no questions about his command of the US military and no
distractions from his leadership.

At about 9:00 in the morning, Churchill boarded the *Augusta* and
clasped hands with FDR. "At last we have gotten together," the president said. "We have," Churchill replied. Churchill presented him with a
letter from King George VI expressing his hope that the meeting "will
prove of great benefit to our two countries in the pursuit of our common goal." The two men thus began a vital alliance that, like FDR's with
Stimson, was based on a bond of trust.

Stimson, remarking in his diary that FDR, Marshall and others
were mysteriously out of Washington at the same time, kept the War
Department moving forward with war preparations. He almost single-
handedly fought a pitched battle with isolationists over the extension
of the military conscription law passed in 1940. Without the extension,
the law's expiration would soon force the US Army to begin discharging soldiers. Stimson had begun building support in Congress for the
bill in June with Speaker of the House Sam Rayburn, a Texas Democrat whom Stimson considered "sensible and friendly."[48] The extension,
however, drew fire from isolationists. Congressman Fish charged that
if the Roosevelt Administration followed the "war policies" of Secretary Stimson, it would need an army of four to five million men.[49] After
a sometimes bitter debate, the House approved the extension measure
on August 12 by a single vote, 203–202, as twenty-one Republicans
voted with a hundred and two Democrats to pass the bill.[50]

As the debate moved to the Senate, Stimson spent much of the next day calling senators, both Democrats and Republicans, to ensure there were sufficient votes to pass the measure. The next morning, the Senate passed the draft extension 37–19, and the final bill was flown to the president—then en route to Washington from Placentia Bay—for his signature.[51]

Finally, more than a week after FDR's mysterious absence began, Stimson learned the mystery was soon to be resolved. He attended a dinner at the British embassy on the evening of August 13, where the British ambassador, Lord Halifax, told him to listen to a broadcast from London the next morning.[52] He would hear the news with the rest of the world. At 9:00 A.M., as Churchill was returning aboard the *Prince of Wales* to England, Clement Attlee in London gave a radio address announcing FDR and Churchill had met secretly at Placentia Bay. Attlee went on to read a joint declaration, which proclaimed principles for restoring world peace after "the final destruction of the Nazi tyranny." The document, called the Atlantic Charter, promised that the United States and the United Kingdom sought no territorial aggrandizement, that they respect the "right of all peoples to choose the form of government under which they will live" and that disarmament of aggressor nations would be necessary to ensure world peace.

Stimson's diary reveals not a hint of jealousy or frustration that at a time of such danger to the nation the secretary of war had been left completely uninformed on the whereabouts of the president and the army chief of staff for ten days. On the joint declaration's points, Stimson later noted in his diary, "So far as they went I thought they were good. They took a peek at the future after the war is over, which is a good thing to get people thinking about that and they did also have the spirit of determination and victory." General Marshall, who had flown back to Washington, came with his wife for dinner at Woodley that night, and afterwards the two men sat outside under the trees discussing the events of Placentia Bay.[53]

The passage of the draft extension was a victory for Stimson and FDR, yet it was achieved by an extremely narrow margin in the House. Isolationism was still powerful in America, a fact driven home September 11 when Charles Lindbergh took the stage at an America First rally in Des Moines, Iowa. He launched a broad attack on those he said were using deception to push the country into the war. "The three most important groups who have been pressing this country toward war are the British, the Jewish and the Roosevelt administration." After accusing the British of spending "great sums of money for propaganda in America," he charged the Jews with conducting a campaign to get America into the war. "Their greatest danger to this country lies in their large ownership and influence in our motion pictures, our press, our radio and our government," he said. He also accused the Roosevelt Administration of tricking America into entering the war. "If any one of these groups—the British, the Jewish or the Administration—stops agitating for war, I believe there will be little danger of our involvement."

Lindbergh's charge that Jews controlled the media—and were using that power to agitate for war—spurred criticism that he was anti-Semitic. White House spokesman Stephen Early said the speech resembled "the outpourings of Berlin."[54] Willkie denounced the aviator's speech as "the most un-American talk made in my time by any person of national reputation."[55] Yet other Republicans, including Alf Landon and Herbert Hoover, readily defended Lindbergh, a sign of the enduring political power of both the aviator and isolationism.

Concerns over war soared in late October 1941 when Nazi submarines torpedoed several US Navy destroyers, which had quietly begun convoying vessels across the Atlantic to Great Britain. The most significant attack came on October 31, when a torpedo sank the US destroyer *Reuben James* in the middle of the night off the west coast of Iceland, killing 101 members of her crew.[56] It was the first US naval ship lost in combat in the war. The father of a sailor who perished in the sinking told reporters, "I think the US should go into the war and wipe the German submarines forever from the sea. If I were young enough I would like to help do the job."[57]

Willkie said at a meeting held by an interventionist group, Fight for Freedom, "This is no time to entertain hopes of peace. This is the time to prepare to enforce our rights, so that freedom may survive in the world." He also called for annulling the last parts of the Neutrality Act, which prohibited merchant vessels from being armed and traveling through a war zone. "The Neutrality Act should be promptly repealed," he said.[58] The group issued its own statement arguing, "Every American citizen must now actively take sides, either with America or Hitler. . . . America has now been challenged as well as attacked. Failure to meet the challenge will have disastrous repercussions throughout the world and upon our own national safety."

FDR continued resisting pressure to take aggressive action against the Nazi attacks. On the day of the sinking of the *Reuben James,* the president announced that the Nazi attack on the destroyer would not change America's relations with Germany.

He also kept a low profile as Congress launched into a tense debate over the remaining restrictions of the Neutrality Act the next day. Senator Theodore Green of Rhode Island, a Democrat, charged the law was "an appeasement of Hitler," and his views drew support from Senator Joseph Ball, a Minnesota Republican, who said "no man can afford to stand on the sidelines in this world-wide fight to the finish between the democratic way of life and the slave system that Hitler calls his new order."[59] Isolationists charged that aggressive naval tactics by FDR and Navy Secretary Knox were pushing the nation into war, and America First denounced the repeal effort and warned it would defeat its supporters in midterm elections of 1942.

Days later, on November 7, the Senate passed a bill revising the Neutrality Act to permit the arming of merchant ships and to allow them to pass through combat zones. The measure passed with a narrow bipartisan vote of 50–37 as six Republicans joined forty-three Democrats and one independent in support. The following week, Republican votes in the House provided the necessary margin of difference when the House voted 212–194 to pass the bill. It was a slim bipartisan victory, but twenty-two Republicans joined a hundred and eighty-nine Democrats in support of the repeal, while a hundred and thirty-seven Republicans sided with fifty-three Democrats in opposition.[60]

Knox swiftly proclaimed that arming merchant vessels would make it possible for weapons and supplies approved by Congress to reach Great Britain and other allies. Willkie called the victory "gratifying," though he paired his praise of the measure with criticism of FDR's handling of labor disputes.[61]

. . .

AMID AMERICA'S TENSE separate peace, scientists were secretly working
on a powerful new weapon, the nuclear bomb, and Stimson would play
a vital role in the project. Physicist Albert Einstein, who fled Germany
to the United States as a refugee, brought the idea for uranium-based
nuclear weapons to FDR's attention in 1939, warning that Germany was
seeking to build such weapons and had even seized uranium mines in
Czechoslovakia.[62] FDR approved scientific research in the area, and in
June 1941 appointed a prominent engineer, Vannevar Bush, to continue the work under the new Office of Scientific Research and Development.[63] In October 1941, FDR established a committee to oversee
nuclear weapons development, the Top Policy Group, whose members
included the president himself, Stimson, Marshall, Vice President Wallace, Bush and James Conant, who led a separate agency on scientific
developments for weapons.[64]

On November 6, 1941, Bush received a report stating that within a
few years nuclear bombs could determine "military superiority." Bombs
containing as little as 220 pounds of uranium could have an explosive
power equal to 300 tons of TNT, the report said. He took the report that
day to Stimson and discussed it with him.[65] Stimson later made a terse
comment in his diary reflecting the bomb's horrific power: "Dr. Vannevar Bush came in to convey an extremely secret statement from the
Scientific Research and Development office—a most terrible thing."[66]

"Let the Negro Masses March!"

In January 1941, civil rights activist A. Philip Randolph launched a new campaign to end segregation in the armed forces and in the war industries. Angered by the Roosevelt Administration's refusal to desegregate the armed forces, Randolph called on Black Americans to march in Washington, DC, to demand desegregation of the armed forces and the manufacturing companies gearing up to produce vast quantities of ships, planes, tanks and other military equipment.

The failure of the desegregation effort in 1940 did not dispirit Randolph, who for three decades had waged vigorous battles for the rights of Black people. He grew up in Jacksonville, Florida, in a home where his father, an African Methodist Episcopal preacher, instilled in him a strong vision of Black leadership.[1] Steeped in the works of Shakespeare and other classic literature, Randolph as a young man performed public readings and contemplated a career on the stage.[2] After moving to New York City in 1911 at the age of twenty-two, he joined the Socialist Party and launched a magazine, *The Messenger,* which called itself the "only radical negro magazine in America."[3] As editor, Randolph blended his socialism with an urgent demand for equal rights for Black people. When President Woodrow Wilson deployed Black soldiers to fight in segregated units in World War I, an editorial in *The Messenger* called out to the president, "Lynching, Jim Crow, segregation, discrimination in the armed forces and out, disfranchisement of millions of black souls in the South—all these things make your cry of making the world safe for democracy a sham, a mockery, a rape on decency and a travesty on common justice."

In 1925, Randolph founded a union, the Brotherhood of Sleeping Car Porters, to represent poorly paid Black porters working on trains for the Pullman Car Company.[4] Pullman, an industrial giant that built and operated sleeper cars for railroads nationwide, refused to recognize the union. For a decade, Randolph demanded that Pullman grant the Brotherhood the right to negotiate wages on behalf of the porters. Randolph finally won recognition of the union in 1935, a victory that increased his renown. From the Brotherhood's New York City headquarters on Harlem's main thoroughfare, 125th Street, he worked with other Black leaders, including Walter White of the NAACP, on a broad array of issues important to Black Americans.

Randolph's role as a leader among those working for civil rights was recognized by Eleanor Roosevelt, who acted informally as the president's representative to the Black community. In September 1940—not long after President Roosevelt, Secretary of War Stimson and Secretary of the Navy Knox rebuffed Randolph's plea for desegregation—the Brotherhood held its annual convention in Harlem. Eleanor addressed the crowd after a dinner, vowing to support any effort "to make this a better country, not for you alone but for all of us."[5]

The limits of the First Lady's support would be tested after Randolph issued a defiant call in January 1941 for a march in the nation's capital demanding civil rights. "No real, actual, bona fide, definite and positive pressure of the Negro masses has ever been brought to bear upon the executive and legislative branches of the city, state, and national governments," he wrote in a proclamation to be published in newspapers.[6] "I suggest that 10,000 Negroes march on Washington, DC, the capital of the nation, with the slogan: We Loyal Negro-American Citizens Demand the Right to Work and Fight for Our Country." The announcement fell flat at first. It apparently ran in no white-owned papers, though there is no sign Randolph even wanted it to do so. The nation's Black-owned newspapers also gave it little attention. *The Pittsburgh Courier,* among the most prominent Black papers, ran its story on Randolph's call for the march on page thirteen. Undaunted, Randolph went to work building a movement.

The fight for desegregation of the armed forces received a boost that same month from Yancey Williams, a twenty-four-year-old Black engineering student at Howard University. Williams had obtained a flying license from the federal Civil Aeronautics Administration in 1940, and he wanted to join the Army Air Corps to serve his country, but he had been rejected. Represented by the NAACP, Williams filed a lawsuit in January 1941 against Secretary of War Henry Stimson over his rejection as an air cadet.[7] Days later, the War Department announced that a pursuit squadron with Black pilots would be created at the Tuskegee Institute in Alabama.

Protesters from the American Youth Congress, a leftist group befriended by the First Lady, picketed outside the War Department against segregation of the army on February 10. Indignant, Stimson emerged from the department building and defended himself to the protesters on the sidewalk. "I am the first Secretary of War to have appointed a colored officer to be a Brigadier General in the United States Army; that is Brigadier General Benjamin C. Davis," he told the group as reporters looked on. "I am the second Secretary of War who has appointed a colored person as a civilian aide to the Secretary of War. This is Judge Hastie. And, finally, I am now starting the organization of a pursuit squadron to be composed of colored personnel, including pilots. That is something that has never been done by the War Department." He then restated the familiar argument of numerically proportionate inclusion in the army, again sidestepping the question of segregation. "I can assure you that the colored population will be represented by its proportionate representation in the Army. Good day!" Having addressed the protesters, he departed for lunch.[8]

Eleanor Roosevelt traveled in March 1941 to visit Tuskegee, where the fighter and bomber pilots soon to be dubbed "the Tuskegee Airmen" were being trained.[9] After flying with Black flight instructor Charles Anderson in the skies over Tuskegee for an hour, the First Lady had her picture taken with Anderson in the plane's cockpit. Yet such signs of progress for Black soldiers were overshadowed by racial violence, particularly in southern states.[10] On March 28, a Black soldier, Private Felix

Hall, was found hanging from a tree on the grounds of Fort Benning in Georgia. His hands were tied behind him, his feet bound by wire.[11] As news of the suspected lynching spread, the Black press and the NAACP called for an investigation and demanded justice for Hall, though no one was charged with the crime.

Randolph brought other groups into his campaign for the march on Washington. He joined with Walter White of the NAACP and other activists to form the Negroes' Committee to March on Washington for Equal Participation in National Defense—of which Randolph was the director. By the end of May, he raised the stakes by calling for a hundred thousand Black people—ten times the original number—to join the march on July 1. "When 100,000 Negroes march on Washington, it will wake up Negro as well as white America," he wrote. "Let the Negro masses march! Let the Negro masses speak!"[12]

With the July 1 protest date fast approaching, Randolph on June 5 sent a flyer on the march and its desegregation goals to Eleanor Roosevelt, urging her to write about it in her regular newspaper column, My Day. Randolph shifted the march's focus from desegregating the armed services to desegregating employment in the war industries. "Negroes are the victims of discrimination in National Defense. Although loyal American citizens, we are denied jobs, not because of lack of merit, but on account of race and color. To fight this un-American and un-Democratic practice, Negro leaders have formed a movement to mobilize 100,000 Negroes to march on Washington for jobs and justice in National Defense," Randolph told the First Lady.[13] He sent similar letters to Stimson, Sidney Hillman and William Knudsen in the Office of Production Management, and Labor Secretary Frances Perkins.[14]

Washington was segregated, and the prospect of one hundred thousand Black protesters marching in the city's streets alarmed officials. When an estimated twenty thousand Army veterans protested for unpaid bonuses in 1932, the Army sent troops to break up the protests and the resulting violence shocked the nation and spurred wide condemnation of President Herbert Hoover. In prior decades, race riots in cities like East St. Louis, Illinois, and Tulsa, Oklahoma, had turned into massacres of innocent Black citizens. The idea that segregated Washington might erupt in opposition to a large protest by Black Americans spurred the First Lady's concerns.

She sent Randolph a letter on June 10 seeking to dissuade him from undertaking the march. "I have talked over your letter with the president and I feel very strongly that your group is making a very grave mistake at the present time to allow this march to take place. I am afraid it will set back the progress that is being made, in the Army at least, towards better opportunities and less segregation." She warned that "any incident" might provoke "even more solid opposition" in Congress.[15] "You know that I am deeply concerned about the rights of the Negro people, but I think one must face situations as they are and not as one wishes them to be. I think this is a very serious decision for you to take."

Stimson told FDR on June 12 that he had received an invitation from Randolph and White to deliver a speech to the protest, but he had declined. The president "approved my refusal," he noted in his diary.[16] "We are doing all we can to try to avoid this march," Undersecretary of War Robert Patterson told Eleanor Roosevelt in a memo the next day.[17] He outlined efforts to encourage war industries not to discriminate against Black people, though he acknowledged that War Department contracts did not set mandatory requirements for labor and left it up to contractors to furnish labor as they wished.

The White House press officer, Stephen Early, surely acting on FDR's orders, appealed to New York City mayor Fiorello La Guardia for help in heading off the march. Noting La Guardia's "great influence with New York Negroes," Early urged him to convince them of a "better means" of presenting their case. La Guardia, indeed, had influence with Randolph. As a congressman in the 1920s, he had steadily supported the Brotherhood of Sleeping Car Porters. He never turned down an invitation to speak at the union's conventions, and he was a personal friend of Randolph and his wife Lucille.[18] And when it was rumored a few months earlier that La Guardia might not seek reelection, Randolph had written him, "Your friends in the Harlem community . . . have a high regard for the best administration any Mayor of New York has ever given."

La Guardia agreed to host a meeting of Randolph, White and the First Lady at City Hall in New York. FDR also asked two administration officials, Aubrey Williams and Anna Rosenberg, to participate and help convince Randolph and White to cancel the march.[19] In the meeting on June 13, Eleanor expressed concern about the Washington police, saying the march should not go on. "Had I considered the problems? she asked. Where would all those thousands of people eat and sleep in Jim Crow Washington," Randolph recalled.[20] She expressed concern that the march could lead to violence. "I replied that there would be no violence unless her husband ordered the police to crack black heads. I told her I was sorry, but the march would not be called off unless the president issued an executive order banning discrimination in the defense industry." The meeting ended with the two Black leaders resolved to proceed with the march.

Mrs. Roosevelt and La Guardia conveyed the results of the meeting to FDR, who called a meeting with Randolph, White, Stimson, Navy Secretary Frank Knox, La Guardia and others to take place the following week.

Randolph, meanwhile, kept promoting the march. Days after the meeting in New York City Hall, he published a column on the front page of New York's prominent Black newspaper, *The New York Age,* calling for "Negro America" to join the march.[21] It began with an exuberant expression of confidence in turnout for the march: "As the day approaches for the all-out, total, dramatic march on Washington and demonstration at the Monument of Abraham Lincoln for jobs and justice in national defense and the abolition of discrimination in Government departments, interest, sentiment and enthusiasm for this movement continues to mount daily." It was a boast designed to ratchet up the pressure on the president and his Republican allies.

Randolph and White went to the White House on June 18 for the meeting with FDR, Stimson, Knox, La Guardia, Hillman and Knudsen. Rosenberg, who had told the president the two men were seeking an executive order banning discrimination in the war industries, also joined the meeting. After welcoming the two Black leaders, FDR said he shared their interest in "human and social justice," but he was concerned that the march would damage, not advance, efforts to increase opportunities for Black citizens.[22] FDR said he could not issue an order for every group that seeks one. He asked the two civil rights leaders to call off the march, according to one account of the meeting. "I'm sorry, Mr. President, the march cannot be called off," Randolph responded. When FDR asked how many people would come to the march, he replied, "One hundred thousand." FDR paused for a moment, perhaps suspecting a bluff, and posed the same question to White, whose NAACP had many chapters across the country and could produce many marchers. "One hundred thousand, Mr. President," White replied. Bluff or not, the threat of a major demonstration by Black protesters on the streets of Washington hung in the air.

The meeting became heated when Knudsen bluntly opposed any order banning discrimination, saying that industry would "hire such negroes as it saw fit to hire." White responded by saying that Knudsen's former employer, General Motors, had a very poor record on racial discrimination, and he offered to document this with a report.[23] Before the exchange could go much further, FDR had to leave for a meeting with Princess Juliana of the Netherlands and was wheeled out of the room. Stimson recalled, "As he went he gaily said that he left the meeting in my charge, which was rather tough—to put it mildly."[24] Stimson's gruff attitude, however, gave him cover to forge a compromise.

The group moved to the Cabinet Room to continue the discussion, which raised the issue of the prominent role of southerners in the armed services, as well as the Navy's refusal to permit Black men to enlist as sailors. "We can't do a thing about it because men live in such intimacy aboard ship that we simply can't enlist Negroes above the rank of messman," Knox said, as White later recalled.[25] These "rather brash remarks" upset the Black leaders, and Knox soon left the meeting, Stimson noted in his diary.

Stimson was struck by the warnings of Randolph and White that communists could inflame the march. The two men cast themselves as moderates trying to avert a major riot, a ploy surely intended to win the favor of Stimson and others. It worked. Stimson wrote later: "These two men are conservatives and they feel that if they are not allowed to march into Washington temperately, the Communists will take charge and do it intemperately. But finally we agreed on certain suggestions which La Guardia undertook to write out a memorandum of."[26]

Within days, La Guardia's draft executive order—hammered out in further negotiations with Randolph—arrived in Stimson's office and he threw his support behind it. At work on Saturday, June 21—working on Saturdays was now routine—he reviewed the draft order with Patterson. It mandated federal agencies to include in contracts with war industries a requirement that the contractor will not discriminate on grounds of race, creed or color. "I had agreed with this suggestion at the meeting on Wednesday," he noted. "Patterson was afraid that it would make great trouble with our contracts but, after thinking it over, I told him we would have to take that chance."[27] Though he remained opposed to desegregating the armed forces, Stimson concluded that ending segregation of the labor force in war industries was the right step, and one that must be taken at that time.

The order would for the first time place the weight and authority of the federal government against the pervasive practice of racial discrimination in employment across America. Crafted quietly behind closed doors for the president by his Republican allies La Guardia and Stimson in collaboration with Randolph and White, the order would be the most significant government action against racial discrimination since the adoption in 1868 of the Constitution's 14th Amendment guaranteeing all citizens equal protection under law. An executive order would have far weaker legal standing than a constitutional amendment, but by issuing the order FDR could avoid—at least temporarily—what likely would have been a brutal and public confrontation with the large bloc of segregationist southern Democrats who had made his rise to the presidency possible. A divisive battle with segregationists in Congress would carry a massive political cost, which FDR surely would have sought to avoid, particularly at a time when the threat of war loomed. Instead, he opted for the executive order, which would enable him to put some teeth in the constitutional promise of equality by opening factory doors to Black workers just as war industries were ramping up production.

Randolph cabled Eleanor Roosevelt on June 24 saying he had learned that the president was preparing to sign the order requiring war industry contractors to "agree that they will not discriminate against any person on account of race, creed, color or national origin." He also noted that the ban on discrimination extended to unions—an important element as Black workers had been widely rejected by white labor unions—and that a committee would be created to enforce the order. He then informed the First Lady that he had decided against holding the march. "On the basis of this statesmanlike action of the president . . . I therefore consider that the proposed negro march on Washington is unnecessary at this time." He added, "I wish to express to you our sincere appreciation for your interest and fine spirit of cooperation and help in securing this action on the part of the president."[28]

The First Lady by then had retreated to the Roosevelt family compound on Campobello Island off the coast of Maine. She thanked Randolph for his cable in a reply. "I am very glad the march has been postponed and delighted that the president is issuing an executive order on defense industries. I hope from this first step, we may go on to others."[29]

On June 25, 1941, FDR signed the executive order, which established a new unit in the Office of Production Management to be called the Committee on Fair Employment Practice to investigate complaints of discrimination and take "appropriate steps to redress grievances which it finds to be valid." The order proclaimed its necessity by stating that "the democratic way of life within the Nation can be defended successfully only with the help and support of all groups within its borders." The White House released the order to the press and—unknown and unaccompanied by any controversy—it ran with little fanfare in the back pages of newspapers.[30] *The New York Times* ran a brief story on page twelve the next day. FDR did not discuss the order at a news conference, ensuring it got almost no attention in the media, except for the Black press. Within days, *The Pittsburgh Courier* ran stories about federal contractors DuPont, Curtiss-Wright and others announcing plans to hire Black workers.[31]

FDR soon appointed the five members of the Fair Employment Practice Committee (FEPC), naming as its chairman Mark Ethridge, a white Mississippian who was general manager of *The Louisville Courier-Journal,* along with two Black men, one of whom was Milton Webster, a Randolph ally who was vice president of the Brotherhood of Sleeping Car Porters. The committee began its work, and by early 1942 it issued a series of orders requiring federal contractors to open their doors to Black workers and others who were Jewish, Italian or German.

The activists were frustrated that the armed forces would remain segregated. White, however, saw the FEPC as a major step forward for Black Americans. In his autobiography published in 1948—before the achievements of the civil rights era that was to follow—White wrote that "more progress was made by the FEPC toward employment on the basis of ability in the face of racial and religious discrimination than at any other period in American history."[32] Randolph won acclaim for his role in the creation of the FEPC. One New York Black newspaper ranked him "along with the great Frederick Douglass" among Black leaders.[33] W.E.B. Du Bois, the Black scholar who helped found the NAACP in 1909, praised Randolph's work "which compelled the issue of Presidential Order 8802" as "the most astonishing in our later leadership."

Creation of the FEPC drew very little comment from Congress. A notable exception was praise by Representative Arthur Mitchell, a Democrat from Chicago who was the only Black member of Congress. Mitchell said in a radio address that he was "gratified" by the president's action, and he named a series of major aircraft and tank manufacturers that had publicly stated their refusal to employ Black workers. He also named many major unions that refused to take Black members.[34] "I point to this defect in our present democracy as the weakest point in our fight for world democracy," he said.

Civil rights leaders had long questioned the president's commitment to civil rights, noting his refusal over years to take a public stand for anti-lynching bills and other civil rights proposals in Congress. Instead, it was the First Lady who, in gestures that were often symbolic, took public steps in support of Black people. Roy Wilkins, editor of the NAACP official magazine *The Crisis*, observed in 1941, "The president reaped the benefit of Mrs. Roosevelt's activities and pronouncements on the Negro. But he never said a word." Commenting gently on the rarity of the president's action creating the FEPC, civil rights activist Mary McLeod Bethune said the order "has come to us as a refreshing shower in a thirsty land."[35]

Quietly, however, FDR had taken a monumental step. In signing

Executive Order 8802 he engaged the machinery of the federal government in breaking down racial segregation, a fundamental feature of American society from its inception. He also broke decisively with his former Democratic mentor and ally, President Woodrow Wilson, who a generation earlier had imposed segregation on the federal work force and promoted white supremacy from the White House. FDR's order put the Democratic Party on the path toward embracing civil rights—and breaking with the white supremacist and segregationist views of Democratic leaders in the southern states. As a result, the president raised the risk that the large and powerful southern bloc of Democrats, who had supported him and helped him win the White House, might now break with him. By signing the executive order, he had set in motion a realignment of the American political parties in which the Democratic Party would gradually abandon its historic role as the oppressor of Black Americans and take from the Republican Party its mantle as their champion.

FDR's exact reasoning for approving the order is lost to history. His words in the June 18 meeting suggest that he shared the First Lady's concern about violence and political opposition that might result from the proposed march. The order itself indicated the president agreed with arguments by Randolph and others that racial discrimination in employment was morally wrong. He also believed the nation needed all workers to contribute for the United States to win the war, as the order stated. As a consummate political strategist, FDR also may have made a calculation: if creation of the FEPC cost the Democratic Party votes of segregationist Democrats in the South, that loss would be compensated by winning the support of Black Americans, other minorities subjected to discrimination and progressive Republicans.

The contribution of FDR's Republican allies to drafting the executive order and creating the FEPC has been largely unknown. In fact, while La Guardia's work on the matter received minor mentions in the Black press at the time, Stimson's role has apparently never been reported—until publication of this book.[36] FDR and his Republican allies were in effect building a coalition that crossed political boundaries. The Democrat-Republican alliance reached across the racial divide to Randolph and

White, who had skillfully and forcefully demanded progress on civil rights in the midst of the war. In backing the creation of the FEPC, this new coalition made an important step toward equality, avoided a potentially dangerous protest in Washington and strengthened the effort to unite America.

Pearl Harbor

In January 1941, Secretary of the Navy Knox sounded an alarm. A surprise attack by British fighters launched from aircraft carriers had devastated Italian ships moored in a Mediterranean port, and the US Navy was examining whether Pearl Harbor was vulnerable to a similar assault. "If war eventuates with Japan, it is believed easily possible that hostilities would be initiated by a surprise attack upon the Fleet or the Naval Base at Pearl Harbor," Knox wrote Secretary of War Stimson on January 24, 1941. "In my opinion, the inherent possibilities of a major disaster to the fleet or naval base warrant taking every step, as rapidly as can be done, that will increase the joint readiness of the Army and Navy to withstand a raid of the character mentioned above."[1] Stimson replied stating his "complete concurrence" with Knox's concerns. He reviewed plans for additional pursuit planes and antiaircraft guns at the base and forwarded Knox's letter to the army's commanding general in Hawaii, Walter Short. The letter also was sent to Admiral Husband Kimmel in February 1941, shortly after Kimmel assumed command of the US Pacific Fleet in Pearl Harbor.

The idea of a surprise attack on Pearl Harbor also occurred to Admiral Isoroku Yamamoto of the Japanese Imperial Navy, who on February 1, 1941, requested a secret study on the feasibility of the idea.[2] After ten days, that study concluded that a surprise attack on Pearl Harbor was risky but had a reasonable chance of success. Yamamoto soon began planning for the attack.

In Washington, the concern raised by Knox and amplified by Stimson was weighed by an array of officials—and it was soon considered resolved. In an April memo to President Roosevelt, General George Marshall said that Oahu, the island where Pearl Harbor was located, "is believed to be the strongest fortress in the world."[3] On April 23, when Stimson and Marshall discussed the idea of moving part of the fleet to the Atlantic to protect shipping to Great Britain, Marshall disagreed with FDR's view that the fleet needed to stay in Hawaii to defend Pearl Harbor. With heavy bombers, pursuit planes and other defenses at the army base, Marshall said the Japanese "wouldn't dare attack Hawaii," particularly because it was so far from Japan, Stimson recorded in his diary.[4] The next day, Knox concurred that Hawaii was "impregnable."

In April 1941, Japan and the Soviet Union concluded a nonaggression pact, enabling both countries to redirect military resources away from the frontier between Russia and Manchuria. With the risk of war with the Soviets curtailed, Japan's military leaders laid plans to move south toward the Philippines, Thailand and the British colonies in Malaysia, Hong Kong, Burma and Singapore. Japan also had designs on two colonies orphaned by the Nazi destruction of France and the Netherlands: the French colony of Indochina, known today as Vietnam, and the Dutch East Indies, now Indonesia. Japan's foreign minister, Yosuke Matsuoka, had called in 1940 for the removal of European colonizers from these countries under the banner of a Japanese-led "Greater East Asia Co-Prosperity Sphere." Chinese nationalists like Chiang Kai-shek decried Matsuoka's strategy as a thinly disguised Japanese effort to dominate all of Asia. Under pressure from the Japanese, the regime of Vichy France, which controlled Indochina and was under the boot of the Nazi regime, agreed in September 1940 to let Japanese troops occupy part of northern Indochina.[5]

Since summer 1940, Stimson had urged FDR to embargo oil shipments to Japan, a measure that would have had a profound impact because Japan obtained most of its oil from the United States. Treasury Secretary Henry Morgenthau also urged FDR to impose an oil embargo on Japan. In July 1940, he wrote: "Thank heavens we have a Stimson with us!"[6] Morgenthau even recommended that FDR nominate Hull to the Supreme Court and make Stimson his secretary of state, but the president rejected the idea.[7] FDR continued resisting the idea of an embargo, fearing it would lead to war.

Unease in Washington ratcheted up after US Army cryptologists in late 1940 deciphered a code that the Japanese government used to communicate with ambassadors and other officials around the world. The decoding effort, dubbed "Magic" by army officials, gave FDR, Stimson, Knox and senior military commanders extraordinary insights into Japanese strategic discussions. Roosevelt told Interior Secretary Harold Ickes in a July 1, 1941, letter that "the Japs are having a drag-down and knock-out fight among themselves trying to decide which way they are going to jump—attack Russia, attack the South Seas . . . or whether they will sit on the fence and be more friendly with us."[8]

FDR asked Stimson and Knox on July 9 to work together to prepare a broad plan estimating the troops and munitions required for the United States to win a war with "our potential enemies."[9] The two men threw themselves into the planning effort, which they gave the optimistic code name Victory Parade.

Stimson constantly sought ways to improve the army's efficiency. On July 22, he approved construction of a vast office building across the Potomac River in northern Virginia to consolidate army departments in nineteen different buildings scattered across Washington.[10] The new structure, the Pentagon, was to have a modern telephone system, including sixty-nine thousand miles of lines linking twenty-seven thousand phones and a vast switchboard, and would provide state-of-the-art communications with US forces around the world. The project was put on a fast track for completion so that Stimson and Marshall could move into their new Pentagon offices within sixteen months—by November 1, 1942.

In late July 1941, the US Army obtained more Magic intercepts showing that Japan had sent an ultimatum to the Vichy government demanding approval for more Japanese troops to occupy Indochina, including certain air force and navy bases.[11] The Japanese prime minister, Prince Fumimaro Konoye, and his minister of war, the extreme nationalist General Hideki Tojo, were seeking to expand Japanese military power. Pressed by Tokyo, the Vichy government announced on July 23 that Japanese troops would occupy the rest of Indochina, a move that gave Japan a new southern strategic position, including the port of Saigon, from which it could launch attacks against other countries such as the Philippines, Thailand, the Dutch East Indies and the British colonies of Hong Kong and Malaya.[12] The Dutch East Indies had productive oil fields, and US officials feared Japan would seize them to keep its army operating in China, Korea and elsewhere.

FDR responded to the rising Japanese threat on July 25 by ordering an immediate halt to all Japanese commerce with the United States, freezing trade in which the US sent 3.3 million barrels of crude oil to Japan the previous year while buying large amounts of Japanese gold and silk.[13] Simultaneously, the British government also froze its trade with Japan. The next day, under urging by Stimson and Marshall, FDR called General Douglas A. MacArthur out of retirement to take command of all US and Filipino armed forces in the Philippines.[14] A former US Army chief of staff with extensive experience in the Philippines, MacArthur was authorized to spend $10 million to improve the weak defenses of the island territory.

Fury rose in Japan over the US trade sanctions, and Japanese officials sounded the alarm over what they saw as aggressive actions by the United States and its allies toward Japan. On July 28, Foreign Minister Teijiro Toyoda warned in a cable to the Japanese embassy in Washington that a "line of encirclement against Japan is being formed."[15] Another decrypted Japanese diplomatic cable called the Philippines "a pistol aimed at Japan's heart."[16]

Days later, Japanese forces were reported to be at the border of Thailand. FDR's embargo had held out the possibility that some trade might be permitted, but on August 1, FDR tightened his stranglehold on Japan's wartime economy by banning export of any aircraft fuel to Japan.[17] Joseph Grew, the US ambassador to Tokyo, wrote in his diary, "The vicious circle of reprisals and counter-reprisals is on. . . . Unless radical surprises occur in the world, it is difficult to see how the momentum of the down-grade movement can be arrested. . . . The obvious conclusion is eventual war."[18]

. . .

As THE RISK of war with Japan rose, Stimson and Marshall scrambled to strengthen the defenses of the Philippines by basing B-17 bombers there—the "Flying Fortress" bombers that the British had been using against Germany. The Philippines were militarily vulnerable. A territory of the United States since the Spanish-American War, the Philippines had virtually no army of its own, and the United States had extremely limited armed forces on the islands. Now, Stimson and Marshall sought to turn the country into a powerful strategic base from which the B-17 bomber force could strike Japan, its naval fleet or other targets across East Asia. Stimson noted in his diary August 4, "We are sending nine of our big flying fortresses to the Philippines to help in the defense there." More would soon be on their way.

Japan's ambassador to Washington, Admiral Kichisaburo Nomura, delivered a proposal to the State Department on August 5 to ease tensions between the two countries. Under the proposal, the United States would end its trade restrictions and suspend its military measures in the Southwest Pacific, and Japan would withdraw its forces from Indochina but only after a settlement was reached between Japan and China. Secretary of State Hull, having recently returned from medical leave, on August 8 rejected the settlement proposal as unresponsive to an earlier proposal by the United States. Admiral Nomura then urged that President Roosevelt and Prime Minister Konoye meet personally to attempt a resolution of the differences between their countries.

On Saturday, August 9, Stimson was at Highhold when an army intelligence officer brought him papers reporting the latest Magic intercepts, which revealed that Japan was intent upon moving south into Indochina and Thailand. "It was another example of Japanese duplicity," Stimson wrote in his diary.[19] "The invitation to the president is merely a blind to try to keep us from taking action. The papers show this right on their face." US officials could not reveal that they knew Japan's plans, as that would have revealed they had cracked the Japanese code, but FDR, Stimson, Hull and other top US officials aware of the Magic intercepts were infuriated.

As Prime Minister Churchill and FDR met aboard the *Augusta* in Placentia Bay on August 11, Churchill pushed the president to confront the Japanese, who were threatening the British colonies of Hong Kong, Malaya and Burma. FDR agreed to keep "in full force" the economic restrictions imposed on Japan, Churchill reported in a cable to London. The prime minister concluded that FDR's position was "a very great advance towards the gripping of Japanese aggression by united forces."[20]

When Stimson, Knox and Hull met in Washington the next day, Hull announced he had abandoned his posture of seeking a negotiated settlement with the Japanese. "We are now back again on the same ground—appeasement is over," Stimson wrote.[21] When FDR returned to Washington a week later, Hull urged him to reject the proposed meeting with Prime Minister Konoye, and on August 17 FDR told Ambassador Nomura that if Japan continued its movements of forces "we could not . . . think of reopening the conversations."[22]

Japan continued secretly preparing for war. On September 2, Japanese navy commanders gathered at the Naval War College in a Tokyo suburb to conduct tabletop maneuvers for the attack on Pearl Harbor and review plans for simultaneous invasions of the Philippines, Dutch East Indies, Malaya, Burma and other Pacific lands.[23] Four days later, Emperor Hirohito instructed the military to complete war plans by late October.[24]

That same evening, Konoye invited US ambassador to Tokyo Joseph Grew to a private dinner and implored him to arrange a meeting of Konoye and FDR to resolve the dispute between the two nations. "Konoye repeatedly stressed the view that time is of the essence," Grew wrote in a cable to Hull.[25] "Konoye feels confident that all problems and questions at issue can be disposed of to our mutual satisfaction during the meeting with the president."

Hull objected to such a meeting as likely to lead to "another Munich," referring to the pact that appeased Hitler in his drive to seize the Sudetenland.[26] Stimson also opposed the idea of FDR meeting with the Japanese prime minister. "I greatly fear that such a conference if actually held would produce concessions which would be highly dangerous to our vitally important relations with China," Stimson told Morgenthau.

The first nine B-17 bombers arrived in the Philippines on September

12. In his diary that day, Stimson reveled in the idea that "this demonstration of our power to place planes which in the narrow seas can completely damage [Japan's] line of ship connection with her expeditionary force is a most powerful factor and we have been busy for the last few weeks in reinforcing the Philippines so that we shall have a vital power of defense there."[27] A week later, on September 22, Stimson brought assistant secretaries John McCloy and Robert Lovett and other senior officers to meet with FDR and review progress on the Victory Parade war planning effort. Stimson reported the president was "in a very amiable frame of mind."[28] He wrote FDR a letter that day proposing two squadrons of Flying Fortresses each for the Philippines and Hawaii by the first half of 1942.[29]

In Japan, anger over the trade embargo rose to a fever pitch. Konoye, seen by nationalists as too eager to negotiate with the Americans, narrowly escaped an assassination attempt on September 18 by four nationalist radicals wielding ceremonial daggers.[30] Convinced that the emperor backed Minister of War Tojo's call for war against the United States, Konoye resigned October 16.[31] Tojo became prime minister the next day.

FDR canceled his regular cabinet meeting on October 16 and instead summoned Stimson, Knox, Hull, Marshall, Stark and Hopkins to the White House to discuss Japan. Stimson described the discussion in his diary: "The Japanese Navy is beginning to talk almost as radically as the Japanese Army, and so we face the delicate question of the diplomatic fencing to be done so as to be sure that Japan was put into the wrong and made the first bad move—overt move."[32] His remarks reflected the reasoning that, with isolationists likely to oppose a declaration of war by Congress, the US military could not strike first and, instead, the only way to win support for a war would be for the United States to be a victim of an unprovoked attack by the Japanese. After the war, when this diary entry provoked questions, Stimson explained the dilemma by saying, "If you know that your enemy is going to strike you, it is not usually wise to wait until he gets the jump on you by taking the initiative. In spite of the risk involved, however, in letting the Japanese fire the first shot, we realized that in order to have the full support of the American people it was desirable to make sure that the Japanese be the ones to do this so that there should remain no doubt in anyone's mind as to who were the aggressors."[33]

Preparing for a possible Japanese attack, Stimson told FDR in an October 21 letter that his B-17 bomber force in the Philippines was "a strategic opportunity of the utmost importance." The bombers could strike Japan if arrangements could be made for them to land in Siberia to refuel for the return flight to the Philippines. The force would "have immense powers of warning to Japan. . . . It might well remove Japan from the Axis powers."[34] He acknowledged, however, that the new bomber force remained vulnerable: "The final success of the operation lies on the knees of the gods and we cannot tell what explosion may momentarily come from Japan."

Magic intercepts soon revealed that the Japanese had learned of the US buildup of planes and other reinforcements in the Philippines. Stimson, however, was pleased with this slow revelation of the new US force. "I preferred to have these facts sink into the Japanese of their own impact. . . . They are very much puzzled by the fact that we are so much more secretive in the Philippines about what we are doing there. All of the stuff that is being landed is being landed by night and they are so reporting to their chiefs in Tokyo," he told Hull on October 28.[35] He needed more time to complete the defenses in the Philippines. "I told Mr. Hull that all of my policy might be summed up in the homely old words of Theodore Roosevelt, 'Speak softly but carry a big stick.' What I wanted now, I told him, was a very short time to get that big stick into readiness."

The Japanese, despite their extraordinary military strength, felt threatened. In Tokyo on November 5, Emperor Hirohito presided as the Privy Council heard Tojo describe Japan as caught in the grip of enemies closing in. "Rather than await extinction, it was better to face death by breaking through the encircling ring and find a way for existence," Tojo said.[36] It was decided that Japan would continue negotiations, but if no agreement was achieved by November 25, a final decision for war would be submitted to Hirohito. Ambassador Nomura was instructed to make a final approach to Hull. Under Yamamoto's command, the strike force— consisting of aircraft carriers, destroyers and submarines—continued to plan and train for its attack on Pearl Harbor.

. . .

As TENSIONS ESCALATED between the two countries, Tojo sent a diplomat, Saburo Kurusu, to meet with FDR in what was described in both Japanese and American news accounts as a "last" effort to reach a peaceful settlement. Kurusu left Tokyo on November 5, and his progress through Hong Kong and other ports was reported by the global press until he finally arrived in Washington. On November 20, Kurusu and Nomura presented Hull with a proposed standstill agreement for a six-month period in which both countries would cease further military advances in the southern Pacific region, Japan would withdraw from southern Indochina, and the United States would lift the freeze order on Japanese assets and sell oil to Japan.[37] Hull found the proposal utterly unacceptable. "The commitments we should have to make were virtually a surrender. We on our part should have to supply Japan as much oil as she might require, suspend our freezing measures, and resume full commercial relations with Tokyo. We should have to discontinue aid to China and withdraw our material support from the recognized government of Chiang Kai-shek," Hull wrote in his memoirs. And, in an apparent reference to the bombers, troops and munitions being sent the Philippines, he said, "We should have to cease augmenting our military forces in the western Pacific."[38]

Hull and FDR, after consulting with British and Chinese diplomats, drafted a counterproposal, a temporary modus vivendi pact providing that for three months both countries would make no armed advances into new areas, the Japanese would reduce their forces in Indochina, and the United States would modify the embargo to permit limited trade, including sale of oil to the Japanese for "civilian needs."

Stimson met with Knox and Hull on November 25, and Hull showed the two men the draft modus vivendi. Stimson's view was extremely pessimistic: The document protected US interests, but "I don't think there is any chance of the Japanese accepting it, because it is so drastic." At noon, the three men went to the White House for a meeting of the War Council, which included FDR, Marshall and Stark. FDR said "we were likely to be attacked perhaps next Monday, for the Japanese are notorious for making an attack without warning, and the question was what we should do," Stimson recorded in his diary. "The question was how we should maneuver them into the position of firing the first shot without allowing too much danger to ourselves."[39] There is no evidence that the War Council found any answer to this question.

The negotiations broke down. Instead of proposing the modus vivendi, Hull on November 26 presented to Kurusu and Nomura a ten-point proclamation of the key American objectives in the Pacific, including Japan's complete withdrawal from China and Indochina, recognition of Chiang Kai-shek's government and withdrawal from the Tripartite Pact.[40] The next morning, Hull told Stimson "he had about made up his mind to give up the whole thing in respect to a truce and to simply tell the Japanese that he had no further action to propose."[41]

Events became more alarming when Stimson received an army intelligence report that the Japanese had sent five divisions of soldiers—aboard as many as fifty ships—south past Formosa (now Taiwan) toward Indochina. He called FDR to inform him of the report, and the president "fairly blew up—jumped up in the air, so to speak, and said he hadn't seen it and that that changed the whole situation because it was an evidence of bad faith on the part of the Japanese that while they were negotiating for an entire truce—an entire withdrawal—they should be sending this expedition down there to Indochina."[42]

The next day, Hull told Stimson he had delivered the statement of principles to the Japanese. "He told me now that he had broken the whole matter off. As he put it, 'I have washed my hands of it and it is now in the hands of you and Knox—the Army and the Navy.'"[43] Stimson called FDR and discussed MacArthur, the US commander in the Philippines. "I suggested and he approved the idea that we should send the final alert; namely, that he should be on the qui vive for any attack and telling him the situation." A message also was sent to Admiral Kimmel in Hawaii placing the island's defenses on heightened alert: "This dispatch is to be considered a war warning. Negotiations with Japan . . . have ceased and an aggressive move by Japan is expected within the next few days."[44] General Marshall also sent Walter Short, the army's commanding general in Hawaii, a dispatch warning, "Negotiations with Japan appear to be terminated to all practical purposes with only the barest possibilities that the Japanese government might come back and offer to continue. Japanese future action unpredictable but hostile action possible at any moment."[45]

By this time, Kurusu had extended the deadline for a settlement to November 29. Each day was overshadowed by the imminent threat of war. On Friday morning, November 28, FDR was in bed when Stimson came in carrying the latest intelligence report on Japanese troop movements past Formosa to the south. FDR told Stimson he saw three options: "First, to do nothing; second, to make something in the nature of an ultimatum again, stating a point beyond which we would fight; third, to fight at once." Stimson replied: "I told him my only two were the last two, because I did not think anyone would do nothing in this situation, and he agreed with me. I said of the other two my choice was the latter one." FDR took up the question again when the War Council met at the White House at noon, and the conversation focused entirely on the troop movements.[46] Stimson reported in his diary that the council's consensus was that if the Japanese expeditionary force landed in Thailand, "it would be a terrific blow" to the United States, Great Britain and the Netherlands. FDR suggested that he might send a "special telegram" as a warning to Emperor Hirohito. Stimson, however, advised, "One does not warn an emperor." Instead, Stimson proposed that the president send a private message to Hirohito and also make a speech to Congress and the people of the United States stating what the danger was. "That was the final decision at that time and the president asked Hull and Knox and myself to try to draft such papers."

The president left that afternoon for a Thanksgiving weekend vacation with his family in Warm Springs, Georgia. When Stimson began drafting the messages, he learned that Hull had not come back from lunch and could not be found. "He had evidently gone away for a rest or sleep or something." The president and his top advisers were wracked with anxiety over the threat of war, a fatalistic sense that war was inevitable and sheer physical exhaustion.

THAT SAME DAY, November 27, Admiral Yamamoto's attack force of six aircraft carriers, eight destroyers and other vessels departed from a bay in Japan's Kuril Islands and headed for Hawaii.[47] Four days later, on

December 1, Hirohito met with Tojo and members of his cabinet and the armed forces in the Imperial Palace in Tokyo. Tojo said the United States had refused to make any concessions and continued demanding the removal of Japanese troops from China and increasing "military pressure" against Japan. "Under the circumstances, our Empire has no alternative but to begin war against the United States, Great Britain, and the Netherlands in order to resolve the present crisis and assure survival."[48] The emperor nodded in agreement and later affixed his seal to papers proposing war. Japan's course was set.[49]

FDR returned from Warm Springs to Washington on December 1. Meanwhile, army reports revealed that the Japanese expeditionary force ships appeared to be landing near Saigon, not going farther south to attack Thailand, which Stimson said "gave us a little bit of respite."[50]

The intense focus on Japan was broken briefly on December 4 when the staunchly isolationist *Chicago Tribune* published on its front page a story about the combined army and navy war plans—the Victory Parade effort that Stimson, Knox and top military officers had been preparing for months. The story said the plan called for total armed forces of ten million men, five million of whom would be sent overseas for a final offensive to defeat the Nazi regime in 1943. Stimson was enraged at the revelations, though he also said they might "shake our American people out of their infernal apathy and ignorance of what this war means." He called FDR and found that the president "was full of fight." The president suggested that the first response of the US government "should be the arrest of those responsible for the disclosure, including if possible the managers of the newspapers."[51]

The next morning, December 5, Stimson called FDR and proposed that he discuss the *Tribune* at his news conference later that morning. "Go ahead. Tell them," FDR replied. At the conference, Stimson said the plans revealed by the *Tribune* were "unfinished studies of our production requirements for national defense."[52] He proclaimed that "the chief evil of their publication is the revelation that there should be among us a group of persons so lacking in appreciation of the danger that confronts the country and so wanting in loyalty and patriotism to their government that they would be willing to take and publish such papers."

On December 6, reports came in that a Japanese force of thirty-five troop transport ships, eight cruisers and twenty destroyers was moving from Indochina toward the south, and Stimson, Knox and Hull discussed the reports through the day.[53] Stimson noted in his diary "the news got worse and worse and the atmosphere indicated something was going to happen. . . . We are mainly concerned with the supplies which are on the way to the Philippines and the additional big bombers which we are trying to fly over there and which are to start today."[54] FDR decided at last to send his message to Emperor Hirohito, which praised the long-standing peaceful relations between the two countries and urged the emperor to "give thought in this definite emergency to ways of dispelling the dark clouds."[55] By 9:00 P.M., Hull sent the message to Tokyo, where it required decoding and was delayed for ten hours in a telegraph office before finally reaching Foreign Minister Shigenori Togo by about 12:30 A.M. that night.[56]

About two hours later, aircraft carriers in Yamamoto's strike force, located about 200 miles north of Oahu, began launching 360 dive bombers, torpedo planes and fighters. It was early on the morning of Sunday, December 7. In clear skies, the Japanese planes swept over Pearl Harbor, dropping bombs and torpedoes that sank four battleships—the *Arizona, California, Oklahoma,* and *West Virginia*—and damaged four other battleships and ten other vessels. The fleet's aircraft carriers, submarines and other vessels were not at Pearl Harbor that day, some because they were in the Atlantic. The Japanese also bombed and strafed three army airfields, destroying ninety-six US army aircraft in all. The surprise attack was devastating: 2,280 members of the army, navy and marine corps were killed, and another 1,109 wounded.[57]

The Japanese assault had caught the vaunted Pearl Harbor fortress in a state of unpreparedness: ships were sitting at their moorings, a radar system meant to detect enemy planes was out of operation, and US planes—caught on the ground—were lined up wingtip to wingtip on runways, an effort to reduce risk of sabotage that unfortunately made them easy targets from the air.[58] US forces sent up pursuit planes and quickly began operating antiaircraft guns, bringing down an estimated twenty-eight Japanese planes, and the navy sank two small Japanese submarines.[59] The latest squadron of B-17 bombers en route to join the bomber fleet in the Philippines landed at the Ford Island airfield, located in the middle of Pearl Harbor, just as the attack was taking place. Somehow the Japanese destroyed only one of the squadron's thirteen bombers.[60]

PRESIDENT ROOSEVELT WAS having lunch at the White House that day when Knox called at about 1:40 P.M. to inform him of the attack.[61] By 2:00, FDR called Stimson: "Have you heard the news?" the president asked. "They have attacked Hawaii. They are now bombing Hawaii."[62] Unaware of the destruction wrought by the Japanese, Stimson noted no feelings of shock, horror or anger in his later diary entry. Having expected a Japanese attack for so long, he wrote, "My first feeling was of relief that the indecision was over and that a crisis had come in a way which would unite our people. . . . For I feel that this country united has practically nothing to fear while the apathy and divisions stirred up by unpatriotic men have been hitherto very discouraging."

FDR called Hull and informed him of the reported attack just minutes before Hull received Nomura and Kurusu at the State Department to present a response to the ten-point statement Hull gave them on November 26. The two men gave Hull a memorandum rejecting the ten-point statement and making no comment on Pearl Harbor. Hull, showing extreme diplomatic restraint, denounced the memorandum as "crowded with infamous falsehoods and distortions," and dismissed the Japanese diplomats.[63] In Tokyo, Foreign Minister Togo told Ambassador Grew that after receiving FDR's last-minute letter he had seen Hirohito at 3:00 A.M. The document delivered to Hull in Washington was the emperor's response, Togo said.[64]

FDR called a cabinet meeting on the evening of December 7 in the Oval Office. The president expressed shock over the success of the attack and the unpreparedness of the forces in Pearl Harbor: He told Knox, "Find out, for God's sake, why the ships were tied up in rows."[65] He read a draft of the speech he intended to give the next day asking Congress for a declaration of war against Japan. Stimson urged the president to expand his request to include a declaration of war against Germany, noting that Germany had encouraged Japan to attack. FDR, even at that moment likely fearing isolationist criticism, rejected the idea.

Congressional leaders later joined the meeting—Senate majority leader Alben Barkley, House Speaker Sam Rayburn and two Republicans, House minority leader Joseph Martin and others. Senator Tom Connally, Democrat of Texas, asked the key question: "How did it happen that our warships were caught like sitting ducks at Pearl Harbor?" FDR replied, "I don't know, Tom, I just don't know."[66]

What happened at Pearl Harbor was yet another retelling of the universal tale of hubris begetting death and mayhem in wars throughout history. Hirohito and his nationalist officers, set on a campaign of imperialist expansion, had launched a brutal attack on America at a time when the two nations were in negotiations. The attack was extremely successful, but it would ultimately reap a bitter harvest for Japan. America's military leaders, alerted to the risk of a Japanese attack on Pearl Harbor in early 1941, believed it was an impregnable fortress; they overlooked the weaknesses of their defenses and failed to ensure the highest levels of alertness of defenders. The senior military commanders in Hawaii, Admiral Kimmel and General Short, played critical roles in the error-ridden tragedy, though some would also fault FDR, Stimson and Knox. Stimson, too, had come to believe in his B-17 bomber force as a strategy for intimidating the Japanese and, if necessary, defeating a Japanese offensive. In fact, the bomber force was highly vulnerable.

Ten hours after they attacked Pearl Harbor, the Japanese struck in the Philippines, delivering a knockout blow to Stimson's B-17 strategy. At about 12:30 P.M. Manila time on January 8, Japanese bombers struck Clark Field air base. Despite a general's plea to get the B-17s and other planes in the air, General MacArthur—for reasons unclear to this day—failed to give the order, and American planes once again were caught on the ground. The Japanese assault destroyed almost all of the nineteen B-17 bombers based there along with eighteen P-40 fighters, killing a hundred men and wounding another two hundred fifty.[67] Marshall lamented to a *Time* magazine reporter two weeks later: "I just don't know how MacArthur happened to let his planes get caught on the ground."[68] The attacks on Clark Field and Pearl Harbor were part of a vast offensive in which Japanese forces invaded the Philippines, the Dutch East Indies, Malaya, Singapore, Thailand, Burma, Hong Kong and a series of Pacific islands. The attack on Clark devastated the base and, while sixteen more B-17s remained untouched at another US base in the Philippines, most of the US air defenses were wiped out, leaving the twenty thousand American troops in the Philippines exposed as the Japanese began their land invasion.

AMID DESPAIR OVER the crushing Japanese assault, FDR sought to rally the nation when he appeared before a joint session of the House and Senate the next day to ask that Congress declare war against Japan. "Yesterday, December 7, 1941—a date which will live in infamy—the United States of America was suddenly and deliberately attacked by na-val and air forces of the empire of Japan. . . . No matter how long it may take us to overcome this premeditated invasion, the American people, in their righteous might, will win through to absolute victory. . . . With confidence in our armed forces, with the unbounding determination of our people, we will gain the inevitable triumph. So help us God."[69]

The attack on Pearl Harbor instantly bolstered the unity between Republicans and Democrats in support of the US war effort that FDR, Stimson and Knox had long sought. After meeting with the president and cabinet at the White House on the evening of December 7, House minority leader Martin signaled an end to partisan disputes. "There is no politics here," he said. "There is only one party when it comes to the integrity and honor of the country."[70] And Senator Charles McNary, the Oregon Republican who was leader of the Republican minority in the Senate and the 1940 GOP vice-presidential candidate, said amid discussion of a possible declaration of war that the Republicans "will all go along, in my opinion, with whatever is done." Even Senator Burton Wheeler, the isolationist Montana Democrat who had flung countless barbs at FDR and Stimson, announced that he supported a declaration of war because of the "vicious and uncalled-for attack by the Japanese government upon the United States." He added, "Everyone, regardless of party affiliations, must back up the Administration to the end that we win."[71]

Shortly after FDR's address at the Capitol, Hamilton Fish, the Re-publican and extreme isolationist from New York, revealed just how swiftly the political tides had changed when he spoke on the House floor. "Interventionists and noninterventionists must cease . . . recriminations, charges and countercharges against each other, and present a united front behind the president and the government in the conduct of the war."[72]

Such clear unity would not last long, but on this day it reigned supreme. Both congressional chambers quickly passed the declaration of war. The vote was unanimous in the Senate, 82–0. In the House the tally was 388–1, with just one Republican—Jeannette Rankin of Montana, a pacifist—voting no. Stimson, who with other members of the cabinet came to the House chamber to observe the president's speech, noted with relief in his diary that the rapid passage of the declaration "was very impressive of the unity of the country."[73] FDR signed the declaration into law at 4:10 P.M. The United States was at war.

World War, Internal War

After President Roosevelt signed the declaration of war on December 8, Fiorello La Guardia and Eleanor Roosevelt boarded a flight to Los Angeles to strengthen civilian defenses amid fears that the Japanese might bomb a West Coast city. Before boarding the plane, La Guardia said in a radio broadcast, "I would not trust those Japs anytime, anywhere," displaying the anti-Japanese fervor gripping the nation.[1] At about 10:00 P.M. that night, Secretary of War Stimson got a phone call at Woodley from Assistant Secretary of War John McCloy, who told him an alert had gone out about a group of unidentified aircraft approaching San Francisco from the Pacific Ocean. A short while later, McCloy called back to say it was a false alarm—the planes were American bombers returning from convoy duty.[2]

America was on edge.

At the White House the next day, Stimson told FDR the army was bringing aircraft from around the country to defend the West Coast. If the United States kept some of the planes intended for Great Britain, air defenses for the entire continental United States could be in place by December 31. "He accepted my proposition and said he thought it was reasonable," Stimson noted.[3] He sent General George Marshall a memo authorizing the army to carry out the new air defense plans. He also outlined for FDR plans for $140 billion in spending on arms and equipping soldiers for the war through 1944. Later that evening, the president delivered a radio address to the nation vowing that America's expanded defense production would enable the nation to win the war.[4] He said America faced a long struggle against "crafty and powerful bandits," and he warned that the "attack at Pearl Harbor can be repeated . . . along both our coast lines."

The shockwaves from Japan's attack set off an internal war against a vulnerable minority, Japanese Americans. On the day of the attack, the US Army imposed martial law in Hawaii, a US territory where more than 30 percent of the population was of Japanese descent. In the following days, FBI agents raided the homes of people of Japanese origin in Hawaii and along the US West Coast, arresting hundreds and seizing their belongings.

Outside the United States, invading Japanese forces captured ground in the Philippines and across the Pacific region. On December 10, Japanese bombers sank two British battleships near Malaya, sending some 1,300 sailors to their deaths. One of these ships was the *Prince of Wales*, which four months prior had brought Prime Minister Churchill to Placentia Bay to meet with FDR. Reflecting on these devastating naval attacks in the Pacific and Indian oceans, Churchill later wrote, "Over all this vast expanse of waters, Japan was supreme, and we everywhere weak and naked."[5]

Seizing the global stage, Hitler announced before the Reichstag on December 11 that Germany and Italy would join Japan in its war against the United States.[6] FDR quickly sent a message to Congress requesting declarations of war against Germany and Italy, which were passed without a dissenting vote within forty-five minutes. FDR signed the declarations into law, and America's long-anticipated war against European fascism became a reality.

Secretary of the Navy Knox went to Hawaii to investigate the attack. After returning to Washington, he met with reporters December 15 and released a report admitting the truth that congressional critics had uttered. "The United States forces were not on alert against the surprise air attack on Hawaii," Knox said. His report included multiple accounts of individual bravery by sailors—actions that saved lives and dealt blows to the Japanese attackers. But he also claimed that collaborators in Hawaii had aided the assault, deflecting blame onto an unseen internal enemy sympathetic to Japan. "The most effective fifth-column work in this war was done in Hawaii, with the exception of Norway," he said, without providing evidence.[7] He also announced that the president would name a board to investigate the attack. "We are all entitled to know if there was any error of judgment . . . or dereliction of duty."

Knox met with FDR, who proposed that a five-member commission—composed of two representatives each from the army and navy, and a civilian—investigate Pearl Harbor. Stimson urged the president to name Supreme Court justice Owen Roberts as the civilian appointee.[8] He also named his old friend General Frank McCoy, and the next day he discussed the matter with Marshall, who recommended General Joseph McNarney for his knowledge of the air force. The president agreed that Roberts, McCoy and McNarney would be on the commission, along with Knox's choices, admirals William H. Standley and Joseph M. Reeves.

Stimson and Knox took action the next day against the commanders in Hawaii. Knox relieved Admiral Husband Kimmel of his duty as commander in chief of the Pacific Fleet, replacing him with Rear Admiral Chester W. Nimitz. Stimson replaced Commander of the Hawaiian Department Lieutenant General Short with Lieutenant General Delos Emmons. Stimson concurred with Knox's findings regarding the "unpreparedness" of US forces.[9]

THE UNITED STATES and Great Britain were firmly allied in the world war, but amid the powerful Japanese offensive this alliance, too, began to show signs of internal division over war strategy. On December 22, Churchill arrived in Washington for a visit over the Christmas holiday that was intended to solidify the wartime alliance, bolster the confidence of the two nations and make decisions about war strategy. Churchill stayed at the White House and on his first evening dove into strategic matters with FDR. The prime minister had prepared a memo urging that an American invasion force of at least one hundred and fifty thousand soldiers land in North Africa within six months. After dinner, he raised the proposal, which the British had given the code name Super-Gymnast.[10] He reported the president's support to his War Cabinet with delight in a telegram the next day. "The president said that he was anxious that American land forces should give their support as quickly as possible wherever they could be most helpful, and favoured the idea of a plan to move into North Africa."[11]

Stimson, however, was deeply concerned about British proposals to send US forces into battle in regions that the US Army did not consider strategically significant. Consulting with Army chief of staff General George Marshall, General Hap Arnold and General Dwight Eisenhower, Stimson prepared a memo for FDR on military strategy that objected to the idea of sending US troops to "the Egyptian area."[12] In 1940, fearing an Italian invasion, Churchill had rushed British forces to North Africa to protect Egypt and the British-controlled Suez Canal as well as British colonies of Kenya, Sudan and British Somaliland.[13] Stimson noted that these colonial holdings were "of immense importance psychologically to the British Empire" but "of the least importance to us." He and senior army officers believed the alliance's strategy must be focused on finding the surest path to defeat Hitler—not on concerns for the future of the British Empire.

Having established his relationship with Churchill at Placentia Bay, FDR this time included Stimson and Knox in a strategy discussion with the British prime minister, held at the White House on December 23. The wartime leadership of both countries gathered in the Cabinet Room. Stimson, Marshall and Arnold represented the army. Knox, Admiral Harold Stark and Admiral Ernest King, recently named by Knox to be commander in chief of the fleet, represented the navy. Churchill was accompanied by Lord Beaverbrook, the minister of supply, Air Chief Charles Portal and other senior officials. After the meeting started, FDR read aloud Stimson's memo with its scathing attack on British imperial objectives in North Africa as being strategically unimportant to the United States. FDR likely felt that this discord on strategy must be debated and resolved for the alliance to move forward. In response, Churchill "commented feelingly" on Stimson's view that a key challenge was "the preservation of our communications across the North Atlantic with our fortress in the British Isles." But the prime minister ignored Stimson's objection to defending British colonies in North Africa.[14] This was the first of many disputes in which Stimson opposed Churchill and his British commanders on war strategy.

The next morning, Christmas Eve, Stimson got word that Churchill wanted to discuss the Philippines with him, so he took General Eisenhower to meet with the prime minister in his room upstairs in the White House. Stimson brought maps of the Philippines and pointed out to Churchill locations of the forces on both sides, explaining the battle's "probable outcome" in a retreat to the island of Corregidor off the southern tip of the Bataan Peninsula.

After Eisenhower left, Stimson and Churchill continued discussing Africa and other theaters of war.[15] The two men ought to have been the easiest of allies: both were conservative yet willing to reach across the political aisle, and both had waged sometimes solitary campaigns urging the Anglo-American alliance to prepare for war to defeat fascism and save democracy. Stimson had sought to bolster Churchill's spirits amid the Blitzkrieg with his telegram in May 1940 vowing "the forces of evil will be stopped," to which Churchill had replied "*On les aura.*" Now, nineteen months later, with the United States fully involved in the global conflict, the two men held opposing strategic positions. Stimson saw Churchill as pushing for preservation of the British Empire and distracting FDR from vital strategic goals, while Churchill perceived Stimson as one of the US military men striving to pull FDR away from sound British strategy. The discord between the two men flared the next day.

Christmas morning dawned with grim news from the Philippines: the Japanese had landed troops at three locations near Manila, and MacArthur had cabled that he would retreat down the Bataan Peninsula toward Corregidor. He planned to evacuate the Philippine government from Manila, which would be declared an open city, averting its ruin at the hands of the Japanese. Filipino president Manuel Quezon and his family had already fled from Manila to the American fortress on Corregidor.[16] Stimson was shocked when Marshall, Arnold and Eisenhower brought him a memorandum stating that FDR and Churchill were considering the idea of diverting reinforcements intended for MacArthur's forces to the British. "This astonishing paper made me extremely angry," Stimson wrote in his diary.[17] He called Hopkins, informed him of the document, which was prepared by an assistant to Churchill, and threatened to send a resignation letter to FDR if the subject "was persisted in." Hopkins hung up, then told FDR and Churchill what Stimson had said, and both men denied any such proposal had been made. Hopkins called Stimson back and told him what the two leaders had said; Stimson remained doubtful.

A short while later, FDR called Stimson, Knox and the senior army and navy commanders to the White House, where they discussed the situation in the Far East. In the meeting, FDR said a paper had been "going around" that was nonsense and that "entirely misrepresented a conference between him and Churchill." Stimson did not reply, though he suggested in his diary that he doubted FDR's candor. "I think he felt that he had pretty nearly burned his fingers and had called this subsequent meeting to make up for it."

FDR, meanwhile, met with Churchill privately and devised plans for winning the war. Churchill later noted, "As we both, by need or habit, were forced to do much of our work in bed, he visited me in my room whenever he felt inclined, and encouraged me to do the same to him."[18] Working with their advisers, "Franklin" and "Winston," as they amicably called each other, reached important agreements, including one to form a joint military command called the Combined Chiefs of Staff. They also agreed to have all the pro-democracy nations sign a pact creating an alliance to be called the "United Nations," avowing their commitment to freedom and the defeat of fascism.

On December 26, as news broke that the British had surrendered to the Japanese in Hong Kong, Churchill was driven past cheering crowds on the streets to the Capitol to address a joint session of Congress. After noting the threat from the "dictator states" of Germany, Italy and Japan, he praised America for its "Olympian fortitude," which he said was "only the mask of an inflexible purpose and the proof of a sure, well-grounded confidence in the final outcome."[19] Turning to the "outrages" the Japanese had committed in attacking Pearl Harbor, the Philippines, Malaya and the Dutch East Indies, he thundered: "What kind of people do they think we are? Is it possible they do not realize that we shall never cease to persevere against them until they have been taught a lesson which they and the world will never forget?" At this rhetorical salvo, applause erupted in the chamber. As Churchill left the chamber, he raised his hand to flash a V for victory sign with his fingers, and his audience raised the V sign in enthusiastic response.

· · ·

CHURCHILL'S OMINOUS THREAT to teach the Japanese "a lesson which they and the world will never forget" played on a fear of the Japanese military that was pervasive in America. Anxiety over possible Japanese espionage and sabotage had been building since at least June 1941, when the FBI in Los Angeles arrested two Japanese citizens, Itaru Tachibana and Toraichi Kono, on charges that they attempted to purchase naval secrets from a US sailor, a case that drew wide publicity. Kono, who had once been movie star Charlie Chaplin's chauffeur, was accused of approaching the sailor and asking if he wanted to make some "easy money."[20] Federal investigators had raided the Japanese consulate in Los Angeles and seized documents including maps, lists of army and navy installations and information on defense factories, harbors and power stations. At the time, Secretary of State Cordell Hull was in intense negotiations with Ambassador Kichisaburo Nomura in an effort to avoid war, and Nomura requested that Tachibana be permitted to leave the United States without trial. Hull consented because he considered the negotiations with the Japanese to be at a "crucial stage," and on June 21 Tachibana was allowed to leave the United States on the condition that he never return.[21]

Since early 1941, the US Army's codebreakers had produced a stream of Magic intercepts revealing that Japanese intelligence operatives were using Japanese Americans to gather information on US military sites and important infrastructure. One intercept, dated January 30, 1941, and sent from Tokyo to Washington, said "the focal point of our investigations shall be determination of the total strength of the US . . . political, economic, and military."[22]

The Japanese intelligence operation in California was relying in part on "second generations," the children of first-generation immigrants. A May 1941 Magic intercept stated, "We shall maintain connection with our second generations who are at present in the (US) Army, to keep us informed of various developments in the Army. We also have connections with our second generations working in airplane plants for intelligence purposes."

Another intercepted cable revealed Japanese espionage efforts targeting the US Navy's Bremerton Naval Yard near Seattle.[23] The cable said a Japanese naval officer serving in the United States, Lieutenant Commander Sadatomo Okada, was a key contact for the intelligence operation. US officials expelled Okada and another naval officer working with Tachibana's espionage ring from the United States on July 5, 1941.[24]

FDR had long been concerned about a perceived security threat posed by Japanese espionage. In August 1936 he sounded an alarm about a navy investigation of Japanese ships visiting Hawaii. The president wrote in a memo to a senior naval commander at the time: "One obvious thought occurs to me—that every Japanese citizen or non-citizen on the island of Oahu who meets these Japanese ships or has any connection with their officers or men should be secretly but definitely identified and his or her name placed on a special list of those who would be first to be placed in a concentration camp in the event of trouble."[25]

After the Tachibana case arose in 1941, the president pushed for more information about the risks of sabotage and espionage by Japanese Americans. He engaged a journalist, John Franklin Carter, to prepare a stream of intelligence reports.[26] In early November 1941, Carter sent FDR a report on the risk of espionage by Japanese people on the West Coast. The report, prepared by a Chicago businessman working for Carter named Curtis Munson, said that the vast majority of American Japanese are loyal, but cautioned, "There will be undoubtedly some sabotage financed by Japan and executed largely by imported agents."

The report said, "Dams, bridges, harbors, power stations etc. are wholly unguarded everywhere. The harbor of San Pedro could be razed by fire completely by four men with hand grenades and a little study in one night. Dams could be blown and half of lower California might actually die of thirst."[27] FDR sent the Munson report to Stimson on November 8, asking him to have the army investigate its warning on the vulnerable sabotage targets.

FDR also asked Carter to discuss the Munson report with spy chief Bill Donovan and FBI director J. Edgar Hoover. Carter began pushing the departments toward an operational plan for arresting "suspects on the West Coast."[28]

After the Pearl Harbor attack three weeks later, the FBI conducted sweeping searches and arrests in the homes and businesses of Japanese Americans on the West Coast. The FBI reported seizing 2,592 guns, 199,000 rounds of ammunition, 1,652 sticks of dynamite, 1,458 radios, and 2,015 cameras. "We have not, however, uncovered through these searches any dangerous persons," the Justice Department reported to FDR. "We have not found a single machine gun nor have found any gun in any circumstances indicating it was to be used in a manner helpful to our enemies."[29] In fact, most of the weapons came from Japanese-owned sporting-goods stores.

On December 9, FDR issued a proclamation that subjected citizens of Japan, Germany and Italy age fourteen and older to immediate arrest as "alien enemies" if they were deemed "dangerous" by Stimson or Attorney General Francis Biddle. FDR approved the sweeping powers of arrest by issuing the proclamation under a First World War–era law that permitted arrests in case of a declaration of war against an enemy nation. By the end of December 9, more than four hundred German and Italian citizens had been added to the nine hundred Japanese under arrest.[30] FDR's proclamation forbade enemy aliens from possessing weapons, explosives and shortwave radios, and also authorized the army to ban their presence from forts, power plants, airports, arms factories or any area "in which residence by an alien enemy shall be found to constitute a danger."

The next day, in the midst of the resulting wave of arrests and searches, Attorney General Francis Biddle assured non-citizens that "every effort will be made to protect them from discrimination or abuse."[31] Eleanor Roosevelt voiced concern in her regular newspaper column, My Day, about the rights of minorities. "If we cannot meet the challenge of fairness to our citizens of every nationality, of really believing in the Bill of Rights and making it a reality for all loyal American citizens, regardless of race, creed or color; if we cannot keep in check anti-Semitism, anti-racial feeling as well as anti-religious feelings, then we shall have removed from the world the one real hope for the future on which all humanity must now rely," the First Lady wrote.[32]

America, however, was in the grip of fear. Along the West Coast, jumpy citizens reported supposed sightings of Japanese aircraft and naval vessels to the military, and air raid sirens sounded—all false alarms. Then came real attacks. On December 20, a Japanese submarine torpedoed and sank a freighter off California's coast and then shelled three of her lifeboats, leaving twenty-two of the vessel's fifty-four crew members missing. The next day, a Japanese submarine surfaced and fired its deck guns at an oil tanker, which escaped and arrived safely in San Francisco.[33] Two days later, a Japanese submarine sank an oil tanker halfway between San Francisco and Los Angeles, the crew escaping in lifeboats.[34] Newspapers nationwide ran stories about the attacks on their front pages, fueling public fear of a possible invasion. Heightening concerns, the Japanese military defeated US Navy forces on Wake Island, two thousand miles west of Hawaii, taking more than a thousand Americans prisoner.[35]

At the Presidio, the large army base in San Francisco, Lieutenant General John L. DeWitt, the army commander over the West Coast region, wrote a memo to the War Department December 19 calling for the US Army to "collect" all enemy aliens above the age of fourteen "and remove them to the Zone of the Interior." The Justice Department, however, argued that there was no legal reason to take action against US citizens of Japanese origin. Upon hearing DeWitt wanted to remove enemy aliens from a one-hundred-mile-wide coastal zone, FBI director J. Edgar Hoover told an FBI agent, "I do not believe that they can put over any plan to clean people out of that area unless there is some very imminent prospect of attack. . . . I thought the army was getting a bit hysterical."[36]

FDR soon highlighted a new scare. On December 29, the president alerted Stimson to the latest report he had received from Carter and Munson, which warned of a possible attack on San Pedro Harbor, the industrial port in Los Angeles. "Munson thinks the attack contemplated is the release of gas off-shore with a favoring wind or fog," he told Stimson. "He reports there are no gas masks on the West Coast for the civilian population."[37] Stimson assured the president that the army had already consulted with Munson and was guarding strategic sites.[38]

FDR also raised the specter of an attack on the West Coast when he delivered his State of the Union speech a week later to Congress. The president warned that the Japanese intended to dominate the West Coast of the United States militarily.[39] "Japan's scheme of conquest goes

back half a century," he said in the speech, which was carried nationwide via radio. "It is not merely a policy of seeking living room, it was a
plan which included subjugation of all the peoples in the Far East and in
the islands of the Pacific, and the domination of that ocean by Japanese
military and naval control of the western coasts of North, Central and
South America."

Congress also made fevered calls for action against Japanese Americans. On January 20, Representative Leland Ford, a California Republican, went to the floor of the House and urged for all Japanese Americans
to be placed in concentration camps. "I believe that a patriotic native-
born Japanese, if he wants to make his contribution, will submit himself
to a concentration camp as his contribution, as against the native-born
American, who lays his life down for his country."[40]

Fueling the climate of fear was a toxic mix of racism and economic
interest. In California, where Japanese Americans operated vegetable
farms, the manager of the Grower-Shipper Vegetable Association admitted openly, "We're charged with wanting to get rid of the Japs for selfish
reasons. We might as well be honest. We do. It's a question of whether
the white man lives on the Pacific Coast or the brown man."[41]

As THE INVESTIGATIVE Pearl Harbor Board wrapped up its work, Stimson met privately with Justice Roberts. On the evening of January 20,
Stimson went to Felix Frankfurter's home for dinner with Assistant
Secretary of War McCloy, who had been working on the issue of the
Japanese Americans, and Roberts. Roberts said he considered the large
Japanese American population in Hawaii "a great menace," Stimson
noted. "He did not think that the FBI had succeeded in getting under
the crust of their secret thoughts at all and he believed that this great
mass of Japanese, both aliens and Americanized, existed as a great potential danger."[42]

The Roberts commission issued its report four days later, finding
that Admiral Kimmel and General Short had failed to take warnings
about the threat of war seriously and failed to confer with each other
regarding defense of Pearl Harbor. The board noted that Admiral Stark
and General Marshall had sent specific warnings of war to Kimmel and

Short on November 27. If the commanders had heeded those warnings, the army's radar system would have been operating, army and navy air patrols would have been active, and antiaircraft batteries would have been manned and ready. "None of these conditions was in fact inaugurated or maintained for the reason that the responsible commanders failed to consult and cooperate as to necessary action based upon the warnings," the board said.[43] It also found that while many military leaders believed the Japanese assault would likely occur in the Southwest Pacific, that did not relieve the commanders of their responsibility to prepare for war. The board absolved Stimson, Knox, Marshall and Stark of blame for the failure.

The Roberts board also said a Japanese spy ring operating in Hawaii before the attack sent "information to the Japanese Empire respecting the military and naval establishments and [military] dispositions on the island." Japan had two hundred officials at its consulate in Hawaii in the summer of 1941. It was later revealed that consular official Takeo Yoshikawa, working with a German spy on Oahu, had sent numerous cables to Tokyo with critical details used to plan the attack, and that those cables had been revealed prior to the attack by Magic intercepts that US officials overlooked.[44] The Roberts report, still guarding the highly sensitive secret that the US Army's Magic system had broken Japan's code, said only that the spy ring included "persons having no open relations with the Japanese foreign service."

The Roberts report's alert about Japanese espionage at Pearl Harbor further stoked public fears about Japanese Americans. In Los Angeles, county manager Wayne Allen on January 27 announced he was firing all workers of Japanese descent because the Pearl Harbor "debacle had been facilitated by wide-spread espionage and fifth column work" by Japanese in Hawaii. "It is difficult if not impossible, to distinguish between loyal and disloyal Japanese," he said.[45]

DeWitt's plan to remove the Japanese from coastal areas won support from General Allen Gullion, the army's provost marshal general and top law enforcement officer. A meeting of Gullion, McCloy and Justice Department officials on February 1, however, revealed a sharp divide. One official warned, "There is too much hysteria about this thing."[46] Attorney General Biddle proposed that the army and Justice

Department issue a joint press release saying the FBI raids had discovered no evidence of sabotage and "the present military situation does not at this time require removal of American citizens of the Japanese race." McCloy proposed delaying the press release to allow DeWitt ten days to submit his views in writing, and the meeting ended in discord.

Two days later, Gullion met with Stimson and urged the removal of Japanese Americans from San Diego, Los Angeles, San Francisco and Puget Sound, where important military installations and factories were located. He said the removal also had to go beyond the arrest of enemy aliens because second-generation Japanese Americans were considered more dangerous than the non-citizen first-generation Japanese.[47] Stimson acknowledged his own concerns about violations of civil liberties when he wrote later that day in his diary, "We cannot discriminate among our citizens on the ground of racial origin."[48]

Biddle made another attempt to block DeWitt's evacuation plan on February 9, sending Stimson a letter saying, "No reasons were given for this mass evacuation." If there is to be a mass evacuation, it "would have to be done on the military necessity in the particular area. Such action, therefore, should in my opinion be taken by the War Department and not by the Department of Justice."[49] Biddle indicated the Justice Department saw no reason for the mass evacuation. The issue weighed on Stimson.

IN THE PHILIPPINES, General MacArthur led a grim retreat of the US Army and allied Filipino forces from a massive Japanese invasion force on the Bataan Peninsula. As army forces ran out of food, Stimson turned for help to Patrick Hurley, a Republican friend who had been secretary of war under President Hoover. Hurley, who had offered Stimson his assistance in 1941, was swiftly made a general, appointed ambassador to New Zealand and sent to the South Pacific to expedite supplies to army forces.[50]

Filipino president Manuel Quezon, on Corregidor, asked FDR to grant immediate independence to the Philippines so its armed forces could surrender to the Japanese, who had promised independence to the Filipinos. On February 8, MacArthur cabled General Marshall seeking guidance on how to respond to Quezon and pointing out that US forces, who had no air and naval defenses, were running low on water. "The troops have sustained practically 50% casualties from their original strength," he reported. The bleak prospects warranted at least some consideration of a withdrawal of American troops from the Philippines, but MacArthur did not suggest it. The general said stoically, "You must be prepared at any time to figure on the complete destruction of this command."[51]

Stimson and Marshall went to the White House the next day to discuss the Philippines with FDR. Stimson was a friend of Quezon, and as a former governor-general he had a long history with the Philippines, including his support for the US plan to grant it independence in 1946.[52] The Japanese attack stirred in him a belief that America must not withdraw its troops but be prepared for a profound sacrifice to protect the island nation. In FDR's study, Marshall asked Stimson to present their views. "The president listened very intently and, when I got through, he said he agreed with us."[53]

Stimson and Marshall drafted the cables for the president. FDR's cable to Quezon said, "So long as the flag of the United States flies on Filipino soil . . . it will be defended by our men to the death. Whatever happens to the present American garrison we shall not relax our efforts until the forces which we are now marshalling outside the Philippine Islands return to the Philippines and drive the last remnant of the invaders from your soil."[54]

In the cable to MacArthur, FDR urged him to let the Filipino troops surrender but ordered the general to fight on. "American forces will continue to keep our flag flying in the Philippines so long as there remains any possibility of resistance," FDR said. The cable underscored the importance of MacArthur's stand:

```
THERE HAS BEEN GRADUALLY WELDED INTO A COMMON
FRONT A GLOBE-ENCIRCLING OPPOSITION TO THE
PREDATORY POWERS THAT ARE SEEKING THE DESTRUCTION
OF INDIVIDUAL LIBERTY AND FREEDOM OF GOVERNMENT.
WE CANNOT AFFORD TO HAVE THIS LINE BROKEN IN ANY
PARTICULAR THEATER. AS THE MOST POWERFUL MEMBER OF
THIS COALITION WE CANNOT DISPLAY WEAKNESS IN FACT
OR IN SPIRIT ANYWHERE. IT IS MANDATORY THAT THERE
```

BE ESTABLISHED ONCE AND FOR ALL IN THE MINDS OF
ALL PEOPLES COMPLETE EVIDENCE THAT THE AMERICAN
DETERMINATION AND INDOMITABLE WILL TO WIN CARRIES
ON DOWN TO THE LAST UNIT.

Stimson later wrote that his work that day, with its demand of sacrifice by MacArthur's forces, consigned "a brave garrison to a fight to the finish."

With MacArthur's troops facing annihilation at the hands of the Japanese in the Philippines, Stimson met with McCloy on February 10 to discuss General DeWitt's plans to evacuate Japanese Americans from the West Coast. Later, Stimson noted in his diary that taking action against Japanese Americans who were US citizens "will make a tremendous hole in our constitutional system."[55] He added, "It is a terrific problem, particularly as I think it is quite within the bounds of possibility that if the Japanese should get naval dominance in the Pacific they would try an invasion of this country; and, if they did, we would have a tough job meeting them. The people of the United States have made a terrible mistake in underestimating the Japanese."

Stimson faced the stark reality of DeWitt's plan the next day: "This is a stiff proposition. General DeWitt is asking for some very drastic steps, to wit: the moving and relocating of some 120,000 people including citizens of Japanese descent." He called President Roosevelt to discuss the matter "and fortunately found that he was very vigorous about it and told me to go ahead on the line that I myself thought the best."[56] That brief remark is the only known comment on this key conversation between Stimson and FDR; there is no evidence they discussed the civil liberties of Japanese Americans. FDR had repeatedly raised fears of sabotage and espionage, and now he wanted Stimson to be the one to decide what was "the best." The two men—stunned by the Pearl Harbor attack, facing defeat in the Philippines by the powerful Japanese war machine and eager to prevent a Japanese attack on the US mainland— were poised to take a sweeping action against Japanese Americans.

Three days later, General DeWitt sent a memo to Stimson outlining his proposed Japanese evacuation and internment plan. The memo focused heavily on race and bore the overtones of genetic racial theories widely held in the first half of the twentieth century. "The Japanese race is an enemy race and while many second and third generation Japanese born on United States soil, possessed of American citizenship, have become 'Americanized,' the racial strains are undiluted," DeWitt wrote.[57] He called for excluding all Japanese and alien enemies from "military areas," and the mandatory placement of non-citizen Japanese in "internment facilities."[58]

The concern over Japan's vast military threat in the Pacific rose on February 15, when approximately a hundred thousand British soldiers surrendered in Singapore.[59] In the United States, public clamor for removal of Japanese Americans from the West Coast reached a crescendo.[60] In Congress, a bipartisan group of legislators from the West Coast on February 18 urged mass removal and detention of Japanese Americans. Democratic representative John Costello of Los Angeles said, "We have to move before any sabotage takes place, and, if you do not move in advance of that sabotage, Pearl Harbor will be insignificant compared to what could happen on the Pacific Coast."[61]

On that same day, Stimson met with McCloy, Gullion, Biddle and others to review a proposed executive order drafted by Biddle for the president to sign, authorizing the evacuation and internment plan. He suggested some changes to the order and then approved it.[62] Stimson wrote in his diary, "I have no illusions as to the magnitude of the task that lies before us and the wails which will go up in relation to some of the actions which will be taken under it."

FDR signed Executive Order 9066 the next day, authorizing Stimson, as Secretary of War, to designate "military areas . . . from which any or all persons may be excluded" to prevent sabotage and espionage. The order made no mention of Japanese Americans or any ethnic group, but authorized Stimson to use his "discretion" to determine who could be excluded from the military areas. It also empowered the secretary of war to use federal troops and agencies to provide transportation, food and shelter as necessary to carry out the order.[63] On February 21, Stimson signed an order commanding DeWitt to carry out the removal of Americans of Japanese ancestry and German aliens from designated military zones.[64]

Amid the wave of false alarms came another real attack. On February 23, a Japanese submarine surfaced in San Pedro Harbor, Los Angeles, and fired a series of shells into an oil refinery located on the shore.

The incident caused minimal damage, but it was the first attack by a foreign armed force on the continental US since the War of 1812—and seized national attention.[65]

Before he could issue evacuation orders, DeWitt concluded that he needed a new law making it a misdemeanor crime to resist them. On March 9, Stimson sent a letter to Congress urging prompt passage of draft legislation.[66] A bill won swift passage by the House and Senate on March 19 with no dissent and no recorded vote; two days later FDR signed it into law.[67] FDR also signed an executive order creating the War Relocation Authority to manage the mass evacuation, and construction began immediately on camps to hold internees.[68] On March 24, DeWitt issued the first evacuation order, which required all Japanese Americans living near Bremerton Naval Yard to leave their homes and report to an internment facility. More than a hundred other evacuation orders followed in the ensuing months.

As the internment machinery worked, complaints arose that the army would also seize vast numbers of German and Italian Americans across the country. Attorney General Biddle once again raised objections, but Stimson assured him in a cabinet meeting on May 15 that there would be no mass evacuations of Germans and Italians, which might sweep up very large numbers of people. Stimson told FDR that no evacuations could take place without his approval, and that he would not authorize them without telling the president. "The president professed himself as perfectly satisfied with the situation," he wrote in his diary.[69]

FDR and Stimson continued working together on the internment of Japanese Americans, and by October 1942 there were nearly one hundred and twelve thousand people of Japanese origin under guard in a chain of ten American concentration camps.[70] The internment caused Japanese Americans, many of whom were very patriotic, profound economic loss and personal pain. Some filed lawsuits claiming that their constitutional rights were violated. Roosevelt and Stimson, driven by fear and concerns about national security, created a system that—like America's fascist enemies—used race to divide the country. For the bipartisan alliance, founded on a shared belief in the need to unite the country to fight for democracy and freedom, the internment of Japanese Americans would stand as an infamous injustice and failure.

Women Unite for the War Effort

Five days after the attack on Pearl Harbor, representative Edith Nourse Rogers, a Massachusetts Republican, called for passage of her bill to permit women to volunteer to perform noncombat duty for the army.[1] She had filed the bill in May 1941, but it had stalled as Congress awaited a report from the War Department. On December 12, 1941, Rogers went to the floor of the House to argue that it was time for women—historically excluded from military service—to join the war effort: "We—the women—want to do our part."[2]

The Republican's bill would create the Women's Army Auxiliary Corps (WAAC), an agency separate from—yet controlled by—the army. WAAC volunteers would be paid the same wage as men in the army—$21 per month. The army and navy already had large numbers of women serving as nurses, but Rogers's bill would open the door for women to perform military-related activities. Secretary of War Stimson urged Congress to pass Rogers's proposal, saying that women could serve in a broad array of noncombat positions. "There are a great many types of duty . . . for which women are better fitted than men, and the employment of women on such duty would increase efficiency and release men for more intensive combat service."[3] The jobs ranged from aircraft warning system operators to clerks, bakers and telephone operators, said Stimson, who would write rules governing the WAAC and appoint its director. Army chief of staff General George Marshall also vigorously supported creation of the new women's corps.[4] Stimson's support was critical, but with Democrats firmly in control of the House, Rogers's bill still required bipartisan support to pass.

Rogers's office in Washington was soon swamped with letters from thousands of women across the country seeking to join the WAAC. One said she wanted to be the first to volunteer since her brother had been killed on the USS *Arizona* at Pearl Harbor. "I am willing to go anywhere in or out of the United States," she wrote. A schoolteacher from Muncie, Indiana, wrote, "The moment I heard of the attack on our country on Dec. 7, I thought to myself that I would like to join the United States Army and do my part, if possible, to preserve our democracy." A housewife from Shrewsbury, Massachusetts, wrote, "I am 58 and can drive and work as good, if not better, than some men."[5] In New York, the state Federation of Republican Women's Clubs called for the bill's passage. Despite this outpouring of support, Rogers's bill became bogged down in Congress.

Rogers had volunteered for the Red Cross during World War I, when she worked with the British Women's Army Auxiliary Corps and was impressed by the contribution of British women to the war effort. In 1926, her husband, a member of Congress, died and she was appointed to his seat and then went on to win reelection repeatedly. The first woman elected to Congress from New England, she ultimately served thirty-five years in the House. As a Republican, Rogers was a sharp critic of President Roosevelt's New Deal, but she supported his foreign policy. She vigorously condemned Hitler's persecution of Jews and in 1938 joined with a Democratic ally of FDR's, Senator Robert Wagner of New York, in sponsoring a bill to let twenty thousand Jewish refugee children enter the country outside the government's restrictive quota system.[6] But FDR, apparently concerned about an anti-immigrant and anti-Semitic backlash in America, had refused to support the refugee bill, which failed to pass.

In 1942, half of the ten women in Congress were Republicans. Among them was Representative Jeannette Rankin of Montana, who in 1916 became the first woman ever elected to Congress, where she was a strong proponent of the constitutional amendment giving women the right to vote. A pacifist, she had opposed the draft in 1940 and the declarations of war shortly after Pearl Harbor. Now, however, she supported Rogers's bill to create the WAAC.

Rogers worked across the aisle, too, and her idea won support from Eleanor Roosevelt. In fact, the First Lady went further than Rogers, predicting in a February 15 radio broadcast that women would be registered for the draft: "I feel quite certain that if the war lasts long enough, we will register women and we will use them in many ways as England has done," she said.[7]

Many Americans had recently learned of the work of English women—including Prime Minister Churchill's daughter Mary and the king's daughter, the young Princess Elizabeth—in the British Women's Army Auxiliary Corps service. In Washington, however, Rogers's bill ran into political headwinds from men in both parties. Some found the bill, which would create a WAAC force of up to one hundred and fifty thousand women, to be an unacceptable change in the roles of women in society. When the bill came up for a vote on March 17, 1942, Representative Clare Hoffman, a Michigan Republican, spoke in opposition:

> Take the women into the armed service, in any appreciable number, who then will maintain the home fires; who will do the cooking, the washing, the mending, the humble, homey tasks to which every woman has devoted herself; who will rear and nurture the children; who will teach them patriotism and loyalty; who will make men of them, so that, when their day comes, they too may march away to war? To me this bill seems to strike at and destroy the very foundation—the base—which supports and maintains our fighting men.

Representative Jennings Randolph, a West Virginia Democrat, warned that "to put the women of the country into a conflict of this kind is absolutely against my idea of the American way of doing business." Representative Mary Norton, a New Jersey Democrat, however, urged passage of the bill. "I know the womanhood of America will respond to the call and that we shall have reason to feel proud of their service," she said on the House floor.[8] Ultimately, many Democrats crossed the aisle to support the Republican bill and it passed the House in a strong bipartisan vote of 249–86.[9]

Rogers's proposal to create a new force of women in the army drew the attention of Walter White, executive secretary of the NAACP, and he privately urged Rogers to amend her bill to include a provision banning racial discrimination in the WAAC.[10]

As Congress wrestled with the bill, Rogers met with Stimson at his office and voiced support for the woman that Stimson wanted to become director of WAAC—Oveta Culp Hobby, a War Department spokeswoman whose husband was a former Democratic governor of Texas. "I was relieved to find that she was in favor of Mrs. Hobby," Stimson noted in his diary.[11] Civil rights activists, however, voiced concerns that Hobby would impose segregation on the new WAAC organization. Given that Stimson and the army opposed desegregating troops, segregation was likely to be the WAAC's policy, too. Edgar G. Brown, director of the National Negro Council, commented that the woman expected to head WAAC "is known to share 'lily white' traditions and 'Jim Crow' practices of her native state."[12] He also said thousands of Black women had sought to serve in the WAAC but were already being met with rejection, and publicly urged FDR to veto the bill if it did not include an anti-discrimination amendment. The Senate, however, advanced the House bill without any anti-discrimination language.

Once again, the idea of changing women's roles in society drew fire. Senator Francis Maloney, a Connecticut Democrat, was among those opposing the bill. He charged that it "casts a shadow over the sanctity of the home." The bill's sponsor, Senator Warren Austin, a Vermont Republican, dismissed Maloney's arguments and the bill passed by a vote of 38–27 on May 12.[13] Support for the bill was bipartisan, with twenty-four Democratic senators joining fourteen Republicans to vote yes.

With the passed bill headed to the White House, Brown again urged FDR to veto it or send it back to the Senate for inclusion of the anti-discrimination amendment. He also asked Stimson to name a WAAC director "in whom the mothers, daughters and sisters of the 200,000 Negro soldiers now in the United States Army" could have confidence. With a racial dispute simmering over the WAAC even before it was launched, Eleanor Roosevelt, the administration's strongest defender of civil rights, said at a news conference that she did not believe an anti-discrimination amendment was necessary, voicing confidence that the WAAC would not show prejudice against Black women volunteers. FDR signed the bill into law on May 15. The next day, before a crowd of reporters and photographers, Hobby took the oath of office and shook hands with Stimson and Marshall.[14]

Later that month, Mary McLeod Bethune, the civil rights activist and friend of the First Lady, met with Hobby, who announced that among the first 450 women to attend the WAAC training school at Fort Des Moines, Iowa, "40 will be Negro candidates."[15] This mirrored the army's previous plan to enlist African Americans at a ratio of roughly 9 percent of all draftees, their approximate percentage of the US population at the time, while maintaining segregation. Yet Hobby also appeared to take a stand against discrimination, saying, "Every care has been taken . . . to see that equality of opportunity is given every woman, regardless of race or creed." Bethune responded by endorsing the WAAC. She said her organization, the National Council of Negro Women, "reasserts its determination to stand shoulder to shoulder with all other women of the country in bearing our part of the responsibility for winning this war."

Bethune had long fought segregation, but over her decades of experience she had become a realist about how much she could change Jim Crow, the legally enforced system of discrimination that the white majority had imposed in the South and other parts of the country. As a young woman, she had founded a school for Black girls in 1904 in Florida, where Black children had few opportunities for education because of segregation. Now, with the nation at war, she remained committed to ending segregation, which she called "the other half of our battle." She added, "It must not, in any way, lessen our support or participation in our country's victory effort."[16]

THE PASSAGE OF Rogers's bill set the stage for other Republican bills to open the military to women, which won bipartisan support and passed the Democrat-controlled Congress and were signed into law by FDR. Inspired by Rogers's proposal for the WAACs, Secretary of the Navy

Knox in January 1942 recommended creating a women's division of
the Naval Reserve. In Congress, Representative Melvin Maas, a Minnesota Republican, filed a bill to establish a women's force in the US
Naval Reserves, the Women Accepted for Volunteer Emergency Service
(WAVES). Maas had been a Marine Corps aviator during World War I
and served in the Marine Corps Reserve. Now the ranking Republican
on the House Naval Affairs Committee, Maas felt it was vital for the war
effort to have women serve in the naval reserve, though his bill limited
their service to shore duty in the United States. Explaining his bill in the
House on April 16, 1942, he said decoding communications was a field
in which women could replace as many as a thousand male officers,
permitting them to go to sea. "There are many other types of work that
can be done as well by women as by men and in many cases better: For
instance, operation of certain devices for airplane detection."[17]

Maas was soon called to active duty for the marines, so when the
bill came to the House floor on July 21, Rogers and another Republican
woman, Frances Bolton of Ohio, spoke in support of it. An amendment
backed by the navy specified that female officers in the WAVES could
not command men: their authority "may be exercised over women of
the Reserve only."[18] Even with this limitation, a male member of the
House, Democrat Beverly Vincent of Kentucky, stepped forward to
condemn the bill: "Let us not come in here and do something in this
war that we have never done before. Let us not embarrass the Navy. . . .
Let us have enough courage to back up our judgment and not become
the laughingstock of the world."[19] Despite such opposition, both chambers of Congress passed the Republican legislation with bipartisan support, and FDR signed it into law on July 30.[20]

Knox named the president of Wellesley College, Mildred McAfee, to
lead the WAVES. Commissioned as a lieutenant commander, she established a training facility on the campus of Smith College in Northampton, Massachusetts. By September, the program had begun training its
first 120 officers.[21] The WAVES would cut a striking figure in American
naval history: Their trim navy-blue uniforms, with a lighter version in
white for summer, were designed by the fashion house Mainbocher.
The WAVES were soon stationed at naval bases around the country,
where they won praise from commanders. Knox opposed admitting

any Black women into the WAVES, and it would not be until 1944 that Black women could enter the navy reserves.[22] Ultimately, more than eighty-one thousand women were serving in the navy by 1945, and the duties of WAVES included training pilots, testing weapons, performing administrative duties and operating the naval radio communications center in Washington, DC.[23]

In the fall of 1942, another bill creating a women's military force, this one a reserve for the US Coast Guard called the SPARS, sailed through Congress without objection.[24] Its first training facility was also at Smith College in Northampton. Dorothy Stratton, a dean and psychology professor at Perdue University in Indiana, became lieutenant commander of the SPARS, saying in a newspaper interview that "it seems fitting for women to be connected with a unit that has as its main purpose the protection and conservation of life and property."[25]

Women also sought to support the US air forces, at the time part of the army. The forceful leader of the effort was Jacqueline Cochran, a former airplane racer who used her aviation skills with tremendous success to promote her own line of cosmetics products. In 1939, Cochran had written Eleanor Roosevelt urging her to support roles for women pilots in the army. The army dragged its feet as it considered the idea, so in late 1941 Cochran led a group of twenty-five American female pilots who joined a British civilian force, the Air Transport Auxiliary, which flew planes wherever the British military needed them. In fall 1942, General Hap Arnold asked Cochran to return to the United States and establish a training program for women pilots.[26] This led to creation of the Women Airforce Service Pilots (WASP), commanded by Cochran.[27] Another former air racer, Nancy H. Love, commanded the Women's Auxiliary Ferrying Squadron (WAFS), which flew military aircraft from factories to bases around the nation. Stimson announced Love's appointment at a news conference on September 10, 1942.[28]

Nearly 1,100 women graduated from the WASP program during the war, and the alums served as training instructors, test pilots and ferrying pilots. They flew a broad array of air force planes—from fighters to big bombers like the B-17 and the B-29 Superfortress. Though the WASPs were not in active combat, their service could be perilous and thirty-eight WASP pilots died in the line of duty during the war.[29] Cochran defended the capabilities of women aviators with flair. "Menstrual cycles didn't upset anyone's cycle," she wrote snappily in her autobiography. "Women had as much endurance, were no more subject to fatigue, flew as regularly and for as many hours as the men."

Women also went to work for the Office of Strategic Services. Owing chiefly to OSS director William Donovan's tendency to fill staff positions through his network of Republican friends and business associates, the OSS took on a Republican elite cast. A joke circulated that the agency's acronym stood for "Oh So Social." Among the women who joined the OSS was Patricia Cutler Fowler, whose husband had died in the battle of Guadalcanal in 1942. From a prominent Boston Republican family, one of her uncles, Robert Cutler, was an attorney brought into the War Department as part of Stimson's Republican team. During her two years in the OSS, Fowler was stationed in Madrid, Spain, gathering information on people suspected of pro-Nazi activities.[30] Another OSS spy was the socialite heiress Gertrude Legendre, whose father was a New York industrialist and Republican member of Congress. Gertie, as she was called, had traveled the world hunting big game before joining the OSS at a time when her husband joined the navy. She was captured inside Germany in September 1944, making her the first US woman captured by the Nazis on the western front.[31] Six months later, she escaped to freedom in Switzerland.

THE WAR BROUGHT vast changes in women's roles in society around the world. In the Soviet Union and other countries, women joined the army and fought in combat. The British equivalent of the WAVES, the WRENS, went to sea on naval vessels, a fact highlighted by stories in the press. In America, combat was still deemed inappropriate for women, but with millions of men away at war women took industrial jobs that previously were not open to them. A federal agency, the War Manpower Commission, sought to place women in industrial positions. Six months after Pearl Harbor, eighty thousand women were working in war industries, and by the end of 1942 that number soared to three million.[32] By the fall of 1943, 36.5 percent of the aviation industry's employees were women, and their massive contribution to production for the war effort was widely recognized. After FDR toured war production plants in late 1942, he told the nation in a Fireside Chat, "I was impressed by the large proportion of women employed—doing skilled manual labor running machines."[33] This new era for working women was captured in a popular song, "Rosie the Riveter." A publicity campaign supporting women in the workforce depicted the fictional Rosie as a woman in work clothes with a bright red polka-dot kerchief on her head, proudly displaying her biceps, under the slogan "We Can Do It!"[34] Images of Rosie, as well as photos of actual working women, quickly spread across popular media.

Congress, however, balked at further steps toward equality. A constitutional amendment guaranteeing women equal rights to men failed to advance, just as it had repeatedly since the 1920s. In 1944, Representative Winifred Stanley, a New York Republican, proposed a narrower bill that would guarantee women pay equal to men's if they were doing the same work under similar conditions. It, too, failed to pass, though the "equal pay" provision would become federal law two decades later.

While women in the workforce drew attention, the WAAC was perhaps the most widely recognized place for women in the armed forces. In July 1942, women from across the country arrived at Fort Des Moines, Iowa, to begin training for their service in the WAAC. When the first 436 graduates completed their training program in late August, Rogers was there to wish them well during a ceremony in which they appeared in uniform. By this time, the public had come to know the women in the corps simply as "WAACs," a name Rogers used, too. "The WAACs more than live up to my expectations," she said. "They all expressed their eagerness to serve their country."[35] The issue of segregation, however, haunted the fledgling agency, and the NAACP received complaints that the training facility was segregated. These prompted Bethune, who also was a vice president of the NAACP, to issue a statement in November 1942 clarifying her objection to the practice: "I have never at any time approved segregation at Fort Des Moines."[36]

After completing their training, WAACs were deployed around the country and overseas in support of the US Army. The corps, which adopted the head of the Greek warrior goddess Pallas Athena as its insignia, operated closely with the army, and its women performed a broad array of roles, from bakers and mechanics to supporting the

secret Manhattan Project building atomic weapons.[37] WAACS and
WAVES worked as cryptologists in highly secret facilities in Washington, deciphering German and Japanese communications to give American strategists an edge.[38] One codebreaker, Elizabeth Smith Friedman,
a member of the elite Coast Guard Cryptanalytic Unit, helped identify
Nazi spies in Brazil and crack multiple versions of the Nazi code known
as "Enigma."[39]

In late 1942, five WAACs were aboard a ship off the coast of Algeria in the middle of the night with soldiers and British and American
nurses when a Nazi torpedo struck the vessel. Many were able to abandon ship on lifeboats, but WAACs Alene Drezmal and Louise Anderson were unable to find room in a lifeboat and stayed on board the
stricken vessel with the remaining soldiers. "We were served tea and
whisky and biscuits. It must have been a strange scene—the ship going down and we cracking jokes and making silly remarks. I think I've
never laughed so much in my life," Drezmal said. Eventually, a destroyer
towed the damaged ship into port on the afternoon of December 21
and the WAACs disembarked before it began to burn.[40] A firsthand
account by Drezmal of the U-boat attack was published in newspapers
across the country, shining a spotlight on the WAAC commitment to
the war effort.

The heroic image of the WAACs, however, would soon be tar-
nished. The *New York Daily News* published a story on June 7, 1943,
asserting that "rumors of sex promiscuity" were circulating about the
women's divisions of the military. Two days later, the newspaper published a story asserting that the War Department and the WAAC had
agreed to distribute contraceptives and "prophylactic equipment" to the
WAACs.[41] The news threatened to disrupt the plan by two members
of Congress, Republican Edith Rogers and Democrat Mary Norton, to
pass a bill ending the WAAC's status as an independent auxiliary and
making it part of the army.

Stimson, Hobby and the First Lady rushed to defend the WAACs
from the attacks on their sexuality and morals. The secretary of war said
at a news conference June 10 that the contraceptives report was "absolutely and completely false." He condemned the press for spreading
"sinister rumors aimed at destroying the reputation of the WAAC."[42] He

said that since June 1942 "approximately 65,000 fine, patriotic women" had joined the corps, releasing men for combat against the enemy. "Anything which would interfere with their recruiting or destroy the reputation of this corps and, by so doing, interfere with increase in the combat strength of our Army, would be of value to that enemy." Rogers depicted the slur against the WAACs as a Nazi plot. "Loose talk concerning our women in the armed services cannot be less than Nazi-inspired," she said. Religious groups that visited the WAAC training facility in Iowa also defended the corps. In her My Day column in newspapers across the country, Eleanor Roosevelt charged that the rumors against the WAACS were intended to aid the enemy. "I have inquired of the authorities and find that there is probably no group of young women anywhere with as high a standard for good behavior."[43]

With the vigorous defense of the WAACs, the bill backed by Rogers and Norton passed Congress with strong bipartisan support, and FDR signed it on July 2.[44] The new law made the women's force part of the army, and so the acronym lost an A for auxiliary and became simply the Women's Army Corps (WAC). Hobby was awarded the rank of a colonel in the army, and WAC officers were given authority over any male soldiers put under their command. Another bill, which would permit WAVES to serve outside the United States, would eventually pass the following year with bipartisan support. As Republicans and Democrats in Washington collaborated, women took greater responsibilities in the American military, along the way challenging attitudes about women's roles in the workplace and in society.

The Double V: Black America's Struggle

As the US war effort expanded, Black Americans found themselves embroiled in a battle on two fronts: fighting against German and Japanese forces overseas—and for racial equality at home. One of the nation's most prominent Black newspapers, *The Pittsburgh Courier,* highlighted this twofold conflict in February 1942 when it launched its "Double V" campaign—an appeal for unity in support of triumph over both fascism and racial oppression.

Unveiling the campaign two months after the Japanese attack upon Pearl Harbor, *The Courier* told its readers: "We, as colored Americans, are determined to protect our country, our form of government and the freedom which we cherish for ourselves and for the rest of the world, therefore we have adopted the Double 'V' war cry—victory over our enemies at home and victory over our enemies on the battlefields abroad."[1] *The Courier* received hundreds of supportive telegrams after unveiling the campaign, and before long several other Black papers joined the effort and scores of local clubs were forming Double V chapters across the country.[2] The Double V even had its own theme song, "Yankee Doodle Tan," which included the lyrics, "America, you can depend on ev'ry native son. . . . To stand by you until the end, his color doesn't run."[3]

The Double V bolstered calls from A. Philip Randolph, the NAACP's Walter White and many other civil rights activists to remove all discriminatory barriers to full Black participation in American society. In the throes of World War II, Black people were vigorously demanding that the nation finally live up to the Constitution's promise of equal justice for all. The Double V called for victory over the horrific reality of American racism. In January 1942, a Black man accused of attacking a white woman in Sikeston, Missouri, was taken from a jail by a white mob. He was then dragged behind an automobile through the Black section of town, and his body was doused with gasoline and set on fire in front of a crowd of about three hundred white people.[4] An editorial in *The New York Times* warned the hideous racial attack would become fodder for Nazi propagandists: "Lynchings are their prize exhibit in proof of the alleged hypocrisy of the free societies."[5]

Centuries of slavery, racism and segregation cast a shadow over an American war effort proclaimed in the name of democracy and freedom. "We are suffering from the persistent legacy of the original crime of slavery," Stimson lamented in his diary that month, "and the section of the country, the South, which foisted that crime upon us is the part of the country which now protests most loudly against being subject to any of the risks which have followed the wrongdoings of their ancestors. I am insisting, however, that we shall create colored divisions and use them."[6] To Secretary of War Stimson's mind, the formation of segregated army units—condemned by civil rights activists as a half-measure—would be a significant blow against the evils of racism and the legacy of slavery. Yet even efforts to develop segregated divisions were posing difficulties in the South, where local officials threatened to prevent Black units from being based in their jurisdictions. "Texas particularly has protested against the stationing of colored troops in that state," he wrote.

Revealing his own prejudices about Black officers, Stimson continued, "I am also insisting that we shall give special attention to the training of colored officers. I am very skeptical about the possible efficiency of such officers but, as it has been determined that we shall have them, I propose that we shall educate them to the highest possible standards and make the best we can of them. Thus far the Army has been slow in taking them into training camps. I am insisting that be remedied. I am also insisting upon the formation of one or two additional squadrons of colored air forces and I am planning to take up with the president the misbehavior of his pet arm—the Navy—which has been acting like a spoiled child in the matter."

While Stimson sought to expand Black participation in the army, he found himself on the defensive over his refusal to desegregate the armed forces. He sought to justify himself to an Office of War Information official a week later, saying, "I had been brought up in an abolitionist family; my father fought in the Civil War, and all my instincts were in favor of justice to the Negro. But I pointed out how this crime of our forefathers had produced a problem which was almost impossible of solution in this country and that I myself could see no theoretical or logical solution for it at war times like these." Like many Americans of his era, Stimson held seemingly contradictory and troubled views on race: he decried the effects of slavery, sounding a note of sympathy for Black Americans, but he also expressed racial prejudice against Black soldiers even though he had limited experience with them. Only six months after he had supported Executive Order 8802 and helped create the Fair Employment Practice Committee, he noted in his diary the "incompetency of colored troops except under white officers." He added, in words that evoked the views of segregationists, "What these foolish leaders of the colored race were seeking is at the bottom social equality, and I pointed out the basic impossibility of social equality because of the impossibility of race mixture by marriage."

AT FIRST, THE navy refused to conscript any Black citizens through the draft, prompting criticism from Stimson.[7] There is little evidence that President Roosevelt said much to Secretary of the Navy Knox on the subject. However, another of his Republican allies, Wendell Willkie, made a public attack on the navy's reticence shortly after he appeared in Congress to call for passage of the Lend-Lease bill. Speaking at a conference in New York on March 19, 1942, he related the stirring story of the heroism of a then-unidentified Black messman during the Pearl Harbor attack.

Early on Sunday, December 7, 1941, twenty-one-year-old Doris Miller had been working belowdecks when his battleship, the USS *West Virginia,* was struck by Japanese torpedoes. As shrapnel flew amid the air attack, he rushed onto an upper deck and carried wounded sailors to safety with a white lieutenant. He was then sent to the bridge to administer aid to the ship's severely injured captain, but it was too late—the captain died of his wounds. Miller immediately went to a .50-caliber antiaircraft gun and, despite never having been trained to use one, began firing at Japanese planes as they screamed by overhead. "I guess I fired her for about fifteen minutes," he said later. "I think I got one of those Jap planes. They were diving pretty close to us."[8] He fired the gun until he was out of ammunition, and then helped more injured men off the ship before it sank to the bottom of Pearl Harbor.

Willkie denounced the fact that the still-unnamed hero was unable to enlist in the navy in any classification other than as a messman in food preparation as a travesty, and called for correction of this "injustice which makes a mockery of all our fine words."[9] He asked the crowd, "Don't you think that as American citizens we should insist that our government and Navy Department eliminate the bar that prohibits any American citizen from serving his country?"[10]

Accounts of Doris Miller's actions reached the NAACP soon after the attack, and in late December 1941 the organization urged Knox to recognize his bravery with a medal. Knox wrote Miller a letter commending his "extraordinary courage," but he later insisted a medal was not merited. The New York Public Library included the "unnamed Negro messman" in its "Honor Roll of Race Relations" the following March, and a week later released his name to the public. Supporters from many quarters demanded Miller receive some recognition for his heroism. In Congress, a bill was filed to award him the Congressional Medal of Honor; it drew support from Senate majority leader Alben Barkley, but it was voted down in early May.[11]

The NAACP urged Knox to permit Black citizens to enlist as sailors as a tribute to Miller, arguing that ending the ban "not only would reward a hero, but would serve dramatic notice that this country is in fact a democracy engaged in an all-out war against anti-democratic forces."[12]

Knox, who had backed Willkie's presidential nomination in 1940, was stung by the barbs the Republican leader flung at him. "I think Wendell

Willkie's attacks on me were perfectly unjustified and unwarranted," he wrote in a letter to Paul Mowrer, editor of Knox's *Chicago Daily News,* who had been in touch with Willkie and offered to bring the two men together.[13] "It is simply impossible in the midst of a war to mix the races on the same ship, and if he had thought on the subject for half a minute, he would have known it. . . . But, despite all this, I am ready to swallow my pride, and I have said, if Willkie shows the slightest disposition to come in and talk things over with me, I will be glad to . . . start afresh." There is no sign the two men met.

Knox finally made a concession to the pressure from Willkie, Stimson, the NAACP and others. On April 7, 1942, he announced that Black men would be permitted to enlist as sailors in the navy and in the naval reserve and the coast guard, and they would have the same opportunities as white sailors to win promotion as noncommissioned officers. However, he restricted the roles for Black sailors, ensuring none would be on vessels with white sailors: they would be assigned to "maritime activities around shore establishments, in navy yards and in the Navy's new construction crews."[14] Willkie nonetheless hailed the decision, saying, "I am glad that Negroes are at last to be given the privilege of fighting for democracy on sea as well as on land."

FDR eventually stepped in to overrule Knox regarding a medal for Miller. On May 11, 1942, the president awarded Miller the navy's highest honor, the Navy Cross, for "distinguished devotion to duty, extraordinary courage and disregard for his personal safety."[15] The Black press lauded the decision; *The Chicago Defender* said, "This is indeed encouraging and will sink deep into the hearts of our people. Let's hear three cheers for Franklin D. Roosevelt."[16]

By late spring 1942, Black soldiers were taking part in many theaters of the war across the world. It was revealed that a Black soldier—who had passed for white and was serving in a tank battalion—had been the first American killed in the Philippines on December 8, 1941.[17] Black troops, however, were chiefly being assigned to noncombat duties, serving in segregated construction battalions in the Philippines, building a highway to Alaska, and constructing ports and airfields in the South Pacific.[18] Stimson commended the Black 810th Engineer Aviation Battalion, which had cleared dense jungle to build an airfield used in the

Battle of the Coral Sea in May 1942, for its "exceptionally meritorious" service.

THE ACHIEVEMENTS OF Black soldiers contrasted sharply with racial violence that broke out at military installations across the country. At Fort Dix, New Jersey, gunfire erupted on the night of April 2, 1942, when white military policemen clashed with Black soldiers at a bar near the fort. The gun battle, which lasted for nearly fifteen minutes, left a white military policeman and two Black soldiers dead, and five Black soldiers wounded.[19] A few weeks later, in the heart of a segregated neighborhood in Little Rock, Arkansas, a white city policeman, A.J. Hay, tried to arrest a drunken Black soldier. When another Black soldier, Sergeant Thomas Foster, resisted arrest, he was struck over the head repeatedly with a nightstick. According to news accounts, Hay shot Foster four times as he lay dazed on the ground, killing him.[20] US attorney general Francis Biddle ordered an investigation, but Hay was never charged.

Alarm in the Black community rose in October 1942 when three lynchings took place in one week in Mississippi. In the town of Shubuta, white men dragged two fourteen-year-old boys from a jail on October 12 and hanged them from a railroad bridge. White authorities claimed that the boys, Charlie Lang and Ernest Green, had confessed to the attempted rape of a thirteen-year-old white girl. Five days later, a man named Howard Wash was awaiting sentencing—having been convicted of murdering his white employer—when a mob took him from a jail. Wash was later found hanging from a bridge.[21] Attorney General Biddle demanded an FBI investigation of the three lynchings. *The New York Times* suggested in an editorial that Hitler-style fascism was operating in Mississippi. "So far as anyone knows, Adolf Hitler's agents were not active in the State of Mississippi, but Hitler's work was being done there. . . . As this news goes around the world—and let us be sure it will do so—our cause will suffer. The Nazi propagandists will not add that the majority of the people of Mississippi detest lynching, nor that these murders outrage the great masses of the American people, though these things are true."[22]

On November 2, 1942, Raymond Carr, a Black military policeman at Camp Beauregard, Louisiana, was killed by a white Louisiana state policeman. Carr was investigating a disturbance involving civilians when state troopers intervened and sought to arrest him. When Carr protested that as a military policeman he could not be arrested, state trooper Dalton McCollum shot and killed him. McCollum was suspended from duty for one day.

The NAACP sent Stimson a letter saying that "unless the War Department takes a definite unequivocal position with respect to this and other attacks by white police and civilians on negro soldiers in the South, there will be inevitable repetition and multiplication of attack."[23] Stimson's assistant secretary, John McCloy, investigated Carr's killing with the Department of Justice, and together they concluded it was a "willful murder." Stimson sent a telegram to Louisiana's Democratic governor, Sam Jones, calling upon him to "vigorously institute prosecution of the matter."[24] State authorities in Louisiana, however, said McCollum would not be charged.

Eleanor Roosevelt, concerned about the morale of Black soldiers, met with Stimson in his office on November 20, 1942, about her recent trip to England and urged that entertainers be sent overseas to perform for soldiers, mentioning in particular singer Paul Robeson.[25] A groundbreaking and highly popular Black performer, Robeson had taken strong positions against fascism and racism. It is unclear whether Stimson took any steps in response to his discussion with the First Lady, but in March 1943 Robeson performed for soldiers in a USO concert at an army base in Wyoming.[26]

SUCH EFFORTS WERE insufficient for William Hastie, Stimson's civilian aide, who had urged desegregation in the Army and opposed, unsuccessfully, the creation of segregated flying units at Tuskegee. Hastie's efforts to expand the role of Black soldiers were met with repeated frustrations. The department's refusal to desegregate had led him to the brink of resigning as early as January 1942.[27] Finally, in January 1943, he announced his resignation and issued a statement recounting his clashes with the Army Air Forces over racial discrimination. Hastie said the problems reached a climax when he learned the Army Air Forces had launched a segregated officer candidate school in Missouri without even consulting with his office. "From the beginning, the Air Command did not want Negro personnel. Resistance bred of that attitude has been met ever since."[28]

Hastie did not point an accusatory finger directly at Stimson, but his criticism of the Army Air Forces necessarily impugned the secretary of war. Years later, Hastie said, "Though Mr. Stimson was entirely well-meaning and I have no reason that he was in any way a prejudiced person, I always felt that he was basically uncomprehending as to the realities of the problems of race in the Army and in the American society generally."[29] Following the resignation, Stimson selected Hastie's assistant, Truman Gibson, to be his civilian aide. Gibson, a Black attorney from Chicago, had represented boxer Joe Louis before the war.

Despite continued segregation and recurring racial violence, civil rights leaders steadfastly encouraged Black Americans to support the war effort while working for equality. "We believe that the fight for democracy on the home front is a part of the fight for democracy on the foreign front," A. Philip Randolph told a labor conference on January 28, 1943. "We stand for all-out support of the war by the Negro. This he is giving with his life, blood and treasure. We also stand for a fight not only against Hitler in Europe, but Hitlerism in Washington, DC, the South and Chicago. The strength of the underpinnings of democracy will make for a stronger national unity in America which will give force and power to our armed forces."[30]

ADVOCATES FOR CIVIL rights found a glimmer of hope in the work of the Fair Employment Practice Committee (FEPC) that FDR had established in 1941. The FEPC had begun requiring the desegregation of war industry businesses, and in April 1942, it ordered ten manufacturers with operations in the Chicago area, including General Motors, to cease segregation of their work forces or face repercussions for violating their contracts with the government. The FEPC also ordered the companies to file monthly reports on the number of Black employees they hired in each type of job.[31] The following month, the committee ordered eight firms in New York and New Jersey, including the prominent Fairchild Aviation company, to cease discrimination.[32]

The FEPC set up regional offices in cities including St. Louis, where the US Cartridge Company, a munitions manufacturer, announced in the spring of 1942 that it was hiring Black workers in compliance with FDR's Executive Order 8082. After white employees voiced opposition, US Cartridge fired several hundred Black workers on May 16 of the same year. The St. Louis chapter of a group founded by A. Philip Randolph, the March on Washington Movement (MOWM), met with US Cartridge executives to demand that the fired workers be rehired.[33] On June 20, the MOWM held a protest at the company's front gates, where marchers carried placards saying "Fight the Axis, Don't Fight Us" and "Racial Discrimination Is Sabotage."[34] The company then rehired three hundred of the laid-off employees, and the following month announced it had hired two hundred more Black workers.

The MOWM drew some twenty-five thousand supporters to Madison Square Garden in New York for a rally on June 25, 1942, where civil rights activist Mary McLeod Bethune enthralled the crowd. "A new Negro has arisen in America," she proclaimed, offering a vision of a Black community that combined unstinting patriotism with a vigorous demand for the constitutional rights due all Americans. "You are seeking full freedom, justice, respect and opportunity. You are militant in spirit. You are unwilling to accept less than the Constitution guarantees you as citizens of the world's greatest democracy. You are no longer begging—you are insisting, because you realize that America, the only country you know and the country you love, cannot be preserved nine-tenths free and one-tenth oppressed." The crowd roared.[35]

President Roosevelt sought to solidify his alliance with this energized Black political movement born in the crucible of a world war. On October 12, 1942, he used a Fireside Chat radio broadcast—the powerful tool that brought his words into homes across America—to argue that ending discrimination in employment was necessary for building the national economy. "In some communities, employers dislike to employ women. In others they are reluctant to hire Negroes. In still others, older men are not wanted," he said. "We can no longer afford to indulge such prejudices or practices."[36] Though this was just one part of a speech about the "home front," the president was urging immense changes to America's racial caste system.

White resistance to FDR's desegregation efforts, however, was stiffening.[37] After the FEPC ordered Washington's main bus company in December 1942 to stop refusing to hire Black drivers, Representative John Rankin, a Mississippi Democrat and a rigid segregationist, warned that such orders were "as certain to bring on race conflicts as the night follows the day."[38] Rankin denounced the FEPC for carrying out "illegal" and "unconstitutional" actions across the country. He warned that the committee would "destroy the confidence of the American people in the administration."[39] Even as it fought a global war, the nation was on the brink of intense internal conflicts over the rights and roles of Black people in American society.

PART III

THE BIPARTISAN
ALLIANCE AT WAR

The US Goes on the Offensive

Early 1942 was a grim time for America. Thousands of US soldiers were retreating from Japanese attackers on the Bataan Peninsula in the Philippines. Japanese forces held a vast swath of the Pacific region and Americans feared an invasion of the West Coast. Germany had seized most of Europe and continued bombing Britain regularly. Nazi submarines cruised the US coastline sinking tankers and cargo ships seemingly at will. A single German U-boat prowling off New York Harbor sank eight vessels in a single day, January 28.[1] German subs sank forty-eight ships off the East Coast in January 1942, and the monthly rate of sinkings soared to ninety-six in March as the US Navy struggled to counter the submarine menace.

Amid these attacks, President Roosevelt and his senior military advisers intensified their efforts to plan a strategic offensive against the Nazis. Secretary of War Stimson, Army chief of staff General George Marshall and the head of war planning, General Dwight Eisenhower, concurred that the US military's chief strategic objective must be a massive invasion of the European mainland to defeat Hitler's armies in Germany. US Army strategists believed the best way to defeat Nazi Germany was by direct invasion across the English Channel into France in 1943. The cross-channel plan would enable air power based in England to protect ground and naval forces, and would provide a direct route of attack across France into Germany. The army men believed that

amassing US forces for this major assault directly aimed at Germany—
rather than dispersing them on secondary objectives—was critical to
the success of their overarching strategy of defeating Germany first,
then Japan. Eisenhower, head of the Army War Plans Division, expressed his opinion tersely in January: "We've got to go to Europe and
fight—and we've got to quit wasting resources all over the world—and
still worse—wasting time."[2]

America's British allies, however, opposed this strategy. During his
Christmas 1941 visit, Prime Minister Churchill urged Roosevelt instead
to invade North Africa, where British forces were battling the German
and Italian armies.[3] FDR, aided by his trusted and highly capable assistant Harry Hopkins, debated war strategy secretly with Churchill,
knowing he would have to bring top US military advisers in later. On
January 12, after Churchill returned to the White House from a visit to
Florida, he argued for the idea of sending American forces to invade
North Africa. He proposed a timetable for putting ninety thousand US
troops and ninety thousand British troops into North Africa. Churchill
said the president "set great store on 'Super-Gymnast,'" the code name
for the combined United States–British expedition to North Africa.[4]

That same night, Stimson voiced opposition to the British strategy
while at dinner with Churchill, Ambassador Lord Halifax and other
British and American officials. During the dinner, held at the British
embassy, Churchill called for "immediate action" on Super-Gymnast,
winning vocal support from Secretary of the Navy Knox. Stimson stood
up for the US Army's opposing view. "I had to put in a few words of
caution, pointing out how thoroughly the matter had been studied by
the War Department and some of the difficulties," he recalled in his
diary.[5] Knox's decision to give quick backing to the idea in a discussion
with the British infuriated Stimson: "I was rather disgusted with Knox's
readiness to talk loosely without careful thought."

Among the critics of Super-Gymnast was Army general Joseph Stilwell, who in his diary faulted FDR for yielding too readily to British
demands for assistance. "Besides being a rank amateur in all military
matters, FDR is apt to act on sudden impulses. On top of that, he has
been completely hypnotized by the British, who have sold him a bill of
goods."[6]

While strategy for defeating the Nazis remained in dispute, Stimson quickly developed a plan for blocking Japan's effort to take control of the British colony of Burma (now Myanmar). In mid-January 1942, Stimson and Marshall began discussing how to strengthen Allied forces in Burma, which the Japanese had invaded. Chinese Nationalist leader Chiang Kai-sheks armies had entered the country and sought to defend the "Burma Road," along which supplies traveled to the southwestern Chinese city of Kunming, held by Chiang. Stimson, long a proponent of China as a force for democracy, wanted the US Army to work with Chiang and British forces to stop the Japanese advance.

Stimson invited Stilwell on the evening of January 14 to Woodley, where they strategized at the fireplace in the library. Known as "Vinegar Joe," Stilwell was a gruff officer whose incisive remarks earned him Stimson's respect and support. He spoke Chinese and had fought with the Chinese against Japan from 1937 to 1939. His understanding of China impressed the secretary of war. "In half an hour he gave me a better firsthand view of the valor of the Chinese armies than I had ever received before. Of this valor he had a very high opinion," Stimson wrote.[7] He described Stilwell as "very quick-witted and alert-minded." Stilwell said the success of Stimson's plan to fight the Japanese in Burma depended on whether Chiang would let an American command Chinese troops. "With that permission Stilwell said that the possibilities of the Chinese proposition were unbounded and he was very enthusiastic about it," Stimson wrote. "I went to bed with a rather relieved feeling that I had discovered a man who will be very useful to us in the problems that are coming."

Stimson promptly named Stilwell commander of the American and Chinese armies in Burma, and as chief of staff of Chiang's Allied headquarters. Though US Army chief of staff Marshall was responsible for the appointments of virtually all top army commanders during the war, he later said without complaint that it was Stimson who appointed Stilwell.[8] Chiang's representative in Washington, his brother-in-law T.V. Soong, agreed on January 21 to Stilwell's appointment. Chiang later opposed Stilwell's command role, but Stimson would remain, as one historian put it, "Stilwell's warmest and steadiest supporter from that day to the end."[9]

Two days later, Stimson met with FDR at the White House and told him of Chiang's consent to giving command to an American chief of staff. He also informed the president "that we had selected General Stilwell for the position." FDR approved the plan a week later and asked Congress to grant a $500 million loan to Chiang's government.[10] Stimson and Knox testified in support of the loan behind closed doors, and Congress swiftly passed the measure. Stilwell went to the White House on February 9 to meet with FDR, who asked him to relay a message to Chiang. "Tell him we are in this thing for keeps, and we intend to keep at it until China gets back all her lost territory."[11] America's strategy for the China-Burma-India theater of war was under way.

As the army continued developing its plan for a cross-channel invasion of Europe, Stimson and Marshall again grew worried that FDR would impulsively embrace ideas that would weaken US forces by dispersing them. On March 24, the two men discussed these tendencies and the need to counter them. "I pointed out that we couldn't delay any longer in trying to bolster up the president from giving away what might be fatal amounts of our munitions and men," Stimson noted in his diary.[12]

The next day, Eisenhower delivered a memorandum to Marshall urging that if the British refused to pursue a major offensive against Germany as soon as one was likely to succeed, the United States should turn away from the Atlantic and go all out against Japan in the Pacific.[13] Marshall and Stimson went to the White House that day to meet with FDR, Hopkins, Knox and Admiral King to discuss strategy in advance of conferring with top British officials. FDR at first appeared to be "going off on the wildest kind of dispersion debauch," Stimson wrote in his diary. The president "toyed a while with the Middle East and the Mediterranean basin," but ultimately "Marshall and I edged the discussion over into the Atlantic and held him there."[14] Marshall presented his plan, which called for a cross-channel invasion by forty-eight divisions in the spring of 1943. It also said an offensive into France could take place as early as September 1942 if Germany's control of France faltered.[15] The president approved the plan as well as a recommendation by Hopkins that it be presented directly to Churchill in London.

Stimson, however, continued to worry that FDR would abandon the army's preferred strategy. "The president's failings as a war leader become evident as we get into the year of crisis. The same qualities which endear him to his own countrymen militate against the firmness of his execution at a time like this," he wrote in his diary two days later. US leaders must "have the courage, even the hardness of heart, to reject appeals for other good purposes," Stimson said.[16] In a letter on March 27, he urged the president to send the plans for the "northern offensive" to Churchill and then pursue the "ruthless rearrangement of shipping allotments and the preparation of landing gear for the ultimate invasion." He concluded, "So long as we remain without our own plan of offensive, our forces will inevitably be dispersed and wasted."

Stimson, once a Republican critic of FDR from outside the administration, was now a tough critic within the administration who readily challenged both the president and Churchill on conduct of the war. He allied himself closely with Marshall and others in the War Department and argued for their views. FDR at times showed signs of irritation with Stimson's tendency to make points forcefully and at length. "I have a fine Secretary of War, but he talks so much when he's here," the president told Joseph Kennedy when the former ambassador visited the White House in April.[17] Yet, as even that frank critique revealed, FDR considered Stimson highly capable.

Stimson often stepped into the breach and acted decisively when difficult or politically sensitive matters arose. For example, after the Pearl Harbor attack, Charles Lindbergh had applied for an appointment in the Army Air Corps. This posed a dilemma. Lindbergh's harsh attacks on FDR had alienated the president and his Republican allies, but millions of Americans still revered the legendary aviator. Comments in the press backed an appointment for Lindbergh. *The New York Times* said in an editorial, "There cannot be the slightest doubt that Mr. Lindbergh's offer should be and will be accepted. It will be accepted not only as a sign of our newfound unity and an effective means of burying the dead past; it will be accepted also because Mr. Lindbergh can be useful to his country. He is a superb air man, and this is primarily and essentially an air war."[18]

Knox also felt the army should find a position for Lindbergh. He wrote FDR on January 1, 1942, urging that Lindbergh be required to start with pilot training because of his lack of military experience. The president forwarded Knox's letter to Stimson, adding a note saying, "I think Frank Knox is right."[19]

Stimson would have none of it. After years of hearing Lindbergh defend Hitler's Germany, he had no use for the former America First spokesman. On January 12—the same day that he'd voiced opposition to Churchill on Super-Gymnast—Stimson met with Lindbergh in his War Department office and abruptly rejected the aviator's request to serve in the army. He told Lindbergh that he could not be placed in command of troops because he "had no faith in the righteousness of our cause."[20] Taken aback, Lindbergh "protested that he was 100 percent American." However, he also acknowledged he had not changed any of the views he had expressed in his speeches. At that, Stimson swiftly reaffirmed his rejection and ended the meeting. The next day, he sent FDR a letter reporting his decision and saying he had told Lindbergh, "I should personally be unwilling to place in command of our troops as a commissioned officer any man who had such a lack of faith in our cause as he had shown in his speeches."[21]

In announcing his meeting with Lindbergh to the public, Stimson diplomatically sidestepped his refusal of any role in the army for the aviator. Instead, he said only that Lindbergh would be working on civilian aviation research "in which the War Department has a vital interest."[22]

MOVING TO RESOLVE the dispute over European war strategy, Marshall presented the army's detailed plan for the cross-channel offensive in 1943 during an April 1 meeting at the White House. The plan called for a combined invasion force of one million soldiers and 5,800 aircraft.[23] FDR approved the plan, and Stimson hailed this decision in his diary as "a memorable one" in the war.[24] FDR also said Hopkins and Marshall should present the plan to Churchill in London. Two days later, the president wrote the prime minister, "What Harry and Geo. Marshall will tell you about has my heart and *mind* in it. Your people and mine demand the establishment of a second front to draw off pressure from the Russians."[25]

After arriving in London on April 8, Marshall and Hopkins met with Churchill at 10 Downing Street, the prime minister's official residence, and began talks with British military leaders including Marshall's counterpart in the British military, General Alan Brooke, chief of the Imperial General Staff. Brooke considered Britain's empire in danger. Singapore and Hong Kong had fallen, British forces were in retreat in Greece and in Burma, and the Germans were gaining ground in North Africa. "I suppose this Empire has never been in such a precarious position throughout its history," Brooke wrote in his diary on April 7.[26] He believed the Americans had not considered the risks of their cross-channel invasion plan, and promptly informed Marshall he had serious concerns.[27]

On the evening of Saturday, April 11, Hopkins and Marshall were invited to Chequers, the official country manor house of the prime minister, where Churchill expounded his reasons for supporting the invasion of North Africa and opposing a cross-channel assault. In keeping with Churchill's habits, the discussion ran into the early hours of the next morning. At 3:00 A.M., a telegram from FDR arrived, causing the prime minister to fly into a rage.

The telegram's subject was India, which was threatened by the movement of the Japanese Navy into the Bay of Bengal. Stimson had spoken with FDR that day about the Japanese forces, which sank twenty-three British ships and bombed two ports of the British colony of Ceylon (now Sri Lanka), threatening an invasion of India.[28]

Indian leaders had vowed not to cooperate with the British in defending against a Japanese invasion unless the British agreed to a plan for Indian independence, which Churchill refused to do. In his telegram, FDR bluntly faulted the British. "The feeling is almost universally held that the deadlock has been caused by the unwillingness of the British Government to concede to the Indians the right of self-government."[29] Furious over FDR's intrusion into British imperial affairs, Churchill erupted in a "string of cuss words" that "lasted for two hours in the middle of the night," Hopkins later told Stimson.[30]

The enraged Churchill drafted an answer to FDR saying the president's proposal would "throw the whole sub-continent of India into utter confusion while the Japanese invader is at its gates."[31] Hopkins, however, convinced Churchill not to send his heated reply.[32] Instead,

Churchill crafted a far more sly and diplomatic cable to the president. The prime minister faced a dilemma: he opposed two major proposals advanced by the president and his commanders—one for the invasion of Europe and the other for India's independence. Rejecting both proposals simultaneously, however, might appear uncooperative. He decided to give a sign that he approved the invasion but stood adamantly opposed to Indian independence. The prime minister began his April 14 cable with a statement that he was "in entire agreement in principle with all you propose" on the invasion, and he then rejected the president's call for Indian independence. "I did not feel I could take the responsibility for the defense of India if everything has again to be thrown into the melting pot at this critical juncture."[33]

Marshall sent Stimson a cable on April 15 happily reporting that in a meeting the prior night Churchill had fully accepted the cross-channel invasion strategy. "Our proposal was formally accepted after oral presentation by me and by Hopkins. . . . PM in impressive pronouncement declared a complete agreement and a deep appreciation of the purpose and time of our visit."[34]

However, two days later Churchill sent another cable to FDR, again signaling support for Marshall's strategy but this time adding a carefully constructed exception. "The campaign of 1943 is straightforward, and we are starting joint plans and preparations at once." He then quickly qualified his support for the plan: "We may, however, feel compelled to act this year." He avoided adding an important point: because of the strength of German defenses in Europe, acting "this year"—in 1942—would likely mean attacking North Africa instead of Europe.[35]

Thus, after leading Marshall and Stimson to think the British were in "complete agreement" with the plan to invade Europe in 1943, Churchill had in fact secretly told FDR that he still might push for a major change in strategy. The prime minister's ploy, later condemned by some as deceptive, set the stage for acrimonious strategy debates in the coming months among the Allies.[36]

WHILE MARSHALL WAS in London, the US forces in the Philippines, surviving on dwindling food supplies, suffered heavy blows.[37] On the morning of April 9, Major General Edward P. King, commander of the combined American and Filipino forces retreating before the Japanese assault on Bataan Peninsula, surrendered with a total of about seventy-six thousand soldiers, including twelve thousand Americans.[38] King had been under orders not to surrender, but at 6:00 A.M. he sent a "flag of truce" to the Japanese commander.

In Washington, Stimson—who two months earlier had joined with FDR in suggesting a fight to the death—decided not to reveal the surrender to the public.[39] At a news conference later that day, he said, "Our troops . . . were outnumbered and worn down by successive attacks as well as lack of food and the diseases peculiar to the tropics. I don't know what happened, but it is evident Bataan has been overthrown. Corregidor is still fighting." The Japanese then began moving about seventy thousand American and Filipino prisoners north roughly sixty miles along the Bataan Peninsula, mostly by foot, to a prison camp. This would come to be known as the "Bataan Death March" because of the inhumane treatment, torture and executions that the Japanese captors perpetrated against their prisoners, of whom an estimated three thousand perished.[40]

The US Navy and the Army Air Corps, meanwhile, were preparing a surprise attack in which bombers launched from an aircraft carrier would strike Japan. Army Air Force lieutenant colonel James Doolittle, an aviation pioneer who had earned a doctorate in aeronautics from the Massachusetts Institute of Technology, had trained five-man crews for a squadron of sixteen B-25 bombers. The pilots were to fly a great distance depleting their fuel, so they planned to land at airfields in China controlled by Chiang's nationalist Chinese forces.[41]

A navy convoy including the aircraft carrier *Hornet* departed San Francisco on April 2 and headed west under command of Admiral William Halsey. On the morning of April 18, when the American ships were still some 620 miles east of Tokyo, Halsey ordered the B-25 bombers to take off from the *Hornet*.[42] The planes flew low, at times as little as two hundred feet above the water, for hundreds of miles to escape detection and finally dropped their bombs on industrial targets in Tokyo and other cities. Most of the crews parachuted from their planes in the dark over China. The Japanese captured eight crew members and eventually executed three of them. Three others died in crashes. Most of the eighty airmen in Doolittle's raid survived with the aid of nationalist Chinese and were sheltered in Chungking.[43]

Doolittle's raid was the first bombing of Japan by the United States in the war. It caused only modest damage to Tokyo factories and killed fewer than a hundred people, yet it undermined Japanese morale while bolstering American spirits. In Washington, FDR was ecstatic over the mission's success. When he returned to Washington a few days later, the press asked him where the planes came from; the president said cryptically with a grin that they had come from "Shangri-La," the fictional realm in a popular novel.[44] Stimson confessed his surprise privately in his diary. "I have always been a little doubtful about this project, which has been a pet project of the president's, because I fear that it will only result in sharp reprisals from the Japanese without doing them very much harm. But I will say that it has had a very good psychological effect on the country both here and abroad."[45] Chiang soon cabled Washington saying that Japanese forces had indeed carried out vicious reprisals against the Chinese, executing thousands of people in places where locals harbored the American aviators.[46]

After Doolittle's raid, Japanese forces intensified their efforts to seize control of northern Burma, where British and Chinese troops had retreated from the Japanese invasion. As pressure from the Japanese intensified, Stilwell proposed moving a hundred thousand Chinese soldiers out of Burma to India, where they could prepare a counterattack. "A telegram came this morning from Stilwell indicating that he was about at the end of his rope," Stimson recorded on April 30. Stimson sent a telegram authorizing him to lead the armies to India.[47] With Stimson, Marshall and FDR backing him, Stilwell's retreat into India swiftly revised the Allied strategy for resisting the Japanese.

In the Philippines, the Japanese intensified their attacks on Corregidor, launching mortar shells from Bataan Peninsula at the island. Japanese commanders celebrated Emperor Hirohito's birthday, April 29, by firing ten thousand shells at Corregidor, where the American and Filipino troops sheltered in a network of tunnels dug deep into the rocky island. On May 2, a Japanese shell penetrated a powder magazine wall, causing an explosion that shook the island, killing fifty-six men and horribly injuring scores of others.[48] Japanese troops landed on the island on the evening of May 5 and began advancing toward the main tunnel entrance. Lieutenant General Jonathan Wainwright concluded further struggle was pointless. He sent a cable early the next morning to General MacArthur, who in March had evacuated his headquarters to Australia: "With broken heart and head bowed in sadness, I report . . . that today I must arrange terms for the surrender of the fortified islands of Manila Bay." This time there was no hiding the capitulation. "General Wainwright has surrendered Corregidor and the other fortified islands in Manila Harbor," MacArthur announced that day.[49] In addition to American soldiers and sailors and Filipino soldiers and civilians, the Japanese took as prisoners fifty-four US Army nurses called the "Angels of Corregidor."[50] With Stimson on vacation at Highhold, FDR revealed the surrender to the American people. He praised Wainwright and his troops for their valor: "In spite of all the handicaps of complete isolation, lack of food and ammunition, you have given the world a shining example of patriotic fortitude and self-sacrifice."[51]

JAPANESE MILITARY LEADERS, meanwhile, planned to target the US Navy's aircraft carriers, which had escaped destruction at Pearl Harbor. Admiral Isoroku Yamamoto, commander in chief of the Imperial Navy, devised a plan to attack Midway Island, a US outpost in the Pacific, and simultaneously lay a trap for the American carriers. Yamamoto hoped the US Navy carriers would rush to defend Midway, enabling Japanese carriers to launch a surprise air attack on them. As a diversionary tactic, Yamamoto ordered Japanese forces to occupy two of the Aleutian Islands in Alaska.

Admiral Chester Nimitz learned of Yamamoto's plans through the cracking of the Imperial Navy's JN-25 code, and he devised a plan to turn the tables on the Japanese admiral. Nimitz ordered US forces to approach Midway and spring their own trap on the Japanese carrier force. Early on June 4, US fighters and dive bombers attacked and destroyed four carriers. It was a severe blow to the Japanese Navy.[52] Japan still had six other carriers, but its limited industrial capacity meant that no new ones would be produced for the Imperial Navy until 1944. Announcing the victory at Midway, Nimitz proclaimed: "Pearl Harbor has now been partially avenged."[53]

The Army Air Force also went on the offensive on the East Coast, equipping a fleet of B-18 bombers with the radar that Stimson had eagerly pursued for hunting Nazi submarines. Stimson flew in a radar-equipped bomber to observe its work and hired a Massachusetts Institute of Technology radar expert to be his assistant and expedite the army's adoption of radar. On July 7, 1942, an army B-18 bombed and sank a Nazi submarine. Nazi submarines soon withdrew from the Atlantic Coast.[54]

By the summer of 1942, FDR, Stimson, Knox and the US Army and Navy had launched significant offensives against the fascist powers, but a dispute was brewing among the Allies over the strategy to defeat the Nazis.

FDR Takes Command

The simmering debate over when and where US forces should invade was poised to erupt again in spring 1942, and this time it threatened to upend President Roosevelt's alliance with his Republican secretary of war. Just one month after Prime Minister Churchill agreed to support an Allied invasion of France in 1943, he began pushing again for an invasion of North Africa in 1942—an operation he now called "Gymnast"—with American troops joining British in the assault. "We must never let ' Gymnast' pass from our minds," he wrote in a cable to Roosevelt on May 28.[1] Secretary of War Stimson and Army chief of staff General George Marshall believed invading France in 1943 was the strategy surest to defeat the Nazis, and they thought the issue had been settled when Marshall met with Churchill in London in April. After learning that Churchill was backing out of his agreement, Stimson became angry. FDR, weighing the arguments of both sides, made no commitment.

With Nazi forces penetrating deep inside the Soviet Union, Joseph Stalin entered the debate over Allied strategy. At Stalin's behest, Soviet foreign minister Vyacheslav Molotov traveled to Washington in late May 1942 to urge the United States to invade Europe. Visiting the White House secretly on May 30, Molotov requested a combined American-British invasion of the European continent in 1942 to pressure Adolf Hitler to move forces away from the Eastern Front. Molotov warned that if FDR delayed the invasion until 1943, Hitler's armies might crush

Soviet resistance, leaving the Nazis in command of all of Europe. "If you postpone your decision, you will have eventually to bear the brunt of the war, and if Hitler becomes master of the continent, next year will unquestionably be tougher than this one," he said.[2]

After the meeting, FDR agreed to release a statement prepared by Molotov saying, "In the course of the conversations full understanding was reached with regard to the urgent tasks of creating a Second Front in Europe in 1942."[3] However, this "Second Front" announcement was not a secret military strategy but a political statement intended to build morale among the Allies and also reassure voters in advance of the elections approaching in November 1942.

The issue of the second front swiftly entered the political debate in America. The implied "First Front," of course, was the battle line between Nazi Germany and the Soviet Union. Representative Carl Vinson, the Democratic chairman of the House Naval Affairs Committee, said, "It is earnestly to be hoped that the United Nations can at the earliest possible date open a second front in Europe. I have been of the opinion for some time that the combined resources of England and the United States should be hurled against the Axis by opening up a second front. It is imperative that this be done immediately."[4] Labor unions, concerned that the Nazis might defeat the Soviets, held rallies calling for a second front.[5] Some isolationists and Republican opponents of FDR, largely muted since Pearl Harbor, raised their voices calling for a focus on defeating Japan. Senator Gerald Nye, the North Dakota Republican, said, "We've got a front or two of our own that we are needing to devote ourselves to most energetically."

Allied military strategy was at the top of the agenda as FDR prepared to receive a visit from Churchill. On June 17, Stimson, Marshall and General Hap Arnold went to the White House to review war strategy with FDR, Secretary of the Navy Knox and Admiral Ernest King. "The president sprung on us a proposition which worried me very much. It looked as if he was going to jump the traces. . . . He wants to take up the case of Gymnast again, thinking he can bring additional pressure to save Russia," Stimson wrote in his diary. Marshall also had prepared a memo opposing Gymnast. The president "met with a rather robust opposition for the Gymnast proposition," Stimson wrote.[6] "I spoke very vigorously against it." FDR pointed to the lack of transportation for troops and the lack of air cover for a 1942 landing in North Africa, and he asked the army to study those problems before Churchill's arrival.

Two days later, Stimson wrote the president, vigorously urging the invasion across the English Channel into France and deriding British strategy in biting terms. "Up to the time when America entered the war, the British Empire had, by force of circumstances, been fighting a series of uphill defensive campaigns with insufficient resources and almost hopeless logistics."[7] He called for pursuing Bolero, the operation to amass troops in England for the cross-channel invasion, saying it offered a direct land route to the "heart" of Germany and also permitted the Allies to provide air cover to the invasion force. He added that amassing troops in England would prevent Hitler from attacking England and also would distract Hitler from his attacks on the Russian front. Marshall wrote his own letter to the president saying Stimson's letter represented his views, and both were dispatched to the president at Hyde Park.

Privately, Stimson worried about Churchill's influence on FDR: "The trouble is Churchill and Roosevelt are too much alike in their strong points and in their weak points. They are both brilliant. They are both penetrating in their thoughts but they lack the steadiness of balance that has got to go along with warfare."[8]

Churchill arrived at Hyde Park on June 19, 1942, armed with his own memo for FDR leaving the agreement reached in April unmentioned and making a strong appeal for Gymnast. Churchill opposed attacking France in late 1942, suggesting that plans for such a move were inadequate and were "certain to lead to disaster."[9] He asked, "Can we afford to stand idle in the Atlantic theater during the whole of 1942?" He suggested an African invasion in 1942 could both gain "positions of advantage" and relieve the pressure on Russia. "It is in this setting and on this background that the French Northwest Africa option should be studied." Left unsaid by the prime minister was the fact that British troops in North Africa were coming under intense pressure from Nazi forces under General Erwin Rommel, known as the Desert Fox.

Churchill and FDR returned to Washington by train overnight, arriving on the morning of June 21. Back in the White House, Churchill took his now-familiar bedroom, this time cooled by an air conditioner, a new device in that era. That morning, a Sunday, the statesmen were together in the president's study when a telegram was delivered reporting that the Germans had captured the city of Tobruk, Libya, and thirty-three thousand British soldiers had surrendered. "This was one of the heaviest blows I can recall during the war," Churchill said later.[10] Rommel had led his Afrika Korps in a staggering defeat of the British, the largest capitulation since Singapore. "What can we do to help?" FDR asked. "Give us as many Sherman tanks as you can spare, and ship them to the Middle East as quickly as possible," Churchill replied. FDR sent for General Marshall, who arrived quickly and began making arrangements to send three hundred Sherman tanks off in ships to British forces at the Suez Canal.

Later that night, Churchill argued for Gymnast in discussions at the White House with FDR, Marshall, Harry Hopkins, chief of the Imperial General Staff Alan Brooke and other senior British commanders.[11] Stimson, though not invited by FDR, loomed over the meeting. FDR had shown Churchill Stimson's letter, with its blunt words about the British Empire's "uphill defensive campaigns" and "hopeless logistics." Accounts of the meeting swiftly reached Stimson. Marshall told him that Churchill "started out with a terrific attack on Bolero," Stimson noted in his diary. "The president, however, stood pretty firm."[12] Hopkins later told Stimson that Marshall made a "very powerful argument for Bolero." Stimson concluded that Churchill urged Gymnast "knowing full well that it was the president's great secret baby and also knowing full well that it was an attack which would have to be carried out by us if it was made at all and entirely by ourselves with all the risks on us." Stimson's acid commentary suggested he feared that Churchill had already slyly secured FDR's support for Gymnast.

Despite Stimson's sharp attacks on British strategy, FDR invited him to the White House the next day to meet with Churchill, Hopkins and Knox. FDR began the discussion by saying that the army had resorted to political reasons for opposing Gymnast. Stimson objected to this, pointing to shortages in shipping and troop carriers, and the "impossibility" of providing air cover for a landing in North Africa. Churchill countered that he had been unable to find a responsible officer who thought it wise to attack the continent in 1942, and that it raised the risk of "sending troops to another Dunkirk."[13]

As the debate grew heated, Stimson responded that "we no more wished to send troops to their deaths than he did." He argued it was best to prepare for the cross-channel invasion in 1943 as planned—"and to do it now with might and main." He warned that if the Allies pursued "diversions" from Bolero, the invasion of the European continent would likely not take place in 1943 and "the whole war effort might be endangered." FDR, however, seemed unconcerned about the possibility and raised the idea of deploying American forces from Egypt to Iran.

Stimson seethed about FDR in his diary after the meeting. "He was talking of a most critical situation and in the presence of the head of another government with the frivolity and lack of responsibility of a child." He later added that FDR "was ready not only to give everything that Churchill asked for but . . . was ready to embark on an entirely new American front from Egypt to Iran, a fantastically impossible project."[14]

Stimson was not alone in doubting the wisdom of Churchill's military strategies. Even General Brooke, who supported Gymnast, later recalled, "Winston never had the slightest doubt that he had inherited all the military genius of his great ancestor [the Duke of] Marlborough! His military plans and ideas varied from the most brilliant conceptions at one end to the wildest and most dangerous ideas at the other. To wean him away from these wilder ideas required superhuman efforts and was never entirely successful in so far as he tended to return to these ideas again and again."[15] Brooke had repeatedly opposed Churchill's "mad plans" for invading Nazi-occupied Norway, and yet the prime minister returned to the idea repeatedly and praised it in a May 1942 cable to FDR.[16]

TAKING A BREAK from the tense debate over war planning, Stimson and Marshall accompanied Churchill, Brooke and other top military men on a train trip to South Carolina to observe American troops in training for the invasion of Europe. They visited Stimson's former artillery regiment, the 305th, and Churchill said "a few very stirring words to the men," Stimson noted.[17] The British delegation flew back to Washington on Stimson's official plane. "Churchill took a good nap in my bunk," Stimson noted. The sturdy American outdoorsman, seventy-four years old, sounded a note of superiority over the sixty-seven-year-old prime minister. "His doctor watched over him the whole day like a hen over a chicken but the little man came along in good shape." Afterwards, Churchill sent a note beginning "My dear Stimson," thanking him and saying he was sorry not to have had time for a longer visit. Stimson replied, saying he enjoyed having the prime minister observe the troops. "My regret is that all of our troops could not have had the great inspiration of your presence and interest in their efforts toward our common cause."[18]

Despite this amicable interlude, Stimson and Marshall remained fiercely opposed to Churchill's military strategy. The dispute flared anew on July 8 when Churchill sent FDR a cable resuming his appeal for a landing in North Africa. "I am sure myself that Gymnast is by far the best chance for effecting relief to the Russian front in 1942. This has all along been in harmony with your ideas. In fact it is your commanding idea," the prime minister cajoled the president. "Here is the true second front of 1942. I have consulted Cabinet and Defense Committee and we all agree. Here is the safest and most fruitful stroke that can be delivered this autumn."[19]

Marshall was infuriated after learning of Churchill's latest push for Gymnast. "I found Marshall very stirred up and emphatic over it," Stimson noted in his diary. "He is very naturally tired of these constant decisions which do not stay made. This is the third time this question will have been brought up by the persistent British and he proposed a showdown which I cordially endorsed. As the British won't go through with what they have agreed to, we will turn our backs on them and take up the war with Japan." Marshall proposed attacking Japan in a memo to the president, which won the support of the navy, as Admiral King was urging Roosevelt to expand the war in the Pacific.[20] "I hope that the threat to the British will work and that Bolero will be revived," Stimson wrote.[21]

FDR, however, flatly rejected the idea of focusing the US war effort on Japan. From Hyde Park, he sent Marshall a cable on July 14 saying that attacking the Japanese would leave the Germans free to concentrate

Henry Stimson, Republican secretary of state to President Herbert Hoover, met with Franklin Roosevelt on January 9, 1933, as FDR—then New York's governor—prepared to take office as president. That day, Stimson convinced the president-elect to continue Stimson's policy against Japan's invasion of Manchuria. The meeting began a relationship that evolved behind the scenes over the following years. (AP Images)

Seven years after their first meeting, Roosevelt and Stimson shook hands on July 10, 1940, after the US Senate confirmed FDR's appointment of Stimson as secretary of war. (Alamy)

FDR's appointment of prominent Republicans Henry Stimson and Frank Knox to cabinet posts in June 1940 prompted outrage among Republicans opposed to FDR's policy toward the war in Europe. A political cartoon in Washington's *Evening Star* newspaper depicted the three men as a small marching band, trying to rouse support for America's broken-down national defense while Republican leaders and isolationists boo them. (Library of Congress)

FDR watched as Supreme Court Justice Felix Frankfurter swore in Frank Knox as secretary of the navy on July 11, 1940. (AP Images)

Republican presidential nominee Wendell Willkie rode in a parade through his hometown of Elwood, Indiana, on August 17, 1940, when he accepted the Republican nomination. At this time, Stimson had already sought the help of Republican editor William Allen White to urge Willkie not to attack key parts of FDR's war policy during the campaign. (AP Images)

Roosevelt and Stimson observed US Army training exercises in upstate New York on the same day that Willkie accepted the Republican nomination. FDR chatted with an army officer while Stimson, seated next to him, and Democratic New York Governor Herbert Lehman looked on. (AP Images) (Another photo from this event is featured on this book's cover.)

To increase the size of the US Army, Stimson led the charge with FDR to win bipartisan passage of the conscription bill in September 1940. On October 29, 1940, Roosevelt looked on from the podium (at left) as Stimson drew the first draft number in a ceremony intended to underscore American unity in support of the army's expansion. (AP Images)

By early 1941, Willkie joined Stimson and Knox in speaking forcefully in support of FDR's proposed Lend-Lease program to send arms to America's allies. A Washington *Evening Star* cartoon portrayed the three Republicans as doing more than Democrats to defend the White House. In the cartoon, FDR calls out, "Let me know, boys, when the time has come for the Democrats to get into action." (Library of Congress)

Prominent Republican attorney William J. Donovan (left) visited the White House with his friend and political ally Frank Knox on June 18, 1941, to confer with President Roosevelt. Donovan won FDR's support to lead a new intelligence unit; he later became director of its successor agency, the Office of Strategic Services. (Getty Images)

Labor and civil rights leader A. Philip Randolph (left), First Lady Eleanor Roosevelt (center), and Republican New York Mayor Fiorello La Guardia (right), attended an event in support of the Fair Employment Practice Committee (FEPC). In 1941, Randolph worked with the First Lady and La Guardia to convince FDR to create the FEPC to end racial discrimination in war industries. Stimson also supported its creation. (Getty Images)

Stimson and the army chief of staff, General George C. Marshall, studied a map in January 1942. The two men developed a close working relationship, and their Pentagon offices were connected by what Stimson called the "door that was never closed." (Library of Congress)

Japanese American families waited at a California railway station for a train to take them to an internment facility on May 20, 1942. Roosevelt and Stimson jointly approved the internment of Japanese Americans, an action the Supreme Court later ruled unconstitutional. (National Archives, War Relocation Authority)

Stimson (at right in pith helmet) reviewed troop exercises with British Prime Minister Winston Churchill (center) and General George C. Marshall (left) in June 1942. Stimson repeatedly clashed with Churchill and urged FDR to reject Churchill's strategic ideas. Stimson was a strong proponent of the idea of invading France across the English Channel, a vision that at times placed him in sharp conflict with Roosevelt and Churchill. (AP Images)

US Representative Edith Nourse Rogers, a Massachusetts Republican, met with members of the first graduating class of the Women's Army Auxiliary Corps (WAAC) on August 28, 1942, at Fort Des Moines in Iowa. Rogers sponsored the bill in Congress to create the WAAC, an important advance for women in US military service. (AP Images)

Willkie and Roosevelt agreed that the 1940 Republican presidential nominee should travel around the world to show that America's two main political parties were united in the fight against fascism. On his trip, Willkie met in September 1942 with Soviet leader Joseph Stalin in Moscow. (From right to left) Willkie, Stalin, journalist Joseph Barnes, and Soviet Foreign Minister Vyacheslav Molotov.

Racial violence erupted in Detroit on June 20, 1943, and the following day a white mob overturned automobiles of Black motorists and set the cars on fire. That night, Roosevelt and Stimson sent US Army troops into Detroit to stop the rioting, which left thirty-four people dead, twenty-five of them Black. (AP Images)

Mayor La Guardia made radio broadcasts throughout the night in an effort to stop the Harlem race riot of August 1–2, 1943. (Getty Images)

Black pilots, all trained at the Tuskegee Institute in Alabama, met after a raid on January 29, 1944. Roosevelt and Stimson called for Black soldiers to join the war effort but rejected appeals by civil rights leaders to desegregate the army. (National Archives)

General Dwight Eisenhower, the supreme Allied commander, spoke with paratroopers on June 5, 1944, shortly before the invasion of France. (National Archives)

Stimson and General Eisenhower met with reporters on July 19, 1944. Then seventy-six years old, Stimson flew to Normandy in July 1944 to observe battlefields as Allied armies advanced toward Paris. (AP Images)

When FDR called for all soldiers to have the right to vote in the 1944 elections, southern Democrats in Congress blocked the president's plan and condemned it as an attack on states' rights and white supremacy. This *Philadelphia Record* political cartoon portrays states' rights as preventing soldiers from casting a ballot. The furor was one of the most heated political disputes of the war years. (*Philadelphia Record*)

Senator "Cotton Ed" Smith, a South Carolina Democrat who proclaimed his "loyalty to white supremacy," expressed his frustration over FDR's policies at a September 1944 meeting in Washington, DC, called to convince Democrats to abandon FDR and support another candidate for president. (Getty Images)

Stimson named a Boston Republican, Robert Cutler, to be his specialist for soldier voting matters. He praised Cutler's handling of the soldier voting dispute in Congress when he awarded him the Distinguished Service Medal at the war's end. (Dwight D. Eisenhower Library)

FDR campaigned with Treasury Secretary Henry Morgenthau Jr., his longtime friend and political ally, on the day before Election Day 1944. Roosevelt initially approved Morgenthau's plan to strip Germany of all industry after the war, but Stimson successfully urged the president to abandon the plan. (Franklin D. Roosevelt Library)

Roosevelt believed bipartisan support was vital to win Senate approval of the treaty creating the permanent United Nations organization. On March 13, 1945, he met with a bipartisan delegation he named to attend the United Nations Conference in San Francisco, including Republican Senator Arthur Vandenberg (second from right), Secretary of State Edward Stettinius Jr. (fourth from right), and Democratic Senator Tom Connally (fifth from right). (AP Images)

FDR died on April 12, 1945, and later that day, Harry Truman, with his wife, Bess, at his side, was sworn in as president in the White House cabinet room. Stimson (far left) and other cabinet members attended. Truman later wrote that immediately after the ceremony Stimson informed him of "a new explosive of almost unbelievable destructive power"—the atom bomb. (National Park Service, Harry S. Truman Library)

Stimson (left) spoke with James Byrnes, the South Carolina segregationist whom Truman appointed secretary of state, in Berlin for the Potsdam Conference on July 15, 1945. Byrnes opposed Stimson's proposal for negotiating an end of the war with Japan. (US Army Signal Corps, Harry S. Truman Library)

An American flag was raised at a ceremony at the US Army headquarters in Berlin on July 20, 1945, during the Potsdam Conference. In the front row were (from left to right) General Dwight Eisenhower, General George Patton, Truman, Stimson (partly obscured), and General Omar Bradley. (US Army Signal Corps, Harry S. Truman Library)

Stimson (at right) reviewed troops on July 20 during the Potsdam Conference with two of his Republican assistant secretaries of war, Harvey Bundy and Jack McCloy (from right to left, both in civilian attire), and General George Patton (in helmet). (US Army Signal Corps, Harry S. Truman Library)

Truman and Stimson met in the Oval Office on August 8, 1945, to discuss the atomic attack two days earlier on Hiroshima. After Nagasaki was bombed, the Japanese on August 10 offered to surrender on the condition they could keep their emperor, an idea that Byrnes rejected. A third atomic bomb was being prepared, but Stimson urged Truman to let the Japanese keep their emperor in order to secure peace. Truman took Stimson's advice, and no additional atomic bombs were dropped on the Japanese. (AP Images)

Truman and Stimson displayed Japanese surrender documents on September 7, 1945. At left was Navy Secretary James Forrestal, and at rear was General Marshall. (US Navy, Harry S. Truman Library)

Truman awarded Stimson the Distinguished Service Medal on September 21, 1945, Stimson's last day as secretary of war. The two men shook hands as Stimson's wife, Mabel, looked on. (Truman Library)

on defeating the Soviet Union. Taking a number of Pacific islands from the Japanese would achieve little, the president added.[22]

The next morning, after flying from Long Island to Washington, Stimson went directly to the White House on a mission to discredit Churchill and Gymnast. Stimson arrived without an appointment, but FDR agreed to receive him. Stimson gave the president a British book on World War I that detailed the tragedy that occurred when Churchill, as first lord of the Admiralty, demanded that the British Navy and Army invade Turkey's Gallipoli peninsula by attacking Turkish forts commanding the Dardanelles strait in early 1915.[23] The risky invasion, which Churchill insisted on, even though it was far from the main theater of the war, was a disastrous defeat and cost some 115,000 British troops their lives.[24] Pilloried for the campaign's failure, Churchill was forced in May 1915 to resign as first lord of the Admiralty.[25] Stimson handed the book to the president, urging him to read particular passages he had marked. The point, he told Roosevelt, was that "Churchill is doing to us now in respect to the Mediterranean and Middle East exactly what he was doing then to his own country."

After hearing Stimson out, FDR told him that, though he had made no decision, he remained in support of Bolero.[26] The president told Stimson he was sending Marshall and King to "thrash the matter out" in discussions with the British in London.

FDR QUICKLY GAVE Marshall and King instructions for their talks with Churchill and his commanders. Critically, in a July 16 memo to them, the president set a time frame for the US Army to start fighting: "It is of the highest importance that US ground forces be brought into action against the enemy in 1942." He urged the two men to give serious consideration to a cross-channel invasion in 1942 as a means of aiding the Soviet Union. In case such an invasion were not possible, the president said Marshall should consider operations in Northwest Africa or the Middle East, where he noted Germany threatened to seize the oil fields of Iran.[27] He thus gave Marshall and King strict guidance that sharply narrowed the possibilities they could consider in their discussions with the British. In a sign FDR was tiring of the protracted debate with the senior army men, he took the unusual step of signing the memo as "C-in-C"—Commander-in-Chief.

His instruction, with its requirement for US military action in 1942, in effect ruled out the plan preferred by Stimson and Marshall to devote all efforts to invading France in 1943. Marshall, King and Hopkins arrived in London on July 18, and quickly sought to develop a plan for a cross-channel invasion in 1942. Working with Eisenhower, who had arrived in England a month earlier, Marshall proposed invading near Cherbourg, France, in September 1942, and holding terrain until a larger invasion could occur the following spring. General Brooke, however, insisted the Germans would respond by concentrating their forces against the 1942 invasion, with the result that the Allied troops would not survive the winter.[28]

After days of negotiations, the two sides recognized on July 22 they were deadlocked. Eisenhower told an aide that the date could go down as "the blackest day in history," underscoring the intensity of his belief that the cross-channel invasion was the correct course.[29] Marshall cabled FDR and Stimson that the two sides were at loggerheads. FDR replied quickly that he was not surprised and urged that they look for another place to attack the Germans—including French North Africa—in 1942.

Stimson went to the White House first thing the next morning to speak with FDR in his bedroom. He argued the British attitude "seemed to me to be the result of a fatigued and defeatist government which had lost its initiative, blocking the help of a young and vigorous nation whose strength had not yet been tapped."[30] Stimson wanted an offensive aimed at the heart of Germany—not a defensive action to protect the British Empire. FDR listened, but it was too late as his mind was made up. That same day, he sent a wire to the British accepting the cancellation of the 1942 invasion in France and saying that he was "in favor of attack in North Africa and was influencing his chiefs in that direction," Brooke recounted in his memoirs.[31]

When Marshall met with Brooke, the American general had already prepared a revised plan that called for invading North Africa in late 1942. The plan also required Roosevelt and Churchill to acknowledge that as a result an invasion of France in 1943 would be "impracticable." Brooke crowed in his diary that Marshall's plan was "almost everything we had asked them to agree to at the start. It is very satisfactory to think that we have got just what we wanted out of the USA chiefs."[32] Marshall sent cables to Stimson and FDR announcing the agreed-upon plan; the US and British war chiefs were at last in accord. That night, Hopkins and Churchill went to a dinner party thrown by British admirals in honor of Admiral Ernest King, after which many gathered around a piano and sang songs, including the national anthems of both countries.

The next morning, Stimson wrote a blistering attack on the Gymnast plan and British motives. "The US has been seeking to establish prompt offensive to ultimately destroy Hitler in Europe and in the meanwhile to keep Russia in the war. The UK, while professing the same purpose, is equally if not more insistent upon a present attempt to preserve its empire in the Middle East."[33] His four-page memo argued that Gymnast was a defensive move that would leave Germany free to defeat the Russians, and would abandon the "sound logistics" of the American plans for a cross-channel invasion in 1942 or 1943. After reviewing his memo with several generals, he took General Hap Arnold, a strong advocate of making a forceful attack on Japan, and General Joseph McNarney, an aide to Marshall, to the White House.

Facing Stimson and the two generals, FDR delivered a blunt message. "The president took the situation in hand and told us that he had decided [the invasion of France] this autumn was definitely out of the question by the direction of the British. In view of that, he had already telegraphed to Marshall and to the others that he accepted the terms of the agreement they had negotiated with Churchill except that he wished a landing made in Gymnast not later than October 30th."[34] Stimson and the generals nonetheless presented their arguments, but it was all to no avail. Stimson told the president that "I recognized that his decision was made and that we must loyally obey it."

FDR and Stimson each sought to diminish the rancor of the dispute. "While he and I met head-on in our discussion, we did it in a semi-humorous way to keep from letting it get too serious, he offering to bet me on his point of view and I offering to bet him on mine." Stimson told the president that at the time the bets were decided, he wanted his memo read. Despite the efforts to quell the emotions of the debate, Stimson later underscored its importance. "This decision marks what I feel to be a very serious parting of the ways. We have turned our back on the path of what I consider sound and correct strategy and are taking a course which I feel will lead to a dangerous diversion and a possible disaster. I hope I am mistaken but my views have been throughout fully concurred in by Marshall and the members of the Army staff." FDR later prepared a point-by-point reply to Stimson's memo, arguing the Gymnast plan and a 1943 offensive have "a good chance of forcing Germany out of the war."[35] Yet with Stimson vowing to loyally follow FDR's decision, the president chose not to prolong the debate. Instead, FDR put his reply memo in his safe at Hyde Park.

In the midst of this heated dispute, FDR had made a key appointment to strengthen his control of US military strategy. Early in 1942, Marshall had suggested that FDR create the post of chairman of the Joint Chiefs of Staff to provide a unified command over the army and navy. Believing the navy would be more likely to approve the idea if the new chairman were a navy officer, Marshall recommended Admiral William Leahy, then serving as ambassador to the Vichy French government, for the role.[36] On July 21, while Marshall was in London, FDR took the first step by appointing Leahy as chief of the president's staff.[37] FDR made it clear that he—the president—was in command of war strategy. Asked by a reporter if Leahy's appointment meant the president was taking more active control of strategic conduct of the war, FDR replied, "That will be almost impossible."[38] Leahy's role quickly expanded when FDR named him the first chairman of the Joint Chiefs of Staff. Leahy would read the president's cable traffic, have free access to the White House Map Room and provide the president with a daily briefing on the war.

FDR and Churchill rejoiced once the North Africa invasion—given the code name Torch—was at last settled upon. Churchill told FDR in a cable on July 27, "I was sure you would be pleased as I am, indeed as we all are here, at the results of this strenuous week."[39] FDR replied: "I am of course very happy in the result, feeling that the past week represented a turning-point in the whole war and that now we are on our way shoulder to shoulder."

Tension between FDR and Stimson persisted. When Stimson took action to help a progressive Republican from Massachusetts, Senator Henry Cabot Lodge, FDR flew into a rage. Lodge, who was serving as a major in a US Army tank unit in North Africa, was seeking reelection in a race against a Democrat. When Lodge's active duty was terminated in accord with an order by Roosevelt applying to all members of Congress in the military, Stimson informed Lodge of the decision in a supportive letter—released to the press on July 8—saying that his military knowledge and experience "will greatly enhance your usefulness to the country as a United States Senator."[40] FDR fumed that Stimson was "practically endorsing" Lodge. "I am going over to my office and will spend the day blowing up various people."[41] One of the victims may have been James Rogers, a Republican whom Stimson had proposed for a War Department post dealing with bacteriological warfare. FDR sent Stimson a note rejecting Rogers, saying "I want to find a liberal minded man . . . who might be said to be in real sympathy with the present Administration."[42] Stimson said it was the first time FDR had "asked me to give weight to political considerations in an appointment and, coming in such a scientific appointment as this, it rather shocked me."

Despite the political tension hanging over their bipartisan alliance, there is no sign that FDR ever suspected that politics was driving Stimson's opposition to the North African invasion. Stimson, likewise, never appeared to suspect political motives for FDR's support of the plan. Marshall, however, saw signs that politics came into play. At the end of the negotiations in July, FDR sent Hopkins a cable saying that the North Africa landing should take place "not later than October 30."[43] That date would place the invasion just four days before the midterm congressional elections in the United States.[44] As planning for the Torch invasion proceeded, Marshall recalled, FDR once clasped his hands in prayer and said, "Please, make it before Election Day."

In a cabinet meeting on August 7, FDR complained sharply that stories had appeared in the press saying that he and Churchill were disregarding their military advisers. He said the charge was false and "as a matter of fact he himself had never departed from the advice of his military advisers except when the army and navy differed and it was necessary for someone to decide between them." Stimson rejected this assertion in his diary, noting that FDR had in fact overridden the US Army and Navy recommendations for an invasion of France in 1943 and an offensive against the Japanese. He concluded the president made his remarks in the cabinet meeting in front of him and Knox "to silence us." He said FDR "must know that we are all against him on Gymnast and yet now that is going to be the first thing probably which is done, and we are all very blue about it."[45]

STIMSON GRADUALLY CAME to accept the plan for Torch, particularly after developments in the war appeared to make it more likely to succeed. On August 23, the Nazis launched an attack on the Russian city of Stalingrad, a massive battle that quickly consumed divisions of troops and significant resources on both sides, making it far less likely that Hitler would send forces from the Russian front to counter an Allied invasion in North Africa. Stimson said of Torch on September 17: "We are embarked on a risky undertaking but it is not at all hopeless and, the Commander in Chief having made the decision, we must do our best to make it a success."[46]

Stimson, seeming to ponder whether he had damaged his relationship with FDR, noted in his diary that he did not see the president as often as he had before. Yet FDR's demeanor revealed no ill will. "My personal relations with the president have not changed in the occasions when I see him. He is always agreeable and ready to listen."[47] As FDR was preparing for a trip in support of Democratic candidates across the country, Stimson called him about a bill in Congress. Both men wanted to reduce the draft age to eighteen, a controversial step that would be enacted two months later. Stimson mentioned that he wanted to see the president more often. FDR was "very cordial and agreeable on that and said that as soon as he got back he wanted to see me about a number of things."[48]

Henry and Mabel Stimson spent the following weekend at Highhold, enjoying some cool weather on Sunday as they took a horseback ride. On Monday morning, September 17, Henry awoke to find an army band at his front door, sent by General Marshall from the nearby Mitchel Field air base in honor of Stimson's seventy-fifth birthday. The band played "Happy Birthday" and an old army song, "The Caissons Go Rolling Along." *The New York Times* ran an editorial that morning praising Stimson's skill and wisdom. "On him has fallen much of the mighty task of raising, training and equipping an enormous army. With General Marshall he reorganized the Army command. . . . He is never afraid to speak his mind. He never yields to any political excuse. Boys of 18 and 19 will have to be drafted; he makes no bones about it."[49] Birthday notes and cables poured in from Churchill, Quezon, Frankfurter, Knox and others.[50] In a cable from London, General Eisenhower wrote, "the entire American army in Europe joins me in felicitations on your anniversary and in expressions of abiding confidence in your administration and leadership in these critical days."[51]

Stimson turned his attention to the constant barrage of War Department demands, including the highly secret nuclear weapons development program, given the code name S-1. In October 1942, as the terrible power of the atom bomb pressed upon Stimson and the close circle of men overseeing S-1, he met with FDR to discuss "ways of meeting the ticklish situation after the war with a view to preventing [the atom bomb] being used to conquer the world."[52] However, with secrecy paramount and the weapons still untested, there was limited debate over their possible postwar use and control.

Another vigorous debate was occurring over US strategy in the Pacific, where Army general Douglas MacArthur sought more forces to attack the Japanese. With FDR insisting on giving the North Africa attack priority, Marshall opposed sending additional army aircraft to the Pacific for the planned invasion of Guadalcanal, which some wryly dubbed "Operation Shoestring."[53] Ultimately, on August 7, a navy armada including three aircraft carriers landed nineteen thousand US Marines on Guadalcanal, the first major island offensive by American forces in the war. The marines encountered ferocious Japanese resistance in the island's thick rain forest. The offensive dragged on for months and would eventually include a series of large naval battles.

For Operation Torch, meanwhile, the Allies had moved quickly into planning the invasion and amassing the necessary troops. Churchill recommended to FDR that Eisenhower, from his post in London, take command of Torch, a move the president approved.[54] As he planned the invasion, Eisenhower's concerns included Vichy France, which had five hundred airplanes and about three hundred thousand soldiers in its North African colonies of Morocco and Tunisia. If the Vichy forces fought the Allies, it might imperil the invasion.[55]

Vichy France, however, was politically fractured. In April 1942, Pierre Laval, a former prime minister who urged closer collaboration with Nazi Germany, pushed aside the aging Marshal Philippe Pétain as the head of the Vichy government. Pétain's ouster alienated many in the French military, and Eisenhower tried to exploit the schism to win the French military's backing for the Allied invasion. Through secret work by American and British diplomats, Vichy French general Henri Giraud, friendly toward the Allies, was spirited away by a British submarine and brought to Ike's headquarters at Gibraltar, setting the stage for Vichy forces to cooperate with the Allies.[56]

In the early morning hours of November 8, an Allied force of two hundred thousand American and British troops began landing at the ports of Casablanca in Morocco and Oran and Algiers in Algeria.[57] At Casablanca, Vichy French fighter planes shot down Allied bombers, and in Oran, ground forces resisted. US casualties mounted. Laval condemned the invasion and cut off relations with the United States. Hitler ordered his forces to take over the remainder of Vichy France that it had not already occupied. Torch's outcome was uncertain.

Eisenhower sent General William Clark on November 9 to negotiate a truce with Vichy's top military commander in North Africa, Admiral Jean Darlan, in the Algerian capital of Algiers.[58] The next day Darlan, recognizing the power of the Allied forces, ordered all Vichy troops to cease fighting. The Allies quickly seized control of the coastal regions of Morocco and Algeria. The fighting, which already had left 526 American and four British soldiers dead, ceased.[59] Three days later, Darlan and Eisenhower entered a formal agreement under which the Allies were granted military control of the colonies. In exchange, Darlan and his officers would escape any prosecution for collaborating with Hitler.[60]

With the agreement in place, the Allies solidified military control and quickly moved eastward to seize Tunisia and attack Rommel's forces.

The invasion of North Africa was a triumph for the US military, and FDR immediately used it to boost the nation's morale. The president announced the tide of the war was turning, and on November 11, Veteran's Day, at Arlington National Cemetery he foretold the "inevitable, final defeat" of German and Japanese militarism. Ultimately, FDR did not get his wish on the timing of the invasion, as it began after Election Day, but the Democrats nonetheless retained control of both the Senate and House of Representatives.

News of the Darlan deal drew fierce criticism from the Fighting French, a group led by Charles de Gaulle, the general who had been operating in exile since the Nazis seized Paris in 1940. The group said US forces should not ally themselves with people who collaborate with Hitler, and that doing so would sap the morale of those resisting Nazi occupation in France and other countries.[61] Edward R. Murrow, the prominent radio journalist, condemned the Darlan deal for its lenient treatment of a man who had turned over opponents to the Nazis.[62] As the criticism mounted, Eisenhower sent Marshall a telegram arguing that the Darlan deal was critical because it permitted sixty thousand troops to fight Germans rather than carry out a military occupation of Morocco.[63]

Stimson learned on November 16 that Republican Party leader Wendell Willkie was poised to condemn the Darlan deal in a radio speech that same evening. He called Willkie on the phone shortly before he was to go on the air and urged him not to criticize it.[64] "Willkie at once flew into a rage, called me names, and wanted to know if I was trying to control his freedom. But I stuck to it and told him flatly that, if he criticized the Darlan agreement at this juncture, he would run the risk of jeopardizing the success of the United States Army in North Africa and would be rendering its task very much more difficult." Willkie calmed down and read Stimson the critical remarks he planned to make. Stimson, in turn, read Willkie the telegram that Eisenhower had sent Marshall. He told Willkie that "I had esteemed and respected him for many years but, if he persisted in doing this, my respect for him would be gravely diminished." Willkie made no commitment to Stimson to revise his speech.

Stimson called FDR to let him know about his talk with Willkie. On the radio a short while later, Willkie condemned "our State Department's long appeasement of Vichy," but made no mention of Darlan or the deal Eisenhower had struck with him.[65] After 11:00 P.M., FDR—having listened to Willkie's speech—called Stimson and congratulated him on "having won a fine victory." Stimson considered the call one of his "characteristic kindnesses which he so often shows to those about him."[66]

FDR issued a statement the next day defending the Darlan deal as only a "temporary expedient, justified solely by the stress of battle," and insisting that people persecuted by the Nazis in North Africa must be freed.[67] Stimson's efforts to bolster Willkie's support of FDR and the war effort likely helped heal the rift between him and the president over the decision to invade North Africa.

Stimson quickly tried to mend fences with Willkie by sending him a letter. "I appreciate deeply your having refrained from making any comment on the Darlan agreement in your speech last evening," he wrote. "On my part I regret that I should have stated my objections in a way which seemed to you rough and uncalled-for. I have been under heavy strain for the last week, for the fighting situation in Africa is critical. Let us both start over again." Willkie sent a note in reply, "I never hold in my mind things that create minor irritations. I appreciate very much your letter. Hope to see you sometime when I am in Washington."[68]

Over a weekend in mid-November, while Henry and Mabel Stimson were at Highhold on Long Island, the contents of Stimson's office were moved from the Munitions Building to the Pentagon. The army had completed the massive structure—the world's largest building by square feet of floor area—with astonishing speed. The number of employees in the new building, many already at work, would reach twenty-two thousand by the following month. But officials in charge of the project were focused on preparing for the arrival of the occupant of room 3E-884, the secretary of war.[69]

The Stimsons arrived at the Pentagon on Monday, November 16. "Mabel and I drove to the Pentagon Building where I found my new office all beautifully prepared and ready for me and Mabel inspected it," Henry wrote in his diary.[70] The spacious third-floor office, with a view across the Potomac to the Washington Monument and the Capitol in the distance, had wood paneling, thick scarlet carpeting, an adjacent dressing room and a nearby dining room that could accommodate twenty-four people. Upon his desk—the same one used by every secretary of war since 1883—was a telephone with a secure line to the White House. Behind his desk hung a portrait of Elihu Root, the former Republican secretary of war, who had been an employer, a mentor and a friend to Stimson. The office had an alcove that held maps showing the location of US forces around the world. It also had a feature of great import to Stimson—a door leading to the office of General Marshall.[71]

As Allied troops fought in North Africa, horrific crimes committed by the Nazis against European Jews were reported. On November 24, 1942, Rabbi Stephen Wise, president of the American Jewish Congress, held a press conference in Washington to announce that sources confirmed by the US Department of State had revealed that about two million Jews had been murdered in a Nazi "extermination campaign" carried out in Poland.[72] Wise said that only about one hundred thousand of the five hundred thousand Jews formerly in Warsaw remained there, and the Nazis were moving Jews from all over Europe to Poland for mass killing. The chief source of the information was an International Red Cross official whom the State Department considered unimpeachable.[73] Other reports, released at about the same time by the Polish government in exile in London and the Jewish press in Palestine, stated that Heinrich Himmler, commander of the Nazi SS security force, had ordered half of Poland's three million Jews killed by the end of 1942, and that in the murderous campaign Jews were being hauled in trains to camps in small towns in Poland including Treblinka, Sobibor and Auschwitz.

Despite the immensity of this human tragedy, the report of Nazi genocide struggled to gain attention in the news media as American troops fought Germans on the ground in North Africa. The New York Times ran a five-paragraph wire story on Rabbi Wise's press conference on page ten the next day.

On December 17, 1942, Secretary of State Cordell Hull released a declaration by the United Nations allies condemning the Nazis for depriving Jews of "the most elementary human rights" and for "now carrying into effect Hitler's oft-repeated intention to exterminate the Jewish people in Europe."[74] This time the story garnered front-page coverage at *The Times* and other papers. Denouncing the "bestial policy of cold-blooded extermination" of Jews, the declaration said the Allies reaffirmed "their solemn resolution to insure that those responsible for these crimes shall not escape retribution and to press on with the necessary practical measures to this end." It was signed by representatives of eleven Allied nations, including the United States, Great Britain and Russia, as well as the French National Committee in London.

The statement depicted the horror unfolding inside the Nazi empire: "From all the occupied countries Jews are being transported in conditions of appalling horror and brutality to Eastern Europe. In Poland, which has been made the principal Nazi slaughterhouse, the ghettoes established by the Nazi invader are being systematically emptied of all Jews except a few highly skilled workers required for war industries. None of those taken away are ever heard of again. The able-bodied are slowly worked to death in labor camps. The infirm are left to die of exposure and starvation or are deliberately massacred in mass executions."

In releasing the United Nations declaration, Hull noted that it came two months after FDR called for the creation of a war crimes tribunal to mete out "just and sure punishment" to the "ringleaders of responsible for the organized murder of thousands of innocent persons and the commission of atrocities which have violated every tenet of the Christian faith."

A week later, Darlan was assassinated by a French royalist at his headquarters in Algiers. The deal with Darlan nonetheless left its imprint on the Allied war effort. When FDR and Churchill met for a victorious summit meeting in Casablanca, Morocco, the following month, FDR announced that the Allies would demand "unconditional surrender" from the Axis nations, a move intended in part to disarm criticism that the Allies were ready to cut deals with fascist sympathizers.[75]

FDR had spent much of the first seven months of 1942 listening to Stimson's arguments against Churchill's plan for the North African

invasion. Stimson's opposition to the invasion, and his alliance with
Marshall and other generals in that opposition, prompted FDR to
tighten his grip over military strategy. Ultimately, the president firmly
and respectfully rejected the reasoning of his Republican ally and General Marshall, taking control of military strategy as a true commander
in chief and guiding US armed forces to success. FDR had taken an
enormous risk, for if the invasion had failed, the blame would fall
largely on him. The president had rejected Stimson's severe attacks on
Churchill's strategy, though he did so only after hearing his secretary
of war's arguments at great length. The alliance of FDR and Stimson,
founded on a bond of trust and a shared belief in defending democracy,
had safely passed through a great trial—and more challenges lay ahead.

Willkie Takes the Stage

Even as he argued with Secretary of War Stimson over war strategy in the summer of 1942, President Roosevelt worked quietly with former Republican presidential nominee Wendell Willkie to craft a plan that would put the bipartisan alliance on display around the world as a reflection of American democracy. The two men agreed that Willkie would go on a global tour, meeting with political leaders and visiting battlefronts to spread the word that America was united in the fight to save democracy.

Willkie announced the trip on August 20, preemptively countering the perception that he was too close to FDR by saying that he arranged it—on his own initiative—out of a desire to learn more about the nations with which the United States was cooperating in the war.[1] FDR clarified the next day that Willkie would act as a "special representative of the president."[2] The voyage posed significant hazards. For Willkie, there were the physical dangers of traveling in war zones, and the political risk that Republican rivals would pillory him as FDR's ally. For FDR, there were the risks that Willkie might somehow disrupt relations with US allies or criticize the administration's conduct of the war. Yet they set such concerns aside in the interest of showing the world that the two major American parties were united in the battle against fascism. FDR told reporters on August 21 that as the leader of the "minority party,"

Willkie would carry a simple message about the US war effort—that "we have unity, and that we are going all-out."

Following the 1940 election, Stimson had worked behind the scenes to bring his old acquaintance Willkie fully into the circle of Republicans supporting Roosevelt. In 1941, Willkie endorsed the Lend-Lease program and traveled to London with a message from FDR. The subject of America's posture toward global issues arose when Willkie and the president began a conversation about a narrow political objective—unseating their common enemy, the extreme isolationist Hamilton Fish, the Republican representative from New York. In February 1942, FDR invited Willkie for lunch to discuss Fish and other matters. Willkie responded in a letter noting the "particular problem" of Fish, and then calling for a wider attack on isolationism. "As you know, I am exceedingly hopeful that all traces of isolationism can be washed out of both Republican and Democratic parties, so that whatever debates may occur hereafter will be within the framework of the recognition of America's necessary position in world affairs and of world leadership."[3]

In April 1942, Willkie urged the Republican Party to abandon isolationism as it prepared for the midterm elections later that year. Battling objections from Senator Robert Taft at a meeting in Chicago, Willkie convinced the Republican National Committee to adopt a resolution committing the United States after the war to recognize its "obligation" to support international cooperation and peace.[4]

Stimson had long carried aloft the banner of internationalism in the Republican Party, a fact that drew public praise from Willkie. Speaking at Union College in New York in May 1942, Willkie recited a litany of isolationist failures while noting Stimson's famed stand against Japanese imperialism. "[A]long with all the other democratic nations, we did nothing when Japan invaded Manchuria, though our own Secretary of State, Henry Stimson, expressed his outrage; we with the other democracies sat by while Italy wantonly invaded Ethiopia, and we let Hitler enter the Rhineland without even a protest. We shut ourselves away from world trade by excessive tariff barriers. We washed our hands of the continent of Europe and displayed no interest in its fate while Germany re-armed."[5] Thus, Willkie praised Stimson while obliquely criticizing FDR and his Republican predecessor, Herbert Hoover, for accommodating isolationism.

In an exchange of letters with FDR in April 1942, Willkie expressed confidence about the outcome of their efforts to see Fish lose his seat in Congress.[6] "My information may be incorrect, but I believe the Hamilton Fish matter is being solved. I am quite confident Fish is going to be eliminated," the Republican leader wrote. "As a matter of fact, I doubt if he even runs."

Fish, indeed, appeared to be in trouble—politically and legally. Federal investigators probing Nazi spies had uncovered evidence linking him to George Viereck, a Nazi propagandist who lived in the United States. In February 1942, one of Fish's aides was convicted of perjury for lying to a grand jury by falsely denying he knew Viereck, who had sent pro-German literature using Fish's congressional mailing privileges. Viereck was convicted in March 1942 of failing to register as a German agent.[7] Fish, however, was never charged with a crime. By June 1942, Willkie reported to FDR in a letter that the efforts to oust Fish were in disarray.[8] Ultimately, despite his pro-Nazi connections, Fish won strong support from local Republican Party groups and later was renominated as the Republican candidate for Congress from the New York district that included Hyde Park.

As he contemplated a wider role with FDR, Willkie issued a manifesto for their alliance in *Look* magazine, whose founder and president was Gardner Cowles Jr., an ardent Willkie supporter. The April 7 *Look* revealed that Willkie had sent FDR a letter praising his speech after the Pearl Harbor attack. "Every American is willing to serve," Willkie wrote the president. However, he also sought to strike a balance—he wanted to support FDR's foreign policy while remaining free to criticize the president and to proclaim his own views.[9] He told *Look,* "I have explained to the president and his advisers that I should prefer not to be associated with the administration because I do not want my right to comment on its policies and conduct curtailed."

FDR evidently accepted Willkie's terms for this arrangement. The president also took steps to assure Willkie that he would receive fair media coverage. In June 1942, FDR created the Office of War Information (OWI), under the executive office of the president, to distribute both factual information about the war and propaganda, including movies and radio programs. Gardner Cowles Jr. was hired to lead its division distributing news domestically.[10]

In this climate of cooperation, on July 29, Willkie wrote FDR saying, "As you know, I would like to take a trip to the Middle East, into Russia, and perhaps China." He suggested departing in late August and returning prior to October 15. "Would it be asking too much of you if the proposed trip is agreeable with you, to refer the matter to persons who could work out the details with me?"

In plain words, Willkie was asking the president to use federal government resources to send the leader of the opposing party—a presumed candidate for the presidency in 1944—on a tour around the globe representing the United States.

Intrigued, FDR promptly wrote General George Marshall asking for his views on Willkie's proposal: "I think that for many reasons Mr. Willkie should take this trip—especially to put some pep talks into the officials of Egypt, Palestine, Syria, Iraq, Iran and China. I do not know what capacity he should go in—perhaps as a special representative of the president. What do you think?"[11] Marshall responded the same day supporting the idea, especially if the purpose of the trip was to boost morale in the countries he planned to visit. He recommended Willkie travel as the president's "unofficial" or "special" representative.

On August 2, FDR sent Willkie a telegram approving the voyage:

```
AM ARRANGING FOR YOU TO LEAVE ANY DAY AFTER AUGUST
15TH AGREEABLE TO YOU AND TO RETURN BETWEEN FIRST
AND FIFTEENTH OF OCTOBER. IT IS MY THOUGHT YOU
WOULD DO THE MIDDLE EAST BUT THAT RUSSIA AND CHINA
WOULD BE SUBJECT TO DEVELOPMENTS WHICH YOU AND I
CAN TALK OVER . . . I HOPE YOU CAN COME TO SEE ME
SO THAT WE CAN HAVE A GOOD TALK IN REGARD TO IT AND
IN REGARD TO A LOT OF OTHER THINGS.

FRANKLIN D. ROOSEVELT
```

Willkie went to the White House on August 7, attending a lunch in honor of Queen Wilhelmina of the Netherlands. Willkie sat on the queen's right and FDR on her left. Afterwards, the two men privately discussed arrangements for Willkie's trip. *The New York Times* revealed the next day that he would travel to Russia and the Middle East "as a private citizen," though he would carry messages from FDR to leaders he would meet on his travels.[12]

FDR wrote to Stalin saying Willkie wished to visit Moscow and learn about "the wonderful progress made by the Russian people" and "the undying unity of thought in repelling the invader and the great sacrifices all of you are making."[13] The president continued:

> He is, as you know, my recent opponent in the 1940 elections and is the head of the minority party today. He is greatly helping in war work and is heart and soul with my Administration in our foreign policy of opposition to Nazism and real friendship with your government.
>
> Personally I think that for the sake of the present and the future a visit by him to the Soviet Union would be a good thing. He would fly to Russia in the first half of September.
>
> Please tell me confidentially and frankly if you would care to have him come for a very short visit.
>
> Roosevelt

The idea of FDR supporting a visit by Willkie may have puzzled Stalin, who had his political rivals murdered or imprisoned rather than sent overseas as diplomats. Republicans had long been among the severest critics of communism, but Willkie's support for the American-Soviet alliance apparently overcame any qualms the dictator had. Stalin sent FDR a terse reply four days later: "The Soviet Government takes a favorable view of Mr. Wendell Willkie's visit to the USSR and I can assure you that he will be most cordially entertained."

INDIA, ONCE CONSIDERED a possible destination for Willkie, now posed a major political problem. Mohandas Gandhi, Jawaharlal Nehru and other Indian leaders demanding immediate independence for their country from British colonial rule were arrested by British police on August 9.[14] Chinese leader Chiang Kai-shek, whose armies had taken refuge in India, sent FDR a cable warning that the arrests "would prove to be a great setback to the Allied cause in the Far East." Chiang urged that the Allies take action to show the world "the sincerity of their professed principle of ensuring freedom and justice for men of all races."[15] FDR forwarded Chiang's message to Prime Minister Churchill on August 11. Churchill responded angrily days later, telling FDR in a cable that Chiang was "most ill-informed" on Indian matters and that the arrests had been approved by "good Indian patriots." India, still a contentious problem for the Allies, would remain stricken from Willkie's itinerary.

When FDR discussed Willkie's tour with reporters on August 21, he said the trip would seek to increase support among many countries for an Allied victory. Willkie would explain to the countries he was to visit "the comparison between an Axis victory and a United Nations victory, as to what would happen to them." The president said this meant Willkie would spread the word that a United Nations victory would give countries "a reasonable opportunity for autonomy, and independence, and development," as was provided for under the Atlantic Charter signed by the United Nations in January 1942.[16] By announcing Willkie's message of "independence" prior to the trip's outset, FDR had set the stage for the Republican leader to spread a message promising self-determination to the colonized nations of the world.

Willkie was to be accompanied by his friend and supporter Gardner Cowles Jr., as well as Joseph Barnes, an OWI staff member and former reporter for the *New York Herald Tribune*. Barnes, who had been a correspondent in Moscow, spoke Russian, a skill that would come in handy during their stay in the Soviet Union.[17] The aircraft the army offered for the trip—a four-engine plane similar to the B-25 Liberator heavy bomber—was named the *Gulliver,* a literary nod to the far-flung travels Willkie would undertake. "Gulliver" was painted on the plane's side in both English and Russian.

On August 26, a limousine picked up Willkie, Cowles and Barnes in New York and took them to Mitchel Field, the army airport on Long Island, where they boarded the *Gulliver*.[18] A US Army major, aided by a crew of six officers, piloted the plane to Brazil for a stopover, then across the Atlantic to Ghana before reaching Egypt.

In Cairo on September 3, Willkie gave his first news conference, announcing that "Nazism has reached the peak of its power and we now are seeing the beginning of its recession, although it will be a long war."[19] He met with King Farouk and visited the British commander, General Bernard Montgomery. Willkie also observed the US Army Sherman tanks that Marshall had ordered so swiftly shipped to Egypt after the fall of Tobruk. After viewing the battlefront at El-Alamein in a British military aircraft with Montgomery, he proclaimed to reporters that "Egypt is saved. Rommel is stopped and a beginning has been made on the task of throwing the Nazis out of Africa."[20]

From Egypt, the *Gulliver* flew to Ankara, Turkey, which was maintaining steadfast neutrality in the war. Talking with reporters about concerns that Germany might seek to disrupt his visit, Willkie launched a sarcastic gibe at Nazi political repression: "Why, if the Germans don't like it, it's easy enough for the Turks to ask them to send along a leader of *their* administration opposition."[21]

After visits in Beirut and Jerusalem, Willkie landed in Moscow on September 20. He walked through the city's streets, visited Red Square, rode the subway and inspected antiaircraft defenses.[22] He was Stalin's guest for dinner September 23 in the Kremlin, where the two men discussed the war for three hours. Churchill had visited Stalin in August and informed him of Operation Torch, which was set for November. Stalin revealed his resentment against Churchill for going back on what he had considered a promise to open a second front in Europe against the Nazis in 1942. Why, he demanded, had FDR "allowed Churchill to run the war"?[23] FDR, however, had provided Willkie with no information about Torch, and so he was unable to respond. Stalin also gave him a list of arms and supplies the Soviets needed from America. Before the evening ended, Willkie complimented the Soviet dictator, suggesting he would have made a good lawyer in America. "Mr. Willkie," Stalin said in return, "you know I grew up a Georgian peasant. I am unschooled in pretty talk. All I can say is I like you very much."

After visiting the battlefront just 130 miles west of Moscow, Willkie on September 26 issued a heartfelt appeal to the American nation for a second front in Europe.[24] He said five million Soviets had already died in the war and another sixty million were living under German occupation. "Personally I am now convinced we can best help by establishing a second front in Europe with Britain at the earliest possible moment our military leaders will approve," he said. "Next year might be too late."[25]

Willkie had thus plunged very publicly into the debate over the American invasion that had so sharply divided senior Allied strategists. In London, Churchill sent Willkie a testy warning via the press: "I welcome this opportunity of again emphasizing the undesirability of public statements as to the time or place of future Allied offensive operations."[26] FDR played down Willkie's comments on the second front issue, telling reporters, "I didn't think it was worth reading the stories."[27]

When the *Gulliver* landed in Chungking, China, Willkie was welcomed in grand style by Chiang Kai-shek and his wife, widely known as Madame Chiang. He was feted with banquets, slept in a lavish guest house and watched Chinese soldiers in training exercises.[28] Willkie also got another perspective on China when he met twice with Chou Enlai, the Chinese Communist leader serving on a council established by the Communists and Nationalists to cooperate in their fight against the Japanese.

Madame Chiang, renowned for her beauty, had spent many years in the United States, was fluent in English, and graduated from Wellesley College in Massachusetts. She lavished her attentions on Willkie, who found her both irresistible and a powerful advocate for the Chinese people. An American diplomat, John Paton Davies, concluded that she had "wound him around her little finger."[29]

Willkie, however, did not require Madame Chiang's persuasion to embrace the anti-imperialist views of her husband. In Chungking on October 6, the Republican leader gave a radio address calling for more military aid to China as well as "ironclad" guarantees by the democracies that they will end imperialism.[30] "We believe this war must mean an end to the empire of nations over other nations. No foot of Chinese soil, for example, should or can be ruled from now on except by the people who live on it." He urged subjugated countries the world over to join the United Nations camp. "We believe it is the world's job to find some system for helping colonial peoples who join the United Nations cause to become free and independent nations." He added: "Mankind is on the march. The old colonial days are past."

On October 9, Japanese planes—apparently targeting Willkie— bombed a train, killing six people.[31] Willkie was not on the train, and the next day the *Gulliver* took off from Chungking for his return—after a forty-nine-day trip covering some 31,000 miles—to the United States.[32]

WILLKIE WENT TO the White House for a private meeting on October 14 with the president. Afterwards, seeking again to underscore his independence from FDR, the Republican leader said of the trip, "This was my own idea. Nobody asked me to do it."[33] He also made a statement saying that the first purpose of the journey was to "demonstrate to our Allies and to a good many neutral countries that there is unity in the United States on the purpose of winning this war."

FDR told reporters two days later only that the two men had had "an exceedingly successful and a very interesting talk."[34] He had to tread lightly on the subject of liberating colonies to avoid irritating Churchill. Ever the strategist, however, the president by his silence quietly endorsed Willkie's anti-colonialist proclamations. Just as FDR benefitted from Stimson's aggressive stances on matters such as the Neutrality Act or starting military conscription, the president now gained from Willkie's ardent appeals for liberation for colonized peoples.

On October 26, Willkie discussed his globe-trotting trip in what he called his "Report to the People," a radio broadcast heard by a vast audience estimated at thirty-six million Americans.[35] Once again, he called for opening a second front and sending more arms to the Allies. Railing against imperialism, he painted the Atlantic Charter as an agreement that promised self-determination for the nations of the Atlantic but turned a blind eye to colonies within the Pacific region. "Is there to be no charter of freedom for the billions of the East? Is freedom supposed to be priceless for the white man, or for the Western World, but of no account to [people] in the East?" He also denounced US policy toward India. "They cannot ascertain from our government's wishy-washy attitude toward the problem of India what we are likely to feel at the end of the war about all the other hundreds of millions of Eastern peoples.

They cannot tell from our vague and vacillating talk whether or not we really do stand for freedom.... I can assure you that the rule of the people by other people is not freedom, and is not what we must fight to preserve."[36]

William Allen White, the Kansas editor and internationalist Republican, swiftly applauded Willkie for challenging FDR and Churchill. "For the first time in human history, a major leader of a great republic spoke out specifically, naming names of nations and races, and demanding in terms definite and certain, freedom for all mankind. Mr. Roosevelt and the Atlantic Charter and Mr. Churchill have spoken of freedom but apparently with crossed fingers for Asia and Africa. The Atlantic charter did not interest 'the yellow and brown and the black,' but Mr. Willkie demanded the end of the colonial system. And he looked square at the remains of the British empire as he said 'the end of the colonial system.' His demand was a forward step in the battle for freedom."[37] The speech also drew support from Clare Boothe Luce—a Republican candidate for Congress in Connecticut, who was a writer and the wife of *Time* magazine publisher Henry Luce. She remarked, "Last night the world heard the message of a global Abraham Lincoln."[38]

FDR responded the next day, reassuring the public that the Atlantic Charter's promises applied to all people around the world—it bore the name "Atlantic" only because of where it was signed. He also insisted that there was no controversy between him and Willkie, attempting to tamp down any discord that could threaten their bipartisan alliance.[39]

Churchill, on the other hand, rebuked Willkie's anti-imperialism. Delivering a speech in London, the prime minister insisted that Great Britain was not fighting to expand its colonial empire. "Let me, however, make this clear, in case there should be any mistake about it in any quarter. We mean to hold our own," he said. "I have not become the King's first minister in order to preside over the liquidation of the British Empire."[40]

The November 3 elections delivered modest gains for Republicans, who seized a net total of nine seats in the Senate and forty-seven in the House of Representatives. The Democrats held on to control of both chambers of Congress, but their majority margins shrank to nineteen senators and only fourteen representatives.[41] Notable Republican victors included Clare Boothe Luce, as well as Henry Cabot Lodge Jr., who was reelected to represent Massachusetts in the Senate. Nationwide, Republicans scored a net gain of three governorships.

These electoral victories, however, did not relieve the pall cast over Willkie's leadership by the fact that the Republicans had failed to take control of either congressional chamber. As Willkie contemplated a run for the presidency in 1944, he faced significant challenges. Hamilton Fish also won reelection, underscoring isolationism's continued strength in the party. And one of Willkie's Republican rivals in the 1940 presidential race, Thomas Dewey, was elected New York governor—a perch from which he would soon prepare another bid for the presidency.

Willkie continued his vigorous advocacy for liberal causes. In November 1942, he argued before the US Supreme Court on behalf of William Schneiderman, a former organizer for the US Communist Party who faced deportation after his citizenship was revoked. In court, Willkie pointed to a dissenting opinion in an earlier case that asserted the American idea of freedom was not "freedom for those who agree with us but freedom for the thought that we hate."[42] When the Supreme Court decided the case in Schneiderman's favor in May 1943, it was a win for Willkie, but it also broadened the rift between him and conservative Republicans.

He also spoke forcefully against the Nazi persecution of the Jews of Europe. In March 1943, the American Jewish Congress brought together a large array of religious and civic leaders in a meeting at Madison Square Garden in New York City to call for rescue of Jews threatened by Hitler. Willkie sent a message to the conference: "Two million human beings, merely because they are Jews, have already been murdered by every fiendish means which Hitler could devise. Millions of other Jews in Central and Eastern Europe face immediate destruction. It is not enough to protest this mass murder of people. Practical measures must be formulated and carried out immediately to save as many Jews as possible."[43]

Willkie refined his vision for human rights around the globe in his book *One World,* a memoir of his travels aboard the *Gulliver* that leapt to the top of bestseller lists after its publication in April 1943. The book denounced as "world-disturbing" Churchill's remark opposing "the liquidation of the British Empire."[44] Willkie also took issue with FDR's defense of the Darlan deal, which he described as diplomacy "trading away the principles which we had proclaimed to the world," and criticized Stalin for failing to state clear plans for Eastern European countries after the war. A chapter entitled "This Is a War of Liberation" condemned Great Britain, France, Belgium, Portugal and the United States for continuing to hold colonies. "In Africa, in the Middle East, throughout the Arab world, as well as in China and the whole Far East, freedom means the orderly but scheduled abolition of the colonial system."[45]

One World went further still, applying Willkie's call for freedom and civil rights to the United States itself and denouncing the country's systemic mistreatment of Black people. "The attitude of the white citizens of this country toward the Negroes has undeniably had some of the unlovely characteristics of an alien imperialism—a smug racial superiority, a willingness to exploit an unprotected people," he wrote.[46] "When we talk of freedom and opportunity for all nations, the mocking paradoxes in our own society become so clear they can no longer be ignored. If we want to talk about freedom, we must mean freedom for others as well as ourselves, and we must mean freedom for everyone inside our frontiers as well as outside."

Even by the standards of progressive Republicans, *One World* trumpeted a powerful liberal message. Some conservative party members—already leery of Willkie's liberalism—raised objections.[47] Stimson, who had hoped that Willkie would draw in broad Republican support for FDR and the war effort, worried in June 1943 that the Republican Party was turning away from Willkie and would once again become "violently isolationist."[48]

Still, the book's idealistic manifesto of internationalism, anti-imperialism and racial equity won wide acclaim in America and around the world. In India, independence activist Jawaharlal Nehru read *One World* in his jail cell and pronounced it "exhilarating."[49] Willkie's supporters soon would call upon him to defend racial equity in America, where racial tension had been building throughout the war and by the summer of 1943 had reached a boiling point.

The 1943 Race Riots:
Hate, Blood and Fire

Although President Roosevelt had kept the initial creation of the Fair Employment Practice Committee (FEPC) relatively quiet in the hope of avoiding a national controversy, before long the news of its work shook white Americans who opposed relaxing segregation's grip. By mid-1943, anti-Black violence reached a crescendo across the country, eroding the sense of shared national purpose that FDR, Secretary of War Stimson and Secretary of the Navy Knox had sought so desperately to build in support of the war effort. The racial turmoil—threatening wider civil unrest and undermining productivity in US war industries at a critical moment—posed stark challenges for the bipartisan alliance.

The racist vitriol unleashed in response to the creation of the FEPC concerned FDR and his allies. Speaking in honor of Abraham Lincoln's birthday in February 1943, Knox noted the bitter condemnations of FDR over racial matters. "Probably no President prior to Franklin D. Roosevelt took the abuse politically and personally that befell Lincoln," Knox said. He uttered these words a year after he himself came under fire for segregation in the navy. Yet now Knox offered a ringing defense of FDR. He said Lincoln was criticized for using the Civil War "to expand opportunity and liberty for not only the white voters of 1860 but the millions of Black men who had been slaves."[1] He continued, "We see history repeating itself with disturbing precision. Our President, our leaders, have been subjected to all the same familiar charges of 80 years ago. We have seen again in these hours of another supreme struggle the same temptations of partisan advantage obstruct our larger purposes." Then, avoiding any specific mention of the FEPC or desegregation, Knox urged the nation to support President Roosevelt. "I fervently hope and pray (and lest you've forgotten, I remind you that I am a Republican), that we can meet the great issues and make the solemn decisions that lie ahead of us without partisanship and prejudice."

The FEPC had ventured south, holding hearings on employment discrimination in Alabama in July 1942 and later issuing desegregation orders to several companies there. In the port city of Mobile, the Alabama Dry Dock and Shipbuilding Company in early 1943 had thirty thousand employees, seven thousand of whom were Black. All Black workers, however, were limited to unskilled positions. The FEPC issued an order requiring the company to end its practice of refusing to hire Black workers in skilled positions, and on May 24, 1943, Alabama Dry Dock announced it would comply and move twelve Black workers to welding jobs. The next morning, white employees attacked their Black coworkers with hammers, crowbars and pieces of steel.[2] Approximately eighty workers, nearly all of them Black, were injured.[3] The army sent troops from a nearby base to stop the violence. The turmoil eased only after the FEPC agreed to permit some segregated working conditions to resume in the shipyard.

Another FEPC order against job discrimination soon sparked trouble in Detroit, Michigan, where competition for employment and a shortage in housing increased racial tensions.[4] An estimated two hundred and fifty thousand southerners, some fifty thousand of them Black, had moved to Detroit in 1942 and early 1943 seeking jobs at booming war industry plants. The city already had a history of extremism; the Ku Klux Klan, the terrorist white-supremacy group, had openly supported a candidate for Detroit mayor as recently as 1924, and prominent political figures in the state were later tied to the Klan. In 1936, sixteen members of a Klan splinter group, the Black Legion, were convicted of murdering a Black man and also a white newspaper publisher who was preparing to reveal that a mayor was a Black Legion member.[5]

In Detroit's auto industry, however, the United Auto Workers union had taken steps toward breaking down racial discrimination in employ-ment. On April 11, 1943, UAW leader Walter Reuther, Detroit NAACP leader James McClendon and others held a rally in the city's Cadillac Square, which was attended by some ten thousand workers, both white and Black, in support of ending workplace discrimination. In a doc-ument to be known as the "Cadillac Charter," the UAW proclaimed its demand that "all industry participating in the war effort treat all labor alike, regardless of race, color, creed, religion, or national origin, in hiring, upgrading and training of men and women, fully observing Executive Order 8802."

On May 24, after the Packard Motor Car Company hired four Black women and promoted three Black men working at its Detroit plant, several hundred white workers went on strike in protest. As such ra-cially motivated actions became more common, they were dubbed "hate strikes." About 1,500 Black workers responded to the Packard hate strike by going on strike in support of the new hires. The strike imper-iled Packard's production of engines for P-51 Mustang fighter planes for the army and motors for navy patrol torpedo boats.

As tensions soared in Detroit, FDR issued an executive order on May 28 strengthening the FEPC and broadening its mandate to fight racial segregation not only of war industry workers but also of government employees. Once again, he made no public comments on the commit-tee, but his actions reaffirmed his support for its mission of breaking down segregation.[6] The president increased the FEPC's size and named as its new chairman a Catholic priest, Francis Haas, who had gained prominence as a mediator in labor disputes.

On June 6, UAW president R.J. Thomas told an NACCP meeting that he had "absolute evidence" that the Ku Klux Klan promoted the hate strike at Packard.[7] "The UAW-CIO will fight for equal rights for all workers regardless of color. If the KKK and the rest of the night-shirt boys want to fight the union on this issue, we are ready and willing to take them on." He informed the group that he'd asked the FBI to investi-gate whether "there is any direct connection between the Klan and Axis agents in Detroit."

. . .

RACIAL TROUBLES ALSO broke out across the country in Los Angeles after a fight between sailors and Mexican American youths wearing the distinctive garb known as "zoot suits." On June 3, about fifty white sailors from a naval base sought revenge for the fight by sweeping through a neighborhood, indiscriminately beating young Mexican Americans.[8] Over the next four nights, mobs of sailors and army soldiers, many armed with wooden bats, swarmed through the city, assaulting Mexican American youths at random, tearing off their zoot suits and proudly displaying the shredded clothing. Los Angeles police accompanied the caravans of rioting servicemen in police cars, watching the beatings and jailing the victims.[9] After five nights of violence, the navy finally stepped in when Admiral David Bagley, commandant of the 11th Naval District, issued an order on June 8 declaring Los Angeles "out of bounds" to all enlisted sailors. He asserted, however, that the sailors had only acted "in self-defense against the rowdy element."[10]

Violence next erupted in Beaumont, Texas, where a shipyard constructed the cargo vessels known as "Liberty Ships" for the navy. The shipyard employed Black workers, and the town's growing population stoked racial tensions as its segregated city buses became crowded. On the afternoon of June 15, 1943, a white woman married to a shipyard worker reported to the Beaumont police that she had been raped by a Black man. That night, some two thousand white shipyard workers put down their tools and walked to the Black part of the city and began assaulting Black citizens. The mob pulled a Black man from his car, beat him, overturned his car and set it ablaze.[11] They smashed stores, looted, and set numerous fires. At a bus depot, attackers set upon fifty-two Black army draftees, including Alex Mouton, who was clubbed mercilessly and later died of his injuries. Another Black man, an ice company employee, died after a white group accosted him and shot him in the chest. A white man also died at the hands of unknown attackers.

Beaumont's eruption was essentially a one-sided riot, with whites—many of them armed—carrying out the savagery. In addition to those who died, an estimated three hundred Black people were injured.[12] The authorities ultimately called the Texas State Guard to help stop the mayhem. In all, 206 people were arrested by the time the riot ended on the morning of June 16, though none was charged with a serious offense.

Officers seized 156 pistols and other weapons. Hundreds of Black residents fled Beaumont. A day after the rioting ended, a Beaumont physician examined the woman who reported the rape and concluded that it was a false accusation.

IN DETROIT, THE hate strike at Packard continued. As summer temperatures reached ninety-one degrees on Sunday, June 20, thousands of citizens, both Black and white, sought relief from the heat in a large municipal park on Belle Isle, an island in the Detroit River connected to the city by a bridge.[13] Late in the afternoon, a series of racial fights broke out. By evening, a large crowd of white people gathered on the bridge, and members of the crowd began chasing and beating Black people. Gladys House, a young Black woman, heard the mob shout, "We don't want any niggers on Belle Isle." The mob assaulted a young Black man accompanying her, but a white policeman took them across the bridge to safety.[14] The crowd at the bridge grew to an estimated five thousand people and spilled into downtown Detroit. Rumors ran wild, spurring angry groups of both races to take to the streets, and the violence intensified. In Paradise Valley, the Black section of town, another mob of Black people stopped a streetcar, stoned the passengers and beat the conductor. By 1:30 A.M., streetcar service in Paradise Valley was halted.

By early Monday morning, the riot had spiraled into mayhem across the city. Gangs of white people roved through the streets, hunting for Black people to assault. On one of the street's main avenues, a white crowd pulled a Black motorist out of his car, beat him and—after pausing as a mounted police officer rode by—turned his car over and set it on fire. About twenty Black people soon lost their cars to similar fires.[15] The intensity of the racial animus was splashed across the front of the next day's *Detroit Free Press* in two photos, each showing a different scene of a white police officer standing between a lone Black man and an angry white mob. "Police come to the rescue of terrified negroes chased and beaten by roving bands of whites," the caption said.[16] Yet police officers also repeatedly opened fire on Black people rioting. When one man, Carl Singleton, refused an order to stop running, a white police officer shot him in the back and killed him.[17] Amid the many tragedies of the day was that of Dr. Joseph De Horatiis, an Italian American doctor who was driving through Paradise Valley to see a patient when a Black man hurled a rock through his open car window, striking him in the head. After De Horatiis crashed his car, the assailant struck the doctor in the head with a rock once again. Horatiis died a few hours later.

As the violence continued into Monday afternoon, Otis Saunders, a Black member of the Detroit Double V Committee, got in a police car and—while being driven slowly through the ravaged areas—used a loudspeaker to implore all citizens to cease fighting. His efforts were met by jeers.[18] Detroit's mayor and police commissioner called all of the city's police officers to duty and state police officers were summoned, but the mob violence continued.

Michigan's Republican governor, Harry Kelly, hesitated to declare martial law and seek the assistance of the US Army. Finally, as a vast white mob gathered in Detroit's Cadillac Square on Monday evening, Kelly declared a "state of emergency" at 6:00 P.M., but he set a curfew to begin only at 10:00 P.M. and he still refused to call for federal troops.[19]

In Washington that evening, Secretary of War Stimson discussed the expected request from Governor Kelly with General Brehon Somervell, chief of the army logistics division. The army had three battalions of military police stationed in Detroit, about 2,500 soldiers in all. "That did not seem enough and I told Somervell to start the Second Division which was four hundred miles away in Wisconsin at Camp McCoy to move at once towards Detroit to be ready to help out," Stimson wrote in his diary.[20] He also called FDR and discussed the unfolding events.

At about ten o'clock that night, General Somervell and Provost General Allen Gullion arrived at Woodley and met with Stimson in his library. Governor Kelly at last called Stimson and requested support from US troops. Stimson immediately called FDR again at Hyde Park. "At ten-thirty I got hold of the president and enumerated to him just what had happened. He was fine about it and ready to back us up." A proclamation was prepared for FDR, who quickly signed it: "I do hereby command all persons engaged in said unlawful and insurrectionary proceedings to disperse and retire peaceably to their respective abodes immediately."[21] Federal troops entered Detroit and began to quell the violence. With bayonets fixed on rifles raised high, military police troops moved into Cadillac Square, launching tear gas grenades to break up the large white mob.[22] About five thousand army troops ultimately patrolled the city—the largest federal force in Detroit since the army quelled a race riot during the Civil War—and the bloody rioting came to an end at last.

The riot's death toll reached thirty-four people—twenty-five Black and nine white. Among the twenty-five Black people who died, seventeen were shot by police, prompting allegations that the police had used excessive force.[23] NAACP chief counsel Thurgood Marshall set up an emergency office in Detroit and took statements from riot victims. The association's executive director, Walter White, declared that many members of the police department were "in sympathy with the mobs." General William Guthner, who led the army's response in Detroit, also cited the police department's brutality, saying, "They have treated the Negroes terribly."[24] Police commissioner John Witherspoon rejected the claims, saying the department's policy was "to treat all alike . . . to avoid discrimination, to attempt in every manner to gain respect and to avoid at all costs any incident which would provide the spark to set off a serious race riot."

Segregationists quickly blamed the rioting on Roosevelt policies and the FEPC. "Detroit has suffered one of the most disastrous race riots in history," said Representative John Rankin of Mississippi. "The trouble has been hastened by the crazy policies of the so-called Fair Employment Practices Committee in attempting to mix the races in all kinds of employment."[25] In Mississippi, the *Jackson Daily News* faulted Eleanor Roosevelt for the rioting: "It is blood on your hands, Mrs. Roosevelt," the newspaper said on June 22. "You have been personally proclaiming and practicing social equality at the White House and wherever you go, Mrs. Roosevelt. In Detroit, a city noted for the growing impudence and insolence of its Negro population, an attempt was made to put your preachments into practice, Mrs. Roosevelt. What followed is history."

The persistent advocate for racial justice in the Roosevelt White House, Eleanor lamented the violence shaking the nation in her My Day newspaper column on June 24, offering a bleak outlook. "The domestic scene," the First Lady wrote, "is anything but encouraging and one would like not to think about it, because it gives one a feeling that, as a whole, we are not really prepared for democracy. We might even fall into the same excesses that some other people whom we look down upon have fallen into, for we do not seem to have learned self-control and obedience to law yet."

A week later, FDR once again deployed his strategy of silently advancing a policy on race: he signaled his continued support for the FEPC's work by appointing six new members to its board, one of whom was a Brotherhood of Sleeping Car Porters official closely allied with Randolph.[26] With the threat of renewed racial violence hanging over the nation, Randolph appeared to embrace the president's quiet tactics. On July 3, two days after FDR strengthened the FEPC, a convention of the March on Washington Movement organized by Randolph voted against holding a march in the nation's capital in 1943.[27]

Stimson was concerned that America's racial tensions might explode again. On July 5, he called General Somervell into his office to discuss transportation of Black soldiers to bases in the South, as the soldiers were using segregated public buses, and "whenever a negro soldier goes into the white portion of the bus, there is trouble. . . . I find there is a great deal of discrimination against them," he wrote in his diary, adding that the Black sections of buses were "insufficient and unpleasant. . . . Consequently I told Somervell I had come to conclusion that we have got to do something at once about that or there will be real trouble in the tense situation that exists among the two races throughout the country."[28] He showed the general a *Life* magazine article about the Detroit riot, noting, "These photographs in every case show the victim was a negro and was being beaten and assaulted by white men."

THE BLOODSHED IN Detroit raised concerns that racial violence might erupt in other cities, including New York. In a radio broadcast on June 27, Mayor Fiorello La Guardia urged all of his city's residents to be skeptical of racial rumors and tolerant of different cultures. "I will not permit, as long as I am mayor of this city, any minority group to be abused by another group," he warned. "I will maintain law and order in this city and I will afford protection to anyone who is attacked as I will prosecute anyone who does the attacking or provoking."[29]

The widespread attacks on Black Americans in Detroit and across the country intensified frustrations and fury among New York's Black community. The writer Langston Hughes expressed his anger in a poem entitled "Beaumont to Detroit: 1943," published July 3 in *The People's Voice,* a newspaper founded a year earlier by a young activist, Adam Clayton Powell Jr.[30] The poem decried the bitter irony of Black Americans fighting a war for freedom against fascism abroad while being subjected to racial discrimination at home. The poem ended trenchantly:

> I ask you this question
> Cause I want to know
> How long I got to fight
> BOTH HITLER AND JIM CROW.

Among those who took a stand against racial violence were entertainers in New York, including clarinetist Benny Goodman, who helped form the Emergency Committee of the Entertainment Industry. Working with Walter White, the group won support from CBS for a thirty-minute radio program on the evening of July 24 calling for an end to the racial violence. White also brought in Wendell Willkie, helping him write a speech for the show.[31]

Called "An Open Letter to the American People," the program began: "Tonight, race hatred is breeding and festering in a score of booming, over-crowded war centers. And so, tonight, we ask you to hear what happened in Detroit, because we believe that no sensible, fully-informed American will allow to happen again here at home what he is fighting against all over the world."[32] The show reenacted scenes from the Detroit riot and then turned the microphone over to Willkie, who had recently announced he was seeking the Republican nomination for president in 1944.

Willkie delivered a sharp condemnation of racism in America, criticizing both major political parties. "One [party] has the tendency to ask the Negro for his vote as recompense for an act of simple justice done 80 years ago," he said, referring to the Republicans and their stance against slavery in the Civil War. He then charged that the "other party"—the

Democratic Party—"retains political power by, in effect, depriving the Negro of his right to vote in one part of the country, while seeking his vote in another, on the plea of great friendship for his race. . . . Both attitudes must be changed. One party cannot go on feeling that it has no further obligation to the Negro citizen because Lincoln freed the slave. And the other is not entitled to power if it sanctions one set of principles in Atlanta, and another in Harlem."[33] He went on to draw a parallel between racism and fascism. "The desire to deprive some of our citizens of their rights—economic, civic, or political—has the same basic motivation as actuates the fascist mind when it seeks to dominate whole peoples and nations." He called for a "bill of rights" that would ensure African Americans equal rights in the realms of justice, voting, education and employment. He warned that the "mob madness" seen in Detroit and other American cities would leave a lasting impression around the world.

On the same day, Vice President Henry Wallace, while visiting Detroit, sounded similar themes when he condemned "American fascists."[34] But it was the 1940 Republican Party leader whom *The Pittsburgh Courier* hailed in a banner headline across its next issue's front page: "Willkie Blasts 'Hate.'"

The efforts of Willkie, La Guardia and White were not enough to prevent more violence. On Sunday night, August 1, a white police officer started to arrest a drunken Black woman in a hotel lobby in Harlem when a Black soldier intervened. The two men fought and the officer shot the soldier in the shoulder.[35] The officer managed to arrest the soldier, whose injury was slight, and walked him to a nearby hospital. Rumors flew that the white officer had shot the Black soldier to death, and Black people in Harlem began rioting, throwing rocks and bottles through windows of vehicles and shops, targeting white-owned businesses in particular. NAACP official Roy Wilkins explained the riot by pointing to the wave of violence against Black soldiers and Black workers by police and others: "The Harlem mob knew all this. It hated this. It could not reach the Arkansas cop who fired a full magazine of his revolver into the prone body of a Negro sergeant, or any of the others, so it tore up Harlem."[36]

Devastation spread through Harlem as looting became rampant. Some shop owners hurriedly posted signs saying their stores were owned by Black people in an attempt to deter the mob. Many white-owned businesses were looted and wrecked. Buildings were set afire. Injured people streamed into hospitals. Writer James Baldwin, who witnessed the riot's fury as a young man living in Harlem, explained the rage: "The mob seems to have been mainly interested in something more potent and real than the white face, that is, in white power."[37] La Guardia ordered a curfew at 10:30 P.M. and, with Walter White at his side, went into the streets of Harlem pleading with rioters to go home—to no avail.[38] At 1:05 A.M. Monday morning, La Guardia went on the radio to report the details of the nonfatal shooting of the soldier, the first of five broadcasts he made during the night.

The violence mounted. Police shot a Black man as he dragged a suitcase from a luggage store; the police said he had drawn a knife.[39] Four other Black men were shot to death while looting. Another Black man was shot by a Black bartender after he allegedly kicked in the bar's window. The city put all of its police officers on duty, and ultimately more than six hundred people were arrested. Nearly 1,500 stores were looted or damaged, and the total loss was estimated at $5 million. In addition to the six slain people, some seven hundred were injured, including forty policemen. At last, by midday Monday, peace was restored.

La Guardia won praise from Powell, White and others. "How different was Detroit!" White said. "There a weak mayor hid while Negroes were beaten on the steps of City Hall itself." La Guardia, in contrast, was "in the thick of the trouble, often at great personal risk," White said.[40] Despite the Black death toll, White praised New York's police, saying that never "during those troubled hours" did he hear "one word about 'niggers,' as I had heard so frequently in Detroit, nor was there any other manifestation of racial animosity. They were simply concerned with restoring order."

Racial discrimination and violence continued across America, but Harlem's explosion on the night of August 1, 1943, was the last race riot to strike an American city during the war. Why no other race riots broke out cannot be known with certainty, but some credit is due to two of FDR's prominent Republican allies, Willkie and La Guardia, and NAACP leader Walter White, who had worked together to restore peace and build unity in America—however imperfect and fractured that unity might be—at a time of tremendous need.

Power, Advice and Dissent

By early 1943, President Franklin Roosevelt and his chief Republican allies, Henry Stimson and Frank Knox, had established an unwritten formula for bipartisan leadership. FDR had joined with the two Republicans to build national unity, secure political power and prepare the nation for war. The secretaries of war and the navy advised him on a broad range of military issues and played critical roles in strengthening US armed forces. They challenged FDR and dissented from his views at times and, in turn, understood that the president welcomed their advice even though he sometimes rejected it. They were guided by an overarching philosophy of placing the national good over partisan interests. The success of this bipartisan formula depended on their relationships of trust and mutual respect, which grew as they faced the trials of wartime leadership.

Roosevelt was, of course, the dominant power in the alliance. Through his masterful conduct of strategic meetings with Prime Minister Churchill and other international leaders, FDR had garnered wide respect as the architect of the global effort to save democracy from fascism. Domestically, his Democratic Party controlled Congress, and he enjoyed a rapport with the American people through his compelling oratory and his reassuring Fireside Chats. However, FDR's alliance with southern Democrats was fracturing over racial politics, while isolationism and opposition to the New Deal persisted. Stimson and Knox, as high-profile Republican leaders in his administration, helped him bring the country together in support for his conduct of the war.

The president informed the American people about the war's progress, but Stimson and Knox often took the lead in releasing news—good and bad—about specific developments in the war. They also played critical roles in building momentum behind key pieces of legislation in Congress, winning the support of Republicans and of the public for a broad array of wartime efforts. On subjects where FDR might be suspected of having a political motive, the two Republicans at his side gave him credibility.

Stimson and Knox ran their departments largely with a free hand, working with commanders to devise military strategy and develop new technologies and weaponry. Although Stimson never publicly proclaimed his theory of holding the War Department as a "hostage" of the Republican Party, he repeatedly named Republicans to War Department posts. The president seldom stepped in to limit Stimson's authority.

The bipartisan alliance followed this formula in addressing the avalanche of issues the administration confronted in early 1943, beginning in January when FDR and Churchill prepared to meet in Casablanca, recently captured by the Allies in the invasion of French Morocco. As with most other strategic conferences, FDR did not invite Stimson or Knox to Casablanca; instead, his advisers included Army chief of staff General George Marshall, General Dwight Eisenhower, General Hap Arnold, Admiral Ernest King and aides Harry Hopkins and Averell Harriman.

As the meeting date approached in January 1943, it became clear that US and British war planners were once again sharply divided. Marshall and Stimson believed that, after the Germans were defeated in Tunisia, the next strategic offensive should be an invasion of the coast of France later in the year.[1] The British, however, considered such an attack too risky because of heavily armored German defenses posted along the French coast. Instead, Churchill and the chief of the Imperial General Staff, General Alan Brooke, advocated for an attack on the Italian island of Sicily.

American views of the cross-channel strategy were not uniform.

Eisenhower, the supreme Allied commander for the European Theater of Operations, had ardently supported the cross-channel invasion in 1942, but had now come to share the British view that invading France in 1943 was not possible because "our original conceptions of the strength required were too low."[2] The army had identified both its own weaknesses and the strengths of the German military. Valuable lessons learned in North Africa made Eisenhower more cautious about attacking Nazi defenses on the French coast. The Combined Chiefs agreed at last, in a January 18 meeting with Roosevelt and Churchill, to invade Sicily after securing the defeat of the Germans in Tunisia, an event expected within a few months. The idea of invading France in 1943 was discarded.

The decision to abandon the 1943 invasion plan angered Stimson, apparently unaware of Eisenhower's views. "It looks as if the British were forcing us to do some more in the Mediterranean," he noted in his diary in Washington.[3] He wrote of the "somber news that . . . it seems to be clear that the British are getting away with their own theories and that the president must be yielding to their views as against those of our own General Staff and Chief of Staff. So it looks as if we were in for further entanglements in the Mediterranean."[4]

The agreement by US commanders to invade Sicily in July 1943 pleased Churchill and Brooke. The British commander crowed in his diary, "We have gotten practically all we hoped to get when we came here!" He had utter disdain for his American counterpart: "Marshall has got practically no strategic vision, his thoughts revolve around the creation of forces and not on their employment. He arrived here without a single real strategic concept, he has initiated nothing in the policy for the future conduct of the war."[5] Churchill joyfully wrote his wife, Clementine: "It is in every respect as I wished & proposed."[6]

Once Marshall returned from Casablanca, he met with Stimson on January 30 to discuss the conference. The US Army's success thus far in North Africa surely tempered Stimson's willingness to challenge FDR's military strategy. There is no evidence that Stimson and FDR ever revisited their long argument over the North African invasion, but Stimson likely conceded at some point—perhaps privately, to himself—that FDR had been proved right. After learning from Marshall that the president had made up his mind on the invasion of Sicily, Stimson ceased urging an invasion of France for 1943. A few days later, the secretary of war met at the White House with FDR. "The president was in fine form and I had one of the best and most friendly talks with him I have ever had," Stimson recalled.[7] "He was full of his trip, naturally, and interspersed our whole talk with stories and anecdotes."

THE TWO MEN soon moved to revise their treatment of Japanese Americans, whom they had sent to concentration camps almost a year earlier despite the attorney general's warnings and Stimson's own concerns about constitutional rights. John McCloy, the assistant secretary of war who was one of Stimson's top aides, had begun exploring the idea of permitting Nisei, the generation of US citizens born to parents who immigrated from Japan, to volunteer for the army. McCloy met in January with two members of the Japanese American Citizens League, an organization of Japanese Americans that vigorously supported the US government and opposed Japanese fascism.[8]

On January 28, Stimson announced publicly that the army would recruit Nisei volunteers. "It is the inherent right of every faithful citizen, regardless of ancestry, to bear arms in the nation's battle. When obstacles to the free expression of that right are imposed by emergency considerations those barriers should be removed as soon as humanly possible."[9]

Days after this announcement, the White House released a letter from FDR to Stimson supporting the recruitment of Japanese Americans into the army. "The proposal of the War Department to organize a combat team consisting of loyal American citizens of Japanese descent has my full approval," FDR said, noting that five thousand people of Japanese descent were already serving in the armed forces. He went on to downplay the importance of ancestry—a concept that had been at the center of the army's internment orders. "No loyal citizen of the United States should be denied the democratic right to exercise the responsibilities of his citizenship, regardless of his ancestry. Americanism is not, and never was, a matter of race or ancestry."[10]

Tied together in the 1942 decision to intern Japanese Americans,

FDR and Stimson were now united in support of an effort to bring Japanese Americans into the war effort. This was a minor correction of a vast injustice—about eighty thousand Japanese Americans remained in concentration camps two years later.[11] US Army recruiters soon appeared in the camps and began accepting applications from young Nisei deemed loyal after completing a two-page questionnaire.[12]

The new Nisei recruits took roles in the army's Military Intelligence Service (MIS), where they served as interpreters, and in the 100th Infantry Battalion, which soon would win recognition for fighting with extraordinary valor in Italy. One Nisei interpreter decoded a radio message relaying flight plans for Japanese admiral Isoroku Yamamoto, the chief planner of the Pearl Harbor attack. The navy then tracked Yamamoto's movements in the South Pacific, and on April 18, 1943, US Army Air Force P-38 fighters shot down his plane, killing him.[13]

THE BIPARTISAN ALLIANCE's method of handling war news drew attention in February 1943, when American and British forces encountered ferocious attacks by German and Italian divisions under General Erwin Rommel in the Atlas Mountains of western Tunisia. From February 14 to 16, Rommel's Panzer tank forces tore through American infantry, devastating the 168th Infantry Regiment and overrunning airfields and supply depots.[14] In Washington, Stimson told reporters on August 18 that Rommel's assault had caused Allied troops to retreat by as much as thirty-five miles and to evacuate three airfields. He described it as a "sharp reverse." He sought to strike a balance by saying it was an event that "should not be minimized but still less should it be exaggerated."[15]

In Germany, Joseph Goebbels, Hitler's propaganda minister, who routinely dispensed false information, noted in his diary that Stimson's conference was "extraordinary in its frankness."[16]

Rommel quickly sought to drive for further gains with his mobile spearhead force, the Afrika Korps, including a Panzer division and Italian armored vehicles, which attacked US tank and infantry forces at the Kasserine Pass in the Atlas Mountains. By the evening of February 20, US forces defending the pass had retreated, casualties mounted, survivors dispersed in disarray, and two hundred US tanks lay wrecked on the battlefield.[17] Two days later, US and British forces stiffened their defenses against Rommel's salient. An American infantry division, supported by the 1st Armored Division and highly accurate artillery fire, exacted a severe toll on Rommel's advance. With Flying Fortresses and Spitfires attacking from the air, the Allies pushed the Axis troops out of the Kasserine Pass and Rommel's forces were in full retreat, a success for the Allies.[18]

At a news conference on February 25, Stimson announced that the Allies had achieved a "clean-cut repulse" to the enemy at Kasserine Pass. "Despite initial reverses the prospects continue favorable," he told reporters at the Pentagon. "However, the current fighting serves to remind us that there is no easy road to victory and that we must expect some setbacks and considerable casualties."[19] News reports had already revealed the military success, but Stimson's official voice confirmed the events and put them in perspective for the American people.

Stimson also released a statement from Eisenhower praising US troops and saying they were "thoroughly mad and ready to fight." FDR spent the day at the White House in bed, perhaps due to illness or exhaustion.[20] Stimson's role in bringing war news to the public, in the authoritative tones of an experienced secretary of war, relieved the stress on the president, enabling him to rest, recuperate and address other priorities.

The following month, when critics in Congress opposed the army's plan to raise its troop level, Stimson waged a public campaign for its passage. He argued in a radio broadcast that the increase from five million soldiers at the end of 1942 to 8.2 million in 1943 was necessary to enable the US military to "take the offensive and seize a number of priceless opportunities which are already opening up for us to end the war as quickly as possible."[21] Stimson prevailed, and the army's expansion won congressional approval.

Bipartisan support in Congress for the administration's war policies remained strong. On March 11, 1943, two years after Stimson, Knox and Willkie fought for passage of the Lend-Lease bill in a bitter debate with isolationists, an expansion of the program was debated for less than three hours before the Senate voted 82–0 to pass it. The House passed the measure, which would boost Lend-Lease spending to $9.6 billion, by a vote of 407–6.[22] FDR signed it immediately, saying Lend-Lease "will contribute increasingly to the defeat of the Axis."

STIMSON'S VITAL ROLE in developing new types of weapons was most evident in the race to stop the Nazi submarines that were sinking Allied vessels at an astonishing pace. From December 1941 to March 1943, German submarines had sunk seven million tons of Allied shipping.[23] The secretary of war tracked the evolution of radar technology through regular conversations with his cousin Alfred Loomis, and he energized the army's deployment of radar by hiring a radar consultant, Massachusetts Institute of Technology professor Edward Bowles.[24] At Stimson's request, Bowles set up a "combat laboratory" at Langley Field, Virginia, to equip the B-24 Liberator and other bombers with radar devices.[25] In 1942, Stimson worked with General Marshall and General Arnold to create an antisubmarine command using B-24 bombers to attack submarines off the US coast. In fall 1942, a submarine-killer B-24 squadron was sent to Morocco and then began operating from St. Eval, England, in collaboration with the British Coastal Command's submarine-hunting force.

Stimson also called for the army and navy to create a joint antisubmarine command to confront the Nazi submarine force, but the navy bluntly rejected the proposal. Admiral King, the chief of Naval Operations, thought the idea of going on the offensive against submarines was like hunting for needles in a haystack. The surest way to defeat Nazi submarines, King believed, was for navy ships to escort merchant vessels as they crossed submarine-infested waters. King told General Marshall in a letter in June 1942 that "escort is not just one way of handling the submarine menace; it is the only way that gives any promise of success."[26] Though escorts had shown success, they had certainly not ended the devastation by Nazi submarines.

Stimson was furious over the navy's refusal to use aircraft to hunt submarines.[27] He raised the issue with both FDR and Knox, and the pressure on the navy to approve an offensive antisubmarine effort led Admiral King in May 1943 to form a new command, the US Navy's Tenth Fleet, to use aircraft to form "submarine killer groups."[28] This new fleet, however, existed chiefly on paper—it had no planes. To resolve the standoff, Stimson approved what became known as the army-navy "horse trade": the army turned over its force of seventy-seven radar-equipped B-24 Liberators to the navy in exchange for a similar number of navy Liberators with no radar equipment.[29]

The navy's takeover of the army antisubmarine force came amid dramatic successes for the army antisubmarine force that was working with the British Coastal Command. The joint forces launched a series of successful attacks on Nazi submarines off the African coast and in the Bay of Biscay in July and August 1943.[30] Churchill giddily reported to FDR in a brief cable July 13: "Admiralty report 5 U-boats destroyed by our joint forces in the last 24 hours. This is an all-time world high."[31] Churchill followed up the next day with another excited cable: "I was wrong when I said 5 U boats in 24 hours. It is 7 in 36."

When Churchill learned the navy was to take control of the army's B-24 force, he wrote Stimson pleading "earnestly" for the navy's take-over not to upset the successful collaboration of the army antisubmarine force with the British Coastal Command. The navy finally completed the takeover in November 1943.[32] The Nazi submarine threat diminished sharply after the fall of 1943, in part due to the effectiveness of the radar-equipped antisubmarine air force that Stimson had built up.

The secretary of war's role in the development of new weapons came to the attention of Senator Harry Truman, a powerful Missouri Democrat who headed a committee investigating abuses in war contracting. The committee unknowingly probed the highly secret S-1 program—also called the Manhattan Project—which was responsible for building the atomic bomb. On June 17, 1943, Truman began questioning Stimson about a vast industrial project led by the army in the state of Washington. Stimson simply replied, "Now that's a matter which I know all about personally, and I am one of the group of two or three men in the whole world who know about it. . . . It's part of a very secret development." Truman quickly withdrew his inquiry, making a deferential retreat. "You won't have to say another word to me. Whenever you say that to me, that's all I want to hear."[33]

· · ·

STIMSON'S SUPPORT OF both FDR and the war effort won praise from key Democrats, including Attorney General Francis Biddle, who had clashed with him over the Japanese internment. In a letter on January 1, 1943, Biddle wrote:

> My Dear Secretary Stimson:
>
> I cannot let the New Year start without a word to you to express my admiration for what you have done for our country. It is a magnificent army; and you have built it up from a shell, patiently, imaginatively, with vision and fortitude. The country knows this; and recognizes your quiet leadership. . . . Your unswerving loyalty to the president . . . heartens the rest of us who are working under his leadership.[34]

Stimson's loyalty to FDR did not prevent him from arguing forcefully with the president on war strategy and other issues, such as when FDR tried to find a military role for his old friend Fiorello La Guardia, the Republican mayor of New York City, as US forces prepared to invade Italy. Since 1942, La Guardia had been delivering antifascist speeches that the US government broadcast by radio to listeners in Italy. But he was eager to play a greater part in the war. On March 17, he met with FDR at the White House and came away with the promise of a job with Eisenhower's forces.[35] "I saw the Chief yesterday—and I am so happy that I can be of service to my country," he wrote his friend Harry Hopkins the next day. "I am to be assigned to General Eisenhower's staff and am confident that I will be able to do a good job and be really useful."

When Stimson learned that FDR had sent a telegram asking Eisenhower to find a place for La Guardia on his staff, he was irate. "Poor Eisenhower was in a terrible position for of course he, as a soldier, could not question the matter the way Marshall and I would have no hesitation in doing," he wrote in his diary on March 27.[36]

La Guardia was an ally—a patriotic Republican who crossed party lines to support FDR—but Stimson gave him no quarter. When he came to Stimson's Pentagon office three days later to discuss the matter, the secretary of war told him he would be commissioned only as a colonel, no higher, and his options would be to enter the ground forces of the Army Air Forces or go to an army school in Virginia for training.[37] Stimson recounted the conversation in a letter the same day to FDR, noting that he told La Guardia that he could better serve the nation by speaking out as mayor of New York than by being a "make-believe General." La Guardia had replied that he thought Eisenhower had asked for him personally, but Stimson bluntly dismissed that idea. "I told him he was mistaken; that I had looked into it personally and that Eisenhower did not want him in Africa until the fighting was over." He told the president that La Guardia "then said that ended it for he wouldn't dream of going if he was not wanted by Eisenhower."

That same night, La Guardia called FDR, who promptly called Marshall.[38] FDR was incensed that Stimson had blocked his plan. Adding to the tension was the fact that La Guardia's desire for a generalcy was reported in the press and had come under scrutiny in Congress. Despite FDR's objections to his handling of the matter, Stimson announced the next day that the mayor would not be joining the army anytime soon. "It was my view that in his present office as Mayor of New York he is rendering directly to that city, and indirectly to the entire nation, an example of such usefulness that it is very difficult now to find any place in the Army where he could be equally useful," the secretary of war told reporters.[39] *The New York Times* ran the story on its front page the next day, virtually sealing La Guardia's rejection. Now, to get La Guardia the post he wanted, FDR would have to overrule the publicly stated advice of his own secretary of war.

After a cabinet meeting the next day, FDR told Stimson he had "been too hard on the Little Flower," using the mayor's nickname (based on his Italian first name, Fiorello).[40] Later that day Stimson received a letter from the president stating his objections more forcefully. It began, "Dear Harry: Frankly, I think you have this LaGuardia business all wrong." FDR proceeded to list his disagreements with nearly every point in Stimson's previous letter.[41] "I do not like your second paragraph wherein you suggested that he ought not to be a make-believe General. In the strictest sense of the word, you have a great many make-believe generals." As to whether Eisenhower had use for La Guardia, FDR said the general himself had told him that he wanted the mayor not for the battle in Tunisia "but for the next operation that you and I know about," referring to the approaching invasion of Italy.

Stunned, Stimson drafted a five-page reply. "My dear Mr. President," he began. "I have received your letter of April 8th and am deeply grieved that, from my own fault in part at least, I should have caused you the distress of mind which your letter evidences." He explained his first letter had caused misunderstandings because it was a hasty one-page summary, not a verbatim account. For instance, he did not actually use the phrase "make-believe general" in the conversation with La Guardia.[42] He also acknowledged that the phrase was "particularly unfair to you" because of the president's willingness to follow the advice of his military advisers in appointing generals. "The record of your Administration is unique in American war history for its scrupulous abstention from personal and political pressure." Stimson went on to say that "as Mayor of the greatest city in this country [La Guardia] held a pulpit for influencing the people of Italy which in my opinion was far more effective than any pulpit he could have as a soldier and I urged him not to lose that pulpit." He closed by asking if he and FDR could talk the matter over in person.

The two men had lunch together on May 3 at the White House, discussing matters ranging from Tunisia to Italy and Burma. Then FDR raised the La Guardia issue by saying the mayor, who had been an army pilot in World War I, "had a strong sentimental feeling for the Army." But FDR let the matter drop. "He gave me the impression that he has reluctantly come to the opinion that I was right in the position I took in my second letter," Stimson recalled. "He was evidently over his irritation." The tempest having passed, the two men resumed their work running the war.

La Guardia, meanwhile, continued his antifascist broadcasts in Italian, condemning the dictator Benito Mussolini. After the Allies invaded Sicily in early July 1943, La Guardia's words, broadcast by the US Office of War Information, urged Italians to turn against the Nazis. "This is your friend La Guardia speaking," he began a July 25 broadcast. He bluntly proclaimed his "hate for the fascist government," which he said had brought his beloved Italy nothing but "a series of hardships, death, shame and defeat." He implored the country to "get rid of the fascist government before Italy's complete defeat."[43] That very same day, as American troops fought the Nazis in Sicily, Italy's king removed Mussolini from power and put him under arrest.

IF STIMSON'S INTERVENTION in the La Guardia case angered Roosevelt, his actions on another personnel matter likely pleased the president. In the fall of 1942, as General Douglas MacArthur led American forces fighting the Japanese through islands in the Southwest Pacific, powerful conservative publishers including Robert McCormick, owner of the *Chicago Tribune*, and William Randolph Hearst joined radio priest Father Charles Coughlin in supporting the idea of a MacArthur run for the presidency—and suggesting that FDR's administration was cutting the general out of operations to hinder his candidacy in 1944.[44] Stimson, who admired the general's military leadership but criticized him for self-serving behavior, grew concerned about the rumors of his possible candidacy. He wrote in his diary in October 1942: "MacArthur, who is not an unselfish being and is a good deal of a prima donna, has himself lent to the story by . . . playing into the hands of people who would really like to make him a candidate."[45]

Four months later, in February 1943, Stimson issued a rule preventing all active army officers from seeking the nomination of political parties for public office. Republicans in Congress charged that Stimson's rule appeared to be aimed at preventing General MacArthur from running against FDR for president in 1944.[46] Senator Arthur Vandenberg, the prominent Michigan Republican, said, "If a great American emerges . . . as the next most eligible President of the United States, the War Department cannot stop him just because he happens to be a 'member of the military forces on active duty,' and it will make a blunder, as ineffectual as it will be transparent, if it tries."

Peppered with questions by reporters during his press conference on April 8, 1943, Stimson bluntly insisted his rule was unrelated to MacArthur and merely restated various rules issued previously by the War Department. Indeed, the perils of active-duty soldiers entering politics was a lesson learned by the army as far back as 1864, when Union general George McClellan ran as the Democratic candidate for president against his own commander in chief, President Abraham Lincoln. "I can tell you with great explicitness that I did not have General MacArthur in mind," Stimson told reporters.[47] Had this rule been issued by a Democrat, the dispute might have gained momentum, but under Stimson's suasion it subsided. The rule stood—and MacArthur did not run for president in 1944.

FDR's DEPTH OF support for Stimson was evident when members of the Democratic National Committee met with FDR and urged him to fire the secretary of war. It was unclear who exactly led the attempted ouster, but FDR had met on May 19, 1943, with Edward Flynn, the former DNC chairman and Bronx Democratic boss who was the president's longtime ally.[48] John McCloy learned ten days later that FDR had responded to a DNC demand for Stimson's dismissal by saying it was a great thing to have such a capable man head the War Department in the midst of the war.[49] The president said Stimson had courage and a good reputation, and pointed to a whiff of scandal brewing over a war contract lobbyist's home in Washington, DC, where prominent officials had attended dinner parties.[50] FDR said Stimson was the only member of his cabinet he could be certain would never be caught in such a trap, and then "brushed [the DNC members] out the door," according to McCloy, who informed Stimson of the discussion. Two days later, Supreme Court justice Felix Frankfurter confirmed FDR's brusque dismissal of the Democratic bid to oust Stimson.[51]

Stimson was a sharp-tongued, free-thinking Republican who sometimes reserved his fiery opinions for his diary, where he once called the staff of FDR's War Manpower Commission "a lot of callow New Dealers with more ambition than brains."[52] At the age of seventy-five in early 1943, the pressures of war could leave him exhausted, though he continued to take regular exercise in deck tennis—usually a few games per week on the court at Woodley—or horseback riding.[53] For Roosevelt, Stimson sometimes made frustrating decisions and refused to back down, but he was a staunch ally with deep insights whom FDR admired. Stimson would remain in the cabinet.

As their relationship matured—the bipartisan alliance was at the end of its third year in May 1943—Stimson and FDR regarded each other with deepening respect. This bond at the center of the American war effort was founded not on hierarchical authority but on their shared commitment to defending democracy and on their mutual trust built through battles fought together. FDR knew that Stimson would summon his abundant faculties to argue for his point of view, but at some point he would honorably accept and obey the president's decision. Though Stimson remained concerned about Churchill's influence over FDR, the secretary of war's criticism of FDR's management style receded. He was now firmly in the president's camp. In late May, he told an army general about "my experience with two great executives—Theodore Roosevelt and Franklin Roosevelt."[54] A week later, he recounted in his diary how, at a private club, he "tried to combat some of the very stiff prejudice that I find everywhere against the president."

It was at this point—with their relationship the strongest it had ever been—that FDR and Stimson took up the twin challenges of overcoming Allied fears about an invasion of France and of putting in place a commander necessary to ensure that invasion's success.

Forging American Leadership for D-Day

In spring 1943, Allied commanders preparing to invade Sicily foresaw a swift victory on the Italian island in the Mediterranean Sea, and they began a tense debate over their next strategic move. The US Army chief of staff, General George Marshall, wanted to launch an invasion across the English Channel into France no later than the spring of 1944, and he had the strong support of Secretary of War Henry Stimson. On the British side, Prime Minister Winston Churchill and General Alan Brooke, chief of the Imperial General Staff, supported an invasion onto mainland Italy and then perhaps through the nearby Balkan countries north toward Germany. In the middle of this fierce debate sat President Franklin Roosevelt, who held to his practice of reserving his final judgment until he had heard from all sides. Roosevelt invited Churchill and his military leaders to come to Washington in mid-May 1943 to discuss strategy.

Stimson perceived that he and Marshall were once again up against Churchill, a leader of captivating oratorical skill who was urging FDR to embrace an attack on the periphery in the Mediterranean rather than a direct assault on the Nazi forces. "I fear it will be the same story over again," Stimson lamented in his diary on May 10. "The man from London will arrive with a program of further expansion in the Mediterranean and will have his way with our Chief, and the careful and deliberate plans of our staff will be overridden. I feel very troubled by it."[1] Stimson foresaw an intense struggle between the Allies. "Churchill arrived last night with a huge military party, evidently equipped for war on us, determined to get his own way."[2] He added, "I dread his eloquent and vigorous presentation of cases that are themselves unstable and dramatic rather than military."

Thus began a drawn-out struggle with Churchill in which Stimson helped FDR convince the British to carry out the momentous D-Day invasion across the English Channel in 1944—and to name an American commander for the invasion. The opening salvo came quickly. On May 12—the same day that more than a hundred thousand German and Italian soldiers surrendered in North Africa, sealing the Allied victory there—Churchill met with FDR and the Combined Chiefs of Staff at the White House.[3] Asked by the president to make some introductory remarks, Churchill said that after conquering Sicily the Allies should attack mainland Italy, obtain its surrender, and then drive north through Italy and the Balkans. He asserted that the Allies could strengthen their forces by convincing Turkey, until now neutral, to enter the war on their side. He also portrayed the American proposition of a cross-channel invasion as liable to fail: "The difficult beaches, with the great rise and fall of tide, the strength of the enemy's defenses, the number of his reserves, and the ease of his communications, all made the task one which must not be underrated."[4] He allowed that the British remained open to the invasion—but only "if a plan offering reasonable prospects of success could be made." Admiral William Leahy, FDR's chief of staff, said of Churchill: "It is apparently his opinion that adequate preparations cannot be made for such an effort in 1944."[5]

FDR suggested that the idea of invading mainland Italy should be considered, but he quickly turned to the cross-channel invasion, saying it "should be decided upon definitely as an operation for the spring of 1944."[6] It was like a thunderclap in the room. The two chiefs of the United Nations were at odds over the central strategic question facing them—whether and when to cross the English Channel and invade France. The sense of discord was sharp. General Hastings Ismay, Churchill's top military assistant, later said the meeting had "an unmistakable atmosphere of tension . . . it was clear there was going to be a battle royal."[7]

Contrary to Stimson's worries, FDR stood up for an invasion across

the English Channel in 1944, but these were merely the opening remarks of the strategy discussions to come. The next day, May 13, FDR
and Churchill remained at the White House while the Combined
Chiefs of Staff—including Admirals Leahy and King, and Generals Marshall, Brooke and Ismay—opened their talks in the Board of Governors
Room of the Federal Reserve on Constitution Avenue. Brooke argued
that the top priority for the Allies must be attacking further into Italy
and the Mediterranean region, and he disparaged the idea of a cross-
channel invasion in 1944. Brooke asserted that the Allies could only
have fifteen to twenty divisions, or roughly two hundred thousand soldiers, available for a cross-channel invasion by spring 1944—and most
of them would be inexperienced.[8]

Marshall countered that he "felt deeply concerned that the landing
of ground forces in Italy would establish a vacuum in the Mediterranean
which would preclude the assembly of sufficient forces in the United
Kingdom to execute a successful cross-channel operation." This would
delay the invasion of France, in turn delaying the defeat of Germany
and the ultimate defeat of Japan, "which the people of the United States
would not tolerate," he insisted.[9]

Brooke argued that the Allies might be able to secure a position
across the English Channel on France's Brest Peninsula, but the limited
number of Allied troops available meant they would not have the forces
required to push the Nazis back across France toward Germany. In fact,
he said, "No major operations would be possible until 1945 or 1946."

After the meeting ended in discord, Stimson spoke with Marshall.
"A very decided deadlock has come up. The British are holding back
dead from going on" with the buildup of forces for the cross-channel
invasion, Stimson wrote in his diary on May 17.[10] He called FDR to bolster his support for the cross-channel invasion. The president appeared
ready to take a firm stance. "He told me he was coming to the conclusion he would have to read the Riot Act to the other side and would
have to be stiff."

The Combined Chiefs, however, reached a compromise that same
day: Brooke agreed to a cross-channel invasion into France in May or
June 1944, and Marshall agreed that the Allies could launch further attacks
against the Italians after the invasion of Sicily as long as seven divisions

of troops were held in reserve for the invasion of France.[11] Brooke was relieved by the accord and noted in his diary that the Combined Chiefs "at last found a bridge across which we could meet! Not altogether a satisfactory one, but far better than a breakup of the conference!"[12]

The deal fell apart quickly. When Marshall, Brooke and other members of the Combined Chiefs went to the White House on Monday, May 24, to present the final terms of their agreement to FDR and Churchill in the Oval Office, Churchill lashed out at the agreement and refused to accept it. The prime minister "entirely repudiated the paper we had passed, agreed to, and been congratulated on at our last meeting! He wished to alter all the Mediterranean decisions!" Brooke wrote exasperatedly in his diary.[13] "As a result he created [a] situation of suspicion in the American Chiefs that we had been behind their backs, and has made matters far more difficult for us in the future!! There are times when he drives me to desperation!"

Marshall and the other American chiefs were equally shocked. Churchill "spent an hour advocating invasion of Italy with a possible extension to Yugoslavia and Greece," Leahy noted in his diary. This stunning rejection of the agreement confirmed suspicions that US military officials had long held about British strategists seeking to advance the aims of the British Empire.

"The Prime Minister's attitude is an exact agreement with the permanent British policy of controlling the Mediterranean Sea, regardless of what may be the result of the war," Leahy wrote.[14]

After the military leaders left the White House, Churchill and Roosevelt met next with Harry Hopkins, FDR's close aide, who had become a trusted intermediary for the two men. Hopkins succeeded in proposing a revision of the agreement that "only altered details and none of the principles," Brooke said.[15] Churchill finally yielded after FDR agreed to send Marshall with the prime minister on a visit to North Africa to discuss strategy further, Marshall later told Stimson.[16] Speaking with Stimson days later, the president said Churchill "had acted like a spoiled boy and refused to give up on one of the points. . . . He persisted and persisted until Roosevelt told him that he, Roosevelt, wasn't interested in the matter and that he had better shut up."[17]

However, FDR acceded to other demands Churchill had made,

including one relating to the sharing of secret nuclear information from the Manhattan Project. In late 1942, Stimson and other top officials had approved a strict security policy for the Manhattan Project that blocked sharing any nuclear information with the British unless it was necessary for prosecution of the war.[18] British officials became frustrated over being denied Manhattan Project information. While Churchill argued against the cross-channel invasion, he simultaneously pushed FDR to restore the exchange of nuclear information. He also urged the president to send additional ships to the British. On the day after the accord on the cross-channel invasion was approved, he proudly informed a member of his War Cabinet that the "President agreed that the exchange of information . . . should be resumed."[19] The prime minister also won agreement for the United States to send twenty new ships to the Royal Navy each month for ten months.[20]

The high-stakes negotiations had resolved the disputes between the Allies: the agreement on the invasion of France had been secured, the assault across the English Channel was—at least for the time being—set for May 1944, and the British would once again get nuclear information. FDR hosted Churchill, the Combined Chiefs of Staff and top military men from both sides at a lunch at the White House on May 25. Despite the furor and doubt raised by Churchill's objections, the president sought to keep the mood upbeat at the event in the White House dining room. He gave a toast of thanks to the participants, and Churchill responded with his own toast in gratitude to "our American hosts."[21] Stimson, seated between Churchill and Brooke, later remarked dryly: "I had a very pleasant time. Of course Churchill is always pleasant to talk to and so is Brooke."

When FDR and Stimson met privately two days later, FDR related his efforts to get Churchill to back off his demands. "I am very glad that for once the president did stand up to him in the way that he ought to be stood up to. I told him that I thought . . . that the conferences this time had gone better than heretofore and that on the whole they were pretty satisfactory," Stimson noted in his diary.[22] Still, the secretary of war remained vigilant about protecting the invasion strategy so that the Allies could deliver a "knock-out blow instead of having it drizzle down to a negotiated peace."

• • •

STIMSON TOOK UP the Manhattan Project security issue with Churchill in July 1943 when he traveled to England with special assistant Harvey Bundy, his top aide for nuclear matters. In sending Stimson on this trip, FDR could safely assume Stimson would go full-throttle into a debate on war strategy with Churchill, making vigorous arguments in support of the cross-channel invasion.

After arriving in London on July 12, Stimson had dinner at the prime minister's official residence, 10 Downing Street, with Churchill and his wife, Clementine, Foreign Secretary Anthony Eden and US ambassador John Winant and his wife. The Allied invasion of Sicily had begun two days earlier—about a hundred and fifty thousand troops landed by boat on the beaches and by parachute, with some meeting stiff German resistance. Stimson quickly found an opening to voice his concerns on strategy: he told Churchill that there was a risk of the American people not "understanding or approving further penetration of the eastern Mediterranean; the consequent loss of prestige of the president, with the immense consequent damage to the common cause," he noted in his diary. "I don't think he had had that spectacle presented to him before and he gave evidence of being impressed by it."[23]

In the following days, Stimson had tea with King George VI and Queen Consort Elizabeth at Buckingham Palace, and met with officers of the US 8th Air Force in London. Joined by Churchill and Winant, he toured the cavernous defenses on the coast at Dover looking across the English Channel to France.[24]

On July 22, Stimson and Churchill met at 10 Downing Street with Bundy and Vannevar Bush, the Office of Scientific Research and Development director, who had played a critical role in the decision to cease sharing Manhattan Project information with the British. Also present were two of Churchill's top advisers, War Cabinet member John Anderson, who headed the British nuclear program, and Frederick Lindemann, who advised Churchill on matters ranging from radar to aerial bombing of Germany.[25] The prime minister began with a vigorous defense of the British position. He said that unless Great Britain could develop its own nuclear weapons, Germany or Russia might "win the race for something which might be used for international blackmail."[26] He warned of a possible atomic threat from Russia in particular, suggesting Stalin might become an enemy after the war's end.

Bush stated the American view that any nuclear information sharing should be done only for purposes of winning the war—not out of concern for postwar matters. Stimson read aloud a statement he had prepared summarizing the situation.[27] Ultimately, Churchill proposed an agreement that he and Roosevelt would sign providing "free interchange" of atomic information with conditions, including one that neither country would "use this invention against the other." Stimson promised he would convey Churchill's proposed agreement to FDR, and later made a terse entry in his diary: "Satisfactory atmosphere produced."[28]

Stimson and Churchill then spoke privately about the cross-channel invasion. Pointing to fierce German resistance in Sicily, Churchill said that if an Allied invasion force landed on the French coast he "felt that the Germans could rush up in sufficient force to drive them back." He warned of "the disastrous effect of having the Channel full of corpses of defeated allies."[29]

Churchill bluntly questioned the wisdom of the cross-channel invasion, referring to it by its code name, Roundhammer.[30] If he were commander in chief, "he would not figure the Roundhammer operation; but being as it was, he having made his pledge, he would go through with it loyally." This drew an indignant retort from Stimson: "I said to him that was like hitting us in the eye and he said, 'Oh, no, if we start anything, we will go through it with utmost effort.'" Alarmed at the prime minister's defeatist words, Stimson admonished him that "we could never win any battle by talking about corpses."[31]

The conversation ended, and Stimson did not see the prime minister again before departing London two days later for North Africa, where he met with Eisenhower at his villa in the Algerian capital, Algiers, on July 26. Churchill had recently visited Ike to urge him to push his campaign further into Italy and the Balkans. Seeking to inoculate Eisenhower against Churchill's persuasive powers, Stimson warned that the prime minister would likely "seek to avoid" his commitment to invade France the following spring. The secretary of war also said Churchill was pushing his Balkans strategy in an effort to repair the historical record of Gallipoli, "his misfortunes at the Dardanelles in the previous war."[32]

Stimson also visited an army hospital and spoke with wounded soldiers. He flew in a B-17 Flying Fortress to Tunis, met with army officers and visited what US troops called Hill 609, a rocky mountain where two months earlier American troops had won a fierce, decisive battle in the closing days of the North African campaign. Returning to Algiers later that day, the seventy-five-year-old clambered into the bombardier's seat in the plane's glass nose for a better view of Hill 609 and other battlefields below. After meeting again with Eisenhower, he wrote in his diary that while the general "lacks the poise of Marshall for example, he has matured into a very important character."[33] On July 29, Stimson's party departed on its return flight to the United States.

THE ALLIED INVASION of Sicily and aerial bombing of Rome on July 19 shattered the reign of the Italian dictator, Benito Mussolini. On July 25 Italy's king, Victor Emmanuel III, removed Mussolini from his post as prime minister and had him arrested.[34] The king named Marshal Pietro Badoglio, who had led the Italian Army's conquest of Abyssinia, as prime minister. The invasion of Sicily had also prompted Hitler to halt his army's assault on the Russian city of Kursk eight days after it began; he diverted those forces from Russia to defend against the expected Allied assault on the Italian mainland.[35]

Upon returning to Washington, Stimson prepared a report for FDR saying that he and Churchill, in their discussion of Roundhammer, had gone at it "hammer and tongs." The result was "a relation between us of greater mutual respect and friendship than ever before."[36] But he also sounded an alarm that Churchill was arguing for a much larger attack through Italy that would be "time-consuming and costly" and "would be sure to make Roundhammer impossible."[37]

FDR invited Stimson to discuss the matter over lunch two days later. Stimson decided to seize the opportunity to repair the weakness he saw in the leadership proposed for the coming invasion of France. Because an American—Eisenhower—had commanded the invasion of North

Africa, FDR and Churchill had decided that a British commander would lead the cross-channel invasion.[38] After reaching that agreement, Churchill had told General Brooke in early 1943 that he would be the commander.

Preparing for his lunch with FDR on August 10, Stimson wrote a two-page letter to the president calling for an American commander to take control of the invasion from timid British leadership. "First: We cannot now rationally hope to be able to cross the Channel and come to grips with our German enemy under a British commander." Churchill and Brooke are "at variance with such a proposal." He suggested that earlier losses—immense numbers of British casualties in battles at Passchendaele, Belgium, in World War I, and the devastation at Dunkirk in 1940—left Churchill and Brooke emotionally incapable of carrying out the proposed direct assault on the German war machine.

"The shadows of Passchendaele and Dunkirk still hang too heavily over the imagination of these leaders," Stimson wrote FDR. "Though they have rendered lip service to the operation, their hearts are not in it and it will require more independence, more faith, and more vigor than it is reasonable to expect we can find in any British commander to overcome the natural difficulties of such an operation."

As a result, Stimson argued, the United States must take a leading role in the cross-channel invasion. "I believe therefore that the time has come for you to decide that your government must assume the responsibility of leadership in this great final movement of the European war. . . . We cannot afford to begin the most dangerous operation of the war under half-hearted leadership which will invite failure or at least disappointing results."[39] He also advised that strong leadership would stave off critics, hinting at the coming presidential race of 1944. "We are facing a difficult year at home with time and hostile hearts ready to seize and exploit any wavering on the part of our war leadership. A firm resolute leadership, on the other hand, will go far to silence such voices."

Finally, he urged the president to name Marshall as the American leader of the cross-channel invasion. "I believe the time has come when we must put our most commanding soldier in charge of this critical operation at this critical time. General Marshall already has a towering eminence of reputation as a tried soldier and as a broad-minded and skillful administrator. . . . I believe that he is the man who most surely can now by his character and skill furnish the military leadership which is necessary to bring our two nations together in confident joint action in this great operation."

Stimson presented his letter to FDR over lunch at the White House on August 10, and the president read it in his presence. The two men discussed the letter in detail, and FDR said "finally that I had announced the conclusions which he had just come to himself," Stimson wrote in his diary. After discussing antisubmarine defenses and other matters, FDR asked him to stay at the White House for a meeting with the Joint Chiefs of Staff attended by Marshall, Admirals Leahy and King, and others. After the military commanders arrived, FDR spoke forcefully in support of fighting in Italy no further north than Rome. He also said he wanted to build up US forces in Great Britain rapidly so there would be more American than British soldiers in the invasion, and he announced that he wanted the invasion to be led by an American commander. FDR said that "he wanted to have an American commander and he thought that would make it easier if we had more men in the expedition at the beginning."[40]

FDR had swiftly embraced Stimson's recommendation of an American commander and put it before US Joint Chiefs of Staff, adding his own idea of using the superior number of American troops to convince the British to reverse the prior decision about the commander. Stimson recalled that "the military and naval conferees were astonished and delighted." As for his own feelings, he said, "I came away with a very much lighter heart on the subject of our military policy than I have had for a long time."[41]

FDR LEFT WASHINGTON the next day by train to spend a few days with Churchill in Hyde Park prior to the conference set for the following week in Québec, Canada. The prime minister arrived with his daughter Mary on August 12 at FDR's Springwood estate overlooking the Hudson River. FDR drove Winston and Mary to Val-Kill, Eleanor's cottage on the estate, for a convivial summer picnic with Eleanor, Daisy Suckley, Harry Hopkins and other guests.[42]

Churchill left ahead of FDR for Québec City, about a hundred sixty miles northeast of Montreal. Upon his arrival, the prime minister met with Brooke on August 15 and told him about his visit to Hyde Park and the talks he had there with FDR and Hopkins. "Apparently the latter pressed hard for the appointment of Marshall as Supreme Commander of the cross-Channel operations," Brooke noted in his diary. Churchill had told his top general that the Americans demanded that Marshall take over as commander of the invasion—and the prime minister had evidently acquiesced. The news came as a harsh blow to Brooke, who wrote, "As far as I can gather Winston gave in, in spite of having previously promised me the job!!"

Brooke seethed at Marshall in his diary later that day as the generals debated the cross-channel invasion: "It is quite impossible to argue with him as he does not even begin to understand a strategic problem!"[43]

Brooke, Marshall and the other members of the Combined Chiefs of Staff held meetings in the Citadel, the colonial-era fortress overlooking Québec City. Despite any bitter feelings over who would be commander, the group agreed on August 17 that the cross-channel invasion, now given the code name Overlord, would be the top strategic priority and would remain scheduled for May 1, 1944. The two sides agreed that the heavy Allied aerial bombing of Germany must continue with the highest priority, and that Allied forces would be allocated to ensure the success of Overlord.[44]

FDR arrived with Hopkins late that same day and after dinner plunged into discussions with Churchill. On August 19, FDR and Churchill signed the nuclear exchange agreement largely as the latter had proposed to Stimson in London. The agreement had been revised to include creation of a six-person committee, including Stimson and Bush, to oversee the exchange of nuclear information and any joint operations.[45] Some historians have suggested—despite a lack of direct evidence—that FDR approved this agreement as an inducement to Churchill to convince him to proceed with Overlord under an American commander, in essence making the deal a quid pro quo.[46]

FDR invited Stimson to the conference, and he arrived in time for lunch at the Citadel on August 22. Before sitting down, he was quickly ushered into a small room where FDR was waiting for him. The president told him that "Churchill had voluntarily come to him and offered to accept Marshall for the Overlord operation." The president said this "relieved him of the embarrassment of being obliged to ask for it."[47] A short while later, Churchill asked Stimson to walk out on a wall of the fortress overlooking Québec City. "Before he went in to luncheon, Churchill took me out on the parapet ostensibly to show me the view and then he told me that he had suggested Marshall to the president." Tension over the Americans taking command of the cross-channel invasion dissipated amid civility among the Allies. During lunch, Stimson was seated between Churchill and his wife, Clementine, who, he noted in his diary, "were very cordial and friendly."

Stimson's brief meetings with FDR and Churchill upon his arrival at the Citadel appeared to be an orchestrated attempt by the two leaders to get their story straight. Churchill likely would not have wanted his military chiefs to know that he had bowed to the American demand that an American commander lead what all recognized might be one of the most important military invasions in world history. When Churchill recounted the story later in his memoirs, he said he proposed the idea himself, having come to the conclusion that an American commander should lead the invasion because of the large number of American troops to be involved. He wrote, "At Quebec, I myself took the initiative of proposing to the president that an American commander should be appointed for the expedition to France."[48]

The prime minister's account, however, conflicts sharply with his telling Brooke—two days before FDR even arrived in Québec City—that Hopkins wanted Marshall to be the commander, and that Churchill apparently "gave in." What seems most likely is that FDR privately broke the news of the American demand to Churchill at Hyde Park, probably with Hopkins joining in the conversation, and after hearing Brooke's reaction at the Citadel, Churchill concluded the best course was to portray it as his own idea.[49]

Stimson didn't question the matter further. He had obtained the outcome he wanted; an American—apparently Marshall—was to be commander of Overlord.

. . .

In the Mediterranean two weeks later, the Allies assembled an invasion force of more than six hundred ships and landing craft laden with soldiers, tanks, artillery guns, equipment and food. On September 8, this armada stood off Salerno, a city on the southwest coast of Italy. At 6:30 P.M., Eisenhower announced over Radio Algiers that the Italian armed forces had surrendered, and urged Italians to help drive Germans from Italian soil. An hour later, Badoglio, speaking over Radio Rome, at last confirmed the Italian surrender, which he had secretly signed days earlier. The Nazi commander, Field Marshal Albert Kesselring, swiftly implemented a standing plan to disarm Italian forces, seize key fortifications and prepare to defend against an Allied invasion. The 1939 accord between Italy and Germany, the Pact of Steel, collapsed and Italy swiftly went from German ally to occupied nation.[50]

In the early morning hours of September 9, a first wave of fifty-five thousand Allied troops went ashore at Salerno, immediately coming under a withering barrage of artillery shells and machine-gun fire. Mines tore open landing vessels, and Luftwaffe planes bombed and strafed the invaders as they struggled to gain a foothold on the beach.[51] On September 13, Kesselring launched a counteroffensive, shredding the US 143rd Infantry in the center of the beachhead and sending American soldiers in a panicked retreat toward the sea. German forces came within five hundred yards of General Mark Clark's US 5th Army headquarters at the beach, which was defended by a hastily formed line of cooks, clerks and drivers.[52] Clark considered evacuating his troops by sea, briefly raising the specter of an American Dunkirk. At the last moment, however, heavy shelling by US Navy vessels offshore stopped the German counteroffensive.

After two weeks of intense fighting near Salerno, the Germans withdrew to a defensive line beyond Naples, about forty miles north of the city.[53] Kesselring's forces in the mainland campaign had inflicted 8,659 casualties so far—more than double the number it suffered—and taken more than three thousand Allied prisoners.[54] Hitler's SS security service, meanwhile, freed Mussolini from a jail on September 12 and compelled him to launch a new pro-Hitler government in northern and central Italy. The Italian king fled Rome, reestablished his kingdom in Allied territory in the south, and cooperated with the Allies. A civil war, pitting the two Italian governments against each other, thus overlaid the battles between the Nazis and the Allies. After the Germans withdrew from Salerno to their defensive line north of Naples, General Clark rode victorious into Naples on October 1.[55]

The invasion of Salerno marked the start of a long and bloody struggle in Italy with tenacious German forces, who gradually withdrew northwards through the difficult mountainous terrain of the peninsula. Stimson's and Marshall's warnings about the dangers posed by an invasion of Italy proved prescient.

Churchill nonetheless resumed his dogged pursuit of a wider Mediterranean offensive, cabling FDR on October 7 to urge the deployment of a division to capture Rhodes, a Greek island near Turkey. FDR swiftly rejected the idea as a move that would put Overlord at risk. The president sent back a prompt reply later that day telling him he wanted Eisenhower, the Mediterranean commander, not to be distracted by diversions and to remain focused on driving to a line north of Rome. "It is my opinion that no diversion of forces or equipment should prejudice Overlord as planned," FDR wrote. Churchill responded in a cable the next day chiding the president for his disinterest in the Greek island. "I am sure that the omission to take Rhodes at this stage . . . would constitute a cardinal error in strategy."[56]

On October 23, he sent FDR another cable questioning the timing of Overlord and whether the Allies had sufficient forces for the invasion. "Our present plans for 1944 seem open to very grave defects." He asked FDR to hold a meeting of top commanders to review the plans for 1944.[57] Seeking to appease his ally's persistent demands, FDR agreed to meet with Churchill and senior military staff in Cairo in November before proceeding to a meeting scheduled that month with Stalin in Tehran, Iran.

STIMSON LEARNED DAYS later that at a conference in Moscow, British foreign minister Anthony Eden—under instructions from Churchill—had read to Stalin part of a telegram from a British general. Eden did not read the accompanying comments by Eisenhower, the supreme commander for the Allied campaign in Italy. This omission gave a

pessimistic view of Overlord and suggested that the cross-channel invasion should be "delayed or perhaps postponed," Stimson noted in his
diary on October 28. This "shows how determined Churchill is to stick
a knife in the back of Overlord."[58] He went to the White House the next
day and told FDR Churchill's behavior was an "improper act" and "dirty
baseball." He also informed the president that Marshall had sent a telegram to Moscow "rebutting Churchill's intervention against Overlord."
Stimson and Marshall were now on heightened alert against Churchill's
attacks on Overlord.

On November 4, as FDR prepared for his trip to Tehran, Stimson
went to the White House to meet with him over lunch and give the
president a pep talk to bolster him in resisting any push by Churchill
to undo the plans for Overlord. FDR informed Stimson of his expectations for the Tehran meeting, which was to be the first meeting of "the
Big Three"—FDR, Churchill and Stalin. Stimson reiterated the reasons
why Overlord would succeed as planned, including the increasingly
successful amphibious landings by the Allies and development of new
types of landing craft. He also "prophesied that when the attempt finally
came we would be surprised that we had ever been afraid of it."

FDR boarded the battleship USS *Iowa* on November 12 and, joined
by the US Chiefs of Staff, headed out to sea for his trip to Tehran. Marshall, among the commanders on board, remained adamantly opposed
to British efforts to divert forces from Overlord, which he warned
would have the effect of prolonging the war in the Pacific.[59] After arriving in Cairo, FDR met with Churchill on November 24 and fended
off his pleas by saying that no changes in strategy should be made until
after the meeting with Stalin.[60]

In 1941, the Soviet Union and Great Britain had agreed jointly to occupy Iran, a move intended to protect supply routes to the Soviet Union
and to English-owned oil production facilities. Now, two years later, the
Allies had turned the tide of the war against the Nazis, and they were
meeting in Tehran to plot their closing strategy to defeat Hitler. Stalin
and FDR met for the first time on November 28, 1943, at the Soviet embassy compound in Tehran, where the president was staying for security reasons. The five-foot-six-inch Soviet dictator, dressed in a simple
khaki tunic with an Order of Lenin medal pinned on his chest, entered

FDR's sitting room. FDR, in his wheelchair, extended his arm, saying, "I am glad to see you."[61] They shook hands, and began a conversation in which they found common ground in condemning Britain and France for their colonization of India and Indochina, which they agreed deserved independence.

Having begun a friendly dialogue, the two men then joined Churchill and their respective senior military commanders in a plenary meeting.[62] After introductory comments by the three leaders, FDR informed Stalin that the target date for Overlord was May 1, 1944.[63] He said Overlord "should not be delayed by secondary operations," but Churchill countered that some of the attack plans under consideration might cause a delay of two or three months, meeting minutes show.[64] Stalin questioned the wisdom of dispersing Allied forces over multiple operations, saying instead "it would be better to take Overlord as the basis for all 1944 operations."

Meeting at the Soviet embassy the next day, November 29, Churchill announced that he was prepared to delay Overlord in order to pursue operations in Rhodes and open a sea route through the Dardanelles. This drew a resolute objection from Stalin: "Overlord was the most important and nothing should be done to distract attention from that operation." The Soviet dictator added that operations in the Mediterranean were "only diversions." He then asked Churchill pointedly, do "the British really believe in Overlord?" Churchill replied indirectly, saying that—if certain conditions regarding German forces in France were met—it would be the British government's "duty" to "hurl every scrap of strength across the channel."[65] This careful reply suggested the prime minister doubted Overlord's chances of success but would support it nonetheless. Stalin urged that the commander for Overlord be selected promptly, saying it was critical for the invasion's success. FDR agreed.[66]

When the meeting minutes were transmitted to Stimson days later in Washington, he wrote in his diary, "I thank the Lord that Stalin was there. In my opinion, he saved the day. He was direct and strong and he brushed away the diversionary attempts of the prime minister with a vigor which rejoiced my soul."[67]

Before leaving Tehran, the three leaders issued a public statement on December 4 voicing confidence in their eventual victory over Nazi

Germany. They also sounded a note of unity: "We came here with hope and determination. We leave here, friends in fact, in spirit and in purpose."[68]

Upon his return to Cairo, FDR invited Marshall to his villa for lunch to discuss the command of Overlord. Marshall declined to state an opinion on whether he should command the invasion. "I merely wished to make clear that whatever the decision, I would go along with it wholeheartedly; that the issue was too great for any personal feeling to be considered," he recalled. As the conversation ended, FDR confided, "I feel I could not sleep at night with you out of the country."[69] The president had made his decision. On December 6, the last day of his meetings in Cairo, he sent a cable to Stalin informing him that Eisenhower would command Overlord.[70]

FDR landed in Tunisia two days later and was met by Eisenhower at the airport. The president got in a car with the general and said, "Well, Ike, you are going to command Overlord." Ike replied, "Mr. President, I realize that such an appointment involved difficult decisions. I hope you will not be disappointed."[71]

On December 17—more than a month after he had departed Washington—FDR returned to the White House, where he was greeted by Stimson and other cabinet members, as well as a bipartisan array of members of Congress. "Republicans were mixed with Democrats and they all seemed very glad to have him back safe and sound," Stimson recalled.[72] The next day, a Saturday, FDR asked Stimson to the White House for a private lunch. The president recounted Churchill's efforts to reopen the debate on Overlord and expand into the Greek islands.[73] He said he had fought hard for Overlord and with Stalin's help had finally won out, reassuring Stimson: "I have thus brought Overlord back to you safe and sound on the ways for accomplishment."

The president then turned to the issue of Overlord's commander. He mentioned how, when he met with Marshall in Cairo, the general refused to state an opinion on which position he preferred. He said he got the impression that Marshall "perhaps really preferred to remain as Chief of Staff." At this, Stimson replied, "I knew that in the bottom of his heart it was Marshall's secret desire above all things to command this invasion force into Europe." He added with a laugh, "I wish I had been along with you in Cairo. I could have made that point clear." FDR said Ike was a very good soldier who was familiar with the European theater, but he was unfamiliar with events in the Pacific region and "would be far less able than Marshall to handle Congress." As a result, he would "be more comfortable if he kept Marshall at his elbow in Washington and turned over Overlord to Eisenhower." Stimson said he was "staggered" because he thought Marshall's selection was settled in Québec City and—ever ready to advise or even admonish FDR—he reiterated his view that Marshall "was our best man for Overlord."

THE DEBATE, HOWEVER, was over. The two men moved on to other matters, including plans for governing Europe after victory. Then Stimson went home, took a horseback ride and spent a quiet evening with Mabel writing Christmas cards to friends. FDR and Eleanor entertained Harry Hopkins and his wife, Louise, and others for dinner at the White House. But there would be no holiday lull. The following week, FDR announced in a meeting with Stimson, Marshall and Leahy that—with several railroad labor unions calling for strikes—he wanted to prevent those strikes by having the army seize control of the nation's railroads.

On Friday, Christmas Eve, Stimson and his top assistants delivered to the president a plan for the army to seize and operate the railroads. Three days later, FDR signed an executive order instructing Stimson to carry out the plan.[74] Stimson swiftly implemented the order, and he gave a national radio address that night saying that the president of the Pennsylvania Railroad Company would serve as an adviser to the army, and that all schedules, services and personnel would remain unchanged. He said US bombers had been trying to destroy Hitler's vital rail system, but in the United States it was labor strikes that threatened to paralyze the railroads. "We shall not hand to Germany and Japan this great military victory. The railroads will continue to run."[75] Army officers were on duty the next day in train stations.

Stimson had sent a note to Eisenhower on Christmas Eve, expressing full confidence in his skill, judgment and ability to lead Overlord. "I now look forward with confidence to your complete success in one of the most difficult tasks which has ever been placed upon an American soldier." Ike visited Woodley on January 2, where the two men discussed a broad array of matters relating to the invasion.[76]

Returning to London, Eisenhower, as commander in chief of the Allied Expeditionary Force, took charge of a massive planning effort already underway for the invasion. He oversaw development of ingenious solutions to the problems of sending a vast army across the sea to face a deeply entrenched enemy, such as floating ports that would make it possible to offload tanks and trucks from ships onto the shore.[77] The Allies also deployed elaborate deception plans. Dummy aircraft, inflatable tanks, and double agents carrying bogus invasion plans—all created a fog of disinformation to obscure the true invasion plan.[78] To allow more time for aerial bombing to wreck German defenses, the invasion's target date was moved from May 1 to early June.[79]

Eisenhower proved remarkably adept at the diplomacy required to hold together a fractious team of generals, including the tempestuous US general George Patton and the haughty British general Bernard Montgomery. Brooke, ever ready with a bilious remark about other leaders, dismissed Ike, saying he "knows nothing about strategy and is quite unsuited to the post of Supreme Commander."[80]

Eisenhower met periodically with Churchill, who continued to raise his deep-seated doubts about the plan. Once, the prime minister expressed doubt about whether the Allied invasion would succeed in holding its position in France by the coming winter.[81] Ike responded by assuring him that in fact the Allied invasion forces would push across France to the border of Germany, some three hundred miles east of Paris, by the winter. Churchill replied, "I applaud your enthusiasm, but liberate Paris by Christmas and none of us can ask for more."

In the first days of June 1944, the Allies completed their final preparations to assail Hitler's coastal defenses, known as the Atlantic Wall. Cheering news came from Italy, where Allied troops seized Rome on Sunday, June 4. FDR spent that weekend in Virginia at the home of his daughter, Anna, where he wrote a prayer for the American soldiers preparing to invade France.[82] On June 5, Ike held his last round of talks with soldiers ahead of the plan to attack the next morning. In Washington that day, Marshall informed Stimson of the final plan, which called for paratroops to be dropped that night inland from the Normandy beaches, and for the first troops to go ashore at dawn the next morning. Stimson recalled, "So this evening as Mabel and I have sat together we have been thinking of the thousands of young men who are keenly on their toes in Great Britain at this time facing the adventure of their lives or perhaps their death. It is one of the great crises of the world . . . and it has all focused together on tonight."[83] The couple woke up at 4:00 A.M. and listened to radio news accounts of the assault.

In the dawn hours of June 6, an Allied armada crossed the English Channel, sending five thousand landing craft through the waves to disgorge one hundred thirty thousand soldiers from across America, Britain and Canada onto a fifty-mile stretch of Normandy beaches. Amid a deadly torrent of bullets and shells launched by the Nazi defenders, many Allied soldiers perished still aboard their vessels or having just left them.

In an area designated as Omaha Beach, the shore's gentle arc gave Nazi gunners an advantage, and the Allies would suffer some two thousand casualties before fighting their way up a bluff and defeating the German defenders by nightfall.[84] At Utah Beach, the Allies cleared the beach of Germans within an hour of landing. Allied paratroopers who had landed in the middle of the night fought difficult battles to secure bridges to intercept Nazi reinforcements.[85] By the end of the day, the beachheads were largely secured and the Allied Expeditionary Force headquarters issued a statement saying all of the landings had "succeeded."[86]

THAT NIGHT, FDR went to the White House's Diplomatic Reception Room and read his prayer for the American soldiers in the D-Day invasion, carried by radio to homes nationwide and around the world. "Almighty God: Our sons, pride of our nation, this day have set upon a might endeavor, a struggle to preserve our Republic, our religion and our civilization, and to set free a suffering humanity. Lead them straight and true; give strength to their arms, stoutness to their hearts, steadfastness in their faith." Though Roosevelt was not viewed as a very religious person, he intoned the words with a solemnity that evoked deep belief. "And, O Lord, give us faith. Give us faith in Thee; faith in our sons; faith in each other; faith in our united crusade."[87]

The president's prayer harkened to his oft-spoken appeals for national unity. Earlier in the day in the US House of Representatives, Representative Joseph Martin, the Massachusetts Republican who was the House minority leader, sounded his own note of nonpartisan unity. "Partisan politics . . . and other prejudices disappear as we think of the heroic deeds of our men and women in every part of the globe on land, on sea and in the air."[88]

In the following weeks, the Allied forces under Eisenhower fought ferociously to drive the Nazis out of Normandy. By July 1, the Allies suffered 60,771 casualties, of whom 8,975 were killed. They also took 41,000 German prisoners, and they expanded the invasion force rapidly by landing a total of one million men and 171,532 vehicles in France.[89] Stimson's and Marshall's prophecies of victory for the cross-channel invasion were vindicated. The Allies liberated Paris on August 25. Among the first Americans to arrive in the city were members of an intelligence unit authorized by Stimson to secure any materials and scientists in Hitler's nuclear bomb program.[90] The Allies managed to drive the Nazis east across France and into Germany by winter, just as Ike had predicted.

Entering Germany to defeat Hitler, however, would require costly, bloody battles. When Allied forces pushed through the Netherlands and sought to cross the Rhine River into Germany, Nazi resistance blocked the crossing and caused large numbers of casualties. And a Nazi counteroffensive into eastern France and Belgium that began in December 1944, the Battle of the Bulge, left some nineteen thousand American soldiers dead. Soviet armies, meanwhile, were fighting their way westward to Berlin. Despite the terrible losses and the horrors of the war, Allied commanders saw a path to the ultimate destruction of the Nazi empire.

Years later, as D-Day gained glory, Churchill penned his memoirs, omitting most of his fears and his disputes with FDR, Stimson and Marshall over the invasion.[91] Churchill was a mighty ally in the fight against fascism, but FDR and Stimson had to overcome the dark doubts that Churchill and others harbored about the D-Day invasion. In Henry Stimson, FDR found a man whose deep faith in American soldiers and sailors sustained the president and helped him guide the nation's armed forces to victory. In a note to Stimson on November 21, 1944, FDR suggested overcoming doubt was a key to their collaboration: "You and I are facing a long and hard road but we both have faith and that is half the battle."[92]

PART IV

VICTORY
AND BEYOND

The Soldier Voting Schism

With millions of American soldiers in uniform and fighting for democracy in early 1944, President Roosevelt supported legislation to enable them to vote from abroad in that year's presidential election. Democratic senators Theodore Green of Rhode Island and Scott Lucas of Illinois had filed a bill to create a federal balloting system allowing soldiers—without regard to their race— to cast votes in elections for the presidency, the Senate and the House of Representatives. The proposed system was to be overseen by a bipartisan commission composed of two Republicans and two Democrats, with a Supreme Court justice to be named to resolve a tie.

This patriotic-sounding plan, however, sparked a furious challenge by southern Democrats, who attacked it as an unconstitutional violation of their state elections laws. The southern states widely prevented Black people from voting, and this bill raised the prospect that suddenly large numbers of Black soldiers might cast ballots. The initial objections to the Senate's Green-Lucas bill were raised under the banner of states' rights, but as the debate grew heated southern Democrats came forward to openly demand the preservation of "white supremacy." FDR's chief Republican ally, Secretary of War Stimson, was soon plunged into the middle of this racially polarized uproar in the midst of the war.

The stakes were high. As many as 8.6 million military service members of voting age would be in uniform by Election Day. That was 3.5

million more than FDR's margin of victory in the 1940 election, and observers expected many in the armed services to vote heavily in his favor if he ran for a fourth term.[1] Some critics saw the president's support for a federal balloting system as a move aimed at reassuring his own reelection.

In fall 1943, Democratic representative John Rankin, the Mississippi segregationist who condemned FDR's Fair Employment Practices Committee, set his sights on blocking the Senate bill, which he condemned as an attempt to supersede state election laws. On November 13, he filed a competing bill in the House that would recommend that states pass their own legislation to allow soldiers to cast absentee ballots but would neither create a federal ballot system nor impose any requirements on states. He said his bill would enable soldiers to vote "without violating the Constitution, overriding State laws, or wrecking the election machinery of any state."[2]

As the debate intensified, Stimson assigned Colonel Robert Cutler, a member of his Republican team in the War Department, to handle the issue. A lawyer from a prominent Boston Republican family, Cutler had served in the army in World War I. He was comfortable with bipartisan politics; he was close to moderate Republican Henry Cabot Lodge Jr., and had served as his campaign finance chairman when Lodge won election to the US Senate in 1936. He was also friends with a reform-minded Boston Democrat, Maurice Tobin, whom he had helped to unseat James Michael Curley, Boston's notoriously corrupt Democratic mayor. After Tobin was elected mayor in 1940, he hired Cutler to serve as Boston's corporation counsel—the city's chief attorney—until Cutler left to join the War Department in 1942.[3]

On November 16, 1943, Cutler appeared before the House committee on elections to deliver the views of the army and navy on the soldier voting bills. He testified that the army already transported some seven hundred thousand pounds of mail per day, and movement of airmail competed with other uses of aircraft that were critical to the war effort. He said the two services were simply unable to handle all of the additional mailings to war zones around the world that would to enable soldiers to comply with the various absentee voting procedures of each of the forty-eight states.

State absentee voting laws posed serious hurdles to soldier voting. For example, three states banned absentee voting entirely if the voter was outside the United States. In addition, thirty-three states required no more than thirty days to pass between the state's receipt of an application for an absentee ballot and the return of the completed ballot to the state. Cutler told the committee that the minimum time required to complete the necessary mailings would be thirty-seven days for a soldier in the European theater and fifty-two days for a soldier in the Far East. "Even with the use of air mail and air priority, the State absentee balloting procedure, as provided by existing state laws, would not allow any substantial number of votes cast by servicemen overseas to be counted." Cutler later recalled, "I thought it a cruel hoax to carry a ballot to a soldier overseas which could not be returned in time to be counted."[4]

In contrast, Cutler testified, the army and navy were confident they would be able to carry out the simplified voting process proposed for the federal ballot system in the Green-Lucas bill.[5]

Rankin curtly dismissed the northern Republican's testimony: "With all deference to Colonel Cutler, he is a Boston lawyer and a graduate of Harvard, and probably has a different slant on holding elections from that of our people down in the fork of the creek."[6]

THE UPROAR OVER threats to the racial caste system in the South intensified later that month—at a time when FDR was meeting with Stalin and Prime Minister Churchill in Tehran, Iran. On November 30, the FEPC ordered twenty railroads and seven rail worker unions—all in the South—to cease their racially discriminatory employment practices. Days later, Rankin raged on the floor of the House, "While the president is away, a bunch of crackpots down here in what they call the 'Fair Employment Practice Committee' seem to be doing everything they possibly can to drive the white people of the South out of the Democratic Party, by trying to force them to accept Negroes on terms of social equality." He warned that the FEPC's drive for equality would devastate the Democratic Party: "The party would be as dead as a doornail."[7]

The foundation for the states' rights argument in the soldier voting dispute was the clause in the Constitution that gave states the power to set the "times, places and manner" of holding elections. The same clause, however, also says Congress "may at any time by law make or alter such regulations," and the 15th Amendment bars states from preventing people from voting on account of their race. This complex balance between state and federal power over elections set the stage for southern Democrats to argue states' rights were being trampled.

FDR's push for a federal ballot for soldiers threatened to undercut the so-called Jim Crow laws that enforced white supremacy in the southern states. Across the South, poll taxes and literacy tests—along with intimidation and violence—prevented many Black people from voting. In addition, many southern states barred Black people from voting in Democratic Party primary elections. Because the party controlled most political activity in what was often called the "Solid South," winners of Democratic primaries routinely went on to victory in general elections. Thus, it was white primary election voters who chose the ultimate officeholders throughout the region.

Jim Crow election laws had come under challenge by the NAACP, which amplified the tension over military voting. The NAACP had filed a lawsuit alleging the "whites-only" primary in Texas was unconstitutional, and the Supreme Court agreed to hear arguments in the case in January 1944.

In early December 1943, with the Supreme Court battle looming just ahead, three southern Democratic senators proposed an amendment that would gut the Green-Lucas bill, leaving it only to recommend how states might—if they chose to—amend absentee voting laws to facilitate soldier voting. The measure tracked the Rankin bill in the House. Senator John McClellan of Arkansas, one of the amendment's sponsors, insisted in a speech in the Senate on December 3 that he wanted soldiers to vote. But, he said, "I appeal to those who believe in the fundamentals of states' rights, of state sovereignty, of the states controlling their own election machinery, and of the states being able to say who is eligible to vote."[8]

Senator Lucas responded, "I yield to no man in my reverence for states' rights." He added, "From the statement given by Colonel Cutler of the Army . . . not a single boy from the state of Illinois who is now serving beyond the limits of the continental United States, could vote in 1944. Does the Senate want to deny them that privilege?"[9]

The alliance of segregationist southern Democrats with northern Republicans proved too powerful. That same day, the Green-Lucas measure went down in defeat as the McClellan bill passed in the Senate by a vote of 42–37.[10] Senate majority leader Alben Barkley, the Kentucky Democrat and close FDR ally, voted for the administration's preferred Green-Lucas bill, but twenty-four other Democrats abandoned their leader, joining eighteen Republicans to secure a victory for the states' rights bill. Senator James O. Eastland, a Mississippi Democrat who sponsored the amendment, exulted that the vote meant the southerners also had the power to block a separate bill proposed in the Senate to end state use of poll taxes, which they soon did.[11]

It was a defeat for FDR, but the president was still far away from Washington politics that day—he was in Cairo working on the issue of who would command Overlord. The angry dispute, however, would soon draw his attention.

Two days later, newspapers nationwide carried a story by George Gallup, a pioneer in the field of public opinion polling, stoking the political furor over soldier voting. Polling results showed that the fifty million civilians expected to vote in the presidential race were evenly divided between those favoring Democrats and Republicans. If an estimated six million "servicemen" were able to cast ballots, Gallup said, their strong Democratic preference would tip the election "in favor of the Democrats."[12] The Black press, meanwhile, pointed to the political impact of a vote by Black soldiers. *The Pittsburgh Courier* said a federal ballot for soldiers would "represent a real threat" because some four hundred thousand Black soldiers from southern states would gain the right to vote and might oust incumbents in Congress.[13]

THE SENATE'S PASSAGE of the McClellan bill set off a firestorm of controversy that revealed a deep schism in the Democratic Party. Days later, a group of twenty-five progressive House Democrats released a letter calling the bill a "slap in the face" to US soldiers. Senator Joseph Guffey, a Pennsylvania Democrat, charged that southern Democrats had entered "an unpatriotic and unholy alliance" with northern Republicans to defeat the Green-Lucas bill. Guffey accused a Democratic senator,

Harry Byrd of Virginia, of conspiring with northern Republicans to deprive soldiers of the vote. Byrd denied the claim and said Guffey had hurled a "gratuitous insult" at twenty-four fellow Democrats and eighteen Republicans.

Senator Josiah Bailey, a North Carolina Democrat, said that if liberal Democrats continued pushing a Roosevelt bill, the southern Democrats might break free and form their own party, a step that would doom Democratic hopes for reelecting Roosevelt. Speaking on the floor of the Senate, Bailey warned that without southern Democrats, "there would never again be a man elected President of the United States on the Democratic ticket."[14] Expressing the indignation of southern Democrats, he said, "If we must be in a party in which we are scorned as southern Democrats, we will find a party which honors us."

Democratic senator Ellison Smith of South Carolina, an avowed white supremacist known as "Cotton Ed," went to the floor of the Senate two days later to propose Byrd for the presidency and urged southern Democrats to form their own party to elect him. Smith proclaimed his "loyalty to white supremacy," and rejected those who he said were "trying to compel us to take the Negro on an equality, to eat with him, to sleep with him. I am not going to do it."[15] In a rambling rant, he denied there were any lynchings of Black people in his part of the country, flatly ignoring the numerous accounts of lynchings in South Carolina and other southern states. He then menaced his opponents in the debate, "We would lynch some white people if they would go down there—and I think I would join in the lynching."

Smith had once supported FDR, but those days were now long gone. He said it was "the real Democrats" who had "made possible the election of the gang that is now disgracing the party."

Amid the turmoil in the Democratic Party, while FDR was still traveling back from Cairo, the president's longtime aide and speechwriter Samuel Rosenman tried to rescue the Green-Lucas soldier voting bill. On December 8, Rosenman went to the Pentagon, where he met with the undersecretary of war, Robert Patterson, and pleaded with him for the War Department to do more to help win passage of the bill. Patterson reported Rosenman's request to Stimson. The secretary of war concluded the federal bill "has broken down in Congress probably because of an attack by southern Senators who don't want to have the poll tax on the negroes abolished as it would be by the federal law." Stimson noted in his diary that he and Patterson agreed there might be a "political motive underneath those bills in favor of the president in the next election." If the army made the effort that Rosenman sought, Stimson worried, "People would say the Army was going into politics on behalf of the president's re-election."[16]

After FDR returned from his conferences in Tehran and Cairo, he steered clear of the issue in radio talks to the nation around Christmastime, focusing instead on the war. In a press conference broadcast on December 28, he said that if his first two terms during the Great Depression made him like a doctor curing a sick patient, he was now "Dr. Win-the-War," and his "overwhelming emphasis should be on winning the war."

FDR let the issue of soldier voting simmer until January 11, 1944, when he delivered his State of the Union address and urged Congress to pass a bill to create a federal ballot system for the armed forces. "Surely the signers of the Constitution did not intend a document which, even in wartime, would be construed to take away the franchise of any of those who are fighting to preserve the Constitution itself. . . . The Army and Navy have reported that it will be impossible effectively to administer forty-eight different soldier-voting laws." He concluded: "It is the duty of the Congress to remove this unjustifiable discrimination against the men and women in our armed forces—and to do it just as quickly as possible."[17]

Working with Cutler, Stimson wrote a letter that day to the House committee on elections stating his concerns about the states' rights bill passed by the Senate, which the committee had begun considering. Still worried about being drawn into the partisan political conflict over the soldier voting issue, Stimson hewed to the line of providing not political opinion, but a factual assessment of the army's capabilities of carrying out voting by millions of soldiers. "The War Department has already indicated," he wrote, "that it may be possible, weather and military conditions permitting, in respect to one election, to carry in bulk by air, overseas and back, with a short time ballots which are uniformly light in weight and small in size. But the War Department does not believe that such expeditious carriage can be made a matter of daily routine over several months or weeks, as would be required to meet the provisions of the laws of the different states."[18]

His efforts to stay above the fray failed. On January 24, Senator Robert Taft, an Ohio Republican, suggested that Stimson and Secretary of the Navy Knox had falsified their accounts of what the military services could achieve, and that the two secretaries were working to support FDR's reelection. "The truth is that from the beginning the Army and Navy have been determined to have Federal ballots. . . . This week the statement made to the House committee by the Secretary of War is distinctly in that direction," Taft said. "In my opinion Secretaries Knox and Stimson are working for a fourth term . . . they have assumed a partisan position, and . . . I do not believe what they say regarding the inability of the War and Navy Departments to transmit the ballots to soldiers throughout the world."[19]

Cutler brought word of these accusations of partisanship back to Stimson, who three decades earlier had served as secretary of war under Taft's father, President William Taft. With a pained look on his face, Stimson said, "Why the young puppy . . . I loved his father."[20]

Roosevelt went on the attack, pointing to Stimson's January 11 letter to the House and calling for passage of the federal ballot system. "What is needed is a complete change of machinery for absentee balloting, which will give the members of our armed services and merchant marine all over the world an opportunity to cast ballots," the president said in a message to Congress on January 26. He then sharply criticized the states' rights bill that was under consideration in the House: "I consider such proposed legislation a fraud on the soldiers and sailors and marines now in training and fighting for us and our sacred rights. It is a fraud upon the American people."[21]

Republicans and southern Democrats swiftly rejected the president's charge of "fraud" and condemned him for impugning their motives. Taft dismissed the accusation as a "direct insult to the members of this body and a direct insult to the members of the House of Representatives."

In the House, Rankin advanced McClellan's states' rights bill, depicting it as part of a struggle by white people in the South. He cast the bill as a southern bulwark against the federal government, just as the South had opposed Reconstruction after the Civil War. "The one thing that the white people of the South have protested against all these decades is the invasion of the rights of the states by the federal government under any pretense," he said in debate on January 28.[22]

In the Senate, Eastland, the Mississippi Democrat and fierce advocate of segregation, argued three days later that soldiers from the South were "fighting to maintain white supremacy and the control of our election machinery." The senator added, "I assert that so far as the State of Mississippi is concerned, we have fully and finally determined that we shall master our own destiny, that we shall maintain control of our own elections, and our election machinery, and that we will protect and preserve white supremacy throughout eternity. I shall not cast a vote for any bill which would to the least extent tear down those safeguards."[23]

Another overt racist, Louisiana Democratic senator John Overton, told the Senate that preserving state election laws was necessary "to maintain white supremacy." Senator Kenneth Wherry, a Republican from Nebraska, responded that Overton's words would be comforting to Hitler and Hirohito. "I subscribe to the doctrine of our forefathers— that God Almighty created all men equal. There is no such thing as white supremacy, and the whole theory is pure poppycock, shrewdly used to disenfranchise poor whites as well as Negroes."[24]

The sponsor of the federal soldier ballot bill in the House was a Democrat, Representative Eugene Worley, a supporter of the New Deal from Shamrock, Texas. His southern roots did not shield him from attacks by Rankin, who denounced supporters of Worley's bill as Black radicals and communists, lacing his comments with anti-Semitic remarks. After Walter Winchell, the influential columnist, argued in support for Worley's bill in New York City's left-leaning *PM* newspaper, Rankin denounced Winchell on the floor of the House as "the little kike," a jolting use of anti-Semitic speech at a time when Hitler's murderous campaign against the Jews of Europe was well known.[25]

The wrathful debate reached its climax in the House on February 4, when Worley's bill was defeated by a vote of 224–168, as forty-eight Democrats—nearly all from the South—joined with one hundred seventy-six Republicans to reject the measure. A short while later, the House passed Rankin's version of the states' rights bill by a vote of 328–69; the House minority leader, Republican Joseph Martin of Massachusetts, had brought dozens of Republicans across the aisle with him to join southern Democrats in rejecting FDR's effort to create a federal ballot for soldiers. The vote showed that the president's opponents could use bipartisanship against him. The stunning defeat for the president also revealed the wide breach that had opened between him and the southern branch of his party.

Because the House and Senate passed different soldier voting bills, a conference committee—composed of Rankin and others from the House and three senators—was appointed to develop a measure that both chambers could agree upon. They drafted a compromise bill that would permit a soldier to use a federal ballot if the governor of the soldier's home state issued a certificate by July 15, 1944, authorizing use of the federal ballot in that state. The bill also would create a War Ballot Commission—composed of Stimson, Knox and a federal shipping official—to oversee the creation and distribution of the federal ballots.[26]

The new bill opened the bitter debate once again; Senators Green and Lucas urged its defeat while Rankin called for its passage. On March 14, Barkley went to the floor of the Senate to denounce the compromise as likely to enable fewer soldiers to vote than in 1942. Despite this, the Senate that same day passed the bill by a vote of 47–31, with twenty-three Democrats joining twenty-four Republicans to approve it.[27] The next day, the House passed the compromise bill by a lopsided tally of 273–111, again with a large group of southern Democrats joining Republicans to vote in its favor.

FDR FUMED, UNSURE of whether to accept the compromise or veto the bill and push for a full federal ballot for all soldiers. On the same day the House passed the compromise, the president sent telegrams to the governors of the forty-eight states asking whether the use of federal ballots would be authorized in their states.[28] New York's Governor Dewey, vying to become the Republican candidate against FDR in the next election, quickly announced his state would not approve the federal soldier ballot. Within a week, about twenty-two governors had announced they would reject the federal soldier ballot, while twenty-one said they would approve it or might do so, and another five were uncertain.[29]

Stimson saw the role he and Knox would play on the War Ballot Commission as tinged with bipartisan irony. "In view of all the criticisms which have been aimed at Frank and me by the different partisans of our own party, it is rather amusing that . . . he and I are the two men who have been chosen as the ones upon whose honesty both parties can depend in carrying out and administering a very difficult voting problem for President of the United States."[30]

FDR at last announced begrudgingly that he would permit the compromise measure to become law without his signature, though he urged Congress to permit all soldiers to cast the federal ballot, and he denounced the compromise as confusing and "wholly inadequate."[31] He vowed that the US military would do everything possible to distribute state absentee ballots, but he also excoriated Congress for failing to make sure an optional federal ballot could be available to all men and women in the military services. "Our boys on the battlefronts must not be denied an opportunity to vote because they are away from home," he said. "They are at the front fighting with their lives to defend our rights and freedoms."

Days later, Stimson and Knox launched the War Ballot Commission, which would oversee the voting plans of the army, the navy and other agencies. Cutler, the army's soldier voting coordinator, also became executive officer of the War Ballot Commission. When FDR learned later that the army's voting program was entirely run by Republicans, he sent Rosenman to discuss the matter with Stimson. Rosenman asked Stimson what party Cutler and his two assistants were affiliated with. Stimson became red in the face and said angrily, "Damn it, Rosenman, what difference does it make what parties they belong to! Are you suggesting to me sir, that I am rigging something here? Cutler was corporation counsel to a Democratic mayor of Boston. I don't give a damn to what party he belongs. How dare you address such an innuendo to me!" Rosenman swiftly excused himself from the secretary of war's office and departed the Pentagon.[32]

Evidently not dissuaded by this tirade, FDR sent Stimson a memo on May 22, 1944, saying he was getting complaints from Democrats about the War Ballot Commission's staff. The president urged adding a Democrat to the staff. "I think it essential to avoid charges of discrimination," he wrote. "I think something must be done for your and my peace of mind later on."[33] With Stimson's approval, Cutler resolved the matter by hiring a Democratic assistant.

Ultimately, Stimson and Cutler had sought to shield the US military from charges it engaged in partisan politics while also trying to provide Congress with a truthful account of the military's ability to enable service members to cast a ballot. Once the final bill passed, the Republicans then carried out the soldier voting, albeit within the limitations imposed by Congress and the states. In the November 1944 election results, with only twenty of the states approving a federal ballot for soldiers, 2.7 million service member ballots—including only 85,000 federal ballots—were counted by state election officials.[34] Though soldier voting had caused a furious political conflict, it drew little attention after the election itself. At the end of the war, Stimson awarded Cutler the Distinguished Service Medal, saying in a citation, "In discharging his soldier voting responsibilities Colonel Cutler added to the Army's prestige by a clear demonstration of its integrity and nonpartisan character."[35] Stimson said no other job "had held more explosive possibilities, and none was accomplished with less friction."[36]

The fierce struggle over soldier voting—which deepened the divide in the Democratic Party and highlighted southern Democrats' intense devotion to the cause of white supremacy—presaged the battles over voting rights in America in the following two decades. For FDR, the bitter confrontation with the southern Democrats confirmed his view that a realignment of the two major parties was necessary.

A Bipartisan Vision for American Politics

In the midst of the soldier voting dispute, President Roosevelt delivered his State of the Union speech from the White House via radio, sending his message directly into the homes of the American people. Speaking before microphones on the evening of January 11, 1944, he explained he couldn't leave the White House because he had the flu. Though he didn't mention it, avoiding the Capitol also meant he wouldn't have to confront southern Democrats in revolt over his soldier voting plan. FDR forcefully called for a federal ballot for soldiers and he urged Congress to pass an ambitious agenda of tax increases, price controls and a national service act.[1]

With southern Democrats in furious opposition to FDR, his legislative program languished in Congress and even the president's relationship with longstanding allies soured. Stymied in Congress, the president secretly reached out to Republican leader Wendell Willkie to pursue a bipartisan vision for recasting America's political parties. FDR confidant Samuel Rosenman later revealed their plan, which he described as a "Herculean task" that only Roosevelt and Willkie could perform.[2]

Speaking to America over the airwaves that evening, FDR called on Congress to pass bills aimed at taxing "unreasonable profits" of corporations and individuals, removing "undue profit" from war industry contracts, using more food subsidies and price controls to protect consumers from inflation, and creating a national service law that would require adults to contribute to the war effort. He also described his "second Bill of Rights" as a list of ten economic "rights" that he believed Americans should have. "The right to a useful and remunerative job in the industries or shops or farms or mines of the nation," his list of rights began. "The right to adequate medical care and the opportunity to achieve and enjoy good health," he continued. He concluded his list: "The right to adequate protection from the economic fears of old age, sickness, accident and unemployment; The right to a good education."[3] He said the nation should seek to implement these rights after the war was over.

Within months, the president's legislative agenda was in tatters. His preferred tax bill would have raised $10.5 billion in new revenue from corporate income and other taxes, but Congress passed a tax bill that would raise only $2.3 billion. FDR's longtime ally Alben Barkley, the Kentucky Democrat who was the Senate majority leader, urged him not to veto the bill, but the president did so anyway—adding a veto message that sharply rebuked Congress.[4] Barkley denounced the president's message and urged Congress to override the veto, which it promptly did on February 25. The vote in the Senate was 72–14, with large numbers of Democrats joining Republicans to overrule FDR.[5] Barkley resigned as majority leader in protest of the president's attack on Congress. He was quickly reelected Senate majority leader, and he insisted he would support President Roosevelt. But the limits of FDR's power in Congress—and the loss of Democratic support for the president and his proposals—had been exposed for all to see.

Congress extended price controls in a compromise bill, but even as FDR signed it he denounced the measure as one that would "weaken and obstruct" efforts to penalize people who raised prices.[6] The proposed National Service Act, despite vigorous support from Secretary of War Stimson, failed to pass.[7] The loss of the southern Democrats had left FDR virtually powerless to enact new laws.

The southern Democratic revolt took on steam as the states' rights rallying cry and support for segregation echoed across the South. When the US Supreme Court ruled on April 3, 1944, that the whites-only primary in Texas was unconstitutional, Democratic politicians across the South vowed to find ways of evading the ruling and ensuring that whites-only primaries would continue.[8] Segregationist Democrats in Congress launched an effort to kill the Fair Employment Practices Committee (FEPC), the agency that FDR established in 1941 to end discrimination and segregation in war industries.

Southern opposition soared after the FEPC ordered southern railroads to begin hiring Black workers for a variety of positions. Ten of the railroads refused to comply, arguing white employees would revolt and cause rioting and deaths.[9] FEPC supporters, including union leader and civil rights activist A. Philip Randolph, launched a committee urging Congress to pass a law establishing the FEPC as a permanent agency. Southern Democrats intensified their attacks, asserting the committee was backed by communists and was undermining white supremacy and segregation.

Senator Theodore Bilbo of Mississippi went to the Senate floor on June 20 and condemned the FEPC by saying its "hope and dream is to build up a greater race by intermarriage and intermingling of the two races." Two years later, Bilbo would publicly avow his membership in the Ku Klux Klan.[10] A man whose racism was at once virulent and buffoonish, Bilbo linked his campaign to kill the FEPC with his own plan to send Black Americans to West Africa.[11] He mocked Eleanor Roosevelt, the administration's leading figure on civil rights, saying, "If I can succeed eventually in resettling the great majority of Negroes in West Africa, I might entertain the proposition of making her queen of that Greater Liberia."

FDR's Republican alliance, a reliable support to the president, suffered a blow on April 28, when Secretary of the Navy Knox died of a heart attack at his home in Washington. The president sent a personal note to Knox's wife, and to the nation he issued a statement saying, "Truly he put his country first. We shall greatly miss his ability and his friendship."[12] Secretary of War Henry Stimson issued a statement saying, "I am deeply shocked and distressed at the news of Frank Knox's death. Our relations were not merely official; they had grown into a close, affectionate friendship based on the mutual confidence which had arisen between us."[13] FDR promoted Navy Under Secretary James V. Forrestal, who took little interest in party politics, to replace Knox.

FDR's own health had secretly become an increasing concern by early

1944. In November 1943, when he was in Tehran, Iran, the president had become suddenly ill—"He turned green and great drops of sweat began to bead off his face," his translator said—cutting short a meeting with Stalin and Churchill.[14] FDR recovered and managed to work, but once he was back in Washington he continued feeling ill and was diagnosed as having a persistent case of the flu. On March 27, 1944, he went for an examination at Bethesda Naval Hospital, where a cardiologist found alarming signs of a decline in the president's health. In a confidential report, the doctor said the president had significantly elevated blood pressure and congestive heart failure. FDR, who had smoked much of his life, also had acute bronchitis and a persistent cough.[15] The president was prescribed the heart drug digitalis and urged to lose weight. He also was advised to reduce his working hours, and his daughter Anna Roosevelt Boettiger began enforcing his new regimen. With the election of 1944 approaching, any hint of the president's poor health would have political impact. His physician told the press that the exam found his health "satisfactory." In truth, FDR's declining health made it even more burdensome for the president—as he led the Allies in war—to try to mend the schism in the Democratic Party.

The Republican Party, meanwhile, had turned away from its nominal leader, the liberal Wendell Willkie, in his bid for the Republican presidential nomination. After losing key primary elections, he dropped out of the race in early April 1944. His withdrawal left the way open for New York governor Thomas Dewey, who attacked FDR as grabbing power for New Deal programs. At the Republican National Convention in Chicago in late June 1944, Dewey won the presidential nomination.[16] Some Republicans touted the idea of drafting a southern segregationist, Democratic senator Harry Byrd of Virginia, for vice president, but in the end the party nominated Ohio governor John Bricker, a conservative known for his firm opposition to the New Deal.

It was then—at a time when FDR's legislative agenda was scuttled, his breach with southern Democrats was an unmanageable fury, his Republican alliance had lost one of its mainstays and the Republican Party had turned to the right—that the president decided to reach out secretly to Willkie.

One day during the week of the Republican convention, FDR called

Samuel Rosenman, his longtime aide and speechwriter, into his office. The former judge was among FDR's closest advisers. He had coined the phrase "New Deal" in 1932, written key speeches and regularly handled highly sensitive matters.[17] Now FDR wanted to send him on a secret political mission. "Willkie has just been beaten by the conservatives in his party who lined up in back of Dewey," the president said. "Now there is no doubt that the conservatives in our own party are out for my scalp, too—as you can see by what is going on in the South."[18]

"Well," FDR continued. "I think the time has come for the Democratic Party to get rid of its reactionary elements in the South, and to attract to it the liberals in the Republican Party. Willkie is the leader of those liberals." Willkie himself had recently raised this idea with Gifford Pinchot, the former Republican governor of Pennsylvania and ally of President Theodore Roosevelt, and Pinchot had relayed the conversation to FDR. "I agree with him one hundred percent and the time is now—right after the election," the president said.

FDR's concept of recasting America's political parties rested on a fundamental truth about American politics over the prior half century: each of the main parties had two wings, one conservative and one liberal. The Democrats had the reactionaries in the South who were bent on maintaining the Jim Crow status quo, while in the North the Democrats had liberal support from labor unions, immigrants and ethnic minorities. The Republican Party also had its liberals, who carried forward the abolitionist tradition of seeking equal rights for Black citizens, and it had conservative elements in big business and isolationists, including those recently associated with groups like America First. FDR believed this duality of the parties must end—the liberals should join one party, and the conservatives another. "We ought to have two real parties—one liberal and the other conservative," the president said. "As it is now, each party is split by dissenters."[19]

FDR didn't see this as a project he could achieve in time for the upcoming election, which was just five months away, in November 1944. "I'm talking about long-range politics—something that we can't accomplish this year. But we can do it in 1948, and we can start building it up right after the election this fall. Willkie and I together can form a new, really liberal party in America," he told Rosenman.[20] "What I want you to do is to go up to New York to see Willkie and tell him how I feel about this whole idea and get his reaction."

Ever since 1938, when FDR had launched his failed effort to elect more Democratic liberals—the so-called "purge" of conservatives from the party—the president had often spoken about a new alignment of the political parties, Rosenman recalled later. But this was the first time FDR had named a Republican leader he thought was qualified to join him in the project.

ROSENMAN AND WILLKIE arranged a secretive meeting at the St. Regis Hotel in New York City on July 5. Lunch was ordered for the two men in a private suite. They were so anxious for their meeting to remain secret that when a hotel waiter knocked on the door to bring in their lunch, Willkie—whose face was of course widely recognized—stepped into the bedroom of the suite so as not to be seen.[21]

Rosenman began by assuring Willkie that FDR was not seeking an endorsement from Willkie for the 1944 election. He then laid out the president's thinking. "Ever since the unsuccessful 'purge' of 1938," he said, "the idea has been growing in the president's mind that the real future of progressivism in American politics lies in a realignment of the parties rather than intraparty conflict. The trouble is that all Democrats get together in a convention hall and the majority adopts a good liberal platform; then, after election, the southern conservatives, who do not depend for election on anyone outside their own conservative districts, just run out on the platform. The president learned in 1938, the hard way, that he cannot beat them in their own districts. He is now ready to form a new grouping, leaving them out of the new liberal party. You see, you both are thinking along the same lines. He wants to team up with you, for he is sure you can do it together; and he thinks the right time to start is immediately after this election. If it is impossible for you to start talking with him about it before the election, then you can wait until later; but he wants to do it—whether he wins or loses in November."

Willkie indicated he and FDR were thinking alike. He said the recent Republican National Convention demonstrated that reactionaries were in control of his party, and it was also clear that "reactionary elements" of the Democratic Party had nothing in common with the administration, Rosenman recalled. Willkie summarized the situation: "Both parties are hybrids."

Willkie predicted that after the war political conflict in the United States would focus more on pitting liberal forces against conservative forces, rather than Democrats against Republicans. He was particularly interested in a foreign policy of internationalism rather than isolationism, and he looked forward to working with FDR. "You tell the president that I'm ready to devote almost full time to this," he told Rosenman.[22] "A sound, liberal government in the United States is absolutely essential to continued co-operation with the other nations of the world. I know some of these reactionaries—especially those in my own party. They'll run out on the other nations when the going gets tough—just as soon as they can."

Willkie and Rosenman also discussed the groups they believed would fall naturally into a cohesive liberal party: "Labor, racial and religious minorities, small farmers, students, small shopkeepers and businessmen, progressive intellectuals," Rosenman recalled. They also talked about the Republican liberals who might join this new party, as well as the Democrats who would be likely to move to a conservative party.

Willkie made it clear that while he was very interested in the idea, he did not want to meet with FDR until after the election because such a meeting could not be kept secret and would "give rise to many conjectures." As their two-hour meeting drew to a close, Rosenman told Willkie that FDR would contact him in due course, now that it was clear Willkie was prepared to speak with him more fully.[23]

Upon returning to Washington, Rosenman gave FDR a detailed account of his meeting with Willkie. "Fine, fine," FDR said. "I'll arrange to get together with him at the proper time." Rosenman assumed this meant after the election. A week later, without telling Rosenman, FDR sent Willkie a letter asking for a meeting, though "not on anything in relationship to the present campaign." The president urged Willkie to contact him after he returned from a trip he was embarking on to California and Hawaii. "We can arrange a meeting either here in Washington or, if you prefer, at Hyde Park—wholly off the record or otherwise, just as you think best."[24]

FDR's chief Republican ally, Stimson, was at this time making headlines while on a trip to the European theater of war, where Allied armies
were fighting their way up the Italian peninsula and across France. On
the Fourth of July, Stimson visited recently occupied Rome, where an
American flag—the same one that had flown over the US Capitol on
the day Pearl Harbor was attacked—was raised in a symbolic gesture.
A train delivering seven hundred tons of coal entered the city bearing a
celebratory sign: "Fourth of July, Rome, 1944." Stimson assured Italians
in his public remarks that American forces came not as conquerors, but
liberators.[25] After meeting with Pope Pius XII, he traveled to London
to meet with Prime Minister Churchill to discuss the thorny issue of
planning for the occupation of Germany, which had become a pressing
matter.

Stimson then went to France and met with the supreme Allied commander, General Dwight Eisenhower. The seventy-six-year-old secretary traveled 150 miles across Normandy in a jeep to witness the
progress of the invasion. "I've been amazed and thrilled by the spirit
that I've seen in the troops and their attitude toward their allies and
comrades. They are not a bit afraid of the enemy and their one thought
is to get hold of them," Stimson told reporters at Eisenhower's command
post in Normandy.[26] Explaining the rationale for his trip, he pointed to
the troops: "I felt that if I could not cross the ocean and tell them what
I thought of them I would not be fit to be secretary of war." He also
visited the grave of his old friend army general Theodore Roosevelt Jr.,
who had died of a heart attack shortly after the invasion began. Stimson
never mentioned politics or parties in these appearances, and yet his
visits with US forces on seized enemy territory quietly and forcefully
proclaimed the power of America's bipartisan wartime leadership.

FDR REMAINED FOCUSED on the war, but the coming presidential election also demanded his attention. On July 11, he announced that if the
Democratic Party nominated him for a fourth term as president, he
would accept.

Striving to appeal to both Republicans and Democrats, he depicted
his campaign as beyond partisan politics: "I would accept and serve, but

I would not run, in the usual partisan, political sense. But if the people command me to continue in this office and in this war I have as little right to withdraw as a soldier has to leave his post in the line."[27]

With the Democratic National Convention set to start in Chicago on July 19, FDR announced that he would miss the convention because he would be visiting military installations in California and Hawaii. His absence would both highlight his experience as commander in chief and avoid an angry confrontation with southern Democrats. The day before the national convention's start, southern Democrats met in Chicago and counted a total of 120 delegates prepared to vote for Senator Byrd to be the party's presidential nominee.

The NAACP and other Black organizations joined together in publishing an "open letter" to the Democratic and Republican parties warning, "Negroes no longer belong to any one political party." The letter enumerated a list of policies the parties must support to win Black votes, including continuation of the FEPC, ending poll taxes, and the desegregation of the armed forces.[28] At their convention, the Republicans had adopted platform planks condemning racial prejudice, calling for an investigation into segregation and abuse of Black soldiers by the army, supporting passage of a law to create a permanent FEPC, opposing the poll tax and supporting an anti-lynching law. At the Democratic convention, in contrast, the southern Democrats wielded their power and fought bitterly to keep such specific planks out of their party's platform. Ultimately, the Democratic convention adopted a compromise measure that said "racial and religious minorities have the right to live, develop and vote equally with all citizens and share the rights guaranteed by the Constitution."[29]

Despite the strength of the southern Democrats, FDR won the nomination on the first ballot by a vote of 1,086 to just 89 for Byrd. The president decided to let the convention decide whether he should keep his vice president, Henry Wallace, a liberal detested by the southern Democrats threatening to split from the party. This opened the way for FDR's aide James Byrnes, the South Carolina segregationist who was director of the Office of War Mobilization, to seek the vice-presidential nomination. Byrnes asked his friend Senator Harry Truman, a moderate Democrat from Missouri, to prepare a nominating speech.

Labor groups and the NAACP, however, voiced strong opposition to Byrnes. NAACP leader Walter White, who considered Byrnes a staunch proponent of white supremacy, told an NAACP conference in Chicago on July 16 that if the Democratic Party nominated a southerner as vice president it could "kiss the Negro vote good-bye."[30] Days later, with FDR making calls to delegates and his operatives at the convention, a compromise was reached: instead of Byrnes, Truman was chosen to be the vice-presidential nominee.

Delivering his acceptance speech from a US Navy base via radio to the convention hall on July 20, FDR made a direct appeal for bipartisan support. "In the last three elections, the people of the United States have transcended party affiliation. Not only Democratic but also forward-looking Republicans and millions of independent voters have turned to progressive leadership, a leadership which has sought consistently, and with fair success, to advance the lot of the average American citizen who had been so forgotten during the period after the last war. I am confident that they will look to that same kind of liberalism, to build our safer economy for the future."[31] He also depicted himself as a commander in chief: "I am now at this naval base in the performance of my duties under the Constitution. The war waits for no elections. Decisions must be made, plans must be laid, strategy must be carried out."

Four years earlier, Stimson had suggested privately that FDR should not run for a third term; but then came the war, and all the two men had been through—and the work that remained before them. Upon returning from visiting the Allied invasion forces in Normandy, Stimson sent the president a handwritten letter on July 27: "I thoroughly agree with the position you have publicly taken, namely, that you could no more decline the duty which is laid before you now than a soldier could refuse to go on in the face of the enemy. It seems to me that that position is not open to argument, in light of the struggle which faces our country today. Therefore all I can do is to send you my most heartfelt good wishes for your health and strength and to pray that the Lord will guide and preserve you through it all. Ever faithfully, Henry L. Stimson."[32]

The loyal and persistent support of Stimson and other Republicans was buoying for FDR, who wearied of fighting the internecine battle against his southern Democratic opponents. His desire to strengthen his appeal to liberal Republicans likely led FDR to leak his letter to Willkie to *The New York Times,* as Rosenman later speculated.[33] On August 11, the paper carried on its front page a story about the letter, saying the president had invited Willkie to the White House to discuss "foreign relations policies that the United States should follow for the immediate and more distant future."[34] Willkie refused to comment.

The bipartisan plan that FDR was pursuing with Willkie was a big-picture, long-term political strategy that remained a secret. But in the summer of 1944, the president's constant search for Republican support for his policies would lead him to pursue a bipartisan accord with a very concrete objective, and it would rapidly become known to the American people. FDR and Secretary of State Cordell Hull developed this accord with none other than the Republican presidential nominee, Thomas Dewey.

The talks with Dewey stemmed from the president's efforts to create a permanent United Nations organization. In June 1944, FDR announced plans to create a permanent UN "to maintain peace and security," and the idea was key to his vision for the postwar world. The four major powers of the United Nations alliance—the United States, Great Britain, the Soviet Union and China—planned a conference to take place in Washington in late August 1944 to develop a charter for the organization.[35] Looming over this idea, however, was the threat of a repeat of the partisan vitriol that followed World War I, when Republicans attacked Democratic president Woodrow Wilson's plan for the League of Nations, and isolationist opposition helped kill the treaty agreement in the Senate. As the date for the United Nations conference approached, the specter of partisan politics arose. On August 16, Dewey publicly attacked the conference during a campaign speech, suggesting "it is planned to subject the nations of the world, great and small, permanently to the coercive power of the four nations holding this conference." He called it "the rankest form of imperialism" by the four powers to "coerce" the smaller nations.[36]

To FDR and Hull, the idea of creating an international organization to preserve peace after the war's end was too critical to fall prey to partisan attacks. With FDR's approval, Hull contacted Dewey and arranged to discuss the matter with his representative, Republican attorney John

Foster Dulles—brother of Office of Strategic Services official Allen Dulles. After meeting on August 25, the two men reached an agreement to avoid partisan political attacks on the effort to create a permanent United Nations organization.[37] They outlined the accord in a statement released that day:

> The Secretary maintained the position that the American people consider the subject of future peace as a nonpartisan subject which must be kept entirely out of politics. Mr. Dulles, on behalf of Governor Dewey, stated that the Governor shared this view on the understanding, however, that it did not preclude full public nonpartisan discussion of the means of attaining a lasting peace.

Though it was brief, stiff and legalistic, this truce in the partisan political conflict laid the foundation for extraordinary bipartisan support for the nascent United Nations organization over the next year and beyond.

In the end, both Republicans and Democrats largely abided by the accord. Even as Dewey criticized FDR's foreign policy and conduct of the war, amid the fray the Republican candidate corresponded with Hull about the Dumbarton Oaks Conference as it unfolded and even proposed changes that were inserted in the charter being drafted for the organization.[38] The conference ended in October with a plan to hold a subsequent international meeting to finalize and adopt the charter of the new United Nations Organization.

WILLKIE, MEANWHILE, SOUGHT to retain his standing in the Republican Party, which required him to keep his distance from FDR. He continued to refuse to meet with the president until after the election. He drafted a response to FDR's July letter that indicated he was intrigued by the idea of a realignment of the parties. "I have your gracious note of the thirteenth. The subjects concerning which you suggest we have a talk on your return from the West are, as you know, subjects in which I am deeply interested. I am fearful, however, that any talk between us before the campaign is over might well be the subject of misinterpretation and misunderstanding."[39]

Willkie never sent that letter, and the two men would never meet again. On October 8, 1944, after suffering a series of heart attacks, he died in a New York hospital. He was only fifty-two years old, and his untimely death led to a stream of condolences from across the country and around the world to his wife, Edith. From the White House, FDR issued a statement saying, "The nation will long remember Wendell Willkie as a forthright American. Earnest, honest, whole-souled, he also had tremendous courage. This courage, which was his dominating trait, prompted him more than once to stand alone and to challenge the wisdom of counsels taken by powerful interests within his own party."[40]

Stimson, ever leery of dragging the army into politics, issued no public statement on Willkie's death. Public praise of the prominent Republican by the Republican secretary of war less than a month before the election might have led to objections—by either Democrats or Republicans. Instead, he wrote privately to Edith Willkie: "The sad news which I received yesterday morning filled me with distress for I have been living in the confident hope that the inspiration of your husband's broad and tolerant patriotism would be a great boon to this country in the tumultuous years which are sure to follow the war. He was a great citizen, a courageous leader, and to me always a warm and helpful friend."[41] Stimson's words to Edith affirmed the friendship of the two men as well as the liberal Republican values they shared and the political alliance they built with FDR. He offered to have Willkie buried in Arlington National Cemetery, but Mrs. Willkie decided he should be laid to rest in his hometown in Indiana.[42]

In a gesture underscoring the Republican leader's dedication to civil rights, his friend Walter White arranged for the NAACP's new headquarters building in New York City to be named in honor of Willkie.[43]

On Election Day, November 7, Americans went to the polls amid concerns that difficulties in counting ballots cast by soldiers might delay the returns and disrupt the ability of officials to determine the outcome. Eleven of the forty-eight states would not begin counting soldier ballots of any kind until after Election Day, but states that included them in

Election Day early returns were heavily in Roosevelt's favor.[44] Dewey won more votes in some parts of the South than had been won by Republicans since Reconstruction, but it was still not enough to prevent FDR from sweeping the southern states.[45] By the early morning hours the next day, it became clear that FDR had won election to a fourth term as president, and Dewey conceded the race.[46] Ultimately, the president beat Dewey by a margin of 25.6 million to 22.0 million votes, or 54 percent to 46 percent. FDR won thirty-six states, giving him a victory in the Electoral College of 432–99.[47] In elections for the Senate, the Democrats maintained their large majority, and in the House of Representatives they increased their margin of control. One of the Republicans who lost was Representative Hamilton Fish, the New York isolationist whose defeat had been sought by both FDR and Willkie.

FDR praised the election as an achievement of American democracy and renewed his plea for the country to unite. "For the first time in eighty years we have held an election [for president] in the midst of a war," he said on November 8. "What is really important is that after all of the changes and vicissitudes of four score years, we have again demonstrated to the world that democracy is a living, vital force; that our faith in American institutions is unshaken, that conscience and not force is the source of power in the government of man. In that faith let us unite to win the war and to achieve a lasting peace."

ROOSEVELT AND WILLKIE never disclosed their plan to remake the two major American parties. Rosenman, however, later revealed their plan as it was sketched out in their secret talks: the liberals in the Republican Party would join the Democratic Party, and the conservatives and white supremacists among the southern Democrats would join the Republican Party. This inversion of the parties would end their dual, hybrid nature, and would make the Democrats more consistently liberal and the Republicans more consistently conservative.

The plan was bipartisan in that it sprang from the minds of a Democrat and a Republican and it was intended to reshape the two parties. However, the primary goal was not to foster bipartisanship, but to enable a liberal leader like FDR to gain support for liberal policies without having to cross party lines to cobble together a coalition of liberal Republicans and Democrats while fighting a battle within the Democratic Party against reactionaries. The bipartisan leadership of FDR and his Republican allies already had united liberal elements across party lines and set the two major parties on new paths. The alliance, in fact, already had put the Roosevelt-Willkie vision on a trajectory toward realization of a more broadly liberal Democratic Party—and a more broadly conservative Republican Party—in the following decades.

The Holocaust and the Fight
over Postwar Germany

In August 1944, Allied armies prepared to invade Germany amid predictions of a rapid victory over the Nazis, perhaps within a few months. In Washington, a dispute broke out behind closed doors between the secretary of war, Henry Stimson, and the secretary of the treasury, Henry Morgenthau Jr., over how the Allies would mete out justice to a defeated Germany. Outraged over Nazi persecution of Europe's Jews, Morgenthau argued that Germany must be stripped of its industry and reduced to an agrarian state to prevent a resurgence of German militarism. Stimson argued that permitting Germany to retain its industrial base would enable the European economy to recover, thus avoiding the sort of economic collapse that had followed World War I and led to World War II. Morgenthau also urged that Nazi leaders be executed immediately upon capture, while Stimson argued they should stand trial before war crimes tribunals.

The debate tested the bipartisan alliance launched when Stimson joined the Roosevelt Administration four years earlier. Morgenthau was a lifelong Democrat and a close friend and confidant of President Roosevelt. Born into a prominent Jewish family in New York City in 1891, he had supported FDR politically for decades. His father, financier Henry Morgenthau Sr., played a role in Democratic politics and financially supported FDR.[1] Henry Morgenthau Jr. attended Philips Exeter Academy and graduated from Cornell University in New York. He and his wife,

Elinor, later owned a farm near the Roosevelts' estate in Hyde Park, and the two couples spent time together socially.[2] After Morgenthau helped Roosevelt win election as New York governor in 1928, FDR named him state conservation commissioner.[3] Early in FDR's presidency, he appointed Morgenthau as treasury secretary. Morgenthau played a critical role in implementing the New Deal, helping finance Social Security and other programs that the president launched to lift America out of the Great Depression. It was only years later—after FDR and Morgenthau had fought many battles side by side in Washington—that Stimson, a Republican critic of the New Deal, had joined the administration. Now, FDR would sit in judgment of the dispute sharply dividing his two close allies—one a Democrat, one a Republican.

After the large rally at Madison Square Garden in March 1943 called attention to the need to rescue Jews from European countries, Jewish groups had come forward offering to help pay for transportation and other costs for rescue operations. Even amid the war, opportunities arose to get Jewish refugees safely out of France, Italy and other countries. US Department of State officials, however, said they needed to coordinate first with British officials and declined to pursue specific opportunities or make visas available for refugees. Despite reports of the Nazi genocide, the State Department failed to take in even the permitted numbers of refugees and immigrants approved by Congress during the war. In Congress, measures to permit more refugees to enter the country were defeated.

There were divisions among the American Jewish community, too, as became evident when Orthodox rabbis planned to hold a protest march in Washington in fall 1943 to call for the US government to take prompt action to rescue Jewish refugees. The Emergency Committee to Save the Jews of Europe, an activist group that had begun criticizing FDR for indifference to their plight, helped organize the protest.[4] Some Jewish leaders, however, worried that making overt political demands would spur anti-Semitism. Rabbi Stephen Wise, president of the American Jewish Congress, was among those who discouraged the march in Washington. Samuel Rosenman, FDR's longtime aide and speechwriter, told the president the protesters did not represent "the most thoughtful elements of Jewry," and "the leading Jews of his acquaintance opposed this march on the Capitol."[5]

On October 6, 1943, some five hundred rabbis marched to the Capitol, where they gave Vice President Henry Wallace a petition demanding the creation of a special agency to rescue European Jews and the opening of Palestine to Jewish immigration.[6] Wallace said that he was moved, but only an Allied victory would solve the Nazi problem. While US refugee rescue efforts stalled, others succeeded. That same month, Danish citizens helped eight thousand Jews escape from Nazi-occupied Denmark to Sweden.[7]

Anguished over the US failure to help Jews escape from the Nazi genocide, staff members of the Treasury Department prepared a report for Morgenthau in January 1944 documenting delays and excuses by State Department officials. Provocatively entitled "Report to the Secretary on the Acquiescence of this Government in the Murder of the Jews," the eighteen-page document began: "One of the greatest crimes in history, the slaughter of the Jewish people in Europe, is continuing unabated." It charged that some State Department officials were "guilty not only of gross procrastination and willful failure to act, but even of willful attempts to prevent action from being taken to rescue Jews from Hitler."[8] Pointing particularly at the conduct of Assistant Secretary of State Breckinridge Long, the report charged that the department had failed to act for five months after the World Jewish Congress proposed plans to rescue Jews from France and Romania.

Responding to the report, Morgenthau urged the president to create a special board to rescue refugees from the war in Europe. On Sunday, January 15, Morgenthau and two of his staff members who helped prepare the "Acquiescence of this Government" report met with FDR, presenting him a shortened version of the report and a draft of an executive order to establish a board to rescue refugees. In a meeting that lasted just twenty minutes, FDR agreed to sign the executive order and create the War Refugee Board (WRB).[9] Roosevelt made one revision to the draft executive order—he placed Stimson on the board so its members would be Morgenthau, Secretary of State Cordell Hull and Stimson. FDR signed Executive Order 9417 a week later, authorizing the WRB to "take action for the immediate rescue from the Nazis of as many as possible of persecuted minorities of Europe, racial, religious or political, all civilian victims of enemy savagery." It also said that the board could accept private contributions to achieve its goals, and that the government's policy was to help victims of Nazi persecution by rendering "all possible relief and assistance consistent with successful prosecution of the war."

The massive scale of the Nazi genocide continued to emerge. Separate from the murderous camp system in Poland, German forces who invaded the Soviet Union in June 1941 carried out a campaign of extermination, killing as many as a million people—the vast majority of them Jews—through mass shootings and use of poison gas.[10] In a war crimes trial in the Soviet Ukrainian city of Kharkiv, three Germans and a Russian collaborator were convicted and sentenced to death on December 18, 1943, for their roles in the mass slayings.[11] They were hanged the next day before a crowd of fifty thousand spectators, who broke into cheers.

Morgenthau gave the first official US response to the hangings a month later. In a dramatic segment of a broadcast aimed at selling war bonds, a figure depicted as a soldier asked, "What's going to happen to the apes that started this thing . . . the Nazis and fascists?" Morgenthau replied, "You'll find your answer in Russia . . . the Russians are removing some of the worst stains from the face of this earth . . . by stringing the ringleaders of hate up and letting them hang there until they are dead. . . . That is the final assurance of the future of free men."[12]

At the newly created WRB, treasury official John Pehle, one of the authors of the "Acquiescence of this Government" report, became the agency's executive director. On February 1, Stimson and his assistants John McCloy and Harvey Bundy met with Morgenthau and Pehle.[13] Stimson noted in his diary that the board intended to move refugees to an array of possible locations, including a camp recently built by the US Army in Algeria. His days were consumed with operations ranging from the Manhattan Project to the army's preparations for D-Day in France and retaking the Philippines from the Japanese, so he named McCloy and Bundy to serve as his alternates on the board. Morgenthau described Stimson as "very sympathetic" in a phone call the next day with Rabbi Jonah Wise, a founder of the United Jewish Appeal, an organization active in refugee relief efforts.[14]

Under Pehle's leadership, the WRB prepared a declaration for the president to make condemning the Nazi slaughter of innocent people, including the Jews, and urging the German people and other nations to help Jews escape. Morgenthau and McCloy helped draft the statement.[15] On March 24, FDR read the declaration publicly at the White House. "In one of the blackest crimes of all history—begun by the Nazis in the day of peace and multiplied by them a hundred times in time of war—the wholesale systematic murder of the Jews of Europe goes on unabated every hour."[16] FDR continued to urge Germans and people in all Nazi-dominated countries to save the Jews "from the Nazi hangman."

Despite the president's urgent appeal, the limits of what the army would do to save the Jews became clear after reports emerged in the spring and summer of 1944 that the Nazis were killing large numbers of Jews at a massive concentration camp in a Polish town, Auschwitz. The Nazis were preparing to deport the Jewish population of Hungary there on trains. In April 1944, an escapee's account had revealed that the Nazis were using one of the four large Auschwitz gas chambers to kill up to two thousand people at a time. Jewish groups began urging the WRB to bomb the Auschwitz gas chambers and the rail lines used to transport Jews to the camp. On June 21, Pehle transmitted to the War Department a request to bomb the rail lines leading to Auschwitz, and three days later he discussed the request with McCloy.[17] On July 4, McCloy rejected the request in a reply suggesting that the proposed air attack would divert support from important military operations and that the best way to help victims of enemy persecution would be "the early defeat of the Axis."[18] The WRB ultimately would be credited with saving some two hundred thousand Jews from murder at the hands of the Nazis, but its inability to convince the army to bomb Auschwitz underscored the limits of its powers.[19]

More requests to bomb Auschwitz and the rail lines followed. In July, a Jewish group sent FDR a letter arguing that such bombing would actually help the war effort because the rail lines had military uses and bombing the camp could enable prisoners to escape and join resistance forces. In early August, an official of the World Jewish Congress sent McCloy a request from the Czech government in exile that US forces bomb the Auschwitz gas chambers. The idea was once again rejected. An August 14 reply from McCloy said the proposed bombing "would be of doubtful efficacy" and "might provoke even more vindictive action by the Germans."[20]

DURING A TRIP to England and France in early August 1944, Morgenthau obtained a draft of a military handbook intended to guide the Allied forces during the anticipated occupation of Germany. Morgenthau found the handbook contained provisions calling for the Allies to encourage German economic recovery, and he met with FDR at the White House on August 19 to object to the plan.[21] FDR replied that he would resolve the matter in a meeting with Prime Minister Churchill in Québec City planned for the following month. "Give me thirty minutes with Churchill and I can correct this," he told Morgenthau. "We have to be tough" with "the German people, not just the Nazis. You either have to castrate the German people or you have got to treat them in such a manner so that they can't just go on reproducing people who want to continue the way they have in the past."

Morgenthau raised the issue with Stimson over lunch in Stimson's office in the Pentagon on August 23. The treasury secretary recommended that he, Stimson and Hull should prepare a joint proposal for the president before FDR met with Churchill. Stimson liked the idea and suggested that the heart of German industry, the Ruhr and Saar regions, could be placed under international control. Morgenthau replied that he would rather see all industry removed, reducing the Germans "to an agricultural population of small landholders."[22] Stimson retorted that removing German industry might necessitate taking many people out of Germany. Morgenthau responded: "Well, that is not nearly as bad as sending them to gas chambers!"

Morgenthau prepared a memo attacking the military handbook, which FDR read aloud at a cabinet meeting on August 25. The president remarked that Germany could "live happily and peacefully on soup from soup kitchens if she couldn't make money for herself." He also agreed to have Morgenthau, Stimson and Hull form a committee on the occupation of Germany.[23] That afternoon, FDR sent Stimson a letter saying, "This so-called Handbook is pretty bad. . . . It gives me the impression that Germany is to be restored as much as the Netherlands or Belgium, and the people of Germany are to be brought back as quickly as possible to their prewar estate."

Stimson and McCloy went to Morgenthau's home in Washington on September 4 for dinner and to discuss postwar plans for Germany with Morgenthau and White. "Morgenthau is, not unnaturally, very bitter and . . . it became very apparent that he would plunge out for a treatment of Germany which I feel sure would be unwise," Stimson wrote in his diary.[24] Morgenthau's recollection of the debate included Stimson saying, "I think we can't solve the German problem except through Christianity and kindness."[25] Germany, of course, was considered a Christian nation, a fact that had failed to protect the Jews or prevent the war, and Stimson's reasoning seemed to suggest a double standard—that while Germany destroyed European Jewry in a genocide, the German people should receive "Christianity and kindness." The remark stung Morgenthau, who recalled it with irritation the next day in a conversation with Harry Hopkins. Stimson and Morgenthau saw the issues through different lenses, which threatened to upend the usual collegiality of their relationship.

The next day, the committee—joined by Hopkins, whom FDR had added to it—met in Hull's office. Stimson found that Morgenthau and Hull both wanted to destroy the industrial capacity of Germany's Ruhr and Saar regions. While all of the men agreed on dissolution of the Nazi party and demilitarizing Germany, Stimson rejected the idea of dismantling German industry. He argued in vain against his three colleagues.[26] "In all the four years that I have been here I have not had such a difficult and unpleasant meeting although of course there were no personalities. We all knew each other too well for that. But we were irreconcilably divided."[27]

The next day, September 6, FDR called the committee together to discuss the issues. Morgenthau laid out his views on the Ruhr in a memo to the president: "Here lies the heart of German industrial power, the caldron of wars. This area should not only be stripped of all presently existing industries but so weakened and controlled that it can not in the foreseeable future become an industrial area."[28] He urged destruction of all industrial plants and equipment, and called for people with technical skills to be encouraged to emigrate from the region. He also suggested immediate execution for the "arch-criminals" of the Nazi regime as soon as they were seized and identified: "When such identification has been made the person identified shall be put to death forthwith by firing squads made up of soldiers." Stimson again argued the opposing side, although he did agree with part of Morgenthau's plan—international control of the Ruhr region. The president commented that the Germans could easily live with no industry and no luxury, Morgenthau recalled, though no decision was made.[29]

Stimson invited his friend Supreme Court justice Felix Frankfurter to Woodley the next day for dinner with Mabel to discuss the matter. Stimson found that Frankfurter supported him and agreed particularly that the Nazi leaders must not be "railroaded to their death without trial."[30]

FDR reconvened the committee on September 9, their last meeting before he departed to join Churchill in Québec City. Morgenthau bolstered his call for the destruction of German industry by delivering a Treasury Department memo to the president saying it would also help Great Britain recover from the dire financial condition the war had left it in. The British coal industry would recover from a protracted depression, and the iron and steel industries in a number of European nations would grow to meet demand previously met by German industry, the memo argued—"The reduction in German industrial capacity would eliminate German competition for British exports in the world market."[31]

Stimson presented his own memo for the president, first establishing common ground. "It is not a question of a soft treatment of Germany or a harsh treatment of Germany. We are all trying to devise protection against recurrence by Germany of her attempts to dominate the world. We differ as to method." He argued that destroying Germany's industrial capacity would "provoke sympathy for the Germans." Stimson also rejected Morgenthau's call for the immediate execution, without trial, of captured Nazi leaders. The secretary of war urged trials that would include "rudimentary aspects of the Bill of Rights, namely, notification to the accused of the charge, the right to be heard and, within reasonable limits, to call witnesses in his defense." He said the "punishment of these men in a dignified manner consistent with the advance of civilization . . . will have all the greater effect upon posterity." He added that such a trial process "will afford the most effective way of making a record of the Nazi system of terrorism and of the effort of the Allies to terminate the system and prevent its recurrence."[32] The meeting led to no decisions.

The next day, FDR departed by train to Québec City to meet with Churchill and British officials. By Monday, September 11, the president and First Lady were in Québec's Citadel fortress, and that afternoon FDR and Churchill met in FDR's map room—a secret hub of maps, war information and communications that traveled with the president—to get the latest war news. General George Marshall, Admiral William Leahy and other members of the US Joint Chiefs of Staff began meetings with General Alan Brooke, General Hastings Ismay and other senior British commanders.[33] At FDR's request, Morgenthau also traveled to Québec to discuss postwar plans for Germany with Churchill.

On September 13, Morgenthau dined with FDR, Churchill and Admiral Leahy and Churchill's scientific adviser, Frederick Lindemann. Morgenthau presented his argument for shutting down industry in the Ruhr region, arguing particularly that—at a time when Britain was struggling to pay for imports—this would boost British exports of steel and other products. Churchill retorted that he supported disarming Germany but vehemently rejected Morgenthau's proposal. "There are bonds between the working classes of all countries, and the British people will not stand for the policy you are advocating," he said. "You cannot indict a whole nation. . . . Kill the criminals, but don't carry on the business for years."[34] The prime minister likened the idea to "chaining his body to a dead German," Morgenthau recalled.[35] In the end, FDR recommended letting Morgenthau discuss the matter further with Lindemann.

The next morning, Lindemann met with Morgenthau at the Chateau Frontenac hotel near the Citadel. Morgenthau asserted that his plan for deindustrialization of the Ruhr region came down to a simple choice: "Do you want a strong Germany and a weak England or a weak Germany and a strong England?" Lindemann expressed surprise that Churchill had rejected the idea, and suggested it could be "dressed up" in a way to make it more attractive to the prime minister.[36]

Later that morning, FDR and Morgenthau met with Churchill and Lindemann back at the Citadel. Lindemann told Churchill that the intention of deindustrializing the Ruhr region was to prevent Germany from making war in the future. "She would, of course, not starve," he said.[37] "The consequence that her export markets would become available for the U.K. and U.S.A. did not seem a disadvantage." Churchill replied that there was much to be said for this approach, abandoning the stern opposition he voiced the day before. "We were entitled to make sure Germany could not commit wanton acts of aggression and the Russians would probably in any case insist on obtaining any machinery available with which to restore the factories which Germany had ruined in her advance into Russia," the prime minister said. FDR added that Germany could revert to the "agricultural status" that it had had in the previous century. Churchill at last announced that he was "converted" to Morgenthau's plan.

Morgenthau later explained Churchill's reversal of his position: "The thing that attracted Churchill the most was the suggestion that they would get the German export business. That is the bait that he bit and swallowed and got hooked so deep that he couldn't, in my opinion, cough it up."[38]

FDR and Churchill returned to the matter again the next day, September 15, discussing it with British foreign minister Anthony Eden and others at the Citadel. Eden objected vigorously to the idea of destroying Germany's industry. Churchill responded, "Well, if it gets down to whether I am for the German people or the English people, I am for the English people, and you can be for whomever you want!"[39] He then dictated a memorandum spelling out the agreement on a plan to dismantle Germany's industries: "This programme for eliminating the war-making industries in the Ruhr and in the Saar is looking forward to converting Germany into a country primarily agricultural and pastoral in its character."[40] Churchill initialed the document. The president wrote "OK FDR."

The two leaders and their military commanders gathered the next day to close the conference, posing for triumphant photographs on a terrace atop the Citadel. FDR and Churchill issued a joint statement expressing confidence in their defeat of Germany and announcing plans to shift massive resources to achieve "the destruction of the barbarians of the Pacific."[41] No mention was made of the deindustrialization of Germany, but accounts of the dispute over what became called "the Morgenthau Plan" soon appeared in newspapers.[42]

Morgenthau reveled in his success, perceiving the agreement of the two leaders as a blow struck to end the evils of German militarism. He told his staff that his visit to Québec City "was the high spot of my whole career in the Government. I got more personal satisfaction out of those forty-eight hours than with anything I have ever been connected with."[43]

Stimson learned of the Roosevelt-Churchill agreement quickly and invited Frankfurter to dinner at Woodley to discuss it on September 20. Frankfurter said that the agreement "couldn't stand; he was clear the British people wouldn't stand for it." He once again rejected Morgenthau's position on immediate executions of Nazi leaders. "As to the shooting without trial, he said that was preposterous and he agreed wholly with me that I should resist it with all means within my power," Stimson noted in his diary.[44]

Nazi propagandists seized on Morgenthau's vision of postwar Germany as confirmation of a Jewish plot against Germans. A prominent Nazi newspaper proclaimed in a headline: "Roosevelt and Churchill Agree to Jewish Murder Plan!" Propaganda minister Joseph Goebbels warned Germans to make their homes into fortresses to fight the Morgenthau Plan. Critics in the American press, meanwhile, charged the Morgenthau Plan was too easy a target for Nazi propaganda. *The Washington Post* asserted that if Germans thought "nothing but complete destruction lies ahead, then they will fight on. Let's stop helping Dr. Goebbels."[45]

FDR SENT STIMSON a bouquet of roses in honor of his seventy-seventh birthday on September 21, but the two men did not meet until after the president returned to Washington from Hyde Park on September 27. FDR's struggle with his declining health was increasingly taking a toll on the president in this period. When Stimson went to the White House for lunch on October 3, he found the president in the company of his daughter Anna Boettiger, and it was immediately clear to Stimson that he could not discuss the long list of items he had planned to raise. "When I got to the White House and saw him, I saw that it would not be possible. He was ill again with a cold and looked tired and worn." Yet Stimson did raise the difficult issue of the postwar treatment of Germany. FDR "grinned and looked naughty," and then said Morgenthau had "pulled a boner"—made a mistake. The president said he had no intention of turning Germany into an agrarian state, but merely wanted to help Great Britain, which was "broke."[46] Stimson, however, read to the president parts of the agreement that he and Churchill initialed, which called for "converting Germany into a country primarily agricultural and pastoral in its character." The president was aghast, Stimson wrote in his diary. "He was frankly staggered by this and said he had no idea how he could have initialed this; that he had evidently done it without much thought."

Stimson urged the president to reject the idea of meting to Germany a justice based on revenge: "What we were after was preventive punishment, even educative punishment, but not vengeance." He focused on FDR's leadership of America in the postwar period. "I said throughout the war his leadership had been on a high moral plane and he had fought for the highest moral objectives. Now during the postwar readjustment 'You must not poison this position' which he and our country held with anything like mere hatred or vengeance." Stimson also addressed his relationship with Morgenthau. "I told him of my personal friendship for Henry Morgenthau who had been so kind to me when I first came into the Cabinet and that I had shuddered when he took the leadership in such a campaign against Germany, knowing how a man of his race would be misrepresented for so doing." He noted that both FDR and his daughter agreed with this.

Morgenthau continued to urge adoption of his plan, but FDR backed away from it, and news stories appeared saying it had been quietly dropped. Subsequent revisions of the Allied handbook and US military guidelines contained no provisions for stripping Germany of its industry. The agreement signed at the Citadel was ignored. Churchill, in discussions with his War Cabinet, abandoned the idea.[47]

PREPARING FOR THE defeat of Germany, Stimson repeatedly discussed with his staff and with FDR the idea that each of the allies—the United

States, Great Britain and the Soviet Union—would occupy a separate zone of the conquered country.[48] Plans for control of postwar Germany, however, were just one relatively small part of the war, which continued like a whirlwind around FDR and Stimson. In Burma, General Joseph Stilwell had run into sharp opposition from Chiang Kai-shek. Stilwell had discovered that while Chinese troops appeared to be under his own command, they would not act without orders from Chiang. A tense relationship of distrust and suspicion grew between the two men, and Stilwell began calling Chiang by a derisive code name, Peanut. Chiang demanded that FDR remove Stilwell from his post. Stimson vigorously urged FDR to retain Stilwell, who had successfully routed the Japanese from much of Burma, but on October 19 FDR agreed to Chiang's demand and ousted Stilwell from his command.[49] On another front, General Douglas MacArthur waded ashore the next day with US forces to retake the Philippines. The Japanese fought back by sending kamikaze pilots on suicide attacks against US Navy ships. In Washington, Stimson gave testimony in an inquiry into the Pearl Harbor attack mandated by Congress, where some members claimed FDR, Stimson and others had known of the Japanese attack plans but failed to alert US forces in Hawaii.[50] He told FDR in a letter that his voluminous diary provided a "documented record" contrary to such allegations, and "I should be greatly distressed if you were victimized now by ignorant or malicious rumors."[51]

As the November 7 election approached, Republican presidential nominee Thomas Dewey seized on the Morgenthau Plan to bludgeon FDR. On November 4, Dewey charged in a campaign speech in Madison Square Garden that the plan had stiffened German resistance and prolonged the war because it called for "disposing of the German people after the war." The impact, he said, was as if Hitler's armies had gotten "ten fresh German divisions." He charged that it was FDR's "confused incompetence" that led him to embrace the Morgenthau Plan in Québec City.[52]

Morgenthau, having learned from a news reporter what Dewey planned to say, called Stimson earlier that day and urged him to refute Dewey's claims, but Stimson demurred. "I was entirely opposed to allowing the Army to enter last day politics," he said. After hearing Dewey's speech, Stimson said that offering a rebuttal would "only accentuate the attack." Despite the furor over the Morgenthau Plan, the president also chose not to respond.

The decades-old friendship between FDR and Morgenthau survived the controversy. As was their habit over many years, FDR and Morgenthau rode together in an open car up the Hudson River Valley toward Hyde Park, making stops along the way, on the day before Election Day.[53]

After Roosevelt won the election, Stimson sent the president a handwritten note:

Dear Mr. President—

I send you my most earnest and heartfelt good wishes for your success and welfare during the term to which you have been elected. It is a unique opportunity, but it is also full of the most terrific difficulties and dangers which I think have ever confronted an American President.

You will need God's help for the wisdom and courage necessary to overcome them. I pray that you may have it, and that through that help you may be one of the most potent instruments in helping to make secure for our country and for the world a long ride of peace, justice and righteousness.

Affectionately your friend
Henry L. Stimson[54]

Stimson urged him to contemplate a legacy of "justice and righteousness" at a time when FDR again faced the troubling issue of the Japanese American internment. A lawsuit challenging the internment had been argued in the Supreme Court, and a decision by the high court releasing the Japanese Americans from the concentration camps was expected soon. Two days after Stimson wrote his note to FDR, the internment came up for discussion in a cabinet meeting.

Recognition that the mass internment was unjustifiable had been building for a long time. Nearly a year earlier, Attorney General Biddle had urged the earliest possible release of the internees. "The present practice of keeping loyal American citizens in concentration camps on the basis of race for longer than is absolutely necessary is dangerous and repugnant to the principles of our Government," Biddle wrote FDR in late 1943.[55] However, he also acknowledged the political problem the administration faced: the people of California widely opposed return of the Japanese Americans to their homes, in part due to agitation by Hearst newspapers, Biddle said. A Los Angeles newspaper had recently conducted a poll that found that Californians "would vote ten to one against permitting citizens of Japanese ancestry ever to return." Biddle's plea remained in limbo.

Five months later, on May 26, 1944, Stimson told FDR in a cabinet meeting that the War Department favored "freeing those who had been screened and found loyal." But he urged caution based on the potential for violence against the Japanese Americans themselves, and a possible retaliatory attack on American prisoners of war held in Japan: "The only military reason remaining for not setting them free was the fear that, in case of riots in the US against these evacuees, there would be reprisals in Japan against our own prisoners." FDR urged that the internees "be distributed in small numbers over the United States rather than dumped on California."[56]

Critics would later charge that the president's position appeared to be based on his desire for partisan political advantage in the elections of 1944.[57] If so, his strategy succeeded. Democrats in California won four new seats in the US House of Representatives in the November 1944 elections.

Meanwhile, Japanese Americans in the US Army—including men who volunteered from inside the concentration camps after Stimson's January 1943 order made this possible—had been recognized for fighting with valor for their country. The 100th Infantry Battalion, composed chiefly of Nisei from Hawaii, and the 442nd Regimental Combat Team, mostly Nisei from the mainland, helped drive the Germans out of Anzio and then Rome in May and June 1944.[58] In September, the 442nd was shipped to southern France, where the next month they fought through German forces to rescue a battalion that was part of the "Alamo Regiment" from Texas.[59] The rescue of the "Lost Battalion" swept across the newswires. Most stories, though, failed to mention the rescuers were Japanese Americans, such as the article in *The New York*

Times under a headline "Doughboys Break German Ring to Free 270 Trapped Eight Days."[60]

On November 10, three days after the elections, the internment issue came up in a cabinet meeting. Stimson later summarized the discussion in a tellingly perfunctory entry in his diary: "There was a discussion by Biddle, Ickes, the president, and myself and we all agreed it was time let them loose."[61]

It didn't happen immediately. At this time, McCloy was in regular contact with Justice Frankfurter, which enabled him to learn when the court would issue its ruling.[62] On December 13, 1944, Stimson reported to FDR that "the continued mass exclusion from the West Coast of persons of Japanese ancestry is no longer a matter of military necessity." The case of Mitsuye Endo was likely to result in an "unfavorable" ruling in the Supreme Court, so the evacuation order should end promptly, Stimson said.[63]

Four days later, the army revoked the 1942 order that excluded all Japanese from the West Coast, though Japanese Americans deemed disloyal would remain in confinement.[64] The very next day, December 18, the US Supreme Court issued its ruling, finding unanimously that the army violated the constitutional rights of Endo, a citizen of unquestioned loyalty, when it interned her and others like her in the camps. In the second case, brought by Fred Korematsu, the court upheld the order excluding citizens of Japanese ancestry from Pacific Coast areas.

In Korematsu's case, the Supreme Court voted 6–3 for a majority opinion that said military authorities acted legally because they "feared an invasion of our West Coast and felt constrained to take properly constituted security measures." Justice Robert Jackson, a Roosevelt appointee to the court, delivered a blistering dissent: "The Court for all time has validated the principle of racial discrimination. . . . The principle then lies about like a loaded weapon, ready for the hand of any authority that can bring forward a plausible claim of an urgent need."

THE JAPANESE AMERICAN troops who rescued the "Lost Division" were not the only racially segregated troops fighting in Europe. A segregated

Black unit, the 92nd Division, was fighting the Nazis in Italy, as were fighter units of the Tuskegee Airmen. The army in January 1944 had released a movie, *The Negro Soldier*, praising the military prowess and dedication of Black soldiers, and Black boxing champion Joe Louis had toured segregated training camps to bolster the spirits of Black soldiers. Still, most Black soldiers in early 1944 remained in army camps. Walter White, the NAACP executive secretary, visited Black troops at Army bases in England in January 1944 and urged Eisenhower to address racially abusive conditions he found and to deploy Black troops for combat.[65] The Black press and figures including Eleanor Roosevelt also called for Black soldiers to go into action.

Stimson and Marshall acquiesced, and in March 1944 the segregated 93rd Division arrived in the Pacific under command of MacArthur. In July 1944, the 92nd Division, which adopted the historic name of the Buffalo Soldiers, arrived in Italy and joined the effort to push the Nazis north from Rome.[66] The delay in their deployment still rankled, but their combat assignments became a source of pride and were hailed in the Black press.

In the wake of the 1944 election, Hull, who had struggled for years with recurring illness, resigned. FDR named Edward Stettinius to take over the secretary of state post, and in December Stimson resumed his regular weekly meetings with the new secretary of state, Stettinius, and secretary of the navy, James Forrestal, just as he had with their predecessors, Hull and Knox, throughout the war.[67] With Knox's death and Hull's retirement, Stimson was now the sole Republican in the group as well as its dean. The three men discussed preparations for the approaching meeting of FDR, Churchill and Stalin in Yalta, set for early February 1945. When Stimson met alone with FDR in the White House on December 31 and the conversation turned to Yalta, Stimson said he knew the Russians were spying on "S-1," as the top-secret Manhattan Project was called, but they did not have "any real knowledge of it." Stimson, concerned about working with the despotic Soviet regime, said it was not yet time to reveal the nuclear weapons program to the Russians. FDR said he thought he agreed.[68]

Stimson remained concerned about how to handle the top Nazi leaders, a subject expected to arise in Yalta.[69] After a January 19 cabinet meeting, he urged the president to support a "state trial with records . . . that would bring out and show the full nature of the Nazi conspiracy." FDR "assented to what I said." Stimson joined with Attorney General Biddle three days later in signing a memorandum that put the issue bluntly: "After Germany's unconditional surrender the United Nations could, if they elected, put to death the most notorious Nazi criminals, such as Hitler or Himmler, without trial or hearing. We do not favor this method. While it has the advantages of a sure and swift disposition, it would be violative of the most fundamental principles of justice, common to all the United Nations."[70]

FDR was accompanied to Yalta by Stettinius, General George Marshall and other political and military advisers. When the president met with Churchill and Stalin on February 5 in the ballroom of the Livadia Palace on a former estate of the czars, the discussion turned to the occupation of Germany. Stalin demanded heavy reparations including forced German labor and the seizure of industrial machinery. FDR and Churchill, however, urged moderation. Roosevelt said the Germans must have "enough industry and work to prevent her from starving." The Allies agreed to divide Germany into three zones of occupation, but they put off the issue of German industry, deciding that a tripartite commission would meet later in Moscow to decide on seizures of equipment and other nonmonetary compensation.[71] Four days later, after hours of discussion over the future governments of Eastern Europe, the leaders took up the issue of treatment of top Nazi leaders. Churchill said "they should be shot once their identity is established," meeting minutes showed.[72] The discussion moved on, however, with no resolution on how to handle Nazi war criminals. Ultimately, the three leaders issued a joint statement announcing they had made plans for the "final defeat" of Germany and promising to support the liberated countries of Eastern Europe in choosing their own governments through free elections. The leaders kept secret an accord providing for the entry of the Soviet Union into the war against Japan.

After the war ended, the Soviets removed large amounts of industrial equipment from Germany. The Morgenthau plan, however, was never adopted. By mid-1946, the United States and Great Britain shifted their policies on the zones of Germany they controlled toward supporting greater economic growth in tandem with democratization.[73] Stimson's vision of a peaceful industrial Germany rejoining the community of European nations—and his reversal of FDR's agreement with Churchill in Québec City on the Morgenthau Plan—prevailed. His urging of a large trial of Nazi leaders—rather than mass executions—was a key step toward the creation of the international war crimes tribunal that took place in Nuremberg in 1946 and 1947. The Nuremberg trials helped reestablish the rule of law in Germany and provided an important record of the Nazi terror, as Stimson hoped.[74] Stimson's vision of Germany recovering after the war as a prosperous and democratic nation at the center of Europe would ultimately come to pass.

Some critics later argued that the Roosevelt Administration abandoned the Jews through a series of failures, such as refusing to work harder to rescue refugees or bomb Auschwitz. Others, however, would note that when the idea of the WRB was put before FDR he quickly created the agency, which went on to save some two hundred thousand Jews from the Nazi machinery of murder. This searing moral debate— over a slow response that appeared to bow to powerful forces of anti-Semitism—echoes the one over the American concentration camps. FDR and Stimson initiated the Japanese internment and then were slow to dismantle it. The army's 1942 Japanese exclusion orders, issued at the behest of FDR and Stimson, and their affirmation by the Supreme Court in the Korematsu case in 1944 would ultimately be recognized as shameful stains on American democracy.[75] Similarly, the administration's refusal to desegregate the armed forces and slowness in sending Black troops into battle became yet another stigma upon the Roosevelt Administration. Roosevelt and Stimson—with all their human flaws— struggled in addressing the pervasive racism in American society even as they collaborated brilliantly in devising a triumphant strategy for a global war in defense of democracy.

FDR's Last Bipartisan Campaign

As the slaughter and mayhem of the war unfolded, President Roosevelt placed increasing importance on creating a permanent United Nations organization to preserve peace. On January 6, 1945, delivering his twelfth State of the Union address—once again over radio, sending a written version to Congress—he said, "1945 can and must see the substantial beginning of the organization of world peace. This organization must be the fulfilment of the promise for which men have fought and died in this war. It must be the justification of all the sacrifices that have been made—of all the dreadful misery that this world has endured."[1]

Days later, Senator Arthur Vandenberg, the top-ranking Republican on the Senate Foreign Affairs Committee, gave a speech calling for the United States to enter a treaty for mutual security and to take a leading role in international peacekeeping efforts. In a cabinet meeting the next day, Secretary of War Stimson told the president that Vandenberg's speech showed there was an opportunity to create a "proper organization" for the United Nations along the principles of the League of Nations.[2] Vandenberg had once been a leading isolationist, but he had recently become a convert to the idea that the United States must work with other nations to secure peace and prevent wars. James Byrnes, the director of the Office of War Mobilization, who was a top adviser to FDR, told the president he believed Vandenberg's conversion was sincere. FDR "seemed to agree with what we said," Stimson recalled.

The shift in the Republican Party toward international cooperation—and away from isolationism—had begun long before. Wendell Willkie had for years called for his party to back greater US involvement in supporting freedom and democracy around the world after the war. In September 1943, Vandenberg and other Republican leaders held a conference on Mackinac Island, Michigan, where they sought to unify the party behind a foreign policy of collaborating with other nations. Later that year, Republicans joined with Democrats to pass a resolution supporting creation of an international organization to preserve peace. When the Dumbarton Oaks conference on creating a permanent United Nations organization began in August 1944, former secretary of state Cordell Hull worked with Thomas Dewey, then the Republican presidential nominee, to shield the conference from partisan politics.

Roosevelt and Stimson knew only too well how President Woodrow Wilson had failed to secure the US Senate's approval of his League of Nations, the international peacekeeping organization that Wilson hoped would prevent wars after the devastation of World War I. Wilson had included no Republicans in the delegation to the Paris Peace Conference of 1919, and a lack of Republican support doomed US participation in the League when it came up for a vote in the Senate. During a meeting at the British embassy in May 1943, Stimson warned Prime Minister Churchill that the organization must be created before the end of the war, or else isolationism would regain its strength after the war and block it. Stimson "believed that it would be much easier to secure American agreement during the war; indeed, that it was a case of during the war or never," Churchill recalled.[3]

In December 1944, FDR had tasked Settinius with ensuring the successful creation of a permanent United Nations organization. During the conference at Yalta in February 1945, Stettinius proposed to FDR the idea of including three Republicans in the American delegation to the next United Nations conference, set to take place in April 1945 in San Francisco.[4] The Republicans would be Vandenberg, a senator from Michigan; Charles Eaton, a representative who was a harsh opponent of the New Deal but often agreed with FDR's foreign policy; and Harold

Stassen, a liberal Republican who in 1943 had resigned as governor of Minnesota to serve in the navy. The Democrats would be Senator Thomas Connally, chairman of the Senate Foreign Relations Committee; former secretary of state Cordell Hull; and Representative Sol Bloom of New York, chairman of the House Foreign Relations Committee. Adding a woman to the delegation, Stettinius named Virginia Gildersleeve, dean of Barnard College in New York City.

Stettinius, who would be chairman of the seven-member delegation, told the president it was vital to have the top Republican and Democrat on the Senate Foreign Relations Committee in the delegation. Vandenberg, however, was the key. Stettinius believed "it was of the utmost importance, from the point of view of ultimate ratification by the Senate of the Charter of the world organization, to have Senator Vandenberg's full understanding and support from the beginning."[5]

The striking proposal would bring a bipartisan congressional group into the treaty negotiations. The Constitution gives the president the power to negotiate treaties, and gives the Senate the power to approve or reject any treaty the president may propose. As a result, treaties have often been negotiated by the executive branch—chiefly the secretary of state—leaving the Senate out. But that runs the risk that the Senate, having had no hand in the negotiations, will reject the treaty. Roosevelt was not the first president to try to solve this problem by bringing the Senate into a treaty negotiation process. Almost fifty years earlier, for example, Republican president William McKinley sent a bipartisan delegation of senators to negotiate the peace treaty that ended the Spanish-American War.

FDR approved the Stettinius plan and sent out formal invitations to the delegates. Vandenberg sent FDR a letter seeking to ensure the Republicans would be free to express their views. Vandenberg announced he agreed to join the delegation after the president assured him of "my right to free action."[6]

On March 13, Vandenberg and other members of the bipartisan delegation went to the White House and posed for pictures with the president in the Oval Office. Stettinius reassured the Republicans that they would be free to express their opinions during the delegation's work. "We all are prompted by the same desire to succeed," he told them. "I am confident, therefore, that while free in pursuing our personal views and convictions we shall be able to work as one team."[7]

In early April, Republican John Foster Dulles announced that he would act as an adviser to the delegation. "There will be no politics on the American delegation," Dulles told reporters. The bipartisan effort also won support from Dewey, who as the 1944 Republican presidential nominee was the head of the Republican Party. "The invitation to Mr. Dulles to serve as adviser to the American delegation at San Francisco was wisely extended, and I am happy Mr. Dulles has found it possible to accept," Dewey said.[8]

Dewey's support for the bipartisan delegation contrasted sharply with the rancor of 1940, when the decisions of Stimson and Frank Knox to join FDR's cabinet caused fury and calls for their ouster from the Republican Party. Of course, joining a delegation to negotiate a treaty was a bipartisan effort focused on a single international policy matter. Even so, this bipartisan delegation to the United Nations conference was an open and high-profile endeavor fully embraced by both FDR and top Republican leaders.

The US delegation quickly began work on an array of questions. The Soviet Union had demanded one vote for each of its sixteen republics at Dumbarton Oaks, which Stettinius and FDR rejected, but a compromise was under consideration. Other questions concerned which nations would be on the powerful Security Council, how nations would join the organization and its legal framework and authority. Stettinius, hoping to defuse worries about secret international agreements, announced that the conference sessions in San Francisco would be open to the press.

RELATIONS WITH THE Soviets grew tense as the European war's end approached. US Army commanders had become increasingly concerned about American prisoners of war who had fallen into Soviet hands as the Soviet Red Army moved westward. On March 16, Stimson and Stettinius met with FDR and urged him to send Stalin a telegram repeating an earlier request—which the Soviets had rejected—that an American general be permitted to visit Poland to investigate. FDR approved their draft telegram and sent it without changes, ratcheting up discord between Stalin and FDR. "Frankly I cannot understand your reluctance to permit American officers . . . to assist their own people in this matter. This Government has done everything to meet each of your requests. Please call [US ambassador to Moscow Averell] Harriman" to resolve the matter.[9]

Stalin raised furious objections with FDR a week later after learning that US officials had met with German officers to arrange a possible surrender of German troops in Italy. William Donovan, the OSS director, and his top officer in Switzerland, Allen Dulles, had pursued the surrender through secret talks with Nazi general Karl Wolff.[10] Stalin cabled FDR, charging that the Nazis had taken advantage of the talks to shift three divisions of troops out of Italy to defend against Soviet forces. Stalin told FDR that the situation "creates ground for mistrust." FDR replied March 31, denying that the discussions with the Germans were negotiations or permitted the Nazis to shift forces.[11] Amid the tense dispute, Donovan told Dulles to break off his talks with Wolff.[12]

The president and the dictator also quarreled over Eastern Europe, where the Soviets were pushing for a communist-dominated government to take power in Poland, excluding members of the Polish government-in-exile based in London. On March 31, after conferring with British prime minister Winston Churchill, FDR sent Stalin a cable arguing the Soviet leader was failing to abide by the Yalta agreement terms for forming a new Polish government. "I am frankly puzzled as to why this should be and must tell you that I do not fully understand in many respects the apparent indifferent attitude of your Government."[13]

FDR sent this cable to Stalin from Warm Springs, Georgia, where he had gone on March 29 for a rest at the polio treatment facility he founded in 1927. The president's health had declined severely. His personal secretary, William Hassett, noted in his diary on March 30, "He is slipping away and no earthly power can keep him here."[14] FDR, now sixty-three, had recently resumed his relationship with Lucy Mercer Rutherfurd, with whom he had had an affair two decades earlier, and she visited him at Warm Springs. There, at about 1:00 P.M. on April 12, he was in the company of Rutherfurd, his cousins Laura Delano and Daisy Suckley, and an artist making sketches for a portrait of the president when

Suckley noticed suddenly that FDR had leaned forward. He raised his hand to his head and said to her, "I have a terrific pain in the back of my head."[15] He lost consciousness and was carried to a bed. Doctors were called, as was Eleanor, who had remained in Washington. Two hours after the first attack, the president's breathing became labored, and then stopped. He was pronounced dead—the cause identified as a cerebral hemorrhage—at 3:35 P.M.[16]

Vice President Harry Truman, who had been at the Capitol, went to the White House immediately upon being informed of the president's death. When he saw First Lady Eleanor Roosevelt, he asked, "Is there anything I can do for you?" She replied, "Is there anything *we* can do for you? For you are the one in trouble now."[17] Truman assured her she could use the presidential airplane to fly to Warm Springs, which she did that night. Stimson, Navy Secretary James Forrestal and other members of the cabinet and leaders of Congress were summoned to the White House, along with Truman's wife, Bess, and their daughter, Margaret. After all gathered in the Cabinet Room, Truman informed them of FDR's death, expressed his grief and announced his intention to carry out FDR's policies. After Supreme Court Chief justice Harlan Stone arrived, he administered the oath of office and Truman was sworn in as president at 7:09 P.M.[18]

Raised in Independence, Missouri, Truman had served as a US Army artillery officer in World War I. After the war, he opened a clothing shop in Kansas City, but after it ran into financial difficulties in 1922 he decided to run for election as a county executive. Backed by the political machine of Tom Pendergast, a powerful Democratic boss in Kansas City, Truman won the election.[19] Pendergast, who helped gather Democratic votes for FDR's elections, became a friend and political ally of Truman and supported his successful runs for US Senate in 1934 and 1940. Controversy arose when Pendergast was convicted in 1939 of evading taxes on income—including more than $300,000 in alleged bribes—and sentenced to fifteen months in prison. Truman, however, did not let that prevent him from showing his fondness for his old friend. When Pendergast died in January 1945, shortly after Truman became vice president, Truman flew on an army plane to attend his funeral in Kansas City.[20]

Immediately upon FDR's death, Truman and Stimson faced the question of whether they would carry forward the bipartisan alliance that FDR had built with Stimson and other Republicans. Truman answered that question on April 13, the day after FDR's death, when he informed both Stimson and Forrestal in a meeting at the White House that he wanted them to remain at their posts.

America mourned the loss of President Roosevelt. On April 13, Eleanor Roosevelt, who had flown from Washington to Warm Springs the previous night, accompanied her husband's casket on a train to Washington, where the next day an estimated five hundred thousand people lined the streets to watch as the funeral procession moved from Union Station to the White House. Draped in an American flag, FDR's casket rested in state in the White House the afternoon of April 14.[21] In New York City that day, people in neighborhoods across the city—in offices, on squares and sidewalks—paused at 4:00 for five minutes to remember the late president. As a light rain fell just before the City Hall chimes tolled four, Mayor Fiorello La Guardia, FDR's longtime Republican ally, urged a crowd of some thirty-five thousand people: "We will now bare our heads and stand in silent prayer for our departed and beloved president." *The New York Times* reported, "Throughout the city millions of persons stood with bared head and many knelt in the rain in an outpouring of mass sorrow seldom witnessed in American life."[22]

Eleanor and other family members accompanied Roosevelt's casket on a train arriving on the morning of Sunday, April 15, at Hyde Park, where that afternoon FDR was buried in the garden of his Springwood estate. Stimson and other members of the cabinet and the administration, and foreign dignitaries such as Canadian prime minister Mackenzie King, joined family and friends for the funeral service that afternoon.[23]

After returning to Washington, Stimson turned over in his mind Roosevelt's presidency, then poured his thoughts into his diary. "On the whole he has been a superb war president—far more so than any other president of our history," he began. "He has pushed for decisions of sound strategy and carried them through against strong opposition from Churchill, for example, and others. The most notable instance was where he accepted the views of our Staff in regard to the final blow at Germany across the Channel and where he accepted my advice on my return from Europe in July 1943 that he should insist upon having American command of the Normandy invasion. . . . Events have shown that we were right and that our direction was the true road to quick victory over Germany."

Stimson sent a handwritten letter to Eleanor Roosevelt the next day, expressing his condolences and his gratitude for the chance to work for FDR. "I have never received from any chief, under whom I have served, more consideration and kindness than I did from him, even when he was laboring under the terrific strain of a great war and in spite of the fact that I was a newcomer in his Cabinet and a member of another party." After praising FDR as an ideal commander in chief, he said "his vision and interpretations of the mission of our country to help establish a rule of freedom and justice in this world raised a standard which put the United States in the unique position of world leadership which she now holds. . . . You may well hold your head high to have been his worthy helpmate at such a time and in such a task."[24]

Eleanor, inundated with thousands of condolence letters and telegrams from around the world, and busy with moving out of the White House, managed to reply to Stimson in a note two days later: "I was deeply touched by your letter and your wonderful tribute. I know how much Franklin admired and loved you and I am very grateful to you for the help you gave him during these critical times."[25]

TRUMAN ASSURED THE nation he intended to follow FDR's foreign policy, including the drive to win the war, liberate oppressed peoples and secure peace through a permanent United Nations organization. Speaking before both houses of Congress on April 16, he said, "I call upon all Americans to help me keep our nation united in defense of those ideals which have been so eloquently proclaimed by Franklin Roosevelt." He added, "I appeal to every American, regardless of party, race, creed, or color to support our efforts to build a strong and lasting United Nations organization."[26]

With FDR's ambitious bipartisan campaign for the United Nations thrust upon him, Truman chose to carry it forward. The day after Truman became president, he called his old friend James Byrnes to the

White House and told him he would nominate him as secretary of state to replace Stettinius, but this could only happen after Stettinius completed the San Francisco conference. It would not be long. Truman's first decision as president, as he later recalled in his memoirs, was to decide that FDR's death must not upset the schedule for the United Nations conference, which was set to begin April 25.[27]

As delegates from forty-six countries assembled for the conference that day in San Francisco, Truman welcomed them in a radio address from the White House, urging them to pursue the ideals of peace and democracy that FDR had sought to elevate. The president also spoke in support of the American delegation. He made no mention of bipartisanship or of any political party at all, but he underscored the bipartisan nature of the delegation by naming all its members, including Vandenberg and the other two Republicans. "They have my confidence. They have my support," he said.[28]

The war in Europe, meanwhile, was rapidly approaching its revelatory and savage close. As Allied forces liberated Nazi concentration camps, they uncovered the horrors of the Nazi mass murders, and in late April General Dwight Eisenhower invited the United Nations War Crimes Commission to visit Buchenwald and other camps. In Italy, partisans captured Benito Mussolini and his mistress, Clara Petacci, as they tried to flee to Switzerland on April 26. Two days later, they were executed, their bodies hung upside down in a square before being buried in a Milan cemetery.[29] In Germany, as the Soviet Red Army seized parts of Berlin, early on the morning of April 29 Adolf Hitler issued a final testament, spewing attacks on Jews and lashing out at army officers for allegedly betraying him. In a macabre ceremony in his heavily fortified bunker, Hitler and his mistress Eva Braun swore they were "of complete Aryan descent" and were married.[30] The next afternoon they committed suicide in Hitler's quarters.[31] Following Hitler's instructions, his staff took their bodies outside and burned them. Nazi propaganda minister Joseph Goebbels and his wife had their six young children murdered and then committed suicide. Heinrich Himmler, the SS chief who led the Nazi mass murder of the Jews, committed suicide shortly after being captured. On May 2, negotiations led by Allen Dulles resulted in the surrender of Nazi forces in Italy.[32] On May 8, in Berlin, senior Nazi generals signed a surrender agreement. People around the world cele-brated the defeat of Hitlerian fascism and the end of the war in Europe.

As the United States turned its full force against Japan, the bipartisan US delegation in San Francisco debated a broad array of issues. Among the disputes resolved was the one over voting—the Soviet Union would have two additional votes—one each for its republics of Belarus and Ukraine—but only the Soviet Union itself would be among the five per-manent members of the powerful security council. On June 20, confer-ence delegates voted unanimously to approve the charter for the United Nations Organization, sending it to the governments of the fifty partic-ipant countries for final approval.

Stimson cabled Stettinius that day: "You have been confronted by a situation of almost unparalleled difficulties and your tact, skill and courage are bringing about a successful solution of them. We all owe you an immense debt for your unremitting and competent effort." The Democratic secretary of state replied to Stimson: "There is no one in public life in the United States whose respect and confidence I treasure more than I do yours, and to have this word of encouragement at this moment means more to me than you know."[33]

Vandenberg announced his wholehearted support of the United Na-tions treaty and said he would work for its rapid approval by the Senate. "I consider collective security essential to peace with justice in a free world of free men," he said on June 25. Seeking to preempt isolationist criticism, he said, "In my opinion, our intelligent American self-interest indispensably requires our loyal cooperation in this great adventure to stop World War III before it starts. I am confident that Congress and the country will agree."[34]

Truman flew to San Francisco for the conference's closing day and looked on as Stettinius signed the new United Nations charter the next day. The president then delivered a speech praising the charter as a means for humanity to defeat the evils of fascism, which he warned would persist even after the defeat of Hitler and Mussolini. He also urged speedy approval by the US Senate. "Let us not fail to grasp this supreme chance to establish a world-wide rule of reason—to create an enduring peace under the guidance of God."[35]

The Senate opened debate on the treaty days after it was signed, as its supporters hoped it could be passed quickly before the war came to an end. Vandenberg and Connally both gave speeches about their experiences in San Francisco on the Senate floor, but it was Vandenberg—as a member of the Republican opposition and a former strong isolationist—who garnered the most attention. Vandenberg praised Stettinius as an "able and inspiring leader" who was "equal to every emergency we faced." The Michigan Republican also praised Senator Connally, the Democratic chairman of the Foreign Relations Committee: "Without the faintest hint of partisanship at any time, he made it constantly possible for each one of us, representing the minority, to play our full role in these deliberations."[36] Seeking to allay the concerns of isolationists, Vandenberg denied the treaty prevented the United States from defending itself or conducting its own domestic affairs. "In a word, we have not created a super-state. We have not organized a world-government. We have not hauled down the Stars and Stripes from the dome of the Capitol. We have simply agreed to cooperate effectively with 49 other sovereign states in the mutual pursuit of peace and security."

On July 2, Truman addressed the Senate and urged it to approve the treaty so that the nations of the world could live in peace. Pointing to the two world wars, he said, "one generation has failed twice to keep the peace."

While Stettinius had won acclaim from the bipartisan delegation, Truman moved him to a new post as US representative to the United Nations and then announced the appointment of Byrnes as secretary of state. The president and Byrnes then departed on July 6 for a conference with Churchill and Stalin in Potsdam, Germany, leaving Stettinius in Washington to work for passage as the Senate debated the fate of the United Nations.

Truman also had made an appeal for "full bipartisan support" for a bill to create a world bank and an international banking system that would foster economic growth after the war. Henry Morgenthau Jr., who resigned as treasury secretary on July 5, had led development of the banking system plan during a meeting of representatives from more than forty Allied countries in 1944 in Bretton Woods, New Hampshire. On July 20, 1945, Congress gave final approval when the House of Representatives passed the Bretton Woods bill without objection.

Remarking on the bill's broad support, Morgenthau said "there is no
partisan division in Congress or the country on this policy."[37]

After the bitter political feuding over soldier voting and the presidential race that roiled Washington in 1944, the nation's capital enjoyed
a spirit of bipartisan collaboration.

On July 28, with Truman still overseas, the Senate voted 89–2—with
all but two Republicans joining the Democrats in voting yes—to ratify
the United Nations treaty and approve US participation in the international peacekeeping body. It was a soaring victory for bipartisanship in
American politics. The vote, which came 107 days after FDR's death,
also was a crowning achievement for FDR and Stimson, who believed
deeply that America must join an international organization to spread
democracy and peace across the world.

Truman, Stimson and the Atom Bomb

After Harry Truman was sworn in as president on April 12, 1945, Secretary of War Stimson stayed back as all the other officials left the Cabinet Room in the White House. "He asked to speak to me about a most urgent matter," President Truman recalled. "Stimson told me that he wanted me to know about an immense project that was under way—a project looking to the development of a new explosive of almost unbelievable destructive power. That was all he felt free to say at the time, and his statement left me puzzled."[1]

Though President Roosevelt's health had been declining for months, neither FDR nor Stimson had revealed to Vice President Truman the fact that the US Army was building the world's first nuclear bomb. Stimson had reservations about Truman, as he noted in a diary entry after he was sworn in: "The new president on whole made a pleasant impression but it was very clear that he knew very little of the task into which he is stepping and he showed some vacillations on minor matters that came up for a decision a little bit as if he might be lacking in force. I hope not."[2]

In fact, there was a divide between the two men that cast doubt over whether they could continue the strong bipartisan alliance that Stimson had built with FDR. The distance between Truman and Stimson would have profound consequences as the president approached the decision to drop the atomic bomb on Japan.

In prior years, investigations by Truman's Senate committee probed waste in military contracts in Stimson's War Department. Truman had courteously backed off his questioning of Stimson about the Manhattan Project in March 1943, but the outcome was very different later that year when he investigated the Canol Project, an army-funded oil refinery in Canada that was intended to supply gas and oil to US Army forces in Alaska. Truman's committee accused the army of wasteful spending on the Canol Project in late 1943.[3] Stimson and others in the army rejected the charge and insisted the project was necessary for national defense, and Congress approved more funding.[4] But in March 1944 Truman demanded that Stimson cooperate with a Senate investigator and threatened him with "dire consequences" if he did not do so. The secretary of war refused to comply, arguing that he was acting on President Roosevelt's orders.[5] Ultimately, the army agreed to shut down the Canol Project just days before FDR died.[6] Furious over Truman's tactics, Stimson in 1944 issued an acid judgment—albeit a private one in his diary—upon the senator: "Truman is a nuisance and a pretty untrustworthy man. He talks smoothly but he acts meanly."[7]

Stimson's distrust of Truman likely factored into his decision not to inform him of the Manhattan Project. FDR also had held Truman at a distance. After their inauguration on January 20, FDR met with Vice President Truman only twice—apart from cabinet meetings—prior to his death.[8] As vice president, Truman spent most of his time in the Capitol working on legislative matters.

Stimson and Truman were thrust together by FDR's death—and they had little in common. In contrast, FDR and Stimson had gradually built a relationship of trust over a period of seven years before FDR invited Stimson to join his cabinet. They also shared a New England elite background, admiration for Theodore Roosevelt, connections to Wall Street, and extensive experience in international relations. Truman, instead, had cut his teeth in the Democratic political machines of Tom Pendergast in Kansas City, precisely the kind of Democratic machine that Stimson had sometimes condemned.

The day after he became president, Truman turned to his old friend James Byrnes, the former senator who was a close aide to FDR, for information about the Manhattan Project. The new president recalled that "with great solemnity [Byrnes] said that we were perfecting an explosive great enough to destroy the whole world."[9] It was then that he told Byrnes he would make him secretary of state.

Born and raised in Charleston, South Carolina, Byrnes became a lawyer and won election to the House of Representatives where he served from 1911 to 1925.[10] He was elected in 1930 to the US Senate, where a few years later he became a key supporter of the New Deal. As a southern Democrat, he was a segregationist who opposed anti-lynching and anti–poll tax bills. While using a filibuster to block an anti-lynching bill in the Senate in 1938, Byrnes charged that "the Negro has come into control of the Democratic Party."[11] He seethed, "The South has ever been loyal to the Democratic Party," but it has been "deserted by the Democrats of the North."

Seeking to rebuild his ties to southern Democrats, Roosevelt in 1941 appointed Byrnes to the Supreme Court, where he served as a justice for a year until FDR asked him to join his administration. In 1943, FDR appointed Byrnes director of the Office of War Mobilization, which coordinated procurement for the war effort. Byrnes became powerful in the post, which FDR acknowledged in a June 1944 note to Byrnes saying, "You have been called 'The Assistant President' and the appellation comes close to the truth."[12] Stimson in his diary called Byrnes "shrewd and able."[13]

After Truman became president on April 12, he decided to name Byrnes his secretary of state partly because of the reversal of fortune he suffered at the 1944 Democratic convention, when Truman—not Byrnes—became the vice-presidential nominee.[14] "I thought that my calling on him at this time might help balance things up," Truman recalled. But the president also was getting the assistance of a highly capable Democratic partisan who had wide knowledge of the war effort, including the Manhattan Project. While waiting to take over from Stettinius as secretary of state, Byrnes would advise Truman on the nuclear bomb.

Almost two weeks passed from Truman's inauguration to the day when he had a serious discussion about the bomb with Stimson. The secretary of war went to the White House on April 25 with Manhattan Project head General Leslie Groves to give the president an overview of the research. Stimson handed Truman a memorandum that began, "Within four months we shall in all probability have completed the most terrible weapon ever known in human history, one bomb of which could destroy a whole city." Russia would likely begin production of the bomb within the next few years, Stimson warned, and the United States and United Kingdom had already launched efforts to prevent the spread of nuclear bomb technology to other countries.[15]

In apocalyptic tones, Stimson presented a dilemma: "Our leadership in the war and in the development of this weapon has placed a certain moral responsibility upon us which we cannot shirk without very serious responsibility for any disaster to civilization which it would further. . . . On the other hand, if the problem of the proper use of this weapon can be solved, we would have the opportunity to bring the world into a pattern in which the peace of the world and our civilization can be saved."

Byrnes had already told Truman that the bomb "might well put us in a position to dictate our own terms at the end of the war," the president recalled. "Stimson, on the other hand, seemed at least as much concerned with the role of the atomic bomb in the shaping of history as in its capacity to shorten this war."[16] Truman cast Byrnes as focused on the immediate resolution of the war and Stimson as more interested in long-term concerns about nuclear weapons, an appraisal that tended to discount the secretary of war's advice on use of the bomb against Japan. When a top Manhattan Project nuclear physicist, Leo Szilard, tried in late May to urge the president not to drop the bomb on Japan, Truman referred Szilard to Byrnes. Szilard traveled to Byrnes's home in Spartansburg, South Carolina, on May 28 to make his plea, arguing that a nuclear attack on Japan would start a nuclear arms race with the Russians. Byrnes bluntly rejected the idea, arguing that Russia would be "more manageable" if the United States revealed the atomic bomb's power by dropping it on Japan.[17]

AT SEVENTY-SEVEN, STIMSON remained vigorous for a man his age. He still played deck tennis and rode horses at Woodley and Highhold, but bouts of exhaustion occasionally came over him. Doctors at Walter Reed General Hospital examined him in mid-May, and the surgeon general urged him to take a week off to rest.[18] While he was at the Pentagon one day the following month, as he reported in his diary, "I found it was hard to study and read, so I went home early." That evening a doctor summoned to Woodley "said that I was improving and there was no reason for anxiety in regard to my heart."[19] Stimson continued working.

After Germany's surrender on May 8, Victory in Europe (V-E) Day celebrations rang out in America and around the world. In the White House, as Stimson and other cabinet members looked on, President Truman delivered an address to the nation praising the American armies and their allies for liberating Europe but warning that "our victory is but half-won." He said, "The West is free but the East is still in bondage to the treacherous tyranny of the Japanese. When the last Japanese division has surrendered unconditionally, then only will our fighting job be done."[20]

The US military was now fully focused on winning the war with Japan. Since shortly after D-Day in June 1944, the Army Air Forces had been using a new long-range bomber, the B-29 Superfortress, to bomb Japanese cities regularly from Pacific islands. It was the same kind of heavy bombing campaign that had reduced Germany's cities, defenses and infrastructure to rubble, taking thousands upon thousands of lives.[21]

In March 1945, US raids began taking off from an American base on Guam almost daily. Japan's air defenses had been devastated, and the bombers often faced only antiaircraft fire from the ground. On March 10, waves of B-29s dropped 1,665 tons of incendiary bombs on Tokyo, leaving the densely populated city center in flames.[22] The fires devastated fifteen square miles of the city, killing an estimated eighty thousand people and leaving more than one million homeless. Aerial bombing of civilians, which the US had earlier denounced as a sinister Japanese tactic, had become part of the US effort to force Japan to surrender. On March 15, the US Marines announced capture of the island of Iwo Jima after five weeks of intense combat that left seven thousand Marines killed in action.[23] Two months later, as America rejoiced over victory in Europe on May 8, the navy said it was planning a massive air and naval assault on Japan.[24]

Also on V-E Day, Stimson secretly created the Interim Committee, which brought top army and navy officials together with Manhattan Project leaders to make recommendations on use of atomic weapons. The committee held its first meeting in Stimson's office the next day. In addition to Stimson and two of his assistants, Harvey Bundy and George Harrison, its members included General Groves, scientific weapons advisers Vannevar Bush and James Conant, Navy undersecretary Ralph Bard and James Byrnes as President Truman's representative.[25]

US and British officials, meanwhile, became increasingly concerned that the Soviets were blocking free elections in the Eastern European nations controlled by Soviet armies. "An iron curtain is drawn down upon their front," Prime Minister Churchill said in a May 12 telegram to Truman. "We do not know what is going on behind."[26]

As conflict with the Soviets ratcheted up, US officials—who had long sought Soviet assistance in the war against Japan—now began to worry that Stalin would use an attack on the Japanese to spread communism in Asia.[27] Under a secret accord signed by the Big Three at Yalta in February, the Soviets had agreed to enter the war against Japan "within two or three months after Germany has surrendered."[28] With V-E Day on May 8, a Soviet attack on the Japanese three months later would fall on August 8. In early April, the Soviet Union terminated the neutrality pact it had entered with Japan in 1941, setting the stage for such an attack.

Though the Soviets had been America's allies in the war, Stimson saw nuclear weapons as a tool to achieve American strategic advantage against the Soviets. In May, he told Jack McCloy, the assistant secretary of war, that "the method now to deal with Russia was to keep our mouths shut and let our actions speak for words." He described the bomb as a winning hand in poker: "I called it a royal straight flush and we mustn't be a fool about the way we play it."[29]

US armed forces, meanwhile, continued their devastating military assault on Japan. The Army Air Force's 21st Bomber Command, led by General Curtis LeMay, continued dropping vast amounts of incendiary bombs on Japanese cities, including Osaka, Nagoya and Kobe.[30] On the night of May 25–26, waves of B-29s dropped 3,262 tons of incendiaries on Tokyo—more than twice the amount of the March 9–10 firebombing—causing an inferno that burned twenty square miles of the city. The attack set the Imperial Palace ablaze. Soldiers rushed to rescue art works, gilt doors and furnishings from the flames, but after four hours only one of the palace's twenty-seven buildings remained.[31]

Emperor Hirohito and his wife, Empress Nagako, emerged from the wreckage unharmed. For a nation whose emperor was worshiped as a living deity and the high priest of the state-sponsored Shinto religion, the destruction of his palace was a shattering blow.

Japanese officials, meanwhile, began to raise the idea of surrendering. On May 12, Office of Strategic Services director William Donovan sent President Truman a top-secret letter reporting that the Japanese minister to Switzerland, Shunichi Kase, had expressed a desire to negotiate peace between the Japanese and the Allies. Kase said he preferred to negotiate with the Americans or British, fearing that "the whole Far East would become communist." Donovan added, "Kase allegedly believes that one of the few provisions the Japanese would insist upon would be the retention of the Emperor as the only safeguard against Japan's conversion to Communism."[32] Someone—perhaps Donovan—raised a question in handwriting at the bottom of the letter: "Should we pursue this?"

Truman had publicly called for Japan's "unconditional surrender," but McCloy suspected that Hirohito would seek a face-saving way out of the war. McCloy believed that by insisting on "unconditional surrender," US officials were erecting an unnecessary barrier to a Japanese surrender. "Unconditional surrender is a phrase which means loss of face and I wonder whether we cannot accomplish everything we want to accomplish in regard to Japan without use of that term," McCloy wrote in a May 28 memo to Stimson.[33]

Joseph Grew, who was acting secretary of state while Stettinius was in San Francisco, urged President Truman to make a public statement that unconditional surrender would not mean elimination of Japan's imperial dynasty. Grew believed that such a statement by the president, coming shortly after the recent devastating B-29 attacks, could set in motion discussions leading to surrender. Truman asked Grew to discuss the matter with Stimson, Forrestal and the Chiefs of Staff.[34]

Stimson held a meeting May 29 in his Pentagon office with Grew, McCloy, Forrestal, General Marshall and others to discuss the idea of trying to prompt surrender negotiations with Japan by issuing a statement that removed the term "unconditional" and permitted the Japanese to keep their imperial dynasty. Stimson responded positively. "I was inclined to agree with giving the Japanese a modification of the unconditional surrender formula and some hope to induce them to practically make an unconditional surrender without the use of those words." However, he said "the timing was wrong," an idea supported by Marshall.[35] With the battle for Okinawa still on, such a statement might be seen as a "confession of weakness."[36] No decision was reached.

Stimson met with his Interim Committee two days later to discuss principles for use of the bomb. He began the meeting with remarks on the risks and opportunities the bomb presented: "It might be Frankenstein that would eat us or it might be a project by which the peace of the world would be helped in becoming secure."[37] He had invited Marshall, Groves and Bundy to join the meeting. Also attending were senior Manhattan Project physicists including Robert Oppenheimer, the head of the project's laboratory in Los Alamos, New Mexico. The committee explored the idea of exploding the bomb at a remote location to prove its power without harming civilians. However, Oppenheimer and others rejected that idea because a demonstration of the bomb's power would require "a real target of built-up structures." Stimson insisted that "we could not concentrate on a civilian area," though it was also agreed that it was important to produce a psychological impact on the Japanese people. The committee ultimately concluded that the best target would be a "vital war plant employing a large number of workers and closely surrounded by workers' houses," and no warning would be given of the bomb's use.[38] This concept called for selecting a military target, but in effect it provided for an attack that would cause mass civilian casualties.

When the Interim Committee met the following day, Byrnes took charge of the meeting because Stimson was absent. Acting as the president's representative, Byrnes "recommended and the committee agreed that the Secretary of War be advised that . . . the present view of the Committee was that the bomb be used against Japan as soon as possible; that it be used on a war plant surrounded by workers' homes; and that it be used without prior warning."[39] Byrnes had steered the committee to the outcome he desired, and he rushed that same afternoon to inform Truman of what he called "the final decision of the committee."

Stimson went to the White House on June 6 to discuss the use of nuclear weapons with Truman.[40] The two men discussed whether the Soviet Union might be convinced to adopt liberal political reforms in exchange for receiving information about the nuclear bomb. Truman "said he had been thinking of that and mentioned the same things that I was thinking of, namely settlement of the Polish, Rumanian, Yugoslavian and Manchurian problems," Stimson wrote in his diary. Stimson hoped to restore the "Open Door" policy, which would permit international trade by Manchuria. Thus, the two men discussed how to use the bomb as an instrument of geopolitical strategy—but they ignored the issue of seeking a Japanese surrender by permitting Japan to keep its imperial dynasty.

Stimson did, however, tell the president about humanitarian concerns over the bombing of Japan. "I told him how I was trying to hold the Air Force down to precision bombing but that with the Japanese method of scattering its manufacture it was rather difficult," he recalled. "I did not want to have the United States get the reputation of outdoing Hitler in atrocities."[41]

The army and navy prepared plans for the final assault on Japan, and Stimson went to the White House with the Chiefs of Staff to present the plans to Truman on June 18. Marshall told the president that the army and navy proposed November 1 as the target date for an invasion of Kyushu, the southernmost of Japan's five main islands.[42] The group discussed the ferocious battle in Okinawa, where a total of 41,700 US servicemen had been killed, wounded or missing—a number that suggested an equally high casualty rate and a long bloody campaign for US troops invading Japan's main islands. Marshall said the entry of Soviet forces into the war against Japan "may well be the decisive action levering them into capitulation."

Stimson supported the invasion plan but also urged the president to seek to avoid the invasion if possible. He said there were many Japanese people "who do not favor the present war and whose full opinion and influence has never yet been felt." He argued that "something should be done to arouse them and to develop any possible influence they might have."[43] Admiral William Leahy, the chief of staff to Truman, agreed with the importance of avoiding the large casualty numbers expected in an invasion. Leahy said "our insistence on unconditional surrender would result only in making the Japanese desperate and thereby increase our casualty lists." He "did not think that this was at all necessary."

Truman approved the invasion plan, but he rejected the idea of dropping the demand for unconditional surrender, which had long been promised—by FDR and Truman himself—to the American people. Truman said he did not feel that he could "take any action at this time to change public opinion on the matter."

STIMSON PERSISTED IN urging Truman to offer the Japanese a chance to surrender by letting them keep their emperor. On July 2, he met with the president in the White House and presented him with a memo that praised the Japanese people—a striking message from one of the most prominent American critics of Japan's fascist rulers and their brutal military assaults on China, the United States and other nations. At the time, anti-Japanese sentiment in America, enflamed by the attack on Pearl Harbor, remained strong amid the furious battles in the Pacific and reported atrocities by Japanese troops. Thousands of Japanese Americans remained in concentration camps. The slur "Jap" was in wide use. Stimson sought to provide Truman with an antidote to these fevers.

"I believe Japan is susceptible to reason in such a crisis to a much greater extent than is indicated by our current press and other current comment. Japan is not a nation composed of mad fanatics of an entirely different mentality from ours," Stimson wrote. "On the contrary, she has within the past century shown herself to possess extremely intelligent people." He recommended a "carefully timed warning" that would disclose the "overwhelming character of the force we are about to bring to bear on the islands." He then made a personal plea: "I personally think that if in saying this we should add that we do not exclude a constitutional monarchy under her present dynasty, it would substantially add to the chances of acceptance."

Stimson's memo to Truman included a draft declaration, prepared with the navy and Department of State, to be issued to Japan at the Potsdam conference. It warned that the Allies were "poised to strike the final blows upon Japan" unless it surrendered. This declaration also provided for Japan to retain "a constitutional monarchy under the present dynasty if it be shown to the complete satisfaction of the world that such a government will never again aspire to aggression."[44] Truman read the memo as he sat with Stimson, who said the president "was apparently acquiescent with my attitude towards the treatment of Japan." He made no decision on issuing a warning to Japan or the question of preserving the dynasty, though, and said he wanted to discuss Stimson's memo further the next day.

When the two men met at the White House the next day, however, they did not resume their discussion of the warning to Japan, its surrender or its dynasty. Instead, they spoke about what Truman should say to Stalin about the bomb at a strategy meeting planned for mid-July in Potsdam, Germany. Stimson recommended that, if the two men seemed on good terms, the president could say simply that "we were busy with this thing" and that "afterwards" they could have a discussion about "having it make the world peaceful and safe rather than to destroy civilization." This approach was intended to avoid a detailed discussion with Stalin. Truman said he thought it was "the best way to do it," Stimson reported in his diary.[45]

The president, who was leaving for Potsdam in three days, had not asked Stimson to come to the conference. FDR had often left Stimson out of summit meetings with foreign leaders, but in light of Stimson's critical role in development of the bomb the secretary of war decided to suggest that he should go to Potsdam. Truman agreed that he should be nearby so he could "help out"—but he still did not ask Stimson to join the official delegation. Stimson rushed back to the Pentagon to begin preparing for the trip—he would leave with McCloy, Bundy and other War Department personnel on a ship from New York in just three days. Truman, Byrnes and others traveled on a separate vessel, the USS *Augusta*. Despite Stimson's central role in the Manhattan Project, Truman included him in the Potsdam Conference only at the last minute and only at his request. Truman kept Stimson at a distance and sought advice from others, primarily Byrnes, who on July 3 was sworn in as secretary of state.

The devastating US aerial assaults on Japan continued, striking dozens of cities with incendiary bombs. By June 15, in the six largest Japanese cities, the US bombing campaign killed an estimated 127,000 people and destroyed 1.4 million buildings.[46] Yokohama's destruction reached 58 percent of the city.[47] To strangle the Japanese economy, the army in

March had begun Operation Starvation, in which B-29s dropped thousands of mines into the waters at Japanese ports, shutting down imports of food commodities, coal and iron ore.[48] Kamikaze plane attacks inflicted damage on and sank US ships, but the US Navy controlled Japan's coastal waters and shelled ports at will.[49]

Emperor Hirohito made moves seeking peace. The Japanese ambassador in Moscow, Naotake Sato, began discussions with the Soviets in a bid to end the war. On July 12, the Japanese minister of foreign affairs, Shigenori Togo, sent a secret message to Sato saying Hirohito was eager to end the war. Togo said Hirohito was "greatly concerned over the daily increasing calamities and sacrifices faced by the citizens," and that it was "His Majesty's desire to see the swift termination of the war." Hirohito wanted to send a former prime minister, Prince Fumimaro Konoye, as a special envoy to Moscow to discuss peace. Sato bluntly replied to Togo, "If our country truly desires to terminate the war, we have no alternative but to accept unconditional surrender or something very close to it." These messages, monitored through the army's Magic system that cracked the Japanese code years earlier, were promptly delivered to Truman.[50]

Searching for a way to reach the American leaders, the Japanese contacted Prince Carl of Sweden. On July 6, the American ambassador in Sweden sent Byrnes a telegram saying that the Japanese military attaché in Stockholm had told Prince Carl that Japan recognized it was defeated and Hirohito was prepared to negotiate a surrender. The sole condition mentioned by the military attaché was: the "Emperor must be maintained in his position after the capitulation."[51]

THE PRESIDENT, BYRNES, Admiral Leahy and other US officials, having crossed the Atlantic aboard the cruiser USS *Augusta,* arrived on July 15 in Potsdam, where they were greeted by Stimson, Fleet Admiral Ernest King, McCloy and Bundy. All were settled into houses inside a heavily guarded Soviet security perimeter. Truman and Byrnes were quartered together in a three-story stucco villa quickly dubbed the "Little White House."[52]

On Monday, July 16, Stimson and McCloy received news of the

intercepted Japanese communications that indicated Hirohito wanted to send Prince Konoye to Moscow to pursue peace.[53] Amid the flurry of communications between Moscow and Japan, the Japanese ambassador in Moscow asked that the emperor's message be delivered to Mikhail Kalinin, a senior Soviet official, and Stalin.[54] McCloy, writing his diary, voiced optimism over the new intercepts: "News came in of the Japanese efforts to get the Russians to get them out of the war. Hirohito himself was called upon to send a message to Kalinin and Stalin. Things are moving—what a long way we have come since that Sunday morning we heard the news of Pearl Harbor!"[55]

Stimson worked quickly with McCloy and Bundy to prepare a memo for the president urging "prompt delivery of our warning"—the declaration he had presented Truman two weeks earlier at the White House.[56] He once again stated his recommendation that the Japanese be reassured that they could keep their imperial dynasty. He also recommended that if a first warning failed, a "renewed and even heavier warning, backed by the power of the new force and possibly the actual entrance of the Russians in the war."[57] Then, if these double warnings failed, the atomic bomb would be used, the memo concluded.

At 7:30 P.M. that evening, Stimson received a stunning secret message from his aide George Harrison in Washington: the long-awaited atomic test had occurred in the New Mexico desert early that morning and was a success.[58] With a blinding flash, a roar and an immense fireball, the atomic age was born. Harrison added a flourish to the secrecy with a medical metaphor: "Operated on this morning," he wrote. "Diagnosis not yet complete but results seem satisfactory and already exceed expectations."[59] Stimson rushed to show this message to Truman and Byrnes, who he said were "greatly interested."

Early the next morning, July 17, Stimson went again to the Little White House to meet with Byrnes and discuss his proposal for a prompt warning to Japan. "Byrnes was opposed to a prompt and early warning to Japan, which I had first suggested. He outlined a timetable on the subject warning which apparently had been agreed to by the president, so I pressed it no further," he wrote in his diary.[60] In other words, Truman and Byrnes were moving ahead rapidly with decisions concerning the atomic bomb—without consulting Stimson. While FDR and Secretary of State Cordell Hull had sought out Stimson's views and engaged him in long policy discussions, Truman and Byrnes did not.

Later that morning, Truman met Stalin for the first time. The brief conversation, before formal meetings began, revealed much. Stalin, with Foreign Minister Vyacheslav Molotov and an interpreter, came to Truman's house. After shaking hands, they engaged in friendly conversation. "I told Stalin that I am no diplomat but usually said yes and no to questions after hearing all the arguments. It pleased him," Truman recalled in his diary. Stalin said he had some questions. "I told him to fire away. He did and it is dynamite—but I have some dynamite too which I am not exploding right now." The planned Soviet attack on Japan was Stalin's "dynamite," although that attack was already expected. The dynamite that Truman was not exploding was evidently the atomic bomb. Stalin revealed important news: "He'll be in the Jap war on August 15th. Fini Japs when that comes about," Truman wrote.[61]

Stalin and Molotov then joined Truman, Byrnes and Leahy for lunch. They "talked socially, put on a real show drinking toasts to everyone then had pictures made in the back yard," Truman recalled. Stalin had mercilessly destroyed his political opponents, agreed with Hitler in 1939 to seize and divide Poland, and was blocking free elections in Eastern Europe, yet he was negotiating in friendly tones with the leaders of the Western democracies. Truman voiced confidence in the Soviet dictator and—perhaps surprisingly—expressed trust in him. "I can deal with Stalin," the president wrote in his diary. "He is honest—but smart as hell."

Stimson had lunch that day with Churchill and Deputy Prime Minister Clement Attlee. The two British leaders, strong allies for the past five years, were now awaiting the results of British national elections that had become a bitter fight between the Labour and Conservative parties.[62] Despite the tension, Stimson said that on that day in Potsdam the two men "were most cordial and familiar with each other at the luncheon and apparently on the best of personal terms and were poking a great deal of fun at each other." After lunch, Stimson revealed the nuclear bomb test results to Churchill. "He was intensely interested and greatly cheered up," he wrote in his diary.[63]

That night, Truman invited Stimson to dinner at his house with

Byrnes, Marshall and other US military commanders and presidential staff members. Revealing his optimism about Stalin's willingness to ensure free trade with northern China, Truman told Stimson that it appeared he had "clinched the Open Door in Manchuria."

The next morning, July 18, Stimson got another message from Harrison, who extended his medical metaphor in describing the results of the atomic bomb test. "Doctor has just returned most enthusiastic that the little boy is as husky as his big brother," he wrote. The first atom bomb, dubbed "Little Boy," was already aboard a ship headed toward a Pacific island where it could be placed aboard a plane to be dropped.[64] Stimson took Harrison's latest message to the president. Truman was "highly delighted," he noted.

Later that day, Truman went with Byrnes and translator Charles Bohlen to a meeting with Stalin in the Soviet leader's quarters. Stalin handed him a copy of a letter from Sato, the Japanese ambassador in Moscow, with a message from the emperor. This document has been lost, but it likely tracked the intercepted cables stating that Emperor Hirohito was seeking peace and urging talks with Prince Konoye.[65] Stalin asked Truman whether it was "worthwhile to answer this communication," Bohlen recalled.[66] Truman replied that he had no respect for the good faith of the Japanese. Stalin suggested that it might be desirable to "lull the Japanese to sleep" by sending a vague reply objecting that the nature of the Konoye mission was unclear. Truman recounted in his diary that he agreed: "Stalin had told Churchill of telegram from Jap Emperor asking for peace. Stalin read his answer to me. It was satisfactory."[67]

A momentous and crucial decision had been made. Emperor Hirohito had sought to start peace talks, and Truman agreed immediately to a suggestion made by the Soviet dictator—without conferring with his Republican secretary of war or other advisers—to rebuff Hirohito's bid for peace.

Later that night in Moscow, a Soviet foreign ministry official delivered to Ambassador Sato a letter saying that because the message from Hirohito was "general in form" and Konoye's mission was unclear, the Soviet government was "unable to give any definite reply."[68]

• • •

STIMSON, MEANWHILE, FUMED over being shut out of the conference. Even though he had long played the role of the junior member of his bipartisan alliance with FDR, Stimson felt acutely that he and his staff members were being kept in the dark at Potsdam. On July 18, the same day that Truman and Stalin turned their backs on the peace overture from Hirohito, Stimson discussed his frustrations with his Republican assistants, McCloy and Bundy. "We were all troubled by the wastage of time in getting information about what is going on. Informal as well as formal conferences are being held, and we have to wait until they are finished and then McCloy gets hold of some one of the State Department subordinates who has been present, finds out from him what has happened and then brings it to me," he wrote in his diary.[69]

The Big Three conference that day raised questions of the occupation of Germany and elections in Poland, but there was no mention of the critical decision about the reply to Japan's emperor. Truman appeared to have already settled on a course of moving quickly to drop an atomic bomb on Japan before the Russians could invade. He wrote in his diary the next day, "Believe Japs will fold up before Russia comes in. I am sure they will when Manhattan appears over their homeland."[70]

The next morning, July 19, Stimson went to plead with Byrnes for greater access, asking if McCloy could participate in the conference, but Byrnes rejected the request. The collegiality of their discussion two weeks earlier had evaporated. "He gives me the impression that he is hugging matters in this Conference pretty close to his bosom, and that my assistance, while generally welcome, was strictly limited in the matters in which it should be given," Stimson wrote.[71] There is no evidence that he was informed of the decision by Stalin and Truman to rebuff Hirohito's peace overture.

On Friday, July 20, Stimson joined President Truman's procession into Berlin, where the American flag—the same one Stimson saw raised in Rome a year earlier—was raised in a ceremony at the American headquarters.[72] The following day, he received a detailed report by General Groves on the destructive power of the atom bomb, which he reviewed with General Marshall and then took to Truman. There, he read the report in its entirety to Truman and Byrnes. "The president was tremendously pepped up by it and spoke to me of it again and again when I saw him. He said it gave him an entirely new feeling of confidence," Stimson wrote in his diary.[73] Afterwards, he shared the report with Churchill.[74]

On July 22, Stimson and Bundy met with Churchill, who said the Groves report—which estimated the test bomb equaled twenty thousand tons of dynamite and caused a fireball that rose ten thousand feet in the sky—had prompted Truman to take a firm stand in discussions with Stalin the day before. "Now I know what happened to Truman yesterday," Churchill said, "When he got to the meeting after having read this report he was a changed man. He told the Russians just where they got on and off and generally bossed the whole meeting."[75] The Groves report stunned Churchill, too. "Stimson, what was gunpowder?" Bundy recalled Churchill saying. "What was electricity? Meaningless. This atomic bomb is the Second Coming in wrath."[76]

Stimson met that day with General Hap Arnold, commander of the Army Air Forces, and raised concerns about the proposed targets for the bomb and "the killing of women and children."[77] Kyoto had been placed on an early target list on the theory that destroying an ancient city of Japanese cultural heritage would prompt Japan's surrender, but Stimson had vigorously objected to this, demanding military targets be selected. Marshall had urged targeting the city of Kokura, which had a large arsenal. Stimson demanded more information from Washington on the proposed targets.[78]

Stimson now confided to his diary that he felt "crippled" by not knowing what was going on in the Potsdam discussions, and he appealed to Truman the next day, Monday, July 23. The president told him he would be happy to discuss the previous day's events if he would come in the mornings. He also told Stimson he would like to know whether Marshall still felt the Allies needed the Soviets to enter the war against Japan.[79]

Truman and Byrnes wanted to prevent Stalin from extending Soviet power into China. While Truman had until recently sought Soviet entry in the war to help defeat Japan, he shifted his views in the wake of the successful test of the atom bomb. Byrnes believed dropping the atomic bomb on Japan quickly before the Soviets invaded China would both bring the war to a rapid end and reduce the ability of the Soviets to spread communism. Walter Brown, an assistant to Byrnes who accompanied him at Potsdam, wrote in his diary on July 24 that Byrnes believed "that after atomic bomb Japan will surrender and Russia will not get in so much on the kill."[80] To Byrnes, the issue of postwar struggle with the Soviets now was closely tied to the question of whether to drop the bomb on Japan.

On the morning of July 24, Stimson went to see Truman and informed him that Marshall felt that, with use of the atomic bomb, "the Russians were not needed" for the defeat of the Japanese. Marshall also warned, however, that the Russians would enter China anyway. Truman told Stimson that he had just sent Chiang Kai-shek the proposed warning declaration to the Japanese. As soon as Chiang approved it, Truman said, he would release it.[81]

Stimson made yet another appeal to include in the declaration a provision letting the Japanese know they could keep their imperial dynasty. "I then spoke of the importance which I attributed to the reassurance of the Japanese on the continuance of their dynasty." He told Truman that he had "heard from Byrnes that they preferred not to put it in, and that now such a change was made impossible by the sending of the message to Chiang." However, if Truman wanted to, he could revise the warning to include the reassurance on the dynasty and then resend it for Chiang's approval. Yet the date for the expected Soviet invasion was fast approaching, and Truman seemed to be moving quickly to either force a Japanese surrender with the warning or drop the bomb prior to the Soviet invasion.

Stimson then suggested another way to secure a surrender by offering the Japanese the preservation of their dynasty: "I hoped that the president would watch carefully so that the Japanese might be reassured verbally through diplomatic channels if it was found they were hanging fire on that one point." On this, Truman gave Stimson assurance. "He said that he had that in mind, and that he would take care of it."[82]

The two men also discussed targeting the bomb. With Kyoto eliminated from the target list, Stimson recalled, the president agreed that "the bitterness which would be caused by such a wanton act might make it impossible during the long post-war period to reconcile the Japanese to us in that area rather than to the Russians."

Late that afternoon, after the meeting of the Big Three and their advisers ended, Truman walked around the large circular table at which they were seated and approached Stalin. "I casually mentioned to Stalin that we had a new weapon of unusual destructive force," he recalled.[83] Stalin showed no special interest and said he was glad to hear it, the president recalled.

Truman later said he decided to use the bomb on the same day he revealed its existence to Stalin, July 24.[84] He recounted his decision the next day in his diary: "I have told the Sec. Of War, Mr. Stimson to use it so that military objectives and soldiers and sailors are the target and not women and children. Even if the Japs are savages, ruthless, merciless and fanatic, we as the leader of the world for the common welfare cannot drop this terrible bomb on the old Capitol or the new. He [Stimson] and I are in accord. The target will be a purely military one and we will issue a warning statement asking the Japs to surrender and save lives."[85] In fact, the two men had not examined whether the blasts would also kill large numbers of civilians in the targeted cities, nor were the two men in accord on the timing or substance of the warning to the Japanese.

Stalin asked Stimson to meet with him the next day at his quarters in Cecilienhof, the German royal palace in Potsdam. Ushered through the corridors and into Stalin's room, Stimson sat in a chair in front of the dictator's desk. Their conversation was diplomatic—Stimson uttered none of his objections to the Soviet secret police or the spread of communism. Instead, he said he hoped the Soviet entry into war with Japan would bring success, and Stalin replied that he expected a speedy victory that would reduce losses. "I stated this was the one thing we were anxious to have for all," Stimson noted.[86]

In Washington the next day, the army began to put President Truman's plan into action. General Carl Spaatz, commanding general of Army Strategic Air Forces, was ordered to drop the "first special bomb" after August 3 on one of four cities: Hiroshima, Kokura, Niigata or Nagasaki. The order called for additional bombs to be dropped as the army staff prepared them. It also instructed Spaatz that only the secretary of war and the president were to make public statements about the atom bomb.[87]

· · ·

ON JULY 26, Truman, Churchill and Chiang released their warning to Japan, now known as the Potsdam Declaration, which threatened "prompt and utter destruction" of Japan unless the country offered its "unconditional surrender." The declaration made no mention of permitting Japan to keep its imperial dynasty, as Stimson had repeatedly urged Truman.[88] Although Truman had assured Stimson he'd "take care of" communicating that provision to the Japanese verbally, there is no evidence the president did so. The declaration was released to the press, not to Japanese diplomats.

The ultimatum was not signed by Stalin, whose nation was still not at war with Japan. Truman signed the declaration on behalf of both Chiang and Churchill. Churchill and Attlee had left the day before to return to London, where the election results were announced. British voters delivered a landslide to the Labour Party, which for the first time in history held a majority of seats in Parliament, and Attlee was swiftly elected prime minister. Churchill's National Coalition—once an inspiring model of national political unity—ended abruptly. Attlee returned to Potsdam and announced his resolve to maintain support of US policies and "to finish the war with Japan."[89]

Stimson's return trip to Washington began with a stop in Munich, where he visited the headquarters of his old friend General George Patton and reviewed Patton's Third Army.[90] Driving through the Alps, he stopped by a stream and went fishing, catching a trout as his party looked on. After meeting with General Dwight Eisenhower in Frankfurt on July 27, Stimson and his aides departed on their flight to the United States.

On July 28, an American military broadcast in Japanese recounted the Potsdam Declaration to the people of Japan and urged them to surrender and restore peace.[91] Prime Minister Kantaro Suzuki rejected the Potsdam Declaration the next day, saying "so far as the Imperial Government of Japan is concerned, it will take no notice of this proclamation."[92]

In Potsdam, the final negotiating session stretched late into the night of August 1 as the three leaders at last reached agreement on the new western frontier of Poland. Truman left Potsdam August 2, flying to London to meet with King George VI. The conference's final communique—issued that day in Washington, Moscow and London—reported agreements on the occupation of Germany. The Allies remained divided on many issues, setting the stage for tensions that would divide East from West in the coming years.

After meeting King George, Truman, Byrnes and other advisers were crossing the Atlantic aboard the *Augusta* when, on August 6, shortly before noon, the president received a decoded message from Stimson stating that an atom bomb had been dropped on Hiroshima.[93]

The bomb's terrifying power became known to the world that day. The blast's heat, estimated at 5,400 degrees Fahrenheit at its center, incinerated much of the city and many of its inhabitants. Five square miles of the city were flattened or burned.[94] Men, women and children were instantly killed, or severely burned by fires, or left to suffer the agony of radiation poisoning while dying slowly. Eyewitnesses recalled that women, sloughing off their skin "like a kimono," plunged into rivers littered with corpses.[95] At a primary school 1,500 feet from ground zero, all 192 students died immediately.[96] Among the dead were twenty US Army prisoners held in Hiroshima.[97] US War Department officials estimated that the bombing caused the deaths of around seventy thousand people, though later independent estimates put that number at one hundred and forty thousand.[98] Soldiers might have accounted for ten thousand of the dead; the rest were civilians.[99]

Working from Highhold, Stimson helped prepare the president's statement for release that morning at about 11:00 A.M. announcing the use of the atomic bomb and threatening another attack: "We are now prepared to obliterate more rapidly and completely every productive enterprise the Japanese have above ground in any city. . . . If they do not now accept our terms, they may expect a rain of ruin from the air, the like of which has never been seen on this earth."[100]

On August 8, President Truman was back at work in the White House, where Stimson met with him and they reviewed a photograph showing the "total destruction" of Hiroshima, as Stimson put it in his diary. The president permitted press photographers into the Oval Office to take pictures of the two men at the president's desk.[101] The news soon arrived that the Soviet Union had declared war on Japan and invaded Manchuria. It was three months from V-E Day, the time frame provided at Yalta. Truman's race to use the bomb had done nothing to forestall the Soviet invasion.

The next day, August 9, an army plane dropped a second atom bomb on Nagasaki. Once again, a city went up in flames beneath a weapon of staggering power. This time, owing to Nagasaki's hilly geography, the area destroyed was three square miles, less than in Hiroshima.[102] The US War Department initially estimated the bombing left thirty-nine thousand dead, though later independent studies estimated that as many as seventy thousand died as a result of the bombing.[103]

On the morning of August 10, the Japanese government issued a statement saying it accepted the Potsdam demands—on the condition that Japan's emperor could remain "a sovereign ruler." This was the provision Stimson had tried since early July to use to induce Japan's surrender but that Truman and Byrnes had rejected. The news of the Japanese plea for peace caused a joyous crowd to gather in front of the White House.

Truman called Byrnes, Stimson, Forrestal and Leahy to the White House to discuss how to respond to the Japanese plea. At the time, the army was readying a third atomic bomb to drop—the cities of Kokura and Niigata remained on the list to be attacked. Byrnes argued forcefully against accepting the Japanese conditional surrender, saying it was the United States—not Japan—that should be laying down terms.[104] Leahy countered that "the question of the Emperor was a minor matter compared with delaying a victory in the war which was now in our hands."[105]

Stimson, at last, spoke. He argued for accepting the peace offer and permitting the Japanese to retain their emperor. He noted that if the emperor were removed the United States could face "a score of bloody Iwo Jimas and Okinawas all over China" because the emperor's armies might continue fighting. Stimson also urged stopping all bombing.[106] In the end, Truman took the advice of Stimson and Leahy over that of Byrnes; the president accepted Japan's offer and permitted the nation to retain its emperor, although he would have to be under control of an Allied commander. Stimson helped draft surrender papers, and on August 14 Japan agreed to the stipulation that the emperor would submit to the authority of the Allied commander who would be named to control occupied Japan.[107] Soviet armies continued to drive deep into Manchuria, where they took control of cities and would help the Chinese Communist Party's Red Army overthrow Chiang's Nationalist Chinese government.[108]

Truman had faltered in carrying forward FDR's bipartisan alliance; he retained Stimson in his post as secretary of war but kept him at a distance while conferring closely with Byrnes, his Democratic ally. The end result was that—at a time when the secretary of war was advocating a negotiated peace with the Japanese to avoid using nuclear weapons— Truman and Byrnes pushed ahead with dropping the bomb. Stimson's strategy was never tried, and it is unknown whether it would have succeeded. Truman disregarded his recommendations of permitting the Japanese to keep their dynasty—until August 10.

ULTIMATELY, MANY CRITICS would charge the US should never have dropped the atom bomb. Among them was Admiral Leahy, who said the "use of the atom bomb at Hiroshima and Nagasaki was no material assistance in our war against Japan. The Japanese were already defeated and ready to surrender." He added that the United States had "adopted an ethical standard common to the barbarians of the Dark Ages. I was not taught to make war in that fashion, and wars cannot be won by destroying women and children."

General LeMay, whose firebombing of Japanese cities pushed Hirohito to seek peace, said, "The war would have been over in two weeks without the Russians entering and without the atomic bomb."[109]

Stimson defended both himself and Truman in a magazine article in 1947, pointing to the large numbers of soldiers and civilians expected to die if US troops had to invade Japan's home islands.[110] The article, however, omitted any reference to the many Japanese efforts to negotiate peace and left out Stimson's own repeated efforts to insert a provision in the warning to Japan that would permit the country to keep its emperor.

In Japan, Hirohito never faced charges in the war crimes tribunal established in Tokyo. The Allied commander over postwar Japan, General Douglas MacArthur, shielded Hirohito from prosecution and barred him from being called as a witness when the war crimes tribunal began in May 1946.[111] The tribunal eventually sentenced six generals, including Hideki Tojo, and a former prime minister to die by hanging.[112] As at Nuremberg, the narrow scope of the Tokyo war crimes trials spurred wide debate over whether people who committed crimes had escaped punishment.

In October 1945, Hirohito selected Baron Kijuro Shidehara, the moderate diplomat with whom Stimson had hoped to build peace after the Manchurian incident of 1931, as Japan's first postwar prime minister. In 1946, Shidehara's cabinet, working under MacArthur's instructions, proposed a constitution that permanently banned Japan from using war to solve international disputes.[113]

After Japan's surrender, Henry and Mabel Stimson took a vacation for a few weeks in the Adirondack Mountains. Back in his Pentagon office in early September, Stimson urged the president to reach an agreement to share nuclear bomb information with the Soviets and British with a goal of ceasing production of nuclear bombs. The Soviet pursuit of the atomic bomb would result in a "secret armament race of a rather desperate character," he warned the president in a memo, and the solution to this looming problem was to share nuclear information promptly and agree on controls.[114] Truman expressed interest in Stimson's views, but he ultimately rejected this concept. Four years later, the Soviets conducted their first successful nuclear bomb explosion, and the nuclear arms race was born.

Stimson announced he would retire on September 21, his seventy-eighth birthday, and began wrapping up his responsibilities in the War Department. He urged the president to award Marshall "the highest possible American decoration, bar none," saying the general "dominated the global strategy of the war in a way that no other general has."[115] He gave Marshall full credit for carrying out the Normandy invasion: "It was his mind and character that carried through the cross-Channel campaign against Germany in spite of constant and powerful attempts to divert and defeat it."

Stimson also awarded the Distinguished Service Medal to each member of his team of top Republican aides—McCloy, Bundy, Patterson and Lovett—and Colonel Robert Cutler, each with a citation praising their contributions to the war effort in detail. On September 21,

Stimson went to the White House, where President Truman awarded him the Distinguished Service Medal, citing him for his contribution to "the successful mobilization, deployment and operations of an Army in which his countrymen may take everlasting pride." General Marshall accompanied Henry and Mabel Stimson to the airport, where an army band played "Happy Birthday." A nineteen-gun salute was fired, and the Stimsons walked between two lines of generals and bade farewell to Marshall before boarding an army plane for their trip home to Highhold.[116]

Even in retirement, Stimson continued to defend his Democratic allies and condemn Republican extremists. After Senator Joseph McCarthy, a Republican from Wisconsin, began a campaign broadly accusing Truman State Department officials of conspiring with Communists, Stimson in March 1950 publicly denounced the smears as a dubious effort to garner attention and said they created a "feeling that we are frightened and suspicious of each other."[117]

President Truman ultimately gave his own stamp to the bipartisan alliance that FDR, Stimson and Knox had launched in 1940. To replace Stimson, he named Patterson, Stimson's Republican undersecretary, to be secretary of war. After James Byrnes resigned as secretary of state in 1947, Truman named George Marshall, Stimson's rigorously nonpartisan ally, to replace Byrnes, and he named Stimson Republican aide John McCloy as president of the World Bank.

Truman also collaborated closely with his Republican ally, Senator Arthur Vandenberg of Michigan, to reach compromises that secured congressional approval of the Marshall Plan, large loans that Secretary of State Marshall proposed to rescue Europe's economy and fight the spread of communism.[118] In addition, Truman worked closely with Vandenberg to win Senate ratification of the 1949 treaty creating the North Atlantic Treaty Organization, intended to protect Western democracies from attack by communists and other foes.

When Henry Stimson died at the age of eighty-three on October 20, 1950, President Truman's remarks for a memorial service praised him as a man unafraid of crossing political lines for the good of his country. "There was nothing narrow or partisan about Mr. Stimson's public service. . . . Everything about him was big, broad, national, humanitarian.

As a statesman who placed duty to country above party line he scorned unreasoning abuse heaped upon him when he accepted a post with a national administration not of the political party to which he had given long allegiance. So he leaves a full record. Great as a lawyer, great as a statesman, he was also a great patriot—a great American."[119]

Epilogue

The Bipartisan Alliance
and America's Future

In launching their bipartisan alliance in 1940, Franklin Roosevelt and Henry Stimson strove to unite Americans in support of defending democracy in America and around the world in the fight against fascism. Their legacy is a brilliant example of what Democrats and Republicans can accomplish when they reach beyond partisan boundaries, valuing country over party. The two men, working with their Democratic and Republican allies, proved that bipartisanship can produce results of supreme importance for the nation at a time when the stakes are the highest.

The achievements of Roosevelt and Stimson—though forever stained by their failings on racial matters—suggest that American political leaders are at their best when they are guided by a deep desire to defend democracy, brave enough to create alliances across political boundaries and intelligent enough to devise successful strategies to achieve their goals. Had the two statesmen not possessed these qualities, and had they not formed their partnership, the war might have ended very differently. It is possible to imagine that if an isolationist had won the presidency in 1940 and America had turned its back on the European war, Americans might still be struggling with a German fascist empire in control of Europe.

The two men brought different strengths to their alliance, as seen most clearly in their early struggle with isolationism. Stimson, who sounded an early alarm over Japanese fascist imperialism, called for the repeal of the Neutrality Act so that America could build military alliances to defend democracy. Like a hunter facing a bear in the wild, he approached the challenge unflinchingly, taking aim and firing his best shots. FDR, in contrast, appealed to isolationist voters from the Oval Office as he approached the election of 1936, signed the Neutrality Act into law and went on to approve its extensions and voice support for neutrality over the next three years. After Stimson and others repeatedly denounced the act, FDR reversed course in 1939 and joined Stimson in calling for its repeal. FDR and Stimson, the strategist and the hunter, joined forces in allegiance to democracy. Together—bringing a divided American people into their cause—they were indomitable.

Their alliance was founded on trust in each other and a shared belief in the crucial importance of preserving democracy, as shown by FDR's reaction when Stimson sent him Ramsay Muir's article on defending liberty in 1934: "It is a splendid expression of faith." Their alliance, led by FDR and including the highly capable Republican Secretary of the Navy Frank Knox, grew stronger through spirited but respectful debates. As they fostered a climate of unity in Washington, bipartisanship triumphed in vote after vote in Congress and held sway in the alliance's myriad decisions in prosecuting the war.

Stimson worked skillfully with the president to win congressional support for expanding the military, launching conscription and raising the US Army from nineteenth largest in the world to first. He also brought Republican presidential nominee Wendell Willkie and other Republicans in to support key Roosevelt war programs like Lend-Lease. Stimson helped FDR create the Fair Employment Practices Committee and supported its efforts to desegregate war industries; he also supported efforts to bring women into the military. Yet their alliance also yielded too much to the evils of racism through actions such as refusing to desegregate the armed forces and confining Japanese Americans in concentration camps. However, it also can be said that by leading America to victory, they safeguarded for future generations the US Constitution's promise of freedom and equal rights for all.

In confronting American isolationism, Roosevelt and Stimson brought Democrats and Republicans together in a shared belief that the United States must act internationally and support global institutions such as the United Nations to spread peace and democracy across the planet. Their beliefs were embraced by Democratic president Harry Truman, Republican senator Arthur Vandenberg and many others in both political parties. This internationalist philosophy has guided American foreign policy over subsequent decades and, despite significant derelictions and distortions, continues broadly to steer US diplomacy to this day.

How significant is the legacy of the Roosevelt-Stimson alliance today? To answer this, one should consider the evolution of bipartisanship in the executive branch since the Truman Administration. Over the subsequent eight decades, bipartisanship diminished at the same time as the party realignment set in motion by FDR contributed to a trend of polarization in American politics.

Remarkably, the FDR-Stimson bipartisan alliance played a quiet role in the resurgence of the Republican Party and the election of General Dwight D. Eisenhower as a Republican president in 1952. In 1950, when Eisenhower still had not declared himself a member of either party, he voiced deep reverence for Stimson. "His leadership of the Army in World War II was wonderful," Eisenhower said. "I met him in December of 1941 and from that day onward he has for me meant the man who yields not one second to such enemies as deceit, flattery, favor-seeking, or any kind of thing except truth and honesty, and the meaning of our great country that is the world's greatest exponent of freedom, all the blessings that freedom can bring to men, materially, morally and intellectually."

Calling him "this very great man," Eisenhower averred that Stimson brought America through the bleak period after Pearl Harbor. "In a very definite way, he will always be my chief, because he was an inspiration when all the world seemed black, where the psychology of our nation was having a difficult time rising above the difficulties of the moment." Remarking on Stimson's campaign against Japan's 1931 invasion of Manchuria, Eisenhower said, "He stood out and said, 'This is wrong and it must be combated.'"[1]

After World War II ended, Republicans and Democrats vied to convince the general to join their party and run for president. Among those pushing the general to join the Republican Party were Massachusetts senator Henry Cabot Lodge Jr. and Robert Cutler, who had helped Stimson navigate the furor over soldier voting. In 1952, Eisenhower announced his candidacy as a Republican, brought on Cutler as a speechwriter and adviser on national security issues and won the presidency. Ike's election was the first time the Republican Party had won the presidency since 1928. It was the kind of resurgence for the Republican Party that Stimson had hoped for when he created a Republican outpost in the War Department in 1940.

WHEN FDR BROUGHT Stimson and Frank Knox into his cabinet, the two Republicans were prominent political figures. Since their era, no bipartisan appointee has had such a high profile as a leader of the opposition to the president. Nonetheless, through the Truman years and after, bipartisanship continued to play a part in American politics.

Ike took a step in the direction of bipartisanship when he appointed Charles Bohlen, the translator who worked for FDR and Truman at conferences with Stalin, as ambassador to Moscow. Nominally a nonpartisan State Department official, Bohlen was a symbol of FDR-Truman politics who drew the ire of Senator Joseph McCarthy, the right-wing Wisconsin Republican who charged with scant evidence that the State Department had become a nest of communists. McCarthy charged in the Senate that Bohlen had appeased the communists and hinted he was a homosexual. Ike stood by Bohlen and in May 1953 pulled Democratic and Republican senators together to vote overwhelmingly for Bohlen's confirmation, dealing McCarthy a powerful bipartisan defeat.[2]

Democrat John F. Kennedy, elected president in 1960, carried forward a bipartisanship that bore Stimson's imprint when he retained Cutler as head of the Inter-American Development Bank and appointed Republican senator Henry Cabot Lodge Jr. as ambassador to Vietnam. Kennedy hired Republican McGeorge Bundy, son of Stimson right-hand man Harvey Bundy, as his national security adviser.[3] The president also named Republican Robert McNamara as secretary of defense.

The endurance of the American tradition of bipartisanship is personified by William Webster, a Missouri Republican who won strong support from Democrats for his dedication to the rule of law. Webster was appointed US attorney in St. Louis by President Eisenhower, and was later appointed a federal judge by Republican president Richard Nixon. Democratic president Jimmy Carter appointed him to lead the FBI, and later Republican president Ronald Reagan chose him as director of the Central Intelligence Agency.

Webster learned a valuable lesson when he served in the navy during World War II: "I didn't have to prove I was a Republican or prove I was a Democrat. I had to prove I was a good officer."[4] He particularly admired one of Stimson's top Republican assistants, John McCloy, who had graduated from Amherst College three decades before Webster did. He said that in the FDR-Stimson era political differences could exist without devolving into rancorous partisan attacks, but that has changed in recent years. "There'd be some areas of policy differences between Republicans and Democrats, but they didn't have that—'I'll get one on the other guy!'" Webster recalled in 2019. "When did we stray from that?"

For people like Webster, the greatest good in American political life is not a victory by one party over another but ensuring that all Americans enjoy equal justice under laws created in accord with the US Constitution and fairly enforced. Such patriots place the highest value on establishing the truth, ensuring the rule of law and protecting the rights of all Americans under the US Constitution—not on pursuing the objectives of their political party. Their motto often is said to be "country over party." This tradition can be traced from George Washington down through Lincoln, through the alliance of FDR and Stimson, to Webster and on to the political leaders today who urge America to restore and embrace a culture of bipartisanship.

In recent decades, bipartisan appointees have tended to be relatively low-profile. Democratic president Bill Clinton appointed Senator William Cohen, a Maine Republican, as secretary of defense. Democratic president Barack Obama kept President George Bush's secretary of defense, Robert Gates, for three years, and later appointed another Republican, Chuck Hagel, to the post. Obama also appointed Republican Ray LaHood as secretary of transportation. No Republican has ever named a Democrat as secretary of defense. President George W. Bush appointed former Democratic congressman Norman Mineta as secretary of transportation. All of these bipartisan appointees were well respected, but they were neither high-profile critics of the president's policies nor leaders who could be expected to bring the president significant support from the opposing party.

Bipartisan appointments in recent decades have tended more to signal support for political moderation than to build a strategic bipartisan alliance with real impact. They are a kind of reflexive tribute to the immense achievements of the FDR-Stimson alliance—even if those feats are unknown to most Americans today.

The FDR-Stimson alliance thrived from 1940 to 1945—among the most tumultuous years of US history—prosecuting a war that spanned the globe and winning congressional passage of numerous pieces of legislation with broad support. In contrast, bipartisan actions in the legislative branch since the war years have tended to be short-lived and focused on specific pieces of legislation. Republicans in Congress voted in significant numbers to pass the Democrat-sponsored Civil Rights Act of 1964. Republicans joined with Democrats on the Judiciary Committee in the House of Representatives to pass the articles of impeachment against Republican president Richard Nixon in 1974. And House Democrats supported Republican president Reagan's major tax cut bill in 1981.

While the two main political parties in Congress continue to reach bipartisan agreement on legislation, many observers have voiced concern in recent years that partisanship too often prevents Congress from passing laws to address problems that are significant to the majority of Americans.

TODAY'S POLITICAL PARTIES look very different from those of 1940, thanks in part to what may be called the "Roosevelt Inversion." As FDR and Willkie saw it, both the Republican and Democratic parties were hybrids, each with a liberal and a conservative wing. Within each of these polarized parties, the liberals and conservatives regularly communicated and compromised with each other in order to get the full support of their party. When southern Democrats broke with the president in 1944, FDR and Willkie envisioned a realignment of the two American political parties: liberal Republicans should move into the Democratic Party, and conservative Democrats in the South and elsewhere should shift into the Republican Party. By creating the FEPC and calling for universal voting rights for soldiers, FDR led the Democrats—until then the party of segregation and white supremacy in the South—to become the party of civil rights. Southern Democrats who supported segregation and white supremacy then shifted their allegiance to the Republican Party.

This inversion of the parties can be traced through key decisions by party leaders. President Truman, for instance, continued FDR's push to make the Democratic Party an advocate for civil rights through actions such as his 1948 executive order desegregating the army. That year, southern Democrats notably rejected their party when South Carolina Democrat Strom Thurmond ran for president as a candidate of a breakaway segregationist party, the so-called Dixiecrats, winning the popular vote in four southern states.

In 1952, Thurmond and another prominent South Carolina segregationist, former FDR aide and Truman secretary of state James Byrnes, endorsed Eisenhower, delivering southern Democratic votes for the Republican.[5] Eisenhower won in such Democratic strongholds as Texas, Florida and Tennessee. The "Solid South" was no longer solidly Democratic.

President Kennedy, elected in 1960, advanced the Democratic partnership with the civil rights movement that FDR had launched. Kennedy was urging passage of a major civil rights bill at the time of his assassination in November 1963. His Democratic successor, President Lyndon B. Johnson, pushed hard for that bill—and then signed it into law as the Civil Rights Act of 1964. Johnson, indeed, was the very embodiment of the Democratic Party's transformation. As a little-known representative from Texas, he had voted with the southern Democrats against FDR's soldier voting plan in 1944, but two decades later as president, he signed into law the historic Voting Rights Act of 1965, breaking down the barriers to voting by Black citizens.[6]

Senator Thurmond, the South Carolina segregationist, chose the other option facing southern Democrats: he switched to the Republican Party in 1964, the same year he voted against the Civil Rights Act. In a sign of conservatives rising to power in the Republican Party, Republicans selected a senator who opposed the Civil Rights Act, Barry Goldwater of Arizona, as their party's presidential nominee in 1964. Four years later, the Republican appeal to southern segregationists gained steam when Republican presidential candidate Richard Nixon voiced opposition to desegregation, and Byrnes became the architect of a plan to convince southern Democrats to vote for the Republican. Nixon won the presidency with all but one of the former states in the old Confederacy.[7]

The migration of southern segregationists and opponents of civil rights into the Republican Party was by 1968 well underway. The completion of the Roosevelt Inversion—with racial politics as its fulcrum—played out over the decades after the FEPC's creation. The shift of Democratic conservatives into the Republican Party was apparent in the 2000 election, when Republican presidential candidate George W. Bush won every state in the old Confederacy as well as large a bloc of states in the West.

Today, with the exception of the state of Georgia, the Republican Party dominates the South just as solidly as the Democrats did before World War II. Republican policies in 2021 carried the telltale imprint of the racial politics of the old southern Democrats, as Republicans across the South passed a wave of laws to restrict voting rights. Democrats—the *new* southern Democrats of the twenty-first century—argued these laws are chiefly aimed at blocking Black and marginalized people from voting. And as FDR envisioned, liberals have abandoned the Republican Party for the Democratic Party. The Roosevelt Inversion is virtually complete. The hybrid nature of the parties—in which each had significant liberal and conservative wings who sought compromise within the party framework—is a thing of the past. There is still a range of political views in the two parties, but the polarization that was once so strong *inside* each of the two parties has largely been replaced by a polarization *between* the two parties.

TODAY'S REPUBLICAN PARTY mirrors a key trait of the old southern Democratic Party, using racially charged issues regularly to distinguish itself from its opponents. From the inception of his candidacy for the 2016 presidential election, Donald Trump denounced immigrants from Mexico, broadly calling them "rapists," and promising to take swift action against them. He had sown the seeds for his candidacy through his years-long efforts to delegitimize the nation's first Black president, Barack Obama. Trump narrowly won election in 2016, carrying all of the southern states.

Trump's rhetoric also echoed that of the fascist dictators combated by FDR, Stimson and the millions of American soldiers who fought in the war.[8] He repeatedly attacked the free press—the bane of fascists and a hallmark of American democracy enshrined in the Constitution's First Amendment—going so far as to denounce it as the "enemy of the people."[9]

Trump also rejected the internationalism of US foreign policy born in the era of the Roosevelt-Stimson alliance, with its emphasis on defending democracy around the world. He repeatedly criticized America's democratic allies and expressed admiration for repressive dictators like Russia's Vladimir Putin. Trump said in 2018 that he had greater confidence in Putin—a former Soviet KGB intelligence officer—than in American intelligence services.[10] He also had financial ties to Putin's allies, including a Russian oligarch who paid Trump $95 million in 2008 for a Florida mansion that Trump had bought for $41 million just four years earlier.[11] In 2016, Trump's real estate company proposed a plan to build a tower in Moscow, giving Putin himself a penthouse in it worth $50 million.[12]

After Putin ordered Russian armies to invade Ukraine in February 2022—and after President Joseph R. Biden and other democratic leaders around the world denounced the invasion and imposed sanctions on Russia—Trump said Putin's actions were "genius" and "savvy."[13]

Trump's dictatorial tendencies took an ominous turn shortly after Biden won the 2020 presidential election. He refused to acknowledge Biden's victory, claiming without evidence that there was widespread fraud in the election. Numerous state and federal officials rejected the claim, and more than 60 lawsuits filed by Trump supporters ended in no findings of fraud.[14] States that were closely contested recounted their votes, some as many as three times, but the results did not change.

Federal officials—even Trump's own attorney general, William Barr—announced publicly that there was no evidence of widespread fraud in the election.[15] Ultimately, election officials in all fifty states certified the results. Official election results showed Biden received 81.3 million votes to Trump's 74.2 million votes, gaining 306 electoral college votes to Trump's 232.[16]

Hunkered down in the White House, Trump spoke after the election with advisers who concocted a plan to prevent Biden from taking power by blocking the certification of the electoral college votes set to take place in Congress on January 6, 2021. A lawyer supporting Trump, John Eastman, developed a theory that, on that day, Vice President Mike Pence could reject the electoral votes from states Trump lost, throwing the electoral college vote in Trump's favor. Steve Bannon, Trump's adviser who has long voiced rage against the American government, told the president, "We're going to bury Biden on January 6, fucking bury him."[17]

On January 6, Trump held a rally near the White House. The president took the stage, delivering a harangue urging Pence to "stand up for the good of our Constitution," and exhorting the crowd to go to the Capitol and "show strength."[18] Many in the crowd marched to the Capitol, where a mob engaged in a violent brawl with Capitol police, smashed doors and windows, and broke into the House and Senate chambers.[19] Some members of the mob carried the Confederate flag, the enduring symbol of white supremacy.[20] More than a hundred officers were assaulted; some were sprayed with chemicals, including one who died the following day. A woman in the violent mob died after being shot by an officer. Members of the House and Senate, interrupted in the process of certifying the election, fled the chambers.

American democracy was disrupted, threatened and under siege.

Prosecutors later charged more than seven hundred people for their actions that day, accusing them of federal crimes such as assaulting officers, entering a restricted area with a deadly weapon, conspiracy and destruction of government property.[21] The founder and ten members of a right-wing paramilitary group were indicted for seditious conspiracy on charges that they helped carry out the attack and prepared to transport weapons into Washington "in support of operations aimed at using force to stop the lawful transfer of presidential power."[22]

The January 6 assault on the Capitol bears eerie similarities to events in Germany in February 1933, when Adolf Hitler sought to take power. With planning by top Hitler aides, the Reichstag legislature building in Berlin was set on fire, and the Nazis immediately blamed the arson on communists. The similarity only sharpened when Fox News, a right-wing cable channel that consistently favors Trump, broadcast the theory—without providing any evidence—that leftist anti-fascist protesters carried out the Capitol assault.[23]

US Army general Mark A. Milley, chairman of the Joint Chiefs of Staff, saw the parallel. "This is a Reichstag moment," he told aides. "The gospel of the Fuhrer."[24]

There was a critical difference between the two attacks, however. The Nazi burning of the Reichstag was a propaganda ploy aimed at discrediting communists: it occurred at night when the Reichstag was empty and no governmental activities were underway—no police officers were attacked and no one died. In stark contrast, Trump's followers, acting as the president exhorted them to go to the Capitol and "show strength," stormed the Capitol, assaulted police and interrupted Congress as its members worked on one of the most important constitutional function of American democracy—the peaceful transfer of power from one president to the next. It was an attempt to carry out a coup d'état.

After the rioters were finally driven from the Capitol, the certification process resumed late on January 6. Though many Republicans voted to confirm the election, one hundred and forty-seven Republicans in the House and Senate voted to overturn the election results in Arizona, Pennsylvania or both.[25] These included prominent senators Ted Cruz of Texas and Josh Hawley of Missouri, as well as House minority leader Kevin McCarthy.

Vice President Pence, however, refused to knuckle under to Trump's pressure on him to overturn the election. "President Trump is wrong," he said later. "The presidency belongs to the American people, and the American people alone. And frankly there is no idea more un-American than the notion that any one person could choose the American president."[26]

How did America—after more than two centuries of peaceful presidential transitions under the Constitution—come to this? The attempted insurrection and the subsequent votes by Republican legislators to overturn the election results were born of the kind of corrosive partisanship that the nation's first president, George Washington, warned against.[27]

At the end of his second term as president, Washington delivered his Farewell Address in September 1796 warning that the "spirit of party"—partisanship in today's terms—could lead to a despotism depriving Americans of their hard-fought freedoms. He announced he would not seek reelection for a third term, a decision establishing a tradition of peaceful transfers of power from one president to the next. He said that partisanship, "sharpened by the spirit of revenge natural to party dissension," could lead to "the chief of some prevailing faction" rising to power "on the ruins of public liberty."[28]

Political parties were virtually nonexistent at the dawn of the American republic, and the US Constitution made no provision for them. Yet by 1796, Washington had seen enough of the two nascent political parties of his day—the Federalists and the Democratic-Republicans—to conclude that their conduct often resulted in treachery. He warned that the "spirit of party" makes the country vulnerable to foreign influence and corruption, and that it leads to the spread of false information. "One of the expedients of party to acquire influence, within particular districts [of the country], is to misrepresent the opinions and aims of other districts."

He solemnly urged Americans to discourage and restrain partisanship, saying "it agitates the community with ill-founded jealousies and false alarms, kindles the animosity of one part against another, foments occasionally riot and insurrection."[29]

These prophetic words of America's first president ought to set off alarms in our own hyperpartisan era, in which party leaders peddle baseless conspiracy theories and foment hatred against others to advance their personal interests and to spur insurrection.

A small number of Republicans joined those condemning Trump's partisan attack on American democracy, including Representatives Liz Cheney of Wyoming and Adam Kinzinger of Illinois, and Senator Mitt Romney of Utah. In Georgia, Republican secretary of state Brad Raffensperger said Trump's voter fraud claims were "just plain wrong."[30] Another Republican who condemned Trump after the January 6 insurrection was Judge William Webster, who urged Congress to impeach or censure Trump. He said, "We are a land of laws and our United States president, above all others, is expected to revere and protect them."[31]

Trump was impeached—for the second time—by the US House of Representatives later in January 2021 for "incitement of insurrection." But Republican senators, led by Majority Leader Mitch McConnell of Kentucky, fell into line in support of Trump, and the Senate acquitted him of the charges the following month. Trump, by then out of office, brazenly resumed spreading his false claims that the election was stolen.

Republican leaders in lockstep with Trump swiftly punished members of their party who dared to question Trump's false claims. After Cheney condemned President Trump for inciting the assault on the Capitol, the Wyoming Republican Party censured her, and she was voted out of her position as chair of the House Republican Conference.[32]

Standing by her views, Cheney tweeted on May 3, 2021: "The 2020 presidential election was not stolen. Anyone who claims it was is spreading THE BIG LIE, turning their back on the rule of law, and poisoning our democratic system."[33]

Cheney and Kinzinger joined Democrats on a House committee formed to investigate the January 6 attack. This led to a bitter rejection by pro-Trump Republicans. In February 2022, the Republican National Committee issued a formal censure of Cheney and Kinzinger for working on the House committee: "Cheney and Kinzinger are participating in a Democrat-led persecution of ordinary citizens engaged in legitimate political discourse."[34]

Trump's attempt to overturn a presidential election stands among the gravest threats to American democracy in the nation's history. Like Hitler and other fascists, Trump sought to elevate the power of one man—himself—by exploiting partisan divisions to trample on democracy and the rule of law. But Trump's fascism is an internal menace—no foreign army is preparing to land on our shores—and so his threat is all the more insidious. Polling suggests that tens of millions of Americans believe his lies that the election was stolen. His supporters have already demonstrated their willingness to act violently in his name, and he appears likely to run for the presidency again in 2024.

In this climate of extreme and volatile partisanship, it would be natural to think bipartisanship is dead. Its embers, however, are still burning. In the courageous stand taken by Cheney, Kinzinger and other Republicans in defense of American democracy, one can see the legacy of Stimson and other Republicans who bravely asserted their positions and joined with FDR, ignoring the severe criticism they received from their own party. Pence, long seen as an unquestioning Trump supporter, also deserves credit for his defiance of Trump's demands that he overturn the election. The Republicans who boldly defy Trump's falsehoods and stand up to his would-be tyranny are the rightful inheritors of Stimson and other Republicans who united with Democrats in defense of American democracy in 1940.

Crossing party lines to preserve American democracy is just as important today as it was in World War II.

In the hyperpartisan climate of the 2020s, the value of "bipartisanship" has been denigrated by both the right and the left. Some see it as a quaint idea that carries little weight or, worse yet, leads to calamity. "Bipartisanship to young people seems like this kind of vintage fantasy," Representative Alexandria Ocasio-Cortez said in 2020. "But for young people bipartisanship got us the Iraq war, bipartisanship got us endless war, bipartisanship got us bank bailouts and we very rarely see the results of bipartisanship yielding in racial justice, yielding in economic justice for working families, yielding in improvements to health care and in fact the things that have yielded those things have been Democratic majorities."[35]

One reply to such criticism is to recall that in 2017 Senator John McCain, an Arizona Republican who was once his party's presidential nominee, famously strode onto the Senate floor and gave a thumbs-down sign, voting against a Republican bill to repeal President Obama's Affordable Care Act. McCain's dramatic stand—breaking with his party on a very high-profile issue—drew praise from Democrats for protecting a program that provided health insurance to as many as thirty million people who have struggled to pay for their care.

Those who doubt the value of bipartisanship also should recall that it was at the foundation of significant progress in civil rights. Southern Democrats used the Senate's filibuster rule to block passage of the Civil Rights Act for seventy-five days in 1964. That legislative battle ended when the Senate minority leader, Republican Everett Dirksen of Illinois, and twenty-six other Republicans provided the votes necessary to defeat the filibuster and pass the landmark civil rights legislation.[36]

It must be said, however, that bipartisanship alone is not inherently good. The simple fact that two parties agree on something doesn't make it right. Both Democrats and Republicans supported the internment of Japanese Americans in 1942, and members of both parties supported racial segregation for many decades. In other words, bipartisanship is only as good as the cause in which it is employed. Bipartisanship is at its best when it enables leaders to look beyond the narrow interests of political parties—such as posturing for political power or securing campaign contributions—to do what is right for the country and democracy.

President Biden, an admirer of FDR, vocally supports bipartisanship. He called for uniting America in his inaugural address in January 2021, in which he pointed to "a rise in political extremism, white supremacy, domestic terrorism that we must confront and we will defeat. To overcome these challenges—to restore the soul and to secure the future of America—requires more than words. It requires that most elusive of things in a democracy: Unity."

Across the aisle, few Republicans have been willing to say publicly that they are open to reaching agreement with Democrats. Senate majority leader McConnell dismissed the idea of compromising with Biden in May 2021, saying, "One-hundred percent of our focus is on stopping this new administration."[37] With such rigid opposition from Republicans, Biden struggled to win bipartisan support for much of the legislation he hoped to pass, but in November 2021 he won passage of a bipartisan bill to spend $1 trillion to improve the nation's highways, bridges and other infrastructure. Notably, McConnell, despite his professed opposition to Biden's agenda, was among the nineteen Republican senators who voted for the infrastructure bill.[38]

Biden has not followed FDR's template for bipartisan leadership in a key way: at the time of this writing, he has appointed no Republicans to his cabinet. Trump's continuing assault on American democracy, however, raises the question of whether Biden might yet consider this strategy, which worked so well for FDR in 1940. It would demonstrate for all to see that Republicans are uniting with Democrats in the fight to save American democracy.

Hyperpartisanship, which stokes Trumpist fascism, also threatens to prevent Congress from taking substantive action on vital issues such as gun violence, climate change and voting rights. Yet America's leaders today can tackle these challenges by reaching across party lines just as FDR and Stimson did when the country was deeply divided over the war in Europe. To do this, legislators must conceive of themselves not as partisans unyieldingly seeking victory for their party but as representatives of the people entrusted with finding the best path forward for the country. They must engage in genuine debate, be open to compromise and disavow the harmful strains of partisanship—all for the sake of advancing America and defending democracy.

ACKNOWLEDGMENTS

I wish to express my heartfelt thanks to the many people who helped me write this book.

Sally Richardson, publisher at large for St. Martin's Press's parent company Macmillan Publishers Ltd., embraced *Uniting America* from the start and has advocated for it through the publishing process. Thanks also to St. Martin's Editor-in-Chief, George Witte, who strongly backed my project, and to St. Martin's associate editor Kevin Reilly, who edited the manuscript superbly. My agent Jacques de Spoelberch offered sage advice.

Yale University kindly granted me permission to view the voluminous Henry L. Stimson Papers, which consists of almost 300,000 pages. That includes Stimson's diary, which he began keeping in 1909 and totals more than 10,000 pages. When the COVID pandemic forced Yale to close its doors, I received a stellar lesson in the vital role played by America's local public libraries. At the Cranston Public Library, in Cranston, Rhode Island, librarian Dave Bartos spent hours helping me obtain and view dozens of microfilm reels of the Stimson Papers through loans from university libraries.

At the Franklin D. Roosevelt Presidential Library and Museum in Hyde Park, New York, the staff provided remarkable support. At the Library of Congress in Washington, DC, the librarians provided careful answers to my many questions about the library's archives. The Library of Congress's John W. Kluge Center also supported the project by designating me a Kluge Center Scholar. At the George C. Marshall Foundation, Melissa Davis, director of the library and archives, helped me obtain copies of key documents remotely.

Gettysburg College history professor Michael Birkner, who became a friend through our shared interest in President Dwight Eisenhower, read the entire manuscript and provided vital guidance and commentary. Wayne Parent, emeritus professor of political science at Louisiana State University, commented helpfully on the chapters on the "Roosevelt Inversion." William Hitchcock, professor of history at the University of Virginia, read and offered advice on two chapters about the years before Pearl Harbor. These fine scholars offered insights on an array of issues. Of course, any errors in this book, as well as any opinions, are mine alone.

Al Kilborne, author of a history of Woodley, Henry and Mabel Stimson's home in Washington, *Images of America: Woodley and Its Residents*, gave me a tour of the mansion with the kind permission of its current occupant, the Maret School.

My friend Dane Nichols kindly welcomed me to her townhouse in Georgetown—a true home away from home—when research required me to be in Washington.

Clark Russell, my lifelong friend who is both an artist and an astute scholar of history, read the manuscript and offered fine insights and wise counsel.

Louise Blais Ross, my mother-in-law, a Republican outnumbered by a loving but largely Democratic-voting family, over many years set an example of how to conduct oneself civilly in debates with those who hold opposing political views, a personal hint at the dignified relationship between Stimson and FDR.

My wife, Marguerite Ross Shinkle, is my first and most cherished reader. Her love and support made this book possible, and her excellent editing made it better.

Peter Shinkle
Barrington, RI
May 2022

NOTES

ABBREVIATIONS USED IN THE NOTES

FDR Franklin Delano Roosevelt

FDRL Franklin Delano Roosevelt Presidential Library, Hyde Park, New York

FKP Frank Knox Papers, Library of Congress, Washington, DC.

FRUS Foreign Relations of the United States

HLS Henry Lewis Stimson

HLSD Henry Lewis Stimson Diaries, Yale University Library, New Haven, Connecticut

HLSP Henry Lewis Stimson Papers, Yale University Library, New Haven, Connecticut

HSTL Harry S. Truman Presidential Library, Independence, Missouri

MD Henry Morgenthau Jr. Diaries, Franklin Delano Roosevelt Presidential Library, Hyde Park, New York

NARA National Archives and Records Administration, College Park, Maryland

NYT *The New York Times*

OAS *On Active Service in Peace and War*, by Henry L. Stimson and McGeorge Bundy

WSC Winston S. Churchill

INTRODUCTION

1. Congressional Record, June 3, 1940, p. 7395.
2. "Stimson and Knox Are Appointed to Posts in the Cabinet to Aid the Defense Drive," *NYT*, June 21, 1940, 1.
3. The book is *Ike's Mystery Man, the Secret Lives of Robert Cutler,* published in 2018. In full disclosure, I am the great-nephew of both Robert Cutler and Hamilton Fish. Thus, my family embodied the fault line that divided isolationist Republicans from

those Republicans who supported FDR in aiding Great Britain and other democracies.

4. FDR letter to HLS, November 21, 1944, Stimson, Henry L. 1934–1944, President's Personal File, FDRL.

CHAPTER 1: THE HUNTER AND THE STRATEGIST

1. "Roosevelt Hears Views of Stimson on Foreign Policy," *NYT,* January 10, 1933, 1.
2. HLSD, January 9, 1933.
3. Raymond Moley, *After Seven Years* (New York: Harper & Brothers, 1939), 94–95; "Roosevelt Reveals Policy in Far East Will Be Continued," *NYT,* January 18, 1933, 1.
4. Godfrey Hodgson, *The Colonel: The Life and Wars of Henry Stimson 1867–1959* (New York: Alfred A. Knopf, 1990), 27–28.
5. Henry Stimson and McGeorge Bundy, *On Active Service in Peace and War* (New York: Harper & Brothers, 1947 (OAS), xiii.
6. OAS, xvi.
7. Henry L. Stimson, *My Vacations* (privately published, 1949), 13, 19, 29, 34.
8. OAS, xv.
9. Philip C. Jessup, *Elihu Root* (New York: Archon Books), 1964, Volume 1, 183–4.
10. OAS, xviii, 6.
11. Stimson, *My Vacations,* 69–72, 74–78.
12. HLSD, January 17, 1909.
13. OAS, xxii.
14. Decision of the US Supreme Court, New York Central R. Co. v. United States, 212 US 481 (1909); OAS, 9.
15. OAS, 9–14; "Sugar Checkers Are Found Guilty," *NYT,* December 18, 1909, 1.
16. Robert F. Bruner and Sean D. Carr, *The Panic of 1907: Lessons Learned from the Market's Perfect Storm* (Hoboken, N.J.: John Wiley & Sons, Inc., 2007), 37–55.
17. "Morse Back in Jail, His Appeal Denied," *NYT,* October 12, 1909, 1.
18. Felix Frankfurter, with Dr. Harlan B. Phillips, *Felix Frankfurter Reminisces* (New York: Reynal & Company, 1960), 48–49.
19. OAS, 26, 28.
20. "Stimson Fighter of Big Graft Cases," *NYT,* September 29, 1910, 5.
21. Kenneth S. Davis, *FDR: The Beckoning of Destiny, 1882–1928* (New York: G.P. Putnam's Sons, 1971), 28–9.
22. Jean Edward Smith, *FDR* (New York: Random House Trade Paperbacks, 2007), 10, 11, 16.
23. Ibid., 23.
24. Ibid., 29–32.
25. Davis, *FDR,* 141–142.
26. Ibid., 153, 164–167.
27. Ibid, 36–37, 46.
28. Ibid., 38.
29. TR letter to FDR, November 29, 1904, Old Family Papers, Box 20, Roosevelt, Theodore, FDRL.
30. Davis, *FDR,* 192–193.

31. "Murphy's Scalp to Be Taken by Big Democrats," *The Buffalo Enquirer,* May 19, 1911, 12.

32. "Stimson Lost by 67,000 Votes, a Margin of 5%. Final Figures Out on State Election," *NYT,* December 16, 1910, 3.

33. OAS, 30–31.

34. OAS, 86–87.

35. OAS, 89.

36. "St. Louis Men Pledge Support to President," *New York Tribune,* April 13, 1917, 4.

37. OAS, 98.

38. Smith, *FDR,* 160.

39. Ibid., 160–162.

40. "F.D. Roosevelt Ill of Poliomyelitis," *NYT,* September 16, 1921, 1.

41. Smith, *FDR,* 217.

42. OAS, 108–109.

43. Henry L. Stimson, *American Policy in Nicaragua* (New York: Charles Scribner's Sons, 1927), 18.

44. Ibid.

45. "Gen. M'Coy to Guide Poll in Nicaragua," *NYT,* July 3, 1927, 6.

46. Jennet Conant, *Tuxedo Park: A Wall Street Tycoon and the Secret Palace of Science That Changed the Course of World War II* (New York: Simon & Schuster, 2002), 27–28, 40–42.

47. Ibid., 50–80.

48. Ibid., 74, 77–78.

49. *Utility Corporations, Letter from the Acting Chairman of the Federal Trade Commission, No. 52, in Response to Senate Resolution No. 83* (Washington, DC: US Government Printing Office, 1933) 47, 532.

50. OAS, 160.

51. Al Kilborne, *Woodley and Its Residents* (Arcadia Publishing, 2008), 25, 37, 42, 68, 76, 100.

52. "Stimson Urges Election of Tuttle for Clean-Up," *NYT,* October 29, 1930, 1.

53. Smith, *FDR,* 244–245.

54. *Report of the Commission of Enquiry to the League of Nations,* September 4, 1932, 29, 67, 68.

55. "Nanking Will Invoke Kellogg Peace Pact," *NYT,* September 21, 1931, 1.

56. OAS, 227.

57. HLSD, November 19, 1931.

58. "The Secretary of State to the Ambassador in Japan," November 19, 1931, 3 p.m., US Department of State Office of the Historian, website: https://history.state.gov/historicaldocuments/frus1931v03/d467, accessed 9/6/2019.

59. "Stimson Insists on Rights in Manchuria," *NYT,* January 8, 1932, 1.

60. Herbert P. Bix, *Hirohito and the Making of Modern Japan* (New York: Harper Perennial, 2016), 252.

61. "Capital Acclaims Manchurian Ruler," *NYT,* March 9, 1932, 14; Bix, *Hirohito,* 247.

62. Bix, *Hirohito,* 255–256.

63. HLSD, April 17, 1932.

64. Federal Reserve Bank of St. Louis, "Unemployment Rate for United States,"

National Bureau of Economic Research, website: https://fred.stlouisfed.org/series /M0892AUSM156SNBR, accessed 9/9/2019.

65. "National Collapse Averted by Hoover, Stimson Says Here," *NYT,* October 19, 1932.

66. HLSD, December 22, 1932.

67. "Stimson Reasserts Manchuria Policy," *NYT,* January 17, 1933, 1.

68. "Roosevelt Reveals Policy in Far East Will Be Continued," January 18, 1933, *NYT,* 1.

69. HLSD, January 19, 1933.

70. "HLS Telegram to FDR, February 15, 1933," President's Personal File, (X-Ref's 1937–45) 19A 20, Container 2, FDRL.

71. William Shirer, *The Rise and Fall of the Third Reich: A History of Nazi Germany* (New York: Simon & Schuster, 1960), 192.

72. Ibid., 192.

73. Smith, *FDR,* 302.

74. Ibid., 312–313.

75. FDR, "Fireside Chat 1," March 12, 1933, FDR Master Speech File, 1898–1945, FDRL.

76. Smith, *FDR,* 318–330, 332.

77. Shirer, *The Rise and Fall of the Third Reich,* 221–223.

78. Ibid., 226.

79. HLSD, May 17, 1934.

80. Ramsay Muir, "Civilisation and Liberty," *The Nineteenth Century and After,* No. DCXCI, September 1934, 217, 219, 225.

81. FDR letter to HLS, December 8, 1934, President's Personal File, (X-Ref's 1937–45) 19A 20, Container 2, FDRL; HLS letter to FDR, November 15, 1937, President's Personal File, Box 20.

CHAPTER 2: THE FIGHT OVER ISOLATIONISM

1. "Mussolini Warns Powers to Leave Ethiopia to Italy," *NYT,* May 15, 1935, 1.

2. "Roosevelt Agrees to Bar," *NYT,* August 23, 1935, 1.

3. "Neutrality Law Is Signed," *NYT,* September 1, 1935, 1.

4. "Roosevelt Proclaims Embargo on Arms to Italy and Ethiopia," *NYT,* October 6, 1935, 1.

5. "Stimson Criticizes Our War Trade Ban," *NYT,* October 24, 1935.

6. HLSD, November 2, 1935, 2–5.

7. Conant, *Tuxedo Park,* 50–80.

8. John F. Wasik, *The Merchant of Power: Sam Insull, Thomas Edison, and the Creation of the Modern Metropolis* (New York: Palgrave Macmillan, 2006), 199–200, 204–205, 217–218.

9. HLSD, October 26, 1934.

10. HLSD, January 17, 1935.

11. Conant, *Tuxedo Park,* 18;

12. David Levering Lewis, *The Improbable Wendell Willkie: The Businessman Who Saved the Republican Party and His Country, and Conceived a New World Order* (New York and London: Liveright, 2018), 88.

13. "TVA Head Attacks Holding Concerns," *NYT,* January 22, 1935, 20; "Utilities Bill Made Law," *NYT,* August 27, 1935.

14. Shirer, *The Rise and Fall of the Third Reich*, 281–284.
15. Ibid., 233.
16. FDR State of the Union, January 3, 1936, FDR Master Speech File, 1898–1945, FDRL.
17. "Britain Sees Peril in Neutrality Idea," *NYT,* January 6, 1936, 6.
18. "Allied Financing, Arms Plant Deals, Told by Morgan," *NYT,* January 9, 1936, 1.
19. Hans Schmidt, *Maverick Marine: General Smedley D. Butler and the Contradictions of American Military History* (Lexington: University Press of Kentucky: 1987), 236–237.
20. See, for example, "Anti-War Mandate Is Sounded in Poll," *NYT,* January 13, 1936, 10.
21. "Roosevelt Renews Plea Against Profits in War," *NYT,* March 1, 1936, 1.
22. John Toland, *The Rising Sun: The Decline and Fall of the Japanese Empire, 1936–1945* (New York: Random House, 1970), 12–18.
23. David Bergamini, *Japan's Imperial Conspiracy,* Volume II: *How Emperor Hirohito Led Japan into War Against the West,* (New York: William Morrow & Company, Inc., 1971); Toland, 35.
24. Antony Beevor, *The Battle for Spain: The Spanish Civil War 1936–1939* (Penguin Books, 1982), 136–137, 139.
25. "Landon Assails Roosevelt," *NYT,* August 27, 1936, 1.
26. "Democrats Adopt Platform Continuing New Deal," *NYT,* June 26, 1936, 1.
27. "Roosevelt Denounces War and Breakers of Pledges," 1, "President Roosevelt's Chautauqua Address on International Affairs," 4, *NYT,* August 15, 1936.
28. "Embargo on Arms for Spain in Force," *NYT,* January 9, 1937, 3.
29. "Roosevelt Asks Power to Reform Courts," and "Aim to Pack Court, Declares Hoover," *NYT,* February 6, 1937, 1.
30. "9 US Leaders Express Views," *The Indianapolis Star,* February 7, 1937, 2.
31. HLSD, April 3, 1937.
32. Smith, *FDR,* 388.
33. "President Accepts Neutrality Plans," *NYT,* January 31, 1937.
34. "Neutrality Fixed by the President," May 2, 1937, *NYT,* 37.
35. Bix, *Hirohito,* 324.
36. Jay Taylor, *The Generalissimo: Chiang Kai-shek and the Struggle for Modern China* (Cambridge and London: Harvard University Press, 2009), 122–126, 157.
37. "Roosevelt Urges 'Concerted Action,'" *NYT,* October 6, 1937, 1.
38. "Stimson Favors Action on Japan"; and "Text of Former Secretary Henry L. Stimson's Letter," *NYT,* October 7, 1937, 1, 12.
39. "Nye Here, Warns of Danger of War," *NYT,* October 8, 1937, 2.
40. HLS letter to FDR, November 15, 1937, President's Personal File, Henry L. Stimson 1934–1944, FDRL.
41. FDR letter to HLS, November 24, 1937, President's Personal File, Henry L. Stimson 1934–1944, FDRL.
42. Iris Chang, *The Rape of Nanking: The Forgotten Holocaust of World War II* (Penguin Books, 1997), 40.
43. Ibid., 44.
44. Bergamini, *Japan's Imperial Conspiracy,* 21.
45. Ibid., 89–99.
46. Ibid., 101–103.

47. "Butchery Marked Capture of Nanking," *NYT,* December 13, 1937, 1.

48. Shirer, *The Rise and Fall of the Third Reich,* 325–331.

49. Ibid., 351.

50. Winston Churchill, *The Gathering Storm* (Boston: Houghton Mifflin Company, 1948), 326–328.

51. "Nazis Smash, Loot and Burn," *NYT,* November 11, 1938, 1.

52. Shirer, *The Rise and Fall of the Third Reich,* 431.

53. HLSD, March 24, 1938.

54. Cordell Hull, *The Memoirs of Cordell Hull, in Two Volumes,* Volume 1 (New York: The Macmillan Company, 1948), 30, 179; also Irwin F. Gellman, *Secret Affairs: Franklin Roosevelt, Cordell Hull, and Sumner Welles* (Baltimore and London: The Johns Hopkins University Press, 1995), 31, 266–267.

55. "Japan Gets Very Few Planes Since 'Moral Embargo' a Year Ago," *NYT,* August 12, 1939, 2.

56. "Text of President Roosevelt's Message as Read by Him in Congress Session," *NYT,* January 5, 1939, 12.

57. Beevor, *The Battle for Spain,* 232.

58. T.H. Watkins, *Righteous Pilgrim: The Life and Times of Harold L. Ickes, 1874–1952,* Book Two (New York: Henry Holt Company, 1992), 308.

59. Stimson letter to Hull, January 18, 1939, Papers of Cordell Hull, Box 44, LOC.

60. Congressional Record—House, January 26, 1939, 853.

61. "Senator Lewis Opposes Lifting Arms Embargo as Perilous Step," *NYT,* January 26, 1939, 4.

62. For a liberal view of Stimson's letter, see "Isolation Is Not Enough," *The Nation,* March 18, 1939, 307.

63. "Neutrality Is a Defense Problem, Stimson Tells Senate Committee," *NYT,* April 6, 1939, 1.

64. Hull, *Memoirs,* Volume 1, 632.

65. Ibid., 637–639.

66. Robert N. Rosen, *Saving the Jews: Franklin D. Roosevelt and the Holocaust* (New York: Thunder's Mouth Press, 2006), 91–104.

67. *Hearings Before the Joint Committee on the Investigation of the Tennessee Valley Authority, Seventy-Fifth Congress* (Washington: Government Printing Office), Part 10, 4348.

68. "TVA Takes Title to Power for State of Tennessee," *NYT,* August 16, 1939, 1.

69. Susan Dunn, *1940: FDR, Willkie, Lindbergh, Hitler—The Election amid the Storm* (New Haven: Yale University Press, 2013), 34.

70. "Roosevelt in Plea," and "British Liner *Athenia* Torpedoed, Sunk," *NYT,* September 4, 1939, 1.

71. "US Proclaims Emergency to Protect Neutrality," "100,000 More Men," *NYT,* September 9, 1939, 1.

72. Testimony of General George C. Marshall, *Hearings on the Emergency Supplemental Appropriation Bill for 1940,* House Committee on Appropriations, November 27, 1939, 21; Eric Larrabee, *Commander in Chief, Franklin Delano Roosevelt, His Lieutenants & Their War* (New York: Harper & Row, Publishers, 1987),114; "First War Forces Relatively Small," *NYT,* September 4, 1939, 22.

73. "Borah Opens Fight Against Revision of Neutrality Act," September 12, 1939, *NYT*, 1.

74. "Plea by Stimson," *NYT*, September 17, 1939, 1.

75. "Lindbergh Urges We Shun the War," *NYT*, September 16, 1939, 1.

76. Ibid.

77. "2 Senators Blast Embargo Repeal as Leading to War," *NYT*, September 17, 1939, 1.

78. Knox editorial "National Unity—How It May Be Achieved," *Chicago Daily News*, September 12, 1939, Box 7, FKP.

79. "Roosevelt Asks Congress to Repeal Arms Embargo," *NYT*, September 22, 1939, 1.

80. Samuel I. Rosenman, *Working with Roosevelt* (New York: Harper & Brothers Publishers, 1952), 190.

81. "Senate Opens Battle over Embargo," and "Senator Borah's Argument," *NYT*, October 3, 1939, 1, 14.

82. OAS, 317; "Stimson Attacks 'Foolish Embargo,'" *NYT*, October 6, 15.

83. 1939 entry, HLSD, 31–33.

84. Frankfurter letter to Stimson, October 16, 1939, Frankfurter Papers, General Correspondence, Henry L. Stimson, Box 104, LOC.

85. Frankfurter's reference apparently was to the English romantic poet William Wordsworth, whose poem "London, 1802" was a lament of the perceived moral decline of England. The poem expressed the belief that the writer John Milton, who died more than a hundred years before the poem was written in 1802, possessed virtues of the sort England needed to recover from its moral decline. The poem begins: "MILTON! thou shouldst be living at this hour:/England hath need of thee . . ."

86. "Lindbergh Favors a Split Arms Ban," *NYT*, October 14, 1939, 1.

87. "House Dooms Arms Embargo," 243–181, *NYT*, November 3, 1939, 1.

88. FDR Speech to Virginia Military Institute, November 11, 1939, FDR Master Speech File, 1898–1945, FDRL.

CHAPTER 3: CROSSING THE DIVIDE

1. "Ridicules Knox Report," *NYT*, December 13, 1939, 22.

2. Knox letter to FDR, December 15, 1939, FKP, Box 4, 1935–1939.

3. FDR letter to Knox, December 29, 1939, FKP, Box 4, 1935–1939.

4. HLSD, January 10, 1940.

5. "Text of Stimson Letter Asking Ban on War Exports to Japan," *NYT*, January 11, 1940, 4.

6. "Stimson Asks Curb on Arms to Japan," *NYT*, January 11, 1940, 4.

7. Shirer, *The Rise and Fall of the Third Reich*, 685–688.

8. Lynne Olson, *Those Angry Days: Roosevelt, Lindbergh, and America's Fight Over World War II, 1939–1941* (New York: Random House, 2014), 97.

9. Roberts letter to Stimson, March 30, 1940; Stimson letter to Willkie, April 5, 1940, HLS Papers, Box 133.

10. Lewis, *The Improbable Wendell Willkie*, 123–127.

11. Shirer, *The Rise and Fall of the Third Reich*, 702–703.

12. Winston S. Churchill, *The Gathering Storm* (Boston: Houghton Mifflin Company, 1948), 591, 597–599.

13. HLSD, May 8, 1940.

14. "US Striving to Halt Spread of War to Mediterranean," the Associated Press, *The Gazette and Daily* of York, Pennsylvania, May 4, 1940, 1.

15. HLSD, May 8, 1940.

16. Frankfurter letter to FDR, May 3, 1940, FDRL, Papers as President: The President's Secretary's File (PSF), 1933–1945, Box 135, Felix Frankfurter, 1940. Original emphasis was underlined.

17. Hugh Sebag-Montefiore, *Dunkirk: Fight to the Last Man* (Penguin Books, 2015), 59–66.

18. See Churchill letter to FDR, November 1940, introducing Walter Citrine, long-time general secretary of the powerful Trades Union Council. "He worked with me three years before the war in our effort to arouse all parties in the country to the need of rearmament against Germany. At the present time he fills a position in the Labour movement more important to the conduct of the war than many Ministerial offices," Churchill wrote. "He has the root of the matter in him, and I most cordially commend him to your consideration." Map Room Papers, Box 1, Churchill-FDR, October 1939–December 1940, FDRL. See also Churchill, *The Gathering Storm*, 216–217.

19. Isaac Kramnick and Barry Sheerman, *Harold Laski: A Life on the Left* (London: Allen Lane, The Penguin Press, 1993), 417.

20. Laski letter to FDR, April 17, 1939, FDR Papers as President, President's Secretary's Files, Box 38, Great Britain–Laski, Harold, FDRL.

21. John Bew, *Clement Attlee: The Man Who Made Modern Britain* (New York: Oxford University Press, 2017), 241–242.

22. Churchill, *The Gathering Storm*, 662–665.

23. Bew, 90, 91, 119, 128.

24. "Labor Party Votes Aid," *NYT*, May 14, 1940, 6; "Churchill Backed by 'Full War' Vote," *NYT*, May 14, 1940, 1.

25. "Text of Churchill's Commons Speech," *NYT*, May 14, 1940, 6.

26. Dunn, *1940*, 38.

27. Shirer, *The Rise and Fall of the Third Reich*, 722.

28. Winston S. Churchill, *Their Finest Hour: The Second World War* (Boston: Houghton Mifflin Company, 1949), 24.

29. "Text of the President's Address Asking a Great Defense Fund," *NYT*, May 17, 1940, 10.

30. "Landon Supports New Defense Plan," *NYT*, May 18, 1940, 9.

31. Jon Meacham, *Franklin and Winston: An Intimate Portrait of an Epic Friendship* (New York: Random House, 2003), 49.

32. "Willkie Pictures Defense Handicap," *NYT*, May 18, 1940, 9.

33. HLS letter to FDR, May 18, 1940, FDRL, Roosevelt Papers as President, Box 84, War Department, Henry L. Stimson, 1940–41.

34. HLS letter to Churchill, May 18, 1940, HLSP, Box 134, Folder May 18–20, 1940.

35. Radio address by Charles A. Lindbergh 5/19/1940, accessed March 13, 2019, at https://archive.org/details/RadioAddressByCharlesALindbergh.

36. The United States Military Academy, *The West Point History of World War II*, Clifford J. Rogers, Ty Seidule, and Steve R. Waddell, eds., Volume 1 (New York: Simon & Schuster, 2015), 81.

37. Robert E. Sherwood, *Roosevelt and Hopkins: An Intimate History* (New York: Harper & Brothers, 1948), 163.

38. "Coalition Cabinet for US Reported Aim of Roosevelt," *NYT*, May 20, 1940, 1.

39. "Landon Rejects Coalition," *NYT*, May 20, 1940, 1.

40. HLS letter to Frank Knox, May 20, 1940, HLSP, Box 134, Folder May 18–20, 1940. Stimson's letter included both the words "solidarity" and "solidity."

41. Stimson had long hoped for a Republican resurgence. See Stimson's discussion of the need to preserve the Republican Party with his old friend Elihu Root, HLSD, October 19, 1934; and his discussion with Republican National Committee chairman John Hamilton on the need to strengthen the Republican Party by bringing more liberals into it, HLSD, April 14, 1937.

42. FDR letter to HLS, May 21, 1940, FDRL, Roosevelt Papers as President, Box 84, War Department, Henry L. Stimson, 1940–41.

43. *The West Point History of World War II*, Volume 1, 84–85.

44. Shirer, *The Rise and Fall of the Third Reich*, 735–737.

45. "Leopold Orders Belgian Army to Quit," *NYT*, May 28, 1940, 1.

46. J. Garry Clifford and Samuel R. Spencer Jr., *The First Peacetime Draft*, (Lawrence, Kansas: University Press of Kansas, 1986), 27–28.

47. Nancy Peterson Hill, *A Very Private Public Citizen: The Life of Grenville Clark* (Columbia, Missouri: University of Missouri Press, 2014), 139–140; "Colonel Knox to Form Air 'Plattsburgs,'" *NYT*, May 18, 1940, 1.

48. Clifford and Spencer, *The First Peacetime Draft*, 56.

49. Godfrey Hodgson, *The Colonel: The Life and Wars of Henry Stimson 1867–1950* (New York: Knopf, 1990), 222–223.

50. Frankfurter letters to FDR of June 4, 1940, and June 5, 1940, Roosevelt Papers as President: The President's Secretary's File (PSF), 1933–1945, Box 135, Frankfurter, Felix, 1940, FDRL.

51. Churchill telegram to HLS, June 1, 1940, Yale University Library, Stimson Papers, Box 134, Folder June 1–3, 1940.

52. *The West Point History of World War II*, Volume 1, 85–86; Shirer, *The Rise and Fall of the Third Reich*, 735–737.

53. Text of Churchill speech in House of Commons, June 4, 1940. International Churchill Society, https://winstonchurchill.org/resources/speeches/1940-the-finest-hour/we-shall-fight-on-the-beaches/, accessed June 9, 2021.

54. Loeb letter to Stimson, June 10, 1940, Yale University Library, Stimson Papers, Box 134, Folder June 9–11, 1940.

55. "Stimson Hails Boys Facing Issues as They Enter World's 'Darkest Hour,'" *NYT*, June 15, 1940, 11.

56. "France Asks Peace, But Is Fighting On," *NYT*, June 18, 1940, 1.

57. "Stimson Demands Military Training," *NYT*, June 19, 1940, 17.

58. HLSD, June 25, 1940.

59. "Knox and Stimson Are Named to Cabinet," *NYT*, June 21, 1940, 1.

60. "Stimson and Knox Disowned by Party," *NYT*, June 21, 1940, 1.

61. Dunn, *1940*, 99.

62. "Roosevelt Move Pleases the British," *NYT*, June 21, 1940, 4.

63. Frankfurter telegram to FDR, June 20, 1940, Frankfurter Papers, Correspondence with Franklin D. and Eleanor Roosevelt, Box 243, Library of Congress.

64. Frankfurter telegram to HLS, June 20, 1940, HLSP, Box 134, Folder June 20, 1940, D-F.

65. Adler telegram to Stimson, June 20, 1940, HLSP, Box 134, Folder June 20, 1940, D-F.

66. Letters from the public to HLS, HLSP, Box 134, Folder June 18, 1940, Anonymous-A-G; Folder June 20, 1940, A-C.

67. "Giant Army Is Aim," *NYT*, June 21, 1940, 1; and "Both Parties Back Selective Service," *NYT*, June 22, 1940, 1.

68. "Willkie Is Called Chief 'Dark Horse,'" *NYT*, May 17, 1940, 5.

69. Charles Peters, *Five Days in Philadelphia: 1940, Wendell Willkie, and the Political Convention That Freed FDR to Win World War II* (New York: Public Affairs, 2005), 69.

70. Ibid., 101–108.

71. Ibid., 110–113.

72. *Hearing Before the Committee on Military Affairs, on the Nomination of Henry L. Stimson to be Secretary of War*, July 2, 1940, US Government Printing Office, 12–13.

73. "Knox Appointment Is Approved," 9–5, *NYT*, July 4, 1940, 8.

74. "Knox and Stimson Approved in Survey," *NYT*, July 5, 1940, 28.

75. HLSD, July 9, 1940.

76. "Stimson Confirmed by Vote of 56–28," *NYT*, July 10, 1940, 1.

77. "$4,848171,957 More Is Asked by Roosevelt for Defense; Not to Send Men to Europe," *NYT*, July 11, 1940, 1.

78. HLSD, July 10, 1940, and August 1, 1940.

CHAPTER 4: UNITING AMERICA

1. "Willkie's Strength Is Revealed in Survey," *NYT*, July 12, 1940, 16.

2. HLSD, July 16, 1940.

3. Rosenman, *Working with Roosevelt*, 211–212.

4. "Army of 2,000,000 a Minimum Need, Marshall Insists," *NYT*, July 18, 1940, 1.

5. "Third Term Statement," *NYT*, July 17, 1940, 1; "Choice Left Open," *NYT*, July 17, 1940, 1.

6. Stimson letter to FDR, July 19, 1940, FDRL, Roosevelt Papers as President, Box 84, War Department, Henry L. Stimson, 1940–41.

7. Marshall letter to Charles J. Graham, September 23, 1941, Box 69, Folder 18, George C. Marshall Papers, George C. Marshall Library and Archives, Lexington, Virginia.

8. Olson, *Those Angry Days*, 190.

9. HLSD, August 3, 1940, and August 8, 1940.

10. HLSD, August 8, 1940.

11. HLSD, August 9, 1940.

12. HLSD, August 13, 1940.

13. Stimson's communications with White regarding Willkie are recorded in Stimson's diaries, located at Yale University, but the author was unable to locate any published accounts of those communications.

14. Doris Kearns Goodwin, *No Ordinary Time: Franklin and Eleanor Roosevelt: The Home Front in World War II* (New York: Simon & Schuster Paperbacks, 1994), 141–142.

15. HLSD, August 16, 1940.

16. A photograph of FDR and Stimson in the car during this inspection appears on this book's cover.

17. Goodwin, *No Ordinary Time,* 143–144.

18. Wendell Willkie, *This Is Wendell Willkie* (New York: Dodd, Mead & Company, 1940), 259; "Willkie for Draft Training," *NYT,* August 18, 1940, 1.

19. HLSD, August 20, 1940.

20. HLSD, August 17, 1940.

21. "US and Britain in Accord on Bases," *NYT,* August 21, 1940, 1.

22. Olson, *Those Angry Days,* 192.

23. OAS, 340–344.

24. Robert A. Lovett Oral History Interview, Harry S. Truman Library website, https://www.trumanlibrary.gov/library/oral-histories/lovett#11, accessed January 22, 2020.

25. Richard Dunlop, *Donovan: America's Master Spy* (New York: Skyhorse Publishing: 2014), 47, 86–88.

26. Ibid., 106–107, 164–169.

27. Ibid., 190.

28. Ibid., 205–206.

29. Kennedy to Hull, diplomatic dispatch, August 7, 1940, *Hostage to Fortune: the Letters of Joseph P. Kennedy,* Amanda Smith, ed. (New York: Viking, 2001), 458.

30. Dunlop, *Donovan,* 219.

31. HLSD, August 6, 1940.

32. Dunlop, *Donovan,* 220–221.

33. Knox broadcast on Columbia Broadcasting System, August 4, 1940, Box 5, FKP.

34. "Defense Post Goes to N. Rockefeller," *NYT,* August 17, 1940, 6.

35. Stimson's close friend William Chanler, a partner at Stimson's law firm, left the firm in 1938 to accept appointment by La Guardia as corporation counsel of New York City.

36. "The Text of Mayor La Guardia's Speech Backing Roosevelt," *NYT,* September 13, 1940, 14.

37. Joseph P. Lash, *Eleanor and Franklin* (New York and London: W.W. Norton & Co., 1971), 669.

38. Thurgood Marshall letter to HLS, July 26, 1940; and HLS letter to T. Marshall, August 2, 1940, in Records of the Adjutant General's Office, 1917– (Record Group 407), Entry NM-3 363-A, Central Decimal Correspondence Files, 1940–1945 filed under War Department decimal 291.21, NARA.

39. Lash, *Eleanor and Franklin,* 669.

40. Marshall letter to HLS, August 7, 1940, Records of the Adjutant General's Office, 1917– (Record Group 407), Entry NM-3 363-A, Central Decimal Correspondence Files, 1940–1945 filed under War Department decimal 291.21, NARA.

41. HLS letter to FDR, August 20, 1940, Records of the Adjutant General's Office, 1917– (Record Group 407), Entry NM-3 363-A, Central Decimal Correspondence Files, 1940–1945 filed under War Department decimal 291.21, NARA.

42. Lash, *Eleanor and Franklin,* 670.

43. "Congress Votes Conscription, Age Limit 21–35," *NYT,* September 15, 1940, 1.

44. "Roosevelt Signs Draft Law," *NYT,* Sept. 17, 1940, 1.

45. Lash, *Eleanor and Franklin,* 670–671; Stenographer's Diary, September 27, 1940, FDRL website, http://www.fdrlibrary.marist.edu/daybyday/daylog/september-27th-1940/, accessed January 31, 2022; Jervis Anderson, *A. Philip Randolph: A Biographical Portrait* (New York: Harcourt Brace Jovanovich, Inc, 1972), 244.

46. HLSD, September 27, 1940.

47. Lash, *Eleanor and Franklin,* 672.

48. "President Roosevelt Okays Jim Crow Army," *The New York Age,* October 19, 1940, 1.

49. "Joe Louis Tours City for Willkie," *NYT,* November 1, 1940, 20.

50. Lash, *Eleanor and Franklin,* 673.

51. Walter White, *A Man Called White* (Athens and London: University of Georgia Press, 1995), 188.

52. HLSD, October 28, 1940.

53. "Lindbergh Assails 'Present' Leaders," *NYT,* October 15, 1940, 1.

54. "Willkie Cites Duty of Nation in Draft," *NYT,* October 16, 1940, 1.

55. "Stimson Answers Willkie on Army," *NYT,* October 18, 1940, 1. Stimson indicated in his diary entry of Thursday, September 19, 1940, that that was the date of his first regular press conference. He held regular news conferences on Thursdays through the next five years of war.

56. HLSD, October 29, 1940.

57. "First Draft Number Is 1–5–8," *NYT,* October 30, 1940, 1.

58. "Washington Hails Roosevelt Return," *NYT,* November 8, 1940, 1.

59. HLS letter to Willkie, November 10, 1940, Papers of Wendell Willkie, Folder: Stimson, Henry L., Box 67, Lilly Library, Indiana University.

60. "Text of Willkie Address Urging 'Loyal Opposition,'" *NYT,* November 12, 1940, 12.

61. HLSD, November 12, 1940.

62. "Oppose Expanding Civil Air Fleet," *NYT,* November 27, 1940, 11.

63. Winston S. Churchill, *Their Finest Hour* (Boston: Houghton Mifflin Company, 1949), 567, 713–714.

64. HLSD, September 17, 1940.

65. HLSD, December 10, 1940.

66. Smith, 483–484.

67. Smith, 485.

68. FDR, "Fireside Chat 16," December 29, 1940, FDR Master Speech File, 1898–1945. Box 58, FDRL.

69. HLSD, December 18, 1940.

70. "President Names a Four-Man Board for Defense Drive," *NYT,* December 21, 1940, 1.

71. Arthur Herman, *Freedom's Forge: How American Business Produced Victory in World War II* (New York: Random House Trade Paperbacks, 2013), 67–71.

72. HLSD, January 2, 1941.

73. HLS note to FDR, undated, FDRL, FDR Papers as President, Box 84, War Department, Henry L. Stimson, 1940–41.
74. FDR note to HLS, January 4, 1941, HLS Papers, Yale Library, Microfilm Reel 103.

CHAPTER 5: A BIPARTISAN CALL TO ARMS

1. HLSD, January 2, 1941.
2. "FDR State of the Union speech, January 6, 1941," FDR Master Speech File, Box 58, FDRL.
3. "Bill Gives President Unlimited Power," and "Opposition Starts," NYT, January 11, 1941, 1.
4. HLSD, January 8, 1941.
5. HLSD, January 11, 1941.
6. "Willkie Statement on the War Aid Bill," NYT, January 13, 1941, 4.
7. "Willkie Endorses 'All-Out' Aid Bill," NYT, January 13, 1941, 1.
8. "'Rotten', 'Dastardly', Roosevelt Says," NYT, January 15, 1941.
9. HLSD, January 13, 1941.
10. "Stimson Sees Danger of Invasion," NYT, January 17, 1941, 1.
11. HLSD, January 17, 1941.
12. "Stimson Sees Crisis in 90 Days," NYT, January 18, 1941, 1.
13. HLSD, January 17, 1941.
14. Knox editorial in Chicago Daily News, January 1941, FKP, Box 5.
15. "Roosevelt Has a Talk with Willkie," NYT, January 20, 1941, 1.
16. Winston S. Churchill, The Grand Alliance: The Second World War (Boston: Houghton Mifflin Company, 1950), 26.
17. Winston S. Churchill, Their Finest Hour: The Second World War (Boston: Houghton Mifflin Company, 1949), 3–26.
18. HLSD, January 20, 1941.
19. "President's Address," NYT, January 21, 1941, 2.
20. "Lindbergh Sees Stalemate, So Urges Negotiated Peace," NYT, January 24, 1941, 1.
21. "Willkie Arrives in London to 'Learn Things'," NYT, January 27, 1941, 1.
22. "Willkie Sees Churchill, Tours Ruins," NYT, January 28, 1941, 1.
23. "Willkie Pays Visit to Coventry Ruins," NYT, February 3, 1941, 5.
24. "House Votes Lend-Lease Bill, 260–165," NYT, February 9, 1941, 1.
25. "Send Britain Bombers, More Destroyers, Willkie Urges," NYT, February 12, 1941, 1.
26. Steve Neal, Dark Horse: A Biography of Wendell Willkie (Garden City, New York: Doubleday & Co., Inc., 1984), 205–206.
27. Ibid., 206.
28. Ibid., 206–207.
29. "Women Hang Effigy Near British Embassy," NYT, February 14, 1941, 5.
30. "Sentiment for Bill Rising, Survey Finds," NYT, February 14, 1941, 5.
31. Lynne Olson, Citizens of London: The Americans Who Stood with Britain in Its Darkest, Finest Hour (New York: Random House, Inc., 2010), 16.
32. Ibid., 22.
33. Ibid., 3.
34. Winant letter to Knox, March 14, 1941, Folder 5, Box 4, Knox Papers, LOC.

35. HLSD, February 7, 1941.
36. Congressional Record—Senate, March 8, 1941, 2052–2061.
37. "Hitler Holds No Aid Can Save Britain," March 17, 1941, *NYT*, 1.
38. "House Votes 7 Billion Fund," *NYT*, March 20, 1941, 1.
39. "President's Address to Jackson Day Diners," *NYT*, March 30, 1941, 42.
40. Smith, *FDR*, 446.
41. "Lindbergh Joins in Wheeler Plea to US to Shun War," *NYT*, May 24, 1941, 1.

CHAPTER 6: THE SEPARATE PEACE

1. Winston S. Churchill, *The Grand Alliance: The Second World War* (Boston: Houghton Mifflin Company, 1950), 782.
2. "Nazi Flyers Report 16 Convoy Ships Hit," *NYT*, February 28, 1941, 1.
3. Olson, *Those Angry Days, Roosevelt, Lindbergh, and America's Fight Over World War II, 1939–1941* (New York: Random House Trade Paperbacks, 2014), 295.
4. HLSD, April 9 and 22, 1941.
5. See, for instance, Olson, *Those Angry Days*, 298.
6. Eleanor Roosevelt, *The Autobiography of Eleanor Roosevelt* (New York: Harper Perennial, 2014), 129–130.
7. Henry Morgenthau Jr. Diary, May 15, 1942, FDRL.
8. HLSD, April 24, 1941.
9. HLSD, Notes after Cabinet Meeting, April 25, 1941; HLSD, April 28, 1941. See, for instance, HLSD, June 19, 1941, and June 23, 1941.
10. "Roosevelt Plans Patrols," *NYT*, April 30, 1941, 1.
11. "Text of Stimson's Radio Appeal to Defend Seas with Navy," *NYT*, May 7, 1941, 14.
12. "Willkie Assails Defeatism," *NYT*, May 8, 1941, 1.
13. HLSD, May 9, 1941.
14. Olson, *Those Angry Days*, 294.
15. HLSD, May 24, 1941.
16. HLSD, May 25, 1941.
17. Niklas Zetterling and Michael Tamelander, *Bismarck: The Final Days of Germany's Largest Battleship* (Philadelphia and Newbury: Casemate, 2009), 266, 296.
18. "Text of the President's Address," *NYT*, May 28, 1941, 2.
19. HLSD, May 28, 1941.
20. Hull, *Memoirs*, Volume 2, 1004–1011.
21. *Investigation of the Pearl Harbor Attack, Report of the Joint Committee on the Investigation of the Pearl Harbor Attack, Congress of the United States* (Washington: Government Printing Office, 1946) 167.
22. Dunlop, *Donovan*, 231; "Donovan Returns to Aid Defense," *St. Louis Globe-Democrat*, March 19, 1941, 6.
23. "Ships Must Get Goods to Britain to Assure Our Aid, Says Donovan," *NYT*, March 27, 1941, 1.
24. Dunlop, *Donovan*, 259.
25. Shirer, *The Rise and Fall of the Third Reich*, 824–286.
26. Dunlop, *Donovan*, 282.
27. Ibid., 285–286.

28. HLSD, June 22, 1941.
29. Leonard Mosley, *Dulles: A Biography of Eleanor, Allen, and John Foster Dulles and Their Family Network* (New York: The Dial Press/James Wade, 1978), 113–114.
30. HLSD, August 12, 1941.
31. HLSD, June 6, 1941.
32. "Army Opens Struck Aviation Plant," *NYT,* June 10, 1941, 1.
33. HLSD, June 9, 1941.
34. "FDR Returns Plane Plant Rule," *NYT,* July 3, 1941, 1.
35. Shirer, *The Rise and Fall of the Third Reich*, 846.
36. HLSD, June 23, 1941.
37. Smith, *FDR,* 496.
38. Ibid., 497.
39. "US Hits Communism, But May Aid Russia," *NYT,* June 24, 1941, 1.
40. "Press Conference #750, June 24, 1941," Press Conferences of President Franklin D. Roosevelt, 1933–1945, FDRL; "Roosevelt to Give All Possible Aid to Russia," *NYT,* June 25, 1941, 1.
41. HLSD, June 3, 1941.
42. HLSD, Stimson letter to FDR, June 23, 1941.
43. "US Occupies Iceland to Thwart Nazi Peril" and "Most in Congress Approve," *NYT,* July 8, 1941, 1.
44. Susan Butler, ed., *My Dear Mr. Stalin: The Complete Correspondence of Franklin D. Roosevelt and Joseph V. Stalin* (New Haven and London: Yale University Press, 2005), 35–36.
45. HLSD, August 1, 1941.
46. John Morton Blum, *From the Morgenthau Diaries: Years of Urgency, 1938–1941* (Boston: Houghton Mifflin Company, 1965), 264.
47. Meacham, *Franklin and Winston,* 5, 106–108; Jean Edward Smith, *FDR,* 499.
48. HLSD, November 13, 1940, and June 30, 1941; "Emergency Bill on Army Service Sent to Congress," *NYT,* July 25, 1941, 1.
49. "Debate on Draft Opened in House," *NYT,* August 9, 1941, 1.
50. "House Votes for 2½ Years Army Service by One Vote," *NYT,* August 13, 1941, 1.
51. Congressional Record, August 14, 1941, 7126.
52. HLSD, August 13, 1941; Congressional Record—Senate, August 14, 1941, 7126.
53. HLSD, August 14, 1941.
54. "Assail Lindbergh for Iowa Speech," *NYT,* September 13, 1941, 1.
55. A. Scott Berg, *Lindbergh* (Berkley Books: New York, 1999), 428–429.
56. "US Destroyer Sunk," *NYT,* November 1, 1941, 1; "Reuben James Toll Is 101," *NYT,* November 9, 1941.
57. Olson, *Those Angry Days,* 404–405.
58. "Willkie Sees Spur in Ship Sinking," November 1, 1941, *NYT,* 2.
59. "Senator Asks End of Neutrality Act," *NYT,* November 2, 1941,
60. "The Vote in the House on the Neutrality Act," *NYT,* November 14, 1941, 4.
61. "Willkie Pleased by House Action," *NYT,* November 14, 1941, 3.
62. Einstein letter to FDR, August 2, 1939, President's Secretary's Files, Safe File, Alexander Sachs, Box 5, FDRL.
63. Vincent C. Jones, *Manhattan: The Army and the Atomic Bomb* (Washington: Center of Military History, US Army, 1985), 28

64. Ibid., 31.

65. Ibid., 33.

66. HLSD, November 6, 1941.

CHAPTER 7: "LET THE NEGRO MASSES MARCH!"

1. Anderson, *A. Philip Randolph*, 26, 32.

2. Ibid., 36, 47, 49.

3. Ibid., 81–85, 98.

4. Ibid., 168, 220–221.

5. Ibid., 242–244.

6. "Let's March on Capital 10,000 Strong, Urges Leader of Porters," *The Pittsburgh Courier*, January 25, 1941, 13.

7. "Tuskegee Selected to Train Flyers," *The Pittsburgh Courier*, January 25, 1941, 1.

8. For Eleanor Roosevelt's support of the American Youth Congress, see Lash, *Eleanor and Franklin*, 687–694, 761–778; "Stimson Rebukes 18 Youth Pickets," *NYT*, February 11, 1941, 11.

9. J. Todd Moye, *Freedom Flyers: The Tuskegee Airmen of World War II* (Oxford and New York: Oxford University Press, 2010), 50–51.

10. HLSD, January 17, 1942.

11. Alexa Mills, "A Lynching Kept Out of Sight," *The Washington Post*, September 2, 2016.

12. Anderson, *A. Philip Randolph*, 251.

13. Randolph letter to Eleanor Roosevelt, June 5, 1941, Anna Eleanor Roosevelt Papers, Box 748, A. Philip Randolph, 1941, FDRL.

14. Anderson, *A. Philip Randolph*, 251.

15. Eleanor Roosevelt letter to Randolph, June 10, 1941, Anna Eleanor Roosevelt Papers, Box 748, A. Philip Randolph, 1941, FDRL.

16. HLSD, June 12, 1941.

17. Patterson memo to Eleanor Roosevelt, June 13, 1941, Anna Eleanor Roosevelt Papers, Box 748, A. Philip Randolph, 1941, FDRL.

18. Anderson, *A. Philip Randolph*, 252.

19. Lash, *Eleanor and Franklin*, 676–677.

20. Anderson, *A. Philip Randolph*, 255.

21. "March on Washington Will be Powerful Evidence," *The New York Age*, June 14, 1941, 1.

22. Anderson, *A. Philip Randolph*, 256–258.

23. White, *A Man Called White*, 192.

24. HLSD, June 18, 1941.

25. White, 191.

26. HLSD, June 18, 1941.

27. HLSD, June 21, 1941.

28. Telegram of A. Philip Randolph to Eleanor Roosevelt, June 24, 1941, Anna Eleanor Roosevelt Papers, Box 748, A. Philip Randolph, 1941, FDRL.

29. Eleanor Roosevelt message to A. Philip Randolph, June 26, 1941, Anna Eleanor Roosevelt Papers, Box 748, A. Philip Randolph, 1941, FDRL.

30. See for example, "President Orders an Even Break for Minorities in Defense Jobs," *NYT*, June 26, 1941, 12.

31. "DuPont, Others to Hire Colored Workers," *The Pittsburgh Courier*, June 28, 1941, 1.

32. White, *A Man Called White*, 193.

33. Anderson, *A. Philip Randolph*, 262.

34. Congressional Record Bound Edition, Appendix, Volume 87—Part 13, July 24, 1941, A3574–A3575.

35. Andrew Edmund Kersten, *Race, Jobs and the War: The FEPC in the Midwest, 1941–46* (Urbana and Chicago: The University of Illinois Press, 2000), 18.

36. There may be published accounts reporting Stimson's role in creation of the FEPC, but if so the author has been unable to locate them.

CHAPTER 8: PEARL HARBOR

1. Joint Committee, *Investigation of the Pearl Harbor Attack*, 23.

2. Toland, *The Rising Sun*, 151.

3. Smith, *FDR*, 506.

4. HLSD, April 23, 1941, and April 24, 1941.

5. Joint Committee, *Investigation of the Pearl Harbor Attack*, 3.

6. Blum, *From the Morgenthau Diaries: Years of Urgency, 1938–1941*, 351.

7. Ibid., 374–375.

8. Ickes, *The Secret Diary of Harold L. Ickes*, 567.

9. FDR letters to Stimson and Knox, July 9, 1941, Box 84, FDR Papers as President, FDRL.

10. HLSD, July 22, 1941; Steve Vogel, *The Pentagon: A History: The Untold Story of the Race to Build the Pentagon—And to Restore it 60 Years Later* (New York: Random House Trade Paperbacks, 2008), 269, 276.

11. Joint Committee, *Investigation of the Pearl Harbor Attack*, 92.

12. "Deal on Far East," *NYT*, July 24, 1941, 1.

13. "US and Britain Freeze Japanese Assets," *NYT*, July 26, 1941, 1; "Japan Is Likely to Get Crude Oil," *NYT*, August 2, 1941, 5.

14. William Manchester, *American Caesar: Douglas MacArthur 1880–1964* (New York, Boston and London: Back Bay Books, 1978), 188–191.

15. *The "Magic" Background of Pearl Harbor*, Volume II Appendix (Washington, DC: US Department of Defense), A-105.

16. Manchester, *American Caesar*, 190.

17. Herbert Feis, *The Road to Pearl Harbor: The Coming of the War Between the United States and Japan* (Princeton, New Jersey: Princeton University Press, 1950), 247–248.

18. Ibid., 248.

19. HLSD, August 9, 1941.

20. Churchill, *The Grand Alliance*, 439–440.

21. HLSD, August 12, 1941.

22. Joint Committee, *Investigation of the Pearl Harbor Attack*, 23.

23. Toland, *The Rising Sun*, 161.

24. Bix, *Hirohito*, 413–414.

25. Joseph Grew, *Turbulent Era: A Record of Forty Years in the US Diplomatic Service* (London: Hammond, Hammond & Co., Ltd.: 1953), 1328–1329.

26. Smith, *FDR,* 521.

27. HLSD, September 12, 1941.

28. HLSD, September 22, 1941, and HLS letter to FDR, September 22, 1941, in HLSD.

29. HLSD, September 29, 1941, and "Roosevelt Asks $5,985,000,000 More," *NYT,* September 19, 1941, 1.

30. Smith, 522.

31. Bix, *Hirohito,* 417–419.

32. HLSD, October 16, 1941. Stimson's original typed diary entry included the phrase "diplomatic touching," but at some point later he inserted by hand the word "fencing" to replace "touching."

33. *Investigation of the Pearl Harbor Attack,* Volume 11, HLS testimony, 5421.

34. HLS letter to FDR, HLSD, October 21, 1941.

35. HLSD, October 28, 1941.

36. Smith, *FDR,* 524.

37. Ibid., 32–33.

38. Hull, *Memoirs,* Volume 2, 1069.

39. HLSD, November 25, 1941.

40. Hull, *Memoirs,* Volume 2, 1083.

41. HLSD, November 26, 1941.

42. Ibid.

43. HLSD, November 27, 1941.

44. Joint Committee, *Investigation of the Pearl Harbor Attack,* 98.

45. Ibid., 102.

46. HLSD, November 28, 1941.

47. Bix, *Hirohito,* 430.

48. Nobutaka Ike, *Japans's Decision for War, Records of the 1941 Policy Conferences,* (Stanford, California: Stanford University Press, 1967), 263.

49. Toland, *The Rising Sun,* 182.

50. HLSD, December 1, 1941.

51. HLSD, December 4, 1941.

52. Stimson statement to the press, HLSD, December 4 and 5, 1941.

53. Hull, *Memoirs,* Volume 2, 1093.

54. HLSD, December 6, 1941.

55. Hull, *Memoirs,* Volume 2, 1093.

56. Joseph Grew, *Ten Years in Japan* (New York: Simon & Schuster, 1944), 487–489.

57. Joint Committee on the Investigation of the Pearl Harbor Attack, Congress of the United States, *Investigation of the Pearl Harbor Attack,* 1946, 64–65.

58. Ibid., 127.

59. Ibid., 65.

60. "B-17 Pilot Flew Unexpectedly into the Middle of Japanese Attack on Pearl Harbor," *Orange County Register,* December 6, 2017, https://www.ocregister.com/2017/12/06/b-17-pilot-flew-unexpectedly-into-the-middle-of-japanese-attack-on-pearl-harbor/, accessed 2.28.2020.

61. Smith, *FDR,* 536.

62. HLSD, December 7, 1941.

63. Hull, *Memoirs*, Volume 2, 1096.
64. Grew, *Ten Years in Japan*, 493.
65. Smith, *FDR*, 537.
66. Ibid., 538.
67. Walter Edmonds, *They Fought With What They Had* (Boston: Little, Brown and Company, 1951), 3, 68, 70, 83, 108.
68. Forrest C. Pogue, *George C. Marshall: Ordeal and Hope, 1939–1942* (New York: The Viking Press, 1965), 234.
69. "The President's Message," *NYT*, December 9, 1941, 1.
70. "Congress Decided," *NYT*, December 8, 1941, 1.
71. "Wheeler Backs War on Japan," *NYT*, December 8, 1941, 6.
72. Congressional Record, December 8, 1941, 9520.
73. HLSD, December 8, 1941.

CHAPTER 9: WORLD WAR, INTERNAL WAR

1. "La Guardia Details Air Raid Behavior," *NYT*, December 9, 1941, 34.
2. HLSD, December 8, 1941.
3. HLSD, December 9, 1941.
4. "The President's Address," *NYT*, December 10, 1941, 1.
5. Winston S. Churchill, *The Second World War: The Grand Alliance* (Boston: Houghton Mifflin Company, 1950), 620.
6. "US Now at War with Germany and Italy," *NYT*, December 12, 1941, 1; "Text Excerpts from the War Speech of Reichsfuehrer in the Reichstag," *NYT*, December 12, 1941, 4.
7. "Knox Reports One Battleship Sunk at Hawaii," *NYT*, December 16, 1941, 1.
8. HLSD, December 15, 1941.
9. "Hawaii Naval, Army, Air Commanders Ousted," *NYT*, December 18, 1941, 1.
10. David L. Roll, *The Hopkins Touch: Harry Hopkins and the Forging of the Alliance to Defeat Hitler* (Oxford: Oxford University Press, 2013), 169.
11. Churchill, *The Grand Alliance*, 665
12. Stimson Memorandum for the President, December 20, 1941, and diary entry December 20, 1941, HLSD.
13. Winston S. Churchill, *Their Finest Hour* (Boston: Houghton Mifflin Company, 1949), 417–437, 487, 505.
14. HLSD, December 23, 1941.
15. HLSD, December 24, 1941.
16. Manuel Quezon, *The Good Fight* (New York and London: D. Appleton–Century Co., 1946), 208–214.
17. HLSD, December 25, 1941.
18. Churchill, *The Grand Alliance*, 663.
19. "Churchill Predicts Huge Allied Drive in 1943," *NYT*, December 27, 1941, 1.
20. "FBI Holds Two Coast Japanese," *Honolulu Advertiser*, June 10, 1941, 1.
21. Hull, *Memoirs*, Volume 2, 1011–1012.
22. David W. Lowman, *Magic: The Untold Story of US Intelligence and the Evacuation of Japanese Residents from the West Coast During WWII* (Athena Press, 2001), 146.
23. Ibid., 146.

24. Hull, *Memoirs*, Volume 2, 1012.

25. Peter Irons, *Justice at War: The Story of the Japanese American Internment Cases* (Berkeley: University of California Press, 1983), 20.

26. John Carter memo on Japanese "Fifth Column" in the Philippines, May 14, 1941; and Stephen Early note to John Carter, May 19, 1941, both FDR Papers as President, President's Secretary's File, 1933–1945, Box 97, Carter, John F., March–October 1941, FDRL.

27. John Franklin Carter memo, November 7, 1941, with C.B. Munson report "Japanese on the West Coast," and FDR note to Stimson, November 8, 1941, all FDR Papers as President, The President's Secretary's File (PSF), 1933–1945, Departmental Correspondence, Box 84, Stimson, Henry L., 1942, FDRL.

28. John Carter memo "Regarding War Department on West Coast Japanese," November 17, 1941, and memo "Report on West Coast Japanese Situation. (Action at Washington)," November 18, 1941, both in FDR Papers as President, President's Secretary's File, 1933–1945, Box 97, Carter, John F., November–December 1941, FDRL.

29. Richard Reeves, *Infamy: The Shocking Story of the Japanese American Internment in World War II* (New York: Picador, 2015), 26.

30. "Axis Aliens Held with Japanese," *NYT*, December 10, 1941, 30.

31. Irons, *Justice at War*, 23–24.

32. Eleanor Roosevelt, My Day, *The Pittsburgh Press*, December 16, 1941, 25.

33. "US Tanker Tried to Ram Submarine in Pacific Fight," *NYT*, December 22, 1941, 1.

34. Reeves, *Infamy*, 25.

35. "1,400 Prisoners on Wake," *NYT*, December 27, 1941, 5.

36. Irons, 27–28.

37. FDR note to HLS, December 29, 1941, FDR Papers as President, Box 84, Stimson, Henry L., FDRL.

38. HLS letter to FDR, February 5, 1942, FDR Papers as President, President's Secretary's File, 1933–1945, Box 98, Carter, John F., January–February 1942, FDRL.

39. "The President's Message," *NYT*, January 7, 1942, 1.

40. Congressional Record, January 20, 1942, 502.

41. Irons, *Justice at War*, 39–40.

42. HLSD, January 20, 1942.

43. Text of the Report of the Roberts Commission, Congressional Record, Appendix, January 24, 1942, A258–A263.

44. Toland, *The Rising Sun*, 152–154, 165–169, 189, 192–193.

45. Irons, *Justice at War*, 40–41.

46. Ibid., 44.

47. Ibid., 45.

48. HLSD, February 3, 1942.

49. Irons, *Justice at War*, 55.

50. HLSD, October 31, 1941, January 17, 1942, and February 13, 1942; Dwight D. Eisenhower, *Crusade in Europe* (New York: Doubleday & Co., Inc., 1948), 25.

51. MacArthur cable to Marshall, February 8, 1942, HLSD, February 9, 10 and 11, 1942.

52. Quezon, in his book *The Good Fight*, wrote that "no representative of the United

States in the Philippines had won my respect and even my personal affection more than did Governor-General Stimson" (pp. 146–147)

53. HLSD, February 9, 1942.
54. Eric Morris, *Corregidor, the American Alamo of World War II* (New York: Cooper Square Press, 2000), 310.
55. HLSD, February 10, 1942.
56. HLSD, February 11, 1942.
57. *Personal Justice Denied: Report of the Commission on Wartime Relocation and Internment of Civilians* (Seattle and London: University of Washington Press, 1997), 82.
58. Irons, *Justice at War,* 59.
59. *The West Point History of World War II,* 200.
60. "Japanese Are Asked to Help Fight Sabotage," *Sacramento Bee,* February 6, 1942, 4.
61. Congressional Record, February 18, 1942, 1412, 1414, 1415.
62. HLSD, February 18, 1942.
63. Executive Order 9066, February 19, 1942.
64. HLSD, February 21, 1942; *Personal Justice Denied: Report of the Commission on Wartime Relocation and Internment of Civilians* (The Civil Liberties Public Education Fund and the University of Washington Press, 1997), 100.
65. Reeves, *Infamy,* 58.
66. Irons, *Justice at War,* 66.
67. Congressional Record, March 19, 1942, 2729–2730, 1222–1226.
68. Irons, *Justice at War,* 68–69, 73.
69. HLSD, May 15, 1942.
70. Irons, *Justice at War,* 73.

CHAPTER 10: WOMEN UNITE FOR THE WAR EFFORT

1. Congressional Record—House, December 12, 1941, 9738.
2. "Drafting of Women Possible but Remote," *NYT,* December 30, 1941, 36.
3. "Stimson Approves Women for Army," *NYT,* December 30, 1941, 14.
4. Pogue, *George C. Marshall,* 103–114.
5. "Big Rush to Enlist in Women's Army," *NYT,* January 1, 1942, 32; "Women Ask Places in Auxiliary Corps," *NYT,* March 15, 1942, 38; "Club Women Back Army Plan," *NYT,* March 31, 1942, 27.
6. Congressional Record—House, May11, 1933, 3289; "Hoover Backs Bill to Waive Quota Act for Reich Children," *NYT,* April 23, 1939, 1; Rosen, *Saving the Jews,* 83–90.
7. "Draft Registration of Women Urged by Mrs. Roosevelt," *The Philadelphia Inquirer,* February 16, 1942, 8.
8. Congressional Record—House, March 17, 1942, 2591, 2593, 2607.
9. "Bill for Women's Auxiliary Corps of 150,000 Passed by the House," *NYT,* March 18. 1942.
10. Walter White telegram to Edith N. Rogers NAACP Records, Box II A651: Women's Army Auxiliary Corps; General, 1942–1944, LOC.
11. HLSD, March 16, 1942.
12. "WAAC Will Begin Recruiting Soon," *NYT,* May 14, 1942, 16.

13. Congressional Record—Senate, May 12, 1942, 4085–4093.

14. HLSD, May 16, 1942.

15. "Mary Bethune Endorses WAAC," *The Pittsburgh Courier,* June 6, 1942, 9.

16. Ibid.

17. Congressional Record—House, April 16, 1942, 3514.

18. Congressional Record—Senate, July 2, 1942, 5922.

19. Congressional Record—House, July 21, 1942, 6467–6468.

20. "Women Navy Corps Will Enroll 11,000," *NYT,* July 31, 1942, 7.

21. Jean Ebbert and Marie-Beth Hall, *Crossed Currents: Navy Women in a Century of Change* (Washington and London: Brassey's, 1999), 54.

22. Morris J. McGregor Jr., *Integration of the Armed Forces, 1940–1965* (Washington: Center of Military History, United States Army, 2001), 87.

23. Ibid., 99–100.

24. Congressional Record—House, October 14, 1942, 8179–8181.

25. "'SPARS' Taken Over by Miss Stratton," *NYT,* November 24, 1942, 20.

26. Jacqueline Cochran and Maryann Bucknum Brinley, *Jackie Cochran: The Autobiography of the Greatest Woman Pilot in Aviation History* (New York: Bantam Books, 1987), 181–183, 188–190, 196–200.

27. Ibid., 207.

28. HLSD, September 10, 1942.

29. Cochran and Brinley, *Jackie Cochran,* 210.

30. "Patricia Warner, an Unlikely World War II Spy, Dies at 99," *The Boston Sunday Globe,* October 24, 2020. Patricia Cutler Fowler, who later married Charles Warner, was the author's aunt. Her sister, Judith Cutler Shinkle, the author's mother, also briefly served in the OSS.

31. "US Woman Seized at Front by Nazis," *NYT,* October 25, 1944, 9; "First US Woman Seized by Foe in West Escapes," *NYT,* March 25, 1945, 8.

32. Herman, *Freedom's Forge,* 204.

33. FDR, "Fireside Chat 23," October 12, 1942, Miller Center, University of Virginia, https://millercenter.org/the-presidency/presidential-speeches/october-12–1942 -fireside-chat-23-home-front, accessed November 15, 2020.

34. Herman, *Freedom's Forge,* 263.

35. "Sponsor of WAACs to See Graduation," *NYT,* August 29, 1942, 13.

36. "Mrs. Bethune Scores WAAC Segregation, Denies She Approves," *The New York Age,* November 21, 1942, 12.

37. Jones, *Manhattan,* 358.

38. Jason Fagone, *The Woman Who Smashed Codes: A True Story of Love, Spies, and the Unlikely Heroine Who Outwitted America's Enemies* (New York: Dey St., 2017), 252, 253.

39. Ibid., 197–202,

40. "WAAC Captain Describes Torpedoing Off Oran," *Lancaster New Era* (Pennsylvania), January 19, 1943, 1.

41. "Capitol Stuff," *Daily News,* June 7, 1943, 4; "Capitol Stuff," *Daily News,* June 9, 1943, 4.

42. "Stimson Condemns Gossip About WAAC," *NYT,* June 11, 1943, 6.

43. Eleanor Roosevelt, My Day, *Detroit Free Press,* June 12, 1943, 4.

44. "WAACS Now in Army," *NYT,* July 3, 1943, 16.

CHAPTER 11: THE DOUBLE V: BLACK AMERICA'S STRUGGLE

1. "The Courier's Double 'V' for a Double Victory Campaign Gets Country-Wide Support," *The Pittsburgh Courier*, February 14, 1942, 1.
2. "'VV' Clubs and Affiliate Members," *The Pittsburgh Courier*, June 13, 1942, 12.
3. Smithsonian Museum of American History, Behring Center, online, https://americanhistory.si.edu/blog/music-inspiring-objects, accessed July 16, 2020.
4. "Negro Is Lynched by Missouri Crowd," *NYT*, January 26, 1942, 17.
5. "Sikeston Disgraces Itself," *NYT*, January 27, 1942, 20.
6. HLSD, January 17, 1942.
7. HLSD, February 16, 1942.
8. Rawn James Jr., *The Double V: How Wars, Protest, and Harry Truman Desegregated America's Military* (New York: Bloomsbury Press, 2013), 129–130.
9. "MacLeish Assails 'Defeatists' in US as Chief Enemies," *NYT*, March 20, 1942, 1.
10. James, *The Double V*, 132.
11. Ibid., 131.
12. Ibid., 131–132.
13. Knox letter to Paul Mowrer, April 30, 1942, Folder 6, Box 4, FKP.
14. "Navy Combat Units Opened to Negroes", *NYT*, April 8, 1942, 11.
15. "Navy Cross to Negro, A Pearl Harbor Hero," *NYT*, May 12, 1942, 3.
16. James, *The Double V*, 132.
17. Christopher Paul Moore, *Fighting for America: Black Soldiers—the Unsung Heroes of World War II* (New York: Ballantine Books, 2006), 34–38.
18. Ibid., 47, 56–60.
19. "Army Board Sifts Fort Dix Shooting," *NYT*, April 4, 1942, 14.
20. "US Orders Probe in Shooting of Colored Soldier," *The Pittsburgh Courier*, May 16, 1942, 1.
21. "Mississippi Mob Lynches a Slayer," *NYT*, October 18, 1942, 49.
22. "Hitler in Mississippi," *NYT*, October 21, 1942, 20.
23. "Lodges Protest on Slaying of Soldier," *The Pittsburgh Courier*, November 28, 1942, 1.
24. HLSD, December 22, 1942.
25. HLSD, November 20, 1942.
26. "Robeson Entertains Fort Warren Troops," *The Pittsburgh Courier*, March 13, 1943, 20.
27. HLSD, January 13, 1942.
28. "Hastie Says Discriminatory Army Air Force Caused His Resignation," *New York Age*, February 6, 1943.
29. Hastie Oral History Interview, HSTL, https://www.trumanlibrary.org/oralhist /hastie.htm, accessed April 4, 2019.
30. "Status of Negro Called Challenge," *NYT*, January 29, 1943, 28.
31. "10 Holders of Big War Contracts Ordered to Cease Discrimination," *NYT*, April 13, 1942.
32. "Tells 8 Concerns to Life Race Bars," *NYT*, May 27, 1942, 17.
33. Kersten, *Race, Jobs and the War*, 116–118.
34. Ibid., 117; "Training to Begin for All-Negro Ammunition Unit," *St. Louis Post-Dispatch*, June 21, 1942, 4.

35. "25,000 Roar Approval," *The Pittsburgh Courier,* June 27, 1942, 1.
36. FDR, Fireside Chat 23, October 12, 1942, Miller Center, University of Virginia, https://millercenter.org/the-presidency/presidential-speeches/october-12–1942 -fireside-chat-23-home-front, accessed November 15, 2020.
37. "Job Discrimination Debated in the South," *NYT,* July 2, 1942, 44.
38. "Terror Campaign Threatened," *The Pittsburgh Courier,* December 12, 1942, 5.
39. Congressional Record, Appendix, Volume 88—Part 10, December 10, 1942, A4242.

CHAPTER 12: THE US GOES ON THE OFFENSIVE

1. Smith, *FDR,* 542.
2. Pogue, *George C. Marshall,* 304, 306.
3. Nigel Hamilton, *The Mantle of Command: FDR at War, 1941–1942* (Boston and New York: Houghton Mifflin Harcourt, 2014), 102–107.
4. Winston S. Churchill, *The Second World War: The Grand Alliance* (Boston: Houghton Mifflin Company, 1950), 705.
5. HLSD, January 12, 1942.
6. Joseph W. Stilwell, *The Stilwell Papers* (New York: William Sloane Associates, Inc., 1948), 15–16.
7. HLSD, January 14, 1942.
8. Pogue, *George C. Marshall,* 360–361.
9. Barbara Tuchman, *Stilwell and the American Experience in China, 1911–45* (New York: The Macmillan Company, 1970), 243.
10. HLSD, January 23, 1942.
11. Stilwell, 36.
12. HLSD, March 24, 1942.
13. Pogue, *George C. Marshall,* 304, 306.
14. HLSD, March 25, 1942.
15. Roll, 185.
16. HLSD, March 27, 1942.
17. *Hostage to Fortune The Letters of Joseph P. Kennedy*, 545. The abbreviation "Sec'y" in the original has been spelled out for clarity.
18. "Mr. Lindbergh Volunteers," *NYT,* December 31, 1941, 16.
19. Knox letter to FDR, January 1, 1942; FDR memo to HLS, January 12, 1942; both President's Secretary's Files, Box 84, War-Stimson, 1942, FDRL.
20. HLSD, January 12, 1942.
21. HLS letter to FDR, January 13, 1942; President's Secretary's Files, Box 84, War-Stimson, 1942, FDRL.
22. "Lindbergh to Aid in Army Research," *NYT,* January 16, 1942, 15.
23. Marshall, George C., April 1942, Box 61, Folder 49, George C. Marshall Papers, George C. Marshall Foundation, Lexington, VA.; Pogue, *George C. Marshall,* 306.
24. HLSD, April 1, 1942.
25. Roll, 186.
26. Alan Brooke, *War Diaries, 1939–1945: Field Marshal Lord Alanbrooke,* eds. Alex Danchev and Daniel Todman, (London: Phoenix, 2003), 245.
27. Booke, *War Diaries,* 246; Pogue, *George C. Marshall,* 308.

28. Hamilton, *The Mantle of Command,* 240–241; WSC cable to FDR, April 7, 1942, FDR Papers as President, Map Room Papers, Box 2, Churchill to FDR, March–April 1942, FDRL; Admiralty message, April 6, 1942, FDR Papers as President, Map Room Papers, Box 39, Indian Ocean, FDRL; HLSD, April 11, 1942.

29. Winston S. Churchill, *Hinge of Fate* (Boston: Houghton Mifflin Company, 1950), 208–214; Roosevelt, with Welles, telegram to Churchill, April 11, 1942, 2 p.m., Document 530, *FRUS: Diplomatic Papers, 1942, General; The British Commonwealth; The Far East,* Volume I, (Washington, DC: Government Printing Office, 1960).

30. HLSD, April 22, 1942.

31. Warren F. Kimball, ed., *Churchill & Roosevelt, the Complete Correspondence,* Volume I: *Alliance Emerging* (Princeton: Princeton University Press, 1984), 447–448.

32. HLSD, April 22, 1942.

33. WSC cable to FDR, April 12, 1942, FDR Papers as President, Map Room Papers, Box 2, Churchill to FDR, March–April 1942, FDRL.

34. Marshall telegram to Stimson, April 15, 1942, Records of the War Department General and Special Staffs (RG 165), Records of the Operations Division (OPD), Executive File 1, Item 5c, NARA.

35. Marshall had in effect already conceded this point; the War Department cross-channel invasion plan, in recognition of the strength of Nazi defenses in Europe, had said an attack on the European Continent in 1942 would be feasible only if for some reason those Nazi defenses collapsed.

36. For example, Andrew Roberts, in his book *Churchill: Walking with Destiny* (New York: Viking, 2018), termed Churchill's cable to FDR "disingenuous" (p. 727). Pogue, in *George C. Marshall,* noted that Lord Hastings Ismay, a senior military adviser to Churchill, acknowledged that Marshall and Hopkins "went happily homewards under the mistaken impression that we had committed ourselves" to the cross-channel attack plan.

37. Bix, *Hirohito,* 447.

38. Eric Morris, *Corregidor, the American Alamo of World War II* (New York: Cooper Square Press, 2000), 405.

39. Stimson had arrived at his office at 7:00 a.m. on April 9 and been informed of the surrender. HLSD, April 9, 1942.

40. "In Corregidor, Bad Memories for Men of 3 Nations," *NYT,* April 14, 1982, 2.

41. Carroll V. Glines, *The Doolittle Raid, America's Daring First Strike Against Japan* (New York: Orion Books, 1988), 52–54.

42. Ibid., 62, 65–67, 69.

43. Ibid., 79.

44. "President Puts Raiders of Tokyo at 'Shangri-La,'" *NYT,*

45. HLSD, April 18, 1942.

46. Glines, *The Doolittle Raid,* 140–142.

47. HLSD, April 30, 1942.

48. Morris, *Corregidor,* 445–447.

49. "Corregidor Surrenders Under Land Attack," *NYT,* May 6, 1942, 1.

50. Elizabeth M. Norman, *We Band of Angels, the Untold Story of the American Women Trapped on Bataan* (New York: Random House Trade Paperbacks, 2013), 111.

51. "Troops Half-Starved," *NYT,* May 6, 1942, 1.

52. *The West Point History of World War II*, 222–230.

53. "2, Perhaps 3, Japanese Carriers Sunk," *NYT,* June 7, 1942.

54. HLSD, April 23 and May 21, 1942; OAS, 509–510.

CHAPTER 13: FDR TAKES COMMAND

1. Winston S. Churchill, *The Second World War,* Volume IV: *The Hinge of Fate,* (Boston: Houghton Mifflin Company, 1950) 340.

2. Sherwood, *Roosevelt and Hopkins,* 563, 574, 575.

3. Ibid., 577.

4. "Molotoff and Roosevelt Plan for 2d Front," *NYT,* June 12, 1942.

5. "Rally Here Urges Second Front Now," *NYT,* July 23, 1942, 4.

6. HLSD, June 17, 1942.

7. HLSD, June 19, 1942.

8. HLSD, June 20, 1942.

9. Churchill, *The Hinge of Fate,* 381–382.

10. Ibid., 382–383.

11. Ibid., 385.

12. HLSD, June 21, 1942. Before the meeting that night, one of the participants, Sir John Dill, senior British representative on the Combined General Staff, had taken his wife to spend that afternoon with the Stimsons at Woodley.

13. HLSD, June 22, 1942.

14. HLSD, June 22, 1942, and combined entry of 23, 24 and 25, 1942.

15. Brooke, *War Diaries,* 273.

16. Brooke, *War Diaries,* 187; for Churchill's suggestion of the Norway invasion to FDR, see WSC cable to FDR of May 28, 1942, in Churchill, *The Second World War: Volume IV, The Hinge of Fate,* 340.

17. HLSD, June 23–25, 1942.

18. WSC letter to HLS, June 25, 1942, and HLS note to WSC, June 26, 1942, both after diary entry of June 25, 1942, HLSD.

19. WSC cable to FDR, July 8, 1942, FDR Papers as President, Map Room Papers, Box 2, Churchill to FDR, May–July 1942, FDRL.

20. HLSD, July 10, 1942.

21. HLSD, July 12, 1942.

22. Roll, 210.

23. The book was William Robertson's *Soldiers and Statesmen 1914–1918* (London: Cassell and Company, Ltd., 1926); see in particular pages 73–98.

24. Peter Hart, *Gallipoli* (New York: Oxford University Press, 2011), 452.

25. Andrew Roberts, *Churchill: Walking with Destiny* (Viking, 2018), 211–218.

26. HLSD, July 15, 1942.

27. Churchill, *The Hinge of Fate,* 441–444.

28. Brooke, *War Diaries,* 282; Roll, *The Hopkins Touch,* 216.

29. Harry C. Butcher, *My Three Years with Eisenhower: The Personal Diary of Captain Harry C. Butcher, USNR, Naval Aide to General Eisenhower, 1942–1945* (New York: Simon & Schuster, 1946), 29.

30. HLSD, July 23, 1942.

31. Brooke, *War Diaries,* 284.

32. Brooke, *War Diaries*, 285.

33. HLSD, July 25, 1942.

34. HLSD, July 25, 1942.

35. Hamilton, *The Mantle of Command*, 359–361.

36. Forrest C. Pogue, *George C. Marshall*, 298–301.

37. "Leahy Will Do Detail Work to Help President Plan War," *NYT*, July 22, 1942, 1.

38. FDR press conference, July 21, 1942, Press Conferences of President Franklin D. Roosevelt, 1933–1945, FDRL.

39. Churchill, *Hinge of Fate*, 448, 449.

40. "Lodge Is Returned to Inactive Status," *NYT*, July 9, 1992.

41. Margaret Suckley *Closest Companion: The Unknown Story of the Intimate Friendship between Franklin Roosevelt and Margaret Suckley*, Geoffrey C. Ward, ed. (Boston and New York: Houghton Mifflin Co., 1995), 169.

42. HLSD, July 24, 1942.

43. Roll, *The Hopkins Touch*, 217–218.

44. Pogue, *George C. Marshall*, 330, 402.

45. HLSD, August 7 and 9, 1942.

46. HLSD, September 17, 1942.

47. Ibid.

48. Ibid.

49. *NYT*, September 21, 1942, 14.

50. HLSP, Reel 106, 1942 No date to August 30, 1942.

51. There is no record of a card from FDR, though there is no known reason for this. It is possible that FDR sent a birthday note to Stimson but it was not retained in Stimson's files. It also is possible that FDR didn't send a card simply because of his hectic schedule.

52. Sean L. Malloy, *Atomic Tragedy: Henry L. Stimson and the Decision to Use the Bomb Against Japan* (Ithaca and New York: Cornell University Press, 2008), 80.

53. Pogue, *George C. Marshall*, 383; Richard B. Frank, *Guadalcanal: the Definitive Account of the Landmark Battle* (London: Penguin Books, 1990), 53.

54. Churchill, *Hinge of Fate*, 450; FDR cable to Churchill, August 6, 1942, FDR Papers as President, Map Room Papers, Box 2, Churchill to FDR, March–April 1942, FDRL.

55. Eisenhower memo to Marshall, August 15, 1942, quoted in Eisenhower, *Crusade in Europe*, 91–93.

56. Churchill, *Hinge of Fate*, 606–607.

57. George F. Howe, *Northwest Africa: Seizing the Initiative in the West* (US Army Center of Military History: Washington, DC, 1993), 65.

58. Eisenhower, *Crusade in Europe*, 103–104, 107.

59. Butcher, *My Three Years with Eisenhower*, 145–146; Howe, *Northwest Africa*, 173.

60. Mark Perry, *Partners in Command: George Marshall and Dwight Eisenhower in War and Peace* (New York: Penguin Books, 2007), 139.

61. "Roosevelt Eases Fears of French," *NYT*, November 18, 1942, 4; "President Says Darlan Deal Is a 'Temporary Expedient,'" *NYT*, November 18, 1942, 1; Sherwood, *Roosevelt and Hopkins*, 653–654.

62. Transcript of Murrow broadcast, November 15, 1942, Henry Morgenthau Jr. Diaries (MD), Book 584, 116–119, FDRL.

63. Eisenhower, *Crusade in Europe*, 109–110.

64. HLSD, November 16, 1942.
65. "Willkie Demands Frank Discussion of War Aims," *NYT,* November 17, 1942, 1.
66. HLSD, November 16, 1942.
67. "President Says Darlan Deal Is a 'Temporary Expedient,'" *NYT,* November 18, 1.
68. HLS letter to Willkie, November 17, 1942, and Willkie reply to Stimson, November 24, 1942, Folder: Stimson, Henry L., Box 67, Willkie mss., Lilly Library, Indiana University, Bloomington, Indiana.
69. Vogel, *The Pentagon,* 284, 291.
70. HLSD, November 16, 1942.
71. Vogel, *The Pentagon,* 271, 272, 284, 285.
72. "Wise Gets Confirmations," *NYT,* November 25, 1942, 10.
73. David S. Wyman, *The Abandonment of the Jews: America and the Holocaust 1941–1945* (New York: Pantheon Books, 1984), 51–52.
74. "11 Allies Condemn Nazi War on Jews," *NYT,* December 18, 1942, 1.
75. "Roosevelt, Churchill Map 1943 War Strategy," *NYT,* January 27, 1943, 1.

CHAPTER 14: WILLKIE TAKES THE STAGE

1. "Willkie to Start Abroad in 3 Weeks," *NYT,* August 21, 1942, 14.
2. FDR Press Conference, August 21, 1942, Press Conferences of the President, 1933–1945, FDRL.
3. Willkie letter to FDR, March 6, 1942, FDR Papers as President, Box 173, Wendell Willkie, FDRL.
4. "Willkie Wins Republicans to His Anti-Isolation Stand," *NYT,* April 21, 1942, 1.
5. "Text of Mr. Willkie's Address at Union College," *NYT,* May 12, 1941, 9.
6. FDR note to Willkie, April 15, 1942; Willkie note to FDR, April 21, 1942; FDR Papers as President, Box 173, Folder: Willkie, September 1940–September 1942, FDRL.
7. "Hill Gets Prison on Perjury Charge," *NYT,* February 7, 1942, 19; "Fish Shouts 'Lie' at Viereck Trial," *NYT,* February 21, 1942, 7; "Viereck Convicted of False Registry," *NYT,* March 6, 1942, 1.
8. Willkie letter to FDR, June 2, 1942, FDR Papers as President, Box 173, Folder: Willkie, September 1940–September 1942, FDRL.
9. "Wendell Willkie Answers Eighteen Blunt Questions," *Look,* April 7, 1942, 16–17.
10. "Full News of War Promised by Davis," *NYT,* July 11, 1942, 1.
11. Willkie letter to FDR, July 29, 1942; FDR note to Marshall, July 31, 1942; General Joseph McNarney memo to FDR, July 31, 1942; and FDR telegram to Willkie, August 2, 1942, all FDR Papers as President, Box 173, Wendell Willkie, FDRL.
12. "Willkie May Visit Russia, Near East," *NYT,* August 8, 1942, 1.
13. FDR letter to Stalin, August 8, 1942; and Stalin reply to FDR, August 12, 1942, both Butler, *My Dear Mr. Stalin,* 82–83.
14. Arthur Herman, *Gandhi and Churchill: The Epic Rivalry That Destroyed an Empire and Forged Our Age* (New York: Bantam Books, 2009), 494.
15. FDR telegrams to Churchill, August 11 and 13, 1942, FDR Papers as President, Map Room Papers, 1941–1945, Box 2, FDR-Churchill August–October 1942, FDRL.
16. FDR Press Conference, August 21, 1942, Press Conferences of the President, 1933–1945, FDRL.

17. Samuel Zipp, *The Idealist: Wendell Willkie's Wartime Quest to Build One World* (Cambridge, Mass. and London: Belknap, 2020), 52.

18. Ibid., 1.

19. "Willkie in Egypt Says 'Give 'Em Hell,'" *NYT*, September 4, 1942, 3.

20. Zipp, *The Idealist*, 65, 66; "Willkie Terms Blow Dealt Rommel," *NYT*, September 7, 1942, 3.

21. "Turkey Heartened by Willkie's Visit," *NYT*, September 11, 1942, 4. Emphasis is the author's.

22. "Willkie Supports Second-Front Plea," *NYT*, September 22, 1942, 6.

23. Neal, *Dark Horse*, 245–247.

24. Lewis, *The Improbable Wendell Willkie*, 248.

25. "Text of Willkie Statement," *The Minneapolis Star*, September 27, 1942, 12.

26. "Second Front Debate Reaches Thorny Stage," October 4, 1942, *NYT*, 118.

27. FDR Press Conference, October 6, 1942, Press Conferences of the President, 1933–1945, FDRL.

28. Neal, *Dark Horse*, 253, 254.

29. John Paton Davies, *Dragon by the Tail: American, British, Japanese, and Russian Encounters With China and One Another* (New York: W.W. Norton & Company, 1972), 257–258.

30. "Global Offensive Urged by Willkie," *NYT*, October 7, 1942, 1.

31. "Japanese Shoot Twice at Willkie" and "Station Shelled Before Arrival," *NYT*, October 10, 1942, 4.

32. Willkie, *One World*, 1.

33. "Willkie Reports, Then Renews Call for Second Front," *NYT*, October 15, 1942, 1.

34. FDR Press Conference October 16, 1942, Press Conferences of the President, 1933–1945, FDRL.

35. "Willkie Demands Second Front, Burma Drive," *NYT*, October 27, 1942, 1.

36. "Text of Willkie's Address to the Nation," *NYT*, October 27, 1942, 8.

37. "Willkie is New Challenge to FDR," *The Berkshire Eagle*, October 29, 1942, 12.

38. Neal, *Dark Horse*, 261.

39. "Charter Says 'All,' President Replies," *NYT*, October 28, 1942, 4.

40. Zipp, *The Idealist*, 208.

41. Official Congressional Directory, 78th Congress, 1st Session (Washington: Government Printing Office, 1942), 142.

42. "Communist's Case Argued by Willkie," *NYT*, November 10, 1942, 1; "Red's Citizenship Declared Valid," *NYT*, June 22, 1943, 1; Lewis, *The Improbable Wendell Willkie*, 271.

43. "Save Doomed Jews, Huge Rally Pleads," *NYT*, March 2, 1943, 1.

44. Willkie, *One World*, 174.

45. Ibid., 184–185.

46. Ibid., 190–191.

47. See, for example, "Queeny Demands Willkie's Stand on 'Union Now,'" *St. Louis Post-Dispatch*, October 12, 1943, 3.

48. HLSD, June 29, 1943.

49. Manu Bhagavan, *The Peacemakers: India and the Quest for One World* (New Delhi: HarperCollins Publishers India, 2012), 29–30.

CHAPTER 15: THE 1943 RACE RIOTS: HATE, BLOOD AND FIRE

1. Knox address in Springfield, Illinois, on February 12, 1943, Box 7, FKP, LOC; "Knox Asks Sinews to Enforce Peace," *NYT,* February 13, 1943, 7.
2. Bruce Nelson, "Organized Labor and the Struggle for Black Equality in Mobile During World War II," *The Journal of American History,* December 1993, Volume 80, No. 3, 979.
3. "Mobile Race Riot Laid to Company," *NYT,* June 13, 1943, 34.
4. Kersten, *Race, Jobs and the War,* 95, 106. "Detroit Elects Bowles Mayor," *The Baltimore Evening Sun,* November 6, 1929, 1.
5. "Justice and the Black Legion," *The Philadelphia Inquirer,* February 28, 1937, 14.
6. Walter White letter to Eleanor Roosevelt, August 28, 1942, Folder 6, Selected Digitized Correspondence of Eleanor Roosevelt, 1933–1945, FDRL; also, "New Board Set Up to End Hiring Bias," *NYT,* May 29, 1941, 6.
7. "Packard Men Start Back," *Detroit Free Press,* June 7, 1943, 1.
8. Kevin Hillstrom, *Defining Moments: The Zoot Suit Riots* (Detroit: Omnigraphics, Inc., 2012), 78–79.
9. Ibid., 82.
10. "Army Takes a Hand in Zoot Suit Frays," *NYT,* June 12, 1943, 28.
11. James A. Burran, "Violence in an 'Arsenal of Democracy': the Beaumont Race Riot, 1943," *East Texas Historical Journal,* 1976, Volume 14, Issue 1, Article 8, 43, 44.
12. Ibid., 44–47.
13. Robert Shogan and Tom Craig, *The Detroit Race Riot: A Study in Violence* (Philadelphia and New York: Chilton Books, 1964), 34–37.
14. Ibid., 39.
15. Ibid., 56.
16. "Martial Law at 10 P.M.," *Detroit Free Press,* June 22, 1943, 1.
17. Shogan and Craig, *The Detroit Race Riot,* 48.
18. "Six Die in Detroit Race Riots," *Poughkeepsie Journal* (Poughkeepsie, N.Y.), June 21, 1943, 1.
19. "Martial Law at 10 P.M.," *Detroit Free Press* June 22, 1943, 1; Shogan and Craig, *The Detroit Race Riot,* 77.
20. HLSD, June 21, 1943.
21. "Proclamation by President Demands Rioters 'Disperse,'" *NYT,* June 22, 1943, 1.
22. Shogan and Craig, 80–81.
23. Ibid., 89.
24. Ibid., 87, 101.
25. Ibid., 98.
26. "President Adds to C.F.E.P.," *NYT,* July 2, 1943, 11.
27. "Decides Against March on Capital," *NYT,* July 4, 1943, 12.
28. HLSD, July 5, 1942.
29. Shogan and Craig, 91.
30. Nat Brandt, *Harlem at War: The Black Experience in WWII* (Syracuse, N.Y.: Syracuse University Press, 1996), front pages.
31. Correspondence between Willkie and White, Box 109, folder July 24, 1943, Open Letter on Race Hatred, Willkie mss. collection, Indiana University Library.
32. "Willkie Blasts 'Hate,'" *The Pittsburgh Courier,* July 31, 1943, 1.

33. Ibid.
34. "Wallace Assails American Fascists," *NYT*, July 25, 1943, 25.
35. Brandt, *Harlem at War*, 184–186.
36. Ibid., 188.
37. James Baldwin, *Notes of a Native Son* (Boston: Beacon Press, 1955), 111.
38. Brandt, *Harlem at War*, 191–193.
39. Ibid., 197–198, 205–206.
40. Ibid., 208.

CHAPTER 16: POWER, ADVICE AND DISSENT

1. HLSD, January 7, 1943.
2. Forrest C. Pogue, *George C. Marshall: Organizer of Victory, 1943–1945* (New York: The Viking Press, 1973), 31.
3. HLSD, January 19, 1943.
4. HLSD, January 21, 1943.
5. Brooke, *War Diaries*, 364.
6. Meacham, *Franklin and Winston*, 207.
7. HLSD, February 3, 1943.
8. Bill Hosokawa, *JACL in Quest of Justice: The History of the Japanese American Citizens League* (New York: William Morrow & Co. Inc., 1982), 210.
9. "Army Opens Ranks to Japanese Units," *NYT*, January 29, 1943, 9. The plan to create an all-Nisei unit drew objections because it segregated the Nisei, but segregated units were deemed necessary to avoid situations in which white soldiers might attack the Nisei or place them in harm's way.
10. "Praises Army Plan for Japanese Unit," *NYT*, February 5, 1942, 6.
11. Bill Hosokawa, *JACL in Quest of Justice*, 269.
12. Ibid., 214–215.
13. Reeves, *Infamy*, 147–148; Nigel Hamilton, *Commander in Chief: FDR's Battle with Churchill, 1943* (Boston and New York: Houghton Mifflin Harcourt, 2016), 184–186.
14. *The West Point History of World War II*, Volume 2, 114.
15. "Stimson Reports a 'Sharp Reverse,'" *NYT*, February 19, 1943, 1.
16. Hamilton, *Commander in Chief*, 144–145.
17. *The West Point History of World War II*, Volume 2, 115.
18. "Rommel Reels Back, Pounded by Planes," *NYT*, February 25, 1943, 1.
19. "'Clean Cut Repulse' in Tunisia," *NYT*, February 26, 1943, 1; FDR Daily Calendar, FDRL, http://www.fdrlibrary.marist.edu/daybyday/daylog/february-25th-1943/, accessed November 17, 2020.
20. White House Usher's Log, February 25, 1943, FDRL, http://www.fdrlibrary.marist.edu/daybyday/daylog/february-25th-1943/, accessed January 15, 2022.
21. "Peril to Cut Army, Stimson Asserts," *NYT*, March 10, 1943, 1.
22. "Senate Votes 82–0," NYT, March 12, 1943, 1.
23. OAS, 508, 510, 511.
24. Conant, *Tuxedo Park*, 131.
25. "Edward L. Bowles, Engineer," *NYT*, September 7, 1990, D19; "The AAF

Antisubmarine Command," prepared by Assistant Chief of Air Staff, Intelligence, Historical Division, US Department of War, April 1945, 66.

26. King letter to Marshall, June 21, 1942, quoted in OAS, 511.

27. See, for instance, HLSD, April 14, 1942, and March 25, 1943.

28. "The AAF Antisubmarine Command," US Department of War, 22–23.

29. Ibid., 82; Samuel Eliot Morison, *The Atlantic Battle Won: May 1943–May 1945* (Edison, N.J.: Castle Books, 2001), 29.

30. Norman Polmar and Edward Whitman, *Hunters and Killers, Volume 2: Anti-Submarine Warfare from 1943* (Annapolis Md., Naval Institute Press, 2016), 7.

31. Churchill cable to FDR, July 13, 1943, C-362, and Churchill cable to FDR, July 14, 29143, *Churchill & Roosevelt: The Complete Correspondence, Volume 2: Alliance Forged*, Warren F. Kimball, ed. (Princeton, New Jersey: Princeton University Press, 1984), 323.

32. Morison, *The Atlantic Battle Won*, 29.

33. Transcript of Conversation of the Secretary of War and Senator Truman, June 17, 1943, Atomic Bomb Collection, Box 2, HSTL; Harry S. Truman, *1945: Year of Decisions* (New York: Konecky & Konecky, 1955), 10.

34. Biddle letter to HLS, January 1, 1943, Correspondence, 1943 N.D.–1943 April 30, HLSP.

35. Sherwood, 725. For Mayor Fiorello La Guardia's broadcasts, Columbus Day 1944, and La Guardia's broadcasts to Italy during World War II, New York City Department of Records & Information Services, https://www.archives.nyc/blog/2019/10/9/columbus-day-1944-mayor-fiorello-laguardias-broadcasts-to-italy, accessed November 22, 2020.

36. HLSD, March 27, 1943.

37. HLS letter to FDR, April 6, 1943, FDR Papers as President, Box 84, War Department—Henry L. Stimson, FDRL.

38. HLSD, April 7, 1943.

39. "Army Won't Take La Guardia Now; Needed as Mayor, Stimson Says," *NYT*, April 9, 1943, 1.

40. HLSD, April 9, 1943.

41. FDR letter to HLS, April 8, 1943, FDR Papers as President, Box 84, War Department—Henry L. Stimson, FDRL.

42. HLS letter to FDR, April 13, 1943, FDR Papers as President, Box 84, War—Stimson—1943–45, FDRL.

43. La Guardia broadcast to the people of Italy, July 25, 1943, Folder 1, Box 220, New York City Department of Records & Information Services.

44. Manchester, *American Caesar*, 308.

45. HLSD, October 29, 1942.

46. See, for instance, comments of Representative Philip Bennett, Congressional Record—House, April 7, 1943, 3060.

47. "Controversy at Washington," *NYT*, April 9, 1943, 9.

48. FDR also had met two months prior to that with members of the DNC, according to calendars at FDRL.

49. HLSD, May 28, 1943.

50. "Knox Denies Talking of War Contracts at House on R Street," *The Daily Intelligencer*, May 4, 1943, 2.

51. HLSD, May 30, 1943.
52. HLSD, October 15, 1942.
53. OAS, 344.
54. HLSD, May 27, 1943 and June 6, 1943.

CHAPTER 17: FORGING AMERICAN LEADERSHIP FOR D-DAY

1. HLSD, May 10, 1943.
2. HLSD, May 12, 1943.
3. For Axis surrender in North Africa, see "African War Over," *NYT*, May 13, 1943, 1; and *The West Point History of World War II*, Volume 2, 120.
4. Combined Chiefs of Staff Minutes, May 12, 1943, 2:30 p.m., *FRUS: Conferences at Washington and Quebec, 1943*, (Washington, DC: US Government Printing Office, 1970), Document 29.
5. Hamilton, *Commander in Chief*, 209.
6. Combined Chiefs of Staff Minutes, May 12, 1943, 2:30 p.m., *FRUS: Conferences at Washington and Quebec, 1943*, Document 29.
7. Hastings Ismay, *The Memoirs of General Lord Ismay* (New York: The Viking Press, 1960), 296.
8. Combined Chiefs of Staff Minutes, May 13, 1943, 10:30 a.m., *FRUS: Conferences at Washington and Quebec, 1943*, Document 31.
9. Ibid.
10. HLSD, May 17, 1943.
11. Combined Chiefs of Staff Minutes, May 19, 1943, 6:00 p.m., *FRUS: Conferences at Washington and Quebec, 1943*, Document 49.
12. Brooke, *War Diaries*, 407.
13. Brooke, *War Diaries*, 410.
14. Hamilton, *Commander in Chief*, 251–252.
15. Brooke, *War Diaries*, 411.
16. HLSD, May 25, 1943.
17. HLSD, May 27, 1943.
18. Jones, *Manhattan*, 232.
19. Churchill message to John Anderson, May 26, 1943, Churchill, *The Hinge of Fate*, 809.
20. Ibid.
21. HLSD, May 25, 1943.
22. HLSD, May 27, 1943.
23. HLSD, July 12, 1943.
24. HLSD, July 17, 1943.
25. Jones, *Manhattan*, 237–238.
26. Ibid., 238.
27. Ibid.
28. HLSD, July 22, 1943.
29. Stimson report to FDR, August 4, 1943, in HLSD.
30. HLSD, July 22, 1943.
31. Stimson report to FDR, August 4, 1943, in HLSD.
32. Butcher, *My Three Years with Eisenhower*, 373–374.

33. HLSD, July 28, 1943.

34. Shirer, *The Rise and Fall of the Third Reich*, 997.

35. Douglas Porch, *The Path to Victory, The Mediterranean Theater in World War II* (New York: Farrar, Straus and Giroux, 2004), 428.

36. Stimson report to FDR, August 4, 1943, in HLSD.

37. Ibid.

38. Winston S. Churchill, *Closing the Ring* (Boston: Houghton Mifflin Company, 1951), 85.

39. FDR telegram to HLS, August 8, 1943, FDR Papers as President, Box 84, War, Stimson—1943–45, FDRL; Stimson letter to FDR, August 10, 1943, HLSD. Stimson's spelling of "Dunkerque" in the August 10 letter revised to "Dunkirk."

40. HLSD, August 10, 1943.

41. HLSD, August 10, 1943.

42. Suckley, *Closest Companion*, 228–230.

43. Brooke, *War Diaries*, 442.

44. "Note by the Secretaries of the Combined Chiefs of Staff, August 17, 1943," *FRUS: Conferences at Washington and Quebec*, 1943, document 451.

45. "Articles of Agreement Governing Collaboration Between the Authorities of the U.S.A. and the U.K. in the Matter of Tube Alloys, August 19, 1943," *FRUS: Conferences at Washington and Quebec*, 1943, document 521.

46. For one presentation of the case that a quid pro quo took place, see Hamilton, *Commander in Chief*, 313–315.

47. August 12, 1943, to September 5, 1943, HLSD.

48. Winston Churchill, *The Second World War: Closing the Ring* (Boston: Houghton Mifflin Company, 1951), 85.

49. One might speculate endlessly why Churchill chose to say it was his idea to have an American commander. He may have wished to avoid having British officers become angry at their American allies. He may have wished to appear magnanimous. He may have wished to avoid having a British officer blamed if Overlord failed, as he feared it might. There is little support for any of these theories.

50. Atkinson, *The Day of Battle*, 195–196, 203.

51. Ibid., 199, 204–206.

52. *The West Point History of World War II*, Volume 2, 133.

53. "Nazis Wreck Naples Port, Sink Ships," *NYT,* September 24, 1943, 1.

54. Porch, *The Path to Victory,* 504.

55. Ibid., 503.

56. WSC cable to FDR, October 7, 1943, C-438; FDR cable to WSC, October 7, 1943, R-379; WSC reply to FDR, October 8, 1943, C-441, all: *Churchill and Roosevelt, The Complete Correspondence,* Volume II: *Alliance Forged,* 498–503.

57. WSC cable to FDR, October 23, 1943, *Churchill and Roosevelt,* Volume II, 555–558.

58. HLSD, October 28, 29 and 31, 1943.

59. Nigel Hamilton, *War and Peace: FDR's Final Odyssey, D-Day to Yalta, 1943–1945* (Boston and New York: Houghton Mifflin Harcourt, 2019), 59, 63.

60. Meeting Minutes, Combined Chiefs of Staff, November 24, 1943, 11 a.m., Roosevelt's Villa, *FRUS: Diplomatic Papers, the Conferences at Cairo and Tehran, 1943,* (Washington, DC: US Government Printing Office, 1961), 329–334.

61. Hamilton, *War and Peace,* 107.

62. "Bohlen Minutes, First Plenary Meeting, November 28, 1943, 4 p.m., Conference Room, Soviet Embassy," *FRUS: The Conferences at Cairo and Tehran, 1943*, 487. General Marshall was absent due to a scheduling oversight.

63. Hamilton, *War and Peace,* 111.

64. Bohlen Minutes, First Plenary Meeting, 489, 493, 494.

65. "Bohlen Minutes, Second Plenary Meeting, November 29, 1943, 4 p.m., Conference Room, Soviet Embassy," *FRUS: The Conferences at Cairo and Tehran, 1943,* 536–539.

66. Bohlen Minutes, Second Plenary Meeting, 535.

67. HLSD, December 5, 1943.

68. "Agreed Text of Communique, December 4, 1943," *FRUS: The Conferences at Cairo and Tehran, 1943*, Document 411.

69. Robert Sherwood, 803.

70. Butler, *My Dear Mr. Stalin,* 193.

71. Eisenhower, *Crusade in Europe,* 206–207.

72. HLSD, December 17, 1943.

73. HLSD, December 18, 1943.

74. "Army Seized Railroads on President's Order," and "WLB Reverses Pay Ruling," *NYT,* December 28, 1943, 1.

75. "Stimson Explains the Need of Seizure," *NYT,* December 29, 1943, 1.

76. HLS letter to Eisenhower, December 24, 1943, HLSP; HLSD, January 2, 1944.

77. Eisenhower, *Crusade in Europe,* 234–237.

78. Antony Beevor, *D-Day: The Battle for Normandy* (New York: Penguin Books, 2014), 2–4.

79. Eisenhower, *Crusade in Europe,* 230–231, 239.

80. Beevor, *D-Day,* 6.

81. Eisenhower, *Crusade in Europe,* 243.

82. Rosenman, *Working with Roosevelt*, 433.

83. HLSD, June 5, 1944.

84. Beevor, *D-Day,* 74, 75, 112.

85. Ibid., 115–117, 119.

86. "Hitler's Sea Wall Is Breached," *NYT,* June 7, 1944, 1.

87. "'Let Our Hearts Be Stout,'" *NYT,* June 7, 1944, 1.

88. Congressional Record—House, June 6, 1944, 5387.

89. Eisenhower, *Crusade in Europe,* 270.

90. Colin Brown, *Operation Big: The Race to Stop Hitler's A-Bomb* (London: Amberley Publishing, 2016), 156, 160–162.

91. For a discussion of Churchill's recasting of history in his memoirs, see Nigel Hamilton, *War and Peace,* 42–43.

92. FDR letter to HLS, November 21, 1944, Stimson, Henry L. 1934–1944, President's Personal File, FDRL.

CHAPTER 18: THE SOLDIER VOTING SCHISM

1. "Service Vote May Be Decisive in Campaign," *NYT,* July 23, 1944, 6E.

2. Congressional Record—House, November 13, 1943, 9473.

3. Peter Shinkle, *Ike's Mystery Man: The Secret Lives of Robert Cutler* (Hanover, New Hampshire: Steerforth Press, 2018), 19–22.

4. Ibid., 27.
5. Cutler statement of November 16, 1943, Congressional Record—House, November 29, 1943, 10087–10088.
6. Congressional Record—House, November 29, 1943, 10091.
7. Congressional Record—Senate, December 3, 1943, 10295.
8. Congressional Record—Senate, December 3, 1943, 10281.
9. Congressional Record—Senate, December 3, 1943, 10289.
10. Ibid., 10290.
11. "Soldier-Vote Bill Shifted by Senate to Let States Rule," *NYT*, December 4, 1943, 1.
12. "Vote of Soldiers Could Decide '44 Election, Gallup Poll Finds," *NYT*, December 5, 1943, 48.
13. "Congress Faces New Race Issues," *The Pittsburgh Courier*, January 8, 1944, 1.
14. "Senators Clash on Soldier Vote," *NYT*, December 8, 1943, 1.
15. Congressional Record—Senate, December 9, 1943, 10516 and 10517.
16. HLSD, December 8, 1943.
17. Recording of FDR State of the Union Speech, January 11, 1944, https://www.fdrlibrary.org/utterancesfdr#afdr285, *Recorded Speeches and Utterances of Franklin D. Roosevelt, 1920–1945*, FDRL, accessed January 27, 2021.
18. HLSD, January 10, 1944; HLS letter to Eugene Worley, Chairman, Committee on Election of President, Vice President, and Representatives in Congress, January 11, 1944, Congressional Record—House, January 11, 1944, 71.
19. Congressional Record—Senate, January 24, 1944, 612.
20. Robert Cutler, *No Time for Rest* (Boston and Toronto: Little, Brown and Company, 1965), 170.
21. "President Calls Vote Bill 'Fraud,'" *NYT*, January 27, 1944, 1.
22. Congressional Record—House, January 28, 1944, 895.
23. Congressional Record—Senate, January 31, 1944, 908, 911.
24. Congressional Record—Senate, January 31, 1944, 921; for Overton's broad defense of white supremacy, Congressional Record—Senate, January 31, 1944, 983.
25. Congressional Record—House, February 2, 1944, 1087.
26. Congressional Record—Senate, March 9, 1944, 2404–2408.
27. "'State Rights' Bill for Soldiers' Vote Passed by Senate," *NYT*, March 15, 1944, 1.
28. "Vote Bill Passed," *NYT*, March 16, 1944, 1.
29. "856 Call for Veto on Federal Ballot," *NYT*, March 24, 1944, 13.
30. HLSD, March 16, 1944.
31. "Vote Bill Allowed to Become a Law," *NYT*, April 1, 1944, 1; "Soldier Vote Message," *NYT*, April 1, 1944, 9.
32. Cutler, *No Time for Rest*, 179–180.
33. FDR memo to HLS, May 22, 1944, HLSP, Reel 110.
34. Cutler, *No Time for Rest*, note 11, 397.
35. HLSD, September 19, 1945.
36. Shinkle, *Ike's Mystery Man*, 31.

CHAPTER 19: A BIPARTISAN VISION FOR AMERICAN POLITICS

1. "FDR Radio Address to the Nation, January 11, 1944," FDR Master Speech File, 1898–1945, FDRL.

2. Rosenman, *Working with Roosevelt,* 463–470.

3. "FDR Radio Address to the Nation, January 11, 1944," 11, 12.

4. Alben W. Barkley, *That Reminds Me—* (Garden City, N.Y.: Doubleday & Company, Inc., 1954), 170–190.

5. "Taxes Voted Law by 72–14," *NYT,* February 26, 1944, 1.

6. "Roosevelt Signs but Criticizes Changes in OPA Extension Bill," *NYT,* July 1, 1944, 1.

7. "National Service Urged by Stimson to Hasten Victory," *NYT,* January 20, 1944, 1.

8. "High Court Rules Negroes Can Vote in Texas Primary," *NYT,* April 4, 1944, 1.

9. "10 Railroads Balk at Hiring Negroes," *NYT,* March 3, 1944, 11.

10. "Bilbo KKK Avowal Stumps Mississippi," *NYT,* August 14, 1946, 14.

11. "Agency Bill Voted with FEPC Funds," *NYT,* June 21, 1944, 20.

12. "Knox Dies in Home," *NYT,* April 29, 1944, 1.

13. HLSD, April 28, 1942.

14. Hamilton, *War and Peace,* 121–122, 190.

15. Robert Dallek, *Franklin D. Roosevelt: A Political Life* (New York: Viking, 2017), 550–551, 553.

16. "Dewey Challenges New Deal's Ability in Making of Peace," *NYT,* February 13, 1944, 1; "Dewey Nomination Assured by Gain of 129 Delegates," *NYT,* June 25, 1944, 1.

17. Rosenman, *Working with Roosevelt,* 71.

18. Ibid., 463.

19. Ibid.

20. Ibid., 464.

21. Ibid., 465, 466.

22. Ibid., 466.

23. Ibid., 467.

24. FDR letter to Willkie, July 13, 1944, Roosevelt, Franklin Delano, Box 68, Willkie mss., Lilly Library, Indiana University, Bloomington, Indiana. Rosenman later noted that Roosevelt sent this letter without telling him, even though Rosenman accompanied the president on his trip and was likely the only other person to know about his secret meeting with Willkie in New York. Having worked with FDR since 1928, Rosenman knew his boss's predilections: he "loved mystery and secrecy; he was fond of the dramatic and climactic; and having learned that Willkie was receptive to his plans, he apparently decided to play it from then on all alone." Rosenman, *Working with Roosevelt,* 468.

25. "Stimson in Rome on Symbolic Day," *NYT,* July 5, 1944, 10.

26. "Death Took High Post from General Roosevelt," *NYT,* July 19, 1944, 3.

27. "The President's Letter," *NYT,* July 12, 1944, 1.

28. White, *A Man Called White,* 262–264.

29. "Major Parties' Planks," *The Pittsburgh Courier,* July 29, 1944, 1.

30. White, *A Man Called White,* 267–268.

31. "Roosevelt's Acceptance," *NYT,* July 21, 1944, 1.

32. HLS letter to FDR, July 27, 1944, Roosevelt Papers as President, Box 84, War—Stimson—1943–45, FDRL.

33. Rosenman, *Working with Roosevelt,* 468–469.

34. "Willkie Is Invited to Visit President," *NYT,* August 11, 1944, 1.

35. "President Outlines US Plan for World Security Union," *NYT,* June 16, 1944.

36. "Dewey Attacks Four-Power Move to Control World," *NYT,* August 17, 1944, 1.

37. Hull, *Memoirs,* Volume 2, 1689–1693.

38. Ibid., 1693, 1694.

39. Willkie draft letter to FDR, July 20, 1944, Roosevelt, Franklin Delano, Box 68, Willkie mss., Lilly Library, Indiana University, Bloomington, Indiana.

40. "Willkie Funeral to Be Tomorrow," *NYT,* October 9, 1944, 1.

41. HLS letter to Edith Willkie, October 9, 1944, Correspondence, Oct. 2, 1944—November 30, 1944, HLSP.

42. Mary Earhart Dillon, *Wendell Willkie* (Philadelphia and New York: J.B. Lippincott Company, 1952), 354–355.

43. White, *A Man Called White,* 301–303.

44. "Roosevelt Strong in War Vote Tally," *NYT,* November 8, 1944, 1.

45. "South Stays in the Democratic Fold," *NYT,* November 8, 1944, 2; "The Deep South," *NYT,* November 12, 1944, 100.

46. "Roosevelt Wins Fourth Term," *NYT,* November 8, 1944, 1.

47. 1944 Election Results, The American Presidency Project, University of California at Santa Barbara, https://www.presidency.ucsb.edu/statistics/elections/1944, accessed February 5, 2021.

CHAPTER 20: THE HOLOCAUST AND THE FIGHT OVER POSTWAR GERMANY

1. Henry Morgenthau III, *Mostly Morgenthaus: A Family History* (New York: Ticknor & Fields, 1991), 263.

2. Eleanor Roosevelt, *The Autobiography of Eleanor Roosevelt* (New York and London: Harper Perennial, 1961), 123; Morgenthau, *Mostly Morgenthaus,* 244, 258–260.

3. Morgenthau, *Mostly Morgenthaus,* 262–263.

4. Julien Gorbach, *The Notorious Ben Hecht: Iconoclastic Writer and Militant Zionist* (West Lafayette, Ind. Purdue University Press, 2019), 193–195.

5. Richard Breitman and Allan J. Lichtman, *FDR and the Jews* (Cambridge, Mass. Harvard University Press, 2013), 229–230.

6. Ibid., 230.

7. David S. Wyman, *The Abandonment of the Jews,* 153–154.

8. *Report to the Secretary on the Acquiescence of this Government in the Murder of the Jews,* January 13, 1944, MD, Book 693, 212–213.

9. Wyman, *The Abandonment of the Jews,* 203.

10. Einsatzgruppen video, United States Holocaust Memorial Museum website, https://encyclopedia.ushmm.org/content/en/article/einsatzgruppen-and-other-ss-and-police-units-in-the-soviet-union, accessed Feb. 20, 2021.

11. "Russians Send Four to Gallows," *NYT,* December 19, 1943, 1.

12. "Morgenthau Opens Fourth Loan Drive," *NYT,* January 18, 1944, 1.

13. HLSD, February 1, 1944.

14. Phone call transcript, February 2, 1944, MD, Book 693, 212–213.

15. Wyman, *The Abandonment of the Jews,* 256.

16. "Text of Statement by Roosevelt," *NYT,* March 25, 1944, 4.

17. Wyman, *The Abandonment of the Jews,* 290–291.

18. Ibid., 292, 294.
19. Ibid., 285.
20. Ibid., 295, 296.
21. Michael Beschloss, *The Conquerors: Roosevelt, Truman and the Destruction of Hitler's Germany, 1941–1945* (New York: Simon & Schuster, 2002), 85.
22. Ibid., 89–91.
23. Ibid., 95.
24. HLSD, September 4, 1944.
25. MD, Book 769, September 5, 1944, 14.
26. OAS, 570.
27. HLSD, September 5, 1944.
28. Morgenthau top-secret memo to FDR, Suggested Post-Surrender Program for Germany, September 5, 1944, *FRUS: The Conference at Quebec, 1944* (Washington, DC: US Government Printing Office, 1974), 101–108.
29. Revision of Military Handbook, September 6, 1944, MD, Book 769, 118–119.
30. HLSD, September 7, 1944.
31. Top-secret memo, Program to Prevent Germany from Starting a World War III, September 9, 1944, *FRUS: The Conference at Quebec, 1944* (Washington, DC: Government Printing Office, 1974), 128–144.
32. Stimson memo, HLSD, September 9, 1944.
33. Meeting of the Combined Chiefs of Staff, Main Conference Room, Chateau Frontenac, 2:30 p.m., September 12, 1944, *FRUS: The Conference at Quebec, 1944* (Washington, DC: Government Printing Office, 1974), 307–309.
34. Charles Wilson notes, quoted in Roosevelt-Churchill Dinner Meeting, September 13, 1944, 8 p.m., The Citadel, *FRUS: The Conference at Quebec, 1944* (Washington, DC: Government Printing Office, 1974), 324–325.
35. MD, Book 772, September 19, 1944, 208.
36. Morgenthau-Cherwell Meeting, September 14, 1944, 10 a.m., Memorandum by the Treasury Secretary's Assistant, *FRUS: The Conference at Quebec, 1944* (Washington, DC: Government Printing Office, 1974), 328–330.
37. Memorandum by the British Paymaster-General (Cherwell), Québec, September 14, 1944, *FRUS: The Conference at Quebec, 1944*, 343–344.
38. MD, Book 772, September 19, 1944, 209.
39. MD, Book 772, September 19, 1944, 209.
40. Memorandum Initialed by President Roosevelt and Prime Minister Churchill, September 15, 1944, *FRUS: The Conference at Quebec, 1944* (Washington, DC: Government Printing Office, 1974), 466–467.
41. "Roosevelt and Churchill Pledge Quick Shift," *NYT*, September 17, 1944, 1.
42. See, for instance, "Morgenthau Plan on Germany Splits Cabinet Committee," *NYT*, September 24, 1944, 1.
43. MD, Book 772, September 19, 1944, 153.
44. HLSD, September 20, 1944.
45. Beschloss, *The Conquerors*, 144–145.
46. HLSD, September 27, 1944, and October 3, 1944.
47. Winston S. Churchill, *Triumph and Tragedy: The Second World War* (Boston: Houghton Mifflin Company, 1953), 156–157.

48. HLSD, September 14, 1944.

49. HLSD, October 3, 1944. Joseph Stilwell, *The Stilwell Papers,* 345. Barbara Tuchman, *Stilwell and the American Experience in China,* 501–502.

50. HLSD, September 26, 1944.

51. HLS letter to FDR, September 26, 1944, HLSP, Reel 111.

52. "Text of Address by Gov. Dewey at Rally Here," *NYT,* November 5, 1944, 42.

53. Beschloss, *The Conquerors,* 164.

54. HLS letter to FDR, November 8, 1944, President's Personal File, Box 20, folder Henry L. Stimson, 1934–1944, FDRL.

55. Biddle memo to FDR, December 30, 1943, Papers as President, President's Secretary's File, Box 56, Justice Department: Francis Biddle, 1944–1945, FDRL.

56. HLSD, May 26, 1944.

57. See Irons, 273, 277.

58. "100th Infantry Battalion in World War II," US Army Center of Military History online, https://history.army.mil/html/topics/apam/100bn.html, accessed March 8, 2021.

59. Reeves, *Infamy,* 228–231.

60. "Doughboys Break German Ring to Free 270 Trapped Eight Days," *NYT,* 3.

61. HLSD, November 19, 1944.

62. Irons, 344–345.

63. Ibid., 276.

64. "Ban on Japanese Lifted on Coast," *NYT,* December 18, 1944.

65. White, *A Man Called White,* 242–248.

66. James, *The Double V,* 162, 163.

67. HLSD, December 19, 1944.

68. HLSD, December 31, 1944.

69. HLSD, January 18 and 19, 1945.

70. Green Hackworth memorandum, January 22, 1945, attachment, Memorandum for the President, *FRUS: Diplomatic Papers, Conferences at Malta and Yalta, 1945,* Document 271.

71. Beschloss, *The Conquerors,* 180, 184, 187; Protocol on German Reparation, February 11, 1945, *FRUS: Diplomatic Papers, Conferences at Malta and Yalta, 1945,* Document 502.

72. Bohlen Minutes, Leningrad, February 9, 1945, 4 p.m., *FRUS: Diplomatic Papers, Conferences at Malta and Yalta, 1945,* Document 423.

73. "Byrnes for German Regime," *NYT,* September 7, 1946, 1.

74. Telford Taylor, *The Anatomy of the Nuremberg Trials: A Personal Memoir* (New York: Skyhorse Publishing, 1993), 4.

75. In 2018, the Supreme Court rejected as unconstitutional the reasoning in the Korematsu case that the Army's 1942 internment decision on the basis of race was legal. See decision in Trump v. Hawaii, June 26, 2018.

CHAPTER 21: FDR'S LAST BIPARTISAN CAMPAIGN

1. "Text of President's Message," *NYT,* January 7, 1945, 32.

2. HLSD, January 11, 1945.

3. Churchill, *Hinge of Fate*, 807.

4. Edward R. Stettinius Jr., *Roosevelt and the Russians: The Yalta Conference* (New York: Doubleday & Co., Inc., 1949) 186–187.

5. Ibid., 187.

6. "36 Nations Invited to Security Parley at San Francisco," *NYT*, March 6, 1945, 1.

7. "President Greets Parley Delegates," *NYT*, March 14, 1945, 1.

8. "Dulles Takes Post as Parley Adviser," *NYT*, April 6, 1945, 1.

9. HLSD, March 16, 1945; Butler, *My Dear Mr. Stalin*, 300.

10. James Srodes, *Allen Dulles* (New York: Regnery Publishing, Inc., 1999), 342–344.

11. Butler, *My Dear Mr. Stalin*, 302–317.

12. Srodes, *Allen Dulles*, 345.

13. Ibid., 310.

14. Dallek, *Franklin D. Roosevelt*, 618–619.

15. Suckley, *Closest Companion*, 418.

16. Bruenn Notes, April 12, 1945, "Clinical Notes on Illness and Death of President Roosevelt," Box 1, FDRL.

17. Dallek, *Franklin D. Roosevelt*, 619.

18. Harry S. Truman, *1945: Year of Decisions* (New York: Konecky & Konecky, 1955), 8.

19. Ibid., 147–149, 151–166.

20. "Truman Attends Pendergast Rites," *NYT*, January 30, 1945, 20.

21. "500,000 View Parade in Washington," *NYT*, 1.

22. "Millions in City Ignore Rain to Pay Honor to Roosevelt," *NYT*, April 15, 1945, 1.

23. HLSD, April 15, 1945.

24. HLS letter to Eleanor Roosevelt, April 16, 1945, HLSP, Reel 112.

25. Eleanor Roosevelt letter to HLS, April 18, 1945, HLSP, Reel 112.

26. "Truman Asks World Unity to Keep Peace," *NYT*, April 17, 1945, 1.

27. Ibid., 23.

28. "Text of Addresses at Opening of United Nations Conference in San Francisco," *NYT*, April 26, 1945, 4.

29. Shirer, *The Rise and Fall of the Third Reich*, 1131, 1138.

30. Ibid., 1123.

31. Ibid., 1133–1134.

32. Douglas Waller, *Wild Bill Donovan: The Spymaster Who Created the OSS and Modern American Espionage* (New York: Free Press, 2011), 317–318.

33. HLSD, June 25, 1945.

34. "Vandenberg Says He Will Sign Charter," *NYT*, June 26, 1945, 10.

35. "Text of President Truman's Address," *NYT*, June 27, 1945, 10.

36. "Vandenberg's Plea for Charter," *NYT*, June 30, 1945, 10.

37. "Bretton Program, Export Bank Fund, Voted by Congress," *NYT*, July 21, 1945, 1.

CHAPTER 22: TRUMAN, STIMSON AND THE ATOM BOMB

1. Truman, *1945: Year of Decisions*, 10. Stimson makes no mention of this brief conversation in his own diary, but there is no support for a theory that this conversation did not occur.

2. HLSD, April 12, 1945.

3. HLSD, December 22, 1943.

4. "Fight Against Canol Fails," *NYT*, June 22, 1944, 7.

5. HLSD, March 13, 1944.

6. "Canol Project to Close," *NYT*, March 9, 1945, 21.

7. HLSD, March 13, 1944.

8. David McCullough, *Truman* (New York: Simon & Schuster, 1992), 339.

9. Truman, *1945*, 11; David Robertson, *Sly and Able: A Political Biography of James F. Byrnes* (New York and London: W.W. Norton & Co., 1994), 391–393.

10. Robertson, *Sly and Able*, 64, 65, 79, 81.

11. Congressional Record—Senate, January 11, 1938, 310.

12. FDR memorandum to Byrnes, June 10, 1944, FDR Papers as President, President's Secretary's Files, Box 132, Executive Office of the President—Byrnes, James F., FDRL.

13. HLSD, January 9, 1943, and March 27, 1944.

14. Truman, *1945*, 22–23.

15. HLSD, April 25, 1945.

16. Truman, *1945*, 87.

17. Robertson, *Sly and Able*, 402–404; William Lanouette, *Genius in the Shadows: A Biography of Leo Szilard, the Man Behind the Bomb* (New York: Charles Scribner's Sons, 1992), 264–266.

18. HLSD, May 14, 1945.

19. HLSD, June 10–11, 1945.

20. "Truman Warns Victory Is 'But Half Won,'" *NYT*, May 9, 1945, 1.

21. "B-29's Make Debut," *NYT*, June 16, 1944, 1.

22. "Center of Tokyo Devastated by Fire Bombs," *NYT*, March 11, 1945; Richard B. Frank, *Downfall: The End of the Imperial Japanese Empire* (New York: Random House, 1999), 9, 15–18.

23. "Marines Landed on Iwo Jima 75 Years Ago," US Department of Defense website, https://www.defense.gov/Explore/Features/story/Article/2051094/marines-landed -on-iwo-jima-75-years-ago/, accessed March 31, 2021.

24. "Nimitz Sets Plan to Invade Japan," *NYT*, May 9, 1945, 1.

25. HLSD, May 9, 1945.

26. McCullough, *Truman*, 383–384.

27. HLSD, May 13, 1945.

28. Agreement Regarding Entry of the Soviet Union Into the War Against Japan, February 11, 1945, *FRUS: Conferences at Malta and Yalta, 1945*, Document 503.

29. HLSD, May 14, 1945.

30. Frank, *Downfall*, 68–69.

31. Ibid., 68–74.

32. Donovan letter to Truman, May 12, 1945, Office of Strategic Services—Donovan—Secret folder; Subject File, Rose Conway Files, Harry S. Truman Papers, Harry S. Truman Presidential Library.

33. Kai Bird, *The Chairman: John J. McCloy and the Making of the American Establishment* (New York: Simon & Schuster, 1992), 242–243.

34. Grew, *Turbulent Era*, 1423–1424.

35. HLSD, May 29, 1945.

36. Grew, *Turbulent Era*, 1424.

37. HLSD, May 31, 1945.

38. Malloy, *Atomic Tragedy,* 114–115.

39. Robertson, *Sly and Able,* 409–411.

40. HLSD, June 6, 1945.

41. HLSD, June 6, 1945.

42. Minutes of Meeting Held at the White House on Monday, 18 June 1945 at 1530, *FRUS: Diplomatic Papers, the Conference of Berlin (The Potsdam Conference), 1945,* Volume I, document 598.

43. Ibid.

44. HLSD, July 2, 1945; Truman memo and cover letter of July 2, 1945, and attached draft proclamation, *FRUS: Diplomatic Papers, the Conference of Berlin (The Potsdam Conference), 1945,* Volume I, document 592.

45. HLSD, July 3, 1945.

46. Frank, *Downfall,* 76–77.

47. *The West Point History of World War II,* Volume 2, 240–241.

48. Frank, *Downfall,* 77–81.

49. See, for example, "Big Shells Level Muroran Plants," *NYT,* July 16, 1945, 1.

50. McCullough, *Truman,* 413.

51. Minister in Sweden Cable to Secretary of State, July 6, 1945, *FRUS: Diplomatic Papers, the Conference of Berlin (The Potsdam Conference), 1945,* Volume I, document 1420.

52. Robertson, *Sly and Able,* 417–418.

53. Gar Alperovitz, *The Decision to Use the Atomic Bomb* (New York: Vintage Books, 2020), 233–234.

54. Sato telegram to Togo, July 13, 1945, *FRUS: Diplomatic Papers, the Conference of Berlin (The Potsdam Conference), 1945,* Volume I, document 586.

55. Alperovitz, *The Decision to Use the Atomic Bomb,* 234.

56. Bird, *The Chairman,* 251.

57. Alperovitz, *The Decision to Use the Atomic Bomb,* 235–236.

58. HLSD, July 17, 1945.

59. Jones, *Manhattan,* 517.

60. HLSD, July 17, 1945.

61. Truman diary entry, July 17, 1945, National Archives, https://www.archives.gov/historical-docs/todays-doc/index.html?dod-date=717, accessed April 9, 2021.

62. "Churchill Warns Against Socialism," *NYT,* June 5, 1945, 1; "Attlee Ridicules Fear of Socialism," *NYT,* June 6, 1945, 1.

63. HLSD, July 17, 1945.

64. Jones, *Manhattan,* 517.

65. Togo telegram to Sato, July 12, 1945, *FRUS: Diplomatic Papers, the Conference of Berlin (The Potsdam Conference), 1945,* Volume I, document 582.

66. Memorandum by Bohlen, March 28, 1960, *FRUS: Diplomatic Papers, the Conference of Berlin (The Potsdam Conference), 1945,* Volume II, document 1419.

67. Truman diary entry in Frank, *Downfall,* 242.

68. Sato telegram to Togo, July 19, 1945, *FRUS: Diplomatic Papers, the Conference of Berlin (The Potsdam Conference), 1945,* Volume II, document 1226.

69. HLSD, July 18, 1945.

70. McCullough, *Truman,* 427.

71. HLSD, July 19, 1945.

72. HLSD, July 20, 1945.

73. HLSD July 21, 1945.

74. Department of State Minutes, July 21, 1945, *FRUS: Diplomatic Papers, The Conference of Berlin (the Potsdam Conference), 1945,* Volume II, document 710.

75. HLSD, July 22, 1945; Groves memorandum to Stimson, July 18, 1945, *FRUS: Diplomatic Papers, The Conference of Berlin (the Potsdam Conference), 1945,* Volume II, document 1305.

76. Harvey Bundy, "Remembered Words," *The Atlantic,* March 1957, 57.

77. Malloy, *Atomic Tragedy,* 134–135.

78. Ibid.

79. HLSD, July 23, 1945.

80. Brown diary entries of July 20 and July 24, 1945, cited in Alperovitz, 268.

81. HLSD, July 24, 1945.

82. HLSD, July 24, 1945.

83. *Truman,* 416; see also Truman-Stalin Conversation, Tuesday, July 24, 1945, 7:30 p.m., *FRUS: Diplomatic Papers, The Conference of Berlin (the Potsdam Conference), 1945,* Volume II, 378–379.

84. McCullough, *Truman,* 442.

85. Truman diary, July 25, 1945, quoted in Malloy, *Atomic Tragedy,* 135.

86. HLSD, July 25, 1945.

87. General Thomas Handy order to General Carl Spaatz, July 25, 1945, US Department of Energy Website, The Manhattan Project, https://www.osti.gov/opennet/manhattan-project-history/Resources/order_drop.htm, accessed January 17, 2022.

88. "Japanese Cabinet Weighs Ultimatum," *NYT,* July 28, 1945, 1.

89. "Attlee in First Talk Backs Harmony with US, Russia," *NYT,* July 27, 1945, 1; "British Ministers Take Their Oaths," *NYT,* July 29, 1945, 5.

90. HLSD, July 26 and July 27, 1945.

91. "US Aide Advises Japan to Accept," *NYT,* July 29, 1945, 4.

92. "Japan Officially Turns Down Allied Surrender Ultimatum," *NYT,* July 30, 1945, 1.

93. McCullough, *Truman,* 454.

94. Jones, *Manhattan,* 545.

95. McCullough, *Truman,* 457.

96. Alex Wellerstein, "Counting the Dead at Hiroshima," *Bulletin of the Atomic Scientists,* August 4, 2020, website of the Federation of Atomic Scientists, https://thebulletin.org/2020/08/counting-the-dead-at-hiroshima-and-nagasaki/, accessed April 13, 2021.

97. Alperovitz, *The Decision to Use the Atomic Bomb,* 612.

98. Wellerstein, op. cit.

99. McCullough, *Truman,* 457.

100. Ibid., 455.

101. HLSD, August 8, 1945.

102. Jones, *Manhattan,* 545.

103. Wellerstein, op. cit.

104. Truman, *1945,* 428.

105. HLSD, August 10, 1945.

106. Ibid.

107. "Japan Surrenders," *NYT,* August 15, 1945, 1.

108. "Russians Advance 105 Miles in Day," *NYT*, August 11, 1945; Jay Taylor, *The Generalissimo: Chiang Kai-Shek and the Struggle for Modern China* (Cambridge, Mass. and London: Harvard University Press, 2009), 317–318.

109. Alperovitz, *The Decision to Use the Atomic Bomb*, xii.

110. Henry L. Stimson, "The Decision to Use the Atomic Bomb," *Harper's Magazine*, January 1947.

111. Bix, *Hirohito*, 544–545, 559, 586–597, 618.

112. Ibid., 609.

113. MacArthur claimed that Shidehara proposed the idea of the anti-war provision, but critics have suggested it was in fact the Americans who originated the idea. See Toru Takemoto, *Failure of Liberalism in Japan: Shidehara Kijuro's Encounter with Anti-Liberals* (University Press of America, 1978), 179–205.

114. HLSD, September 11 and 12, 1945.

115. HLSD, September 18, 1945.

116. HLSD, September 21, 1945.

117. "Mr. Stimson's Letter," *NYT*, March 27, 1950, 22.

118. Lawrence J. Haas, *Harry & Arthur: Truman, Vandenberg and the Partnership that Created the Free World* (Lincoln, Neb. Potomac Books, 2016), 160–161, 260–273.

119. Henry L. Stimson Memorial Services Program, January 21, 1951, The National Presbyterian Church, Washington, DC, President's Secretary's Files, Mr. and Mrs. Henry L. Stimson folder, Box 275, HSTL.

EPILOGUE: THE BIPARTISAN ALLIANCE AND AMERICA'S FUTURE

1. *Henry L. Stimson: Addresses Made in His Honor, April 6, 1950*, private printing of the Century Association, New York, N.Y., 1950.

2. Shinkle, *Ike's Mystery Man*, 118–124. Ike also appointed a Democrat, union official Martin Durkin, as secretary of labor, though Durkin lasted less than a year in the post.

3. Bundy was son of Stimson aide Harvey Bundy, a friend of Cutler.

4. William Webster interview with the author, May 2, 2019.

5. Robertson, *Sly and Able*, 512.

6. Congressional Record—House, February 3, 1944, 1229.

7. Ibid., 539–540.

8. "With Cross Talk, Lies and Mockery, Trump Tramples Decorum in Debate with Biden," *NYT*, September 30, 1. Trump also expressed support for white supremacists who marched in Virginia chanting "Jews will not replace us." He said there were "very fine people on both sides," a remark interpreted by critics as a defense of white supremacy. Full text: "Trump's Comments on White Supremacists, 'Alt-Left' in Charlottesville," Politico, https://www.politico.com/story/2017/08/15/full-text -trump-comments-white-supremacists-alt-left-transcript-241662, accessed May 4, 2021; for Trump's comments mocking constitutional rights of criminal suspects, see "Trump, on Long Island, Vows an End to Gang Violence," *NYT*, July 28, 2017, 14.

9. See, for instance, "Trump Renews Attacks on Media," *The Washington Post*, October 29, 2018, https://www.washingtonpost.com/politics/trump-renews-attacks-on -media-as-the-true-enemy-of-the-people/2018/10/29/9ebc62ee-db60–11e8–85df -7a6b4d25cfbb_story.html, accessed May 9, 2021.

10. "Trump Sides with Russia against FBI at Helsinki Summit," BBC, https://www.bbc.com/news/world-europe-44852812, accessed May 4, 2021.

11. "'Follow the Money,'" ABC News, February 9, 2018, https://abcnews.go.com/Politics/follow-money-senator-probes-trumps-95-million-palm/story?id=52970095, accessed January 29, 2022.

12. "The Trump Organization Reportedly Wanted to Give Putin the Penthouse in Trump Tower Moscow," Insider, November 29, 2018, https://www.businessinsider.com/trump-organization-putin-penthouse-trump-tower-moscow-2018–11, accessed March 31, 2022.

13. "Trump Calls Putin 'Genius' and 'Savvy' for Ukraine Invasion," Politico, https://www.politico.com/news/2022/02/23/trump-putin-ukraine-invasion-00010923, accessed March 20, 2022.

14. "By the Numbers: President Donald Trump's Failed Efforts to Overturn the Election," *USA Today,* January 6, 2021, https://www.usatoday.com/in-depth/news/politics/elections/2021/01/06/trumps-failed-efforts-overturn-election-numbers/4130307001/, accessed January 28, 2022.

15. "Disputing Trump, Barr Says No Widespread Election Fraud," Associated Press, December 1, 2020, https://apnews.com/article/barr-no-widespread-election-fraud-b1f1488796c9a98c4b1a9061a6c7f49d, accessed January 30, 2022.

16. Official 2020 Presidential General Election Results, Federal Election Commission, https://www.fec.gov/resources/cms-content/documents/2020presgeresults.pdf, accessed May 4, 2021.

17. Bob Woodward and Robert Costa, *Peril* (New York: Simon & Schuster, 2021), 207, 210, 211.

18. Ibid., 240; "Incitement to Riot? What Donald Trump Told Supporters Before Mob Stormed Capitol," *NYT,* January 10, 2021, accessed May 4, 2021.

19. "Proud Boys Leaders in Four States Are Charged in Capitol Riot," *NYT,* March 17, 2021, 22.

20. "Before Wednesday, Insurgents Waving Confederate Flags Hadn't Been Within 5 Miles of the US Capitol," CNN website, https://www.cnn.com/2021/01/07/us/capitol-confederate-flag-fort-stevens/index.html, accessed May 4, 2021.

21. "One Year Since the Jan. 6 Attack on the Capitol," US Department of Justice website, https://www.justice.gov/usao-dc/one-year-jan-6-attack-capitol, accessed January 29, 2022.

22. "Leader of Oath Keepers and 10 Other Individuals Indicted," US Department of Justice website, https://www.justice.gov/opa/pr/leader-oath-keepers-and-10-other-individuals-indicted-federal-court-seditious-conspiracy-and, accessed January 29, 2022.

23. The FBI said that in fact there was no evidence that "antifa" activists were involved in the Jan. 6 insurrection. See "Antifa Didn't Storm the Capital. Just Ask the Rioters," NPR, March 2, 2021, https://www.npr.org/2021/03/02/972564176/antifa-didnt-storm-the-capitol-just-ask-the-rioters, access May 4, 2021.

24. Carol Leonnig and Philip Rucker, *I Alone Can Fix It: Donald J. Trump's Catastrophic Final Year* (New York: Penguin Press, 2021), 437.

25. "The 147 Republicans Who Voted to Overturn Election Results," NYT, January 7, 2021, https://www.nytimes.com/interactive/2021/01/07/us/elections/electoral

-college-biden-objectors.html?searchResultPosition=1, accessed February 10, 2022.

26. "Pence Says Trump Was Wrong That He Could Have Overturned 2020 Election," Reuters, February 7, 2022, https://www.reuters.com/world/us/pence-says-trump -was-wrong-that-he-could-have-overturned-2020-election-result-2022–02–04/, accessed February 10, 2022.

27. "The 147 Republicans Who Voted to Overturn Election Results," *NYT*, https:// www.nytimes.com/interactive/2021/01/07/us/elections/electoral-college-biden -objectors.html, accessed May 4, 2021.

28. George Washington's Farewell Address, *A Sacred Union of Citizens: George Washington's Farewell Address and the National Character,* by Patrick J. Garrity, (Lanham, Maryland: Rowman & Littlefield Publishers, Inc., 1996) 182. The author has modified capitalization to conform with modern usage. Washington was not absolute in his condemnation: he conceded that political parties may be grounded in human nature and in some cases may even help preserve liberty. Yet the "Spirit of Party" poses such a grave risk from its excess that "the effort ought to be, by force of public opinion, to mitigate and assuage it," Washington wrote. "A fire not to be quenched; it demands a uniform vigilance to prevent its bursting into flame, lest instead of warming it should consume."

29. A general in the Revolutionary War, Washington held at a distance the two nascent political parties of his day, the Federalists and the Democratic-Republicans, but by 1796 he had already witnessed their vitriol and perfidy.

   Washington warned that one party may lie about another: "One of the expedients of Party to acquire influence, within particular districts, is to misrepresent the opinions and aims of other Districts. You can not shield yourselves too much against the jealousies and heart burnings which spring from these misrepresentations." Garrity, 179, 182.

30. "Trump 'Just Plain Wrong' on Fraud Claims: Georgia Secretary of State Raffensperger," ABC News, https://abcnews.go.com/Politics/trump-plain-wrong-fraud -claims-georgia-secretary-state/story?id=75032595, accessed January 28, 2022.

31. "William Webster: Congress Must Consider Censure, Impeachment, Removal," *St. Louis Post-Dispatch* website, January 11, 2021, https://www.stltoday.com/opinion /columnists/william-webster-congress-must-consider-censure-impeachment -removal/article_a8b1fe8c-e0c8–5b3b-8313-b6741f9e281d.html, accessed May 5, 2021.

32. "Wyoming GOP Censures Liz Cheney Over Impeachment Vote," Associated Press, February 6, 2021, https://apnews.com/article/donald-trump-capitol-siege-censures -rawlins-wyoming-3d2a5ad3377bb748c22f632642ba23f1, accessed May 4, 2021.

33. Liz Cheney tweet, May 3, 2021.

34. "RNC Votes to Censure Cheney, Kinzinger," ABC News, https://abcnews.go .com/Politics/rnc-vote-censure-cheney-kinzinger-roles-jan-committee/story?id =82671994, accessed February 10, 2022.

35. "Interview of Alexandria Ocasio-Cortez," *New Yorker* Politics and More podcast, October 18, 2020.

36. "Senate Invokes Closure on Rights Bill," 71 to 29 *NYT*, June 11, 1964, 1.

37. "McConnell Says He's '100 Percent' Focused on 'Stopping' Biden's Administration,"

NBC News online, May 5, 2021, https://www.nbcnews.com/politics/joe-biden
/mcconnell-says-he-s-100-percent-focused-stopping-biden-s-n1266443.

38. "Here Are the Republicans Who Voted for the Infrastructure Bill in the Senate," NPR, August 10, 2021, https://www.npr.org/2021/08/10/1026486578/senate
-republican-votes-infrastructure-bill, accessed March 21, 2022.

INDEX